Plt Off Paul Brennar
Plt Off Ray Hessel

SPITFIRES
OVER
MALTA

A Birchington Roundabout Publication

A catalogue record for this book is available from the
British Library
ISBN 978-0-9553646-5-5

Printed and bound in Great Britain
Cover image: Malta-George Cross by Robert Taylor.
Spitfires in combat with Me109s over Valletta in April 1942.
(Aces High Aviation Gallery)

Contents

Acknowledgements Of Thanks

Some years ago I attended a small airshow at Woodchurch, Kent. After the show there was time for another tour of the traders' stalls. On the grass next to one stall was a cardboard box full of various books, all getting wet in the rain that had started to fall, one of these was a small blue book called Spitfires Over Malta. The word Malta caught my eye, for the previous couple of years my aviation interest had moved from the Battle of Britain to a very similar conflict, the Battle of Malta.

The two stories were the same, an island alone, fighting for its survival against an enemy based very close by, and in much greater numbers; a fight that was proudly taken up by a relatively small number of fighter pilots. If either island had fallen the war would have had a very different outcome. Some of the pilots believed that the Battle of Malta was the harder of the two conflicts:

"One lives here only to destroy the Hun and hold him at bay; everything else, living conditions, sleep, food and all the ordinary standards of life have gone by the board. It all makes the Battle of Britain and fighter sweeps seem like child's play in comparison, but it is certainly history in the making and nowhere is there aerial warfare to compare with this."

My book purchase cost me just £2.00; its original price in 1943 had been two shillings. It is an exciting first hand account of the conflict in the air above and around Malta. The authors were two pilots from the British Commonwealth, Pilot Officer Paul Brennan from Australia, and Pilot Officer Raymond Hesselyn from New Zealand. Both had travelled from the other side of the world to help their mother country.

Having enjoyed reading the book I tried to obtain a more recent version than my original copy, with its rusty staples and loose pages, one page at the front proudly declaring that the book had been published to the prevailing War Economy Standard. I found that the book appeared to have been out of print since the war. I thought this a great pity, and decided it would be a nice tribute to those who had been involved in the battle, to return it to print, and so be accessible to all once again.

I considered that the story should be updated, with details that could not be told during the war, including a profile of the sixteen pilots, who, during Operation Spotter, flew the first Spitfires off the aircraft carrier HMS Eagle to Malta on March 7th 1942. Fifteen pilots actually flew off the carrier, the other, Flt Lt John Yarra, followed on with the next delivery, after his Spitfire had been cannibalised to provide spare parts for the other aircraft. Of these 16 pilots, six would be killed on Malta and three others, including Plt Off Paul Brennan, would not survive to see the final victory in 1945.

My first starting point was to trace Lynne Nicholl in New Zealand, a relative of Raymond Hesselyn, she agreed that I could reproduce the original book, for which I am very grateful. I was unfortunately unable to trace a relative from the Brennan family in Australia.

The original UK publishers Jarrold's stated that they now had no record of the original book, having changed ownership and premises several times since the war, but wished me well with my project.

My next contact was the excellent Malta Aviation Museum at Ta' Qali (aka Takali) where my thanks go to Frederick Galea for his assistance with photographs and contact details for some of the pilots relatives. Frederick, in conjunction with Brian Cull, has written one of the definitive books about the conflict in the air above Malta, which is also entitled Spitfires Over Malta. Brian Cull with Christopher Shores and Nicola Malizia produced Malta: The Spitfire Year 1942. These two books are highly recommended for anyone seeking the full story of that time. My thanks to them for allowing me to quote from their works and also to Christopher Shores for the use of a photograph from his book, The Spitfire Smiths. My thanks also to Lex McAulay for his consent to quote and use photographs from his book, Against All Odds. Also to Anthony Rogers for the use of a photograph and consent to quote from his book Battle Over Malta.

My thanks also go to the staff at the National Archives, Kew, and the RAF Museum, Hendon, London. Also to Paul Lazell, for the use of photographs taken by his father Sergeant William (Bill) Lazell. In particular I would like to thank the following relatives of the pilots, or contacts who provided valuable information or photographs:

Rank Shown as held in March 1942

Flight Lieutenant John Yarra- National Archives Of Australia. Australian War Memorial.
Flight Lieutenant Norman Macqueen- Charles Leach.
Flight Lieutenant Philip Heppell- Philip Heppell.
Flight Sergeant David Ferraby- Mrs Pamela Ferraby.
Flight Sergeant Ian Cormack- Ian Boraston, Ron MacGregor.
Flight Sergeant Paul Brennan- National Archives Of Australia.

Australian War Memorial.
Flying Officer Norman Lee- Patrick Lee.
Pilot Officer Douglas Leggo- Gavin Cooper.
Pilot Officer James Guerin- National Archives Of Australia.
Pilot Officer John Plagis- Daphne Ritson, Jason Plagis, Martin Woodhall.
Pilot Officer Kenric Murray- David and Simon Thornton.
Pilot Officer Peter Nash- The National Archives, Kew.
Sergeant John Tayleur- Phyllis Greene (Previously Tayleur), Susie Hanmer, Constance Halford-Thompson.
Sergeant Raymond Hesselyn- Lynne Nicholl, Nathan Nicholl, James Sutherland. Auckland War Memorial.
Sergeant Robert Sim- Errol Martyn. Auckland War Memorial.
Squadron Leader Stanley Grant- The National Archives, Kew. Aces of WW2 Website.

My thanks go also to my good friend Stuart Horner for assistance in the publishing of this book, including page layout and design. Also to Stella my wife for some typing, correcting and also for putting up with me being upstairs on the computer all hours.

Introduction

The island of Malta lies almost centrally in the Mediterranean sea, a small island around 17 miles long by over eight wide. It has two smaller sister islands Gozo, 8 km to the northwest, with the sparsely populated Comino in between. Malta's advantageous setting and deep natural harbours made it a valuable asset, much fought over by many different nationalities from the Phoenicians and Romans, to the Arabs, Normans and the Spanish.

Arriving in 1530 the Knights of St John later held off an attack and siege in 1565 from a Turkish force much greater in number. Napoleon Bonaparte succeeded in seizing the islands in 1798, but the French forces were defeated by the Maltese and British troops two years later, and the subsequent Treaty of Paris confirmed British rule from 1814 until Malta's Independence in September 1964.

In the 1930s doubts about the security of Malta, by then a significant base for the Royal Navy, began to arise when Italy's Dictator Benito Mussolini declared the Mediterranean as 'Mare Nostrum'- Our Sea.

Hal Far airfield had opened in 1924 with aircrew from the Royal Navy flying aircraft to the inland airfield from aircraft carriers. In 1929 a Royal Air Force Station was also established there followed later by a grass airfield at Takali, and in 1935 at Luqa construction began on an all weather airfield of paved runways. In addition there was a seaplane station at Kalafrana with further facilities built at St Paul's Bay and Marsaxlokk.

A series of stone built parabolic sound mirrors were planned as an early warning system of approaching aircraft, but only one was actually constructed in 1935 at Ta' San Pietru, angled towards Sicily and Italy beyond. The 225-foot structure, known locally as Il-Widna, The Ear, survives to this day with traces of its wartime camouflage paintwork still visible. By 1937 it was no longer in use and the task of aircraft detection was passed in 1939 to Malta's first radar station built high on the cliffs at Dingli. The same year saw the Committee of Imperial Defence agree a long term strategy to defend the island by sending up to 122 heavy and 60 light anti-aircraft guns. However, by the outbreak of hostilities only 34 heavy and 8 light guns were in position, although the planned 24 searchlights were in place.

Initially 29 guns of various calibres, operated by the 4th Heavy Regiment Royal Artillery and the Royal Malta Artillery, defended the coastline which had been strewn with barbed wire and explosive devices against a possible invasion, and supplemented with concrete pillboxes many of which had been built earlier in 1935. The island's defence comprised five infantry battalions but many others followed during the course of the war.

Malta's strategically important position meant it had to be held as a base, from which British sea and air forces could attack the reinforcements of men and supplies being sent to the Axis armies in North Africa. These armies threatened an invasion of Egypt, the Suez Canal and Britain's oilfields in the Middle East. The German occupation of most of mainland Europe from the middle of 1940 meant that Malta became isolated, the closest allied bases were at Gibraltar, 1,100 miles to the west, and Alexandria, Egypt, around 1,100 miles to the east.

On the evening of June 10th 1940 Mussolini aligned Italy with Germany and

A cleverly camouflaged defensive pillbox located at Wied iz-Zurrieq.

declared war on Britain and France as from midnight. Britain at that stage was still trying to comprehend the retreat of the British Expeditionary Force two weeks earlier from the beaches of Dunkirk in France. Over 338,000 men were evacuated to England but without all of their heavy equipment. The surrender of France came later that same month.

Within seven hours of the announcement of war the first Italian bombers had left their Sicilian bases 60 miles away and headed for Malta. Eight bombing raids were carried out, causing minimal damage, but the first of many lives were lost both civilian, including several children, and military. The Italian aircraft were fired on by the anti aircraft guns, and intercepted by three of the six Gloster Gladiators biplanes, which were the only fighters on the island at that time. No Italian aircraft were shot down on the first day, although the Gladiators would have their successes later on, but the morale raising affect on the Maltese of seeing the small number of Gladiators taking on the Italians was immense. There were never any more than three Gladiators flown on any interception, these aircraft later became famously known as Faith, Hope and Charity. For nearly two weeks the Gladiators defended the skies until five Hurricanes, heading for the Middle East, stopped off on Malta to refuel and were promptly retained to help with the island's defence.

The first RAF pilot killed was Flight Lieutenant Peter Keeble, his Hurricane was shot down over the island on July 16th 1940, although it is

The Hurricanes were not only shot out of the sky, but also destroyed on the ground by the constant bombing. (B Lazell)

believed he may also have accounted for the destruction of an Italian aircraft during the same dogfight. On the 31st the first Gladiator was lost, the pilot, Flg Off Peter Hartley, was able to bale out into the sea but, having sustained severe burns that left him hospitalised, he was later returned to England due to his injuries.

With the fall of France it was no longer possible for aircraft to over fly the country to Malta, and it was decided that the best alternative was for aircraft to be flown off an aircraft carrier at a range of around 500 miles to the island. On July 23rd 1940 the first such delivery took place when HMS Argus sailed with 12 Hurricanes and 2 Skuas to Gibraltar. The Royal Navy's Force H, a protective force that included another aircraft carrier the Ark Royal, along with several battleships, destroyers and cruisers, then escorted them on their journey towards Malta on July 31st. The Hurricanes all took off from the carrier successfully and were led approximately 380 miles to Malta by the Skuas. One Hurricane and one Skua were subsequently damaged landing at Luqa.

This had been Operation Hurry, one of 14 deliveries of Hurricanes that would be made between August 1940 and November 1941 from the aircraft carriers Argus, Ark Royal and Furious. Between the three carriers 333 Hurricanes, 8 Swordfish and 11 Albacores were safely delivered, 28 Hurricanes and one Swordfish were lost during these operations.

The greatest loss of life was on the second delivery, Operation White. On November 17th Argus once again sailed with 12 Hurricanes and two Skuas along with their naval escort. The Italian Navy were reportedly in the area and the captain of Argus was keen to launch the Hurricanes and return to the safety of Gibraltar. The first six Hurricanes, led by their navigating Skua, took off at around 06:15am when they were believed to be around 400 miles from Malta, this allowed a margin of safety. The aircraft took some time to form up together once airborne, this consumed valuable amounts of fuel. Flt Lt James MacLachlan, a 21-year-old, led the first flight with a second flight of six Hurricanes, following approximately an hour later.

During their flight the direction of the wind changed to almost head on, increasing their fuel consumption even further. The Hurricanes successfully met the Sunderland aircraft that had flown out of Malta to guide them in, but, whilst still around 40 miles away from the island, one of the Hurricanes ran out of fuel. The pilot was able to bale out watched by MacLachlan who followed him down and called the Sunderland in to rescue him. Having successfully retrieved the pilot they attempted to catch up with the rest of the Hurricanes by then barely visible in the distance.

Shortly after, another of the Hurricanes, flown by Sgt Cunnington, also ran out of fuel, he baled out, but by the time the Sunderland arrived he was lost to the sea, his body never being recovered. The four remaining Hurricanes and the Skua safely landed at Takali with only a few gallons of fuel left, the engine of one aircraft stopping through lack of fuel whilst it was still on the runway.

The second flight fared even worse; the Sunderland which was to meet them never appeared, they missed Galite Island, one of their navigating points, and another aircraft sent from Malta to replace the Sunderland subsequently became lost. The Skua pilot attempted to make radio contact but was unable to receive any replies due to a faulty receiver. As they desperately searched for somewhere to land, one by one the six Hurricanes ran out of fuel and fell from the sky. The Skua pilot finally spotted land, which turned out to be Sicily, and, having been fired on by anti aircraft guns, he made a crash landing on the beach.

Aircraft flown out from Malta carried out a five-hour search, but no trace of the six pilots was ever found. The blame for the tragedy was initially put on to the pilots for flying too low at 2,000 feet, instead of 10,000 feet where the air would have been thinner. Later several other reasons were put forward, including poor weather forecasting, insufficient liaison between the Air Force and the Royal Navy, and the decision to release the aircraft too far away from Malta.

During the seven months after the outbreak of hostilities in June 1940, Malta endured 211 air raid alerts; 1941 saw 963 alerts, with attacks now coming from, not only the Italian forces, but also the German Luftwaffe from January onwards. Fliegerkorps X with over 260 aircraft, including 80 Ju87 Stuka dive-bombers and 40 Me109 fighters, had been sent to Sicily to support the Italian assault against Malta, with the emphasis being on attacking convoys bringing in supplies as well as the island itself. This aerial blockade ,in conjunction with naval attacks, would lead to food rationing and severe shortages of medical and other supplies for all those living on Malta.

The build up to the German invasion of Russia saw the withdrawal of the majority of Luftwaffe forces in May 1941, with other units also leaving to be based in Libya the following month. In June Air Commodore Hugh Pughe Lloyd became the new Air Officer Commanding on Malta, tasked with the continued protection of the island and the sinking of Axis supply ships sailing from Italy to North Africa.

Malta now experienced a short period of respite when the Hurricane MkII aircraft were able to fight on an even basis against the Italian Air Force. A small convoy of food and ammunition supplies was able to reach the island but that would no longer be possible from November 1941, with the return of the Luftwaffe from Russia. Luftflotte 2 along with the aircraft of Fligerkorps II and Fliegerkorps X were based in Sicily under the command of Generalfeldmarschall Albert Kesselring. The German forces started to take a heavy toll on the Hurricanes, which were now outclassed and out numbered by the Luftwaffe's superior Me109F fighter. If Malta were to survive the bombing, and the twin threats of starvation and invasion, air supremacy would have to be regained over the island. Only one aircraft was able to dogfight the Messerschmitt fighter on equal terms, the Spitfire.

Operation Spotter: The first Delivery of Spitfires to Malta

The files relating to Operation Spotter are held at the National Archives in Kew and include a document dated May 1941, referring to a meeting held on May 16th between Group Captain Yool and Wing Commander Robert Harston, where the continued supply of fighters to Malta was discussed. The decision at this stage centred on whether more Hurricanes should be despatched or if it were possible to send Spitfires in their place. Up until this time there had been four Hurricane deliveries to Malta by aircraft carrier, including two the previous month with 51 aircraft landing on the island.

It was noted that assembled Spitfires could not be loaded into the aircraft carriers Ark Royal, Formidable and Victorious as the ships lifts to the lower hangar decks were not large enough to accept them. This left the Eagle, Furious, Argus, Hermes and Indomitable as suitable ships. The document states that assembled Spitfires could be sent straight away, but only a small quantity. However, if the aircraft were disassembled, then it would be possible to send twice as many.

A Spitfire with its wings removed would, however, present a problem. The undercarriage wheels of a Spitfire are held within the wings, therefore some form of temporary undercarriage would be required to be able to move the aircraft; no such item existed within the RAF. At this stage also, insufficient personnel with the technical knowledge were available in numbers to be sent abroad to reassemble the Spitfires. It was considered that at least two months notice was required if disassembled Spitfires were to be sent to allow for these two problems to be resolved.

Planning had already been underway for another delivery of Hurricanes during May, and 46 were flown safely to Malta on May 21st. A further 236 Hurricanes had been flown to the island from seven other deliveries before the first Spitfires were sent out to replace them.

Eight months after the initial May 1941 meeting, on the afternoon of January 30th 1942, a conference was held in Room 271 at the Air Ministry at Adastral House, Kingsway, London. On the agenda was the intention to supply Malta with either a further 35 Hurricanes or 15 Spitfires, the maximum number that could be carried by HMS Eagle the aircraft carrier chosen. Under the chairmanship of Air Commodore Robert Musgrave-Whitham, the room contained one other Air Commodore, six Group Captains, seven Wing Commanders, five Squadron Leaders and two Flight Lieutenants. By the end of the meeting the decision to supply Spitfires had been made, and the outline for the, as yet unnamed supply operation, had been decided.

The unassembled Spitfires, packed into crates, would be transported, along with their pilots, the erection party and their equipment, in a merchant ship as part of a convoy to Gibraltar. Once docked, the Spitfires would be assembled on the quay and then loaded on to HMS Eagle. The Admiralty had advised that the maximum number of erected Spitfires that could be carried was 15. It would be advantageous if even just one more Spitfire could be fitted into the carrier so Wing Commander Henry Pearson Rogers was tasked with getting the Navy to agree to this. The proposed date of sailing from England was February 16th 1942.

Wing Commander Edgar Lowe informed the group that the only Spitfires available with the required additional 90-gallon fuel tanks were those being prepared for the Middle East, these were Mark Vbs with tropical filters. It was decided to reduce the weight, and therefore the fuel required during their flight, by removing from the Spitfires their four Browning machine guns, they would fly armed with only their two cannons, each carrying 60 rounds. Checks would be made to ensure that Malta held sufficient Browning guns available to refit to the Spitfires. If not, then the aircraft would retain their machine guns when they flew out, but they would not be loaded. It had been found that the two outer machine guns on the MkVb could suffer from overheating and a modification was required, but time would not allow this to take place before despatch to Malta. The Spitfires were already fitted with VHF radio sets and I.F.F. (Identification Friend or Foe) transmitters.

It was decided that 18 pilots, including two in reserve, would be sent by ship with the Spitfires. A secret telegram sent from the Air Ministry on February 1st to RAF Headquarters in Malta stated that Air Vice Marshall William Sholto Douglas, the Air Officer in Command of Fighter Command, would choose the pilots himself, and they would be **"Specially selected, of the highest quality, experienced and promising pilots."** The pilots chosen would be given time to fly several practise flights in a Spitfire fitted with an additional fuel tank, so they would become familiar with the aerodynamic change it would make to the handling of the aircraft. Time would also allow for the pilots to receive a short period of leave before they left the UK.

An experienced Wing Commander would travel with the group to brief and supervise the pilots once on-board the carrier; he would first report to the Air Ministry for his own briefing. The man chosen was John Sterling McLean DFC. He had joined the RAF in 1932, and was promoted to the rank of Squadron Leader in 1939. Whilst a staff officer at No.7 Operational Training Unit in 1940 he had, as part of a makeshift airfield defence flight, shot down an intruding

German bomber. Later he commanded 111 Squadron with whom he shot down an Me109 and damaged two others. In September 1941 he was promoted to become a Wing Commander at North Weald.

An aircraft erection party, the number of which Wing Commander Royce and Group Captain Oliver Carter would decide upon later, were to travel to Gibraltar to unload the Spitfires, where they would be reassembled and craned on to HMS Eagle. The majority of the party would be taken from RAF Sealand in Wales, a depot for packing aircraft due to be sent abroad. The men would afterwards be returned back to the UK by ship, with a small maintenance group travelling with the Spitfires on-board the aircraft carrier. All personnel were to be issued with tropical kit and in addition the pilots were to have their flying kit, including parachutes and dinghies, given to them before departure. All tools, equipment, and technical manuals on the Spitfire, plus oil and Glycol coolant would be sent out on-board the ship with the erection party. Each Spitfire would also carry a small amount of spares during its delivery flight to Malta.

For security reasons, the personnel involved were not to be told of their destination initially and maps would only be issued once in Gibraltar or at the discretion of Wing Commander McLean. All crates and boxes would state only the Middle East as their destination. To assist with the pilot's navigation to Malta from the carrier, they would be led by eight Bristol Blenheim aircraft flown by experienced crews. These crews would prepare before hand at Bicester, where they would be vaccinated and equipped, before moving down to Portreath, Cornwall. They would then fly out under the command of Wing Commander Graham to Gibraltar on February 12th to be ready to escort the Spitfires, four per flight.

At 21:00 on the same day of the meeting the order was sent from the Air Ministry to Headquarters 41(Maintenance) Group, who were responsible for the supply of aircraft, stating that 16 Mark Vb Spitfires, with jettisonable fuel tanks, were to be taken from those allocated to the Middle East, and, as a priority, were to be packed in crates ready for delivery on February 6th 1942.

The operation to deliver the Spitfires would consist of two separate parts. The first part of the operation to transport the pilots and crated Spitfires to Gibraltar would be known by the code name **Operation Quarter**. The code for the second part, the flight of the aircraft to Malta, would be announced later.

After reporting to the Air Ministry and having the details of the operation explained to him, Wing Commander McLean was issued with a folder containing details of the operation and his own responsibilities. These included the supervision of all RAF personnel involved whilst aboard HMS Eagle and liaising with the ship's Captain. In addition, he was to ensure all the pilots including those of the Blenheims knew the details involved and had studied the information provided. He was also to check the aircraft were ready, and that each pilot was spoken with to confirm that they were fully aware of what was expected of them with regard to cruising speeds and heights flown etc.

The Captain of the aircraft carrier would decide the actual flying off position but this would not be more than 580 nautical miles (670 statute miles) allowing a safety margin of 33% in the air. The additional fuel tanks were to be retained unless it compromised the safety of the aircraft and its range. The aircraft would carry 84 gallons of fuel in the main tanks and 90 in the auxiliary tank along with 6 gallons of engine oil giving an approximate weight of 7,330lbs. The fuel consumed during the take off and climb to cruising height would leave the Spitfires with a range of around 940 miles. The aircraft were to take off using the main fuel tanks and then switch to the additional tank when at a safe height. If the tank was jettisoned when empty it was considered that the range would then be in the region of 1,040 miles.

The radio call signs for the Spitfire formation was to be **LYGON,** but radio silence would be kept except in the case of an emergency. The Blenheims unfortunately carried different radio equipment, which would prevent them from communicating both with the Spitfires and the aircraft carrier.

In January a provisional list of sixteen pilots was put forward for the operation, these were subsequently interviewed by Wg Cdr John McLean, fourteen of those initially listed went on to take part in Operation Spotter:

Original list of pilots

F/Lt Grant	Stanley Bernard Grant
S/Ldr. Acting F/Lt. Macqueen	Norman Carter Macqueen
F/Lt. Heppell, DFC	Philip Whaley Ellis Heppell
Sergeant Sim	Robert James Sim
P/O Leggo	Douglas Cecil Leggo
P/O Plagis	John Agorastos Plagis
P/O Nash	Peter Alfred Nash
Sergeant Fox	Harry Fox
Sergeant Iarra (Incorrect spelling)	John William Yarra
Sergeant Brennan	Virgil Paul Brennan
Sergeant Gas (Incorrect spelling)	Murray Irving Gass
F/Sgt. Cormack	Ian Maxwell Cormack
F/Sgt. Ferraby	David Lake Ferraby

Sergeant Tayleur	John Lovett Tayleur
P/O Geurnan (Incorrect spelling)	James Joseph Guerin
Sergeant Hesselyn	Raymond Brown Hesselyn

It was also noted that Plt Off Blackburn had not reported and Plt Off Seilmer, an American, had been taken off the list. An asterisk had been placed against the names of Sgt Fox and Sgt Gass as having insufficient operational experience and therefore not being suitable. A hand written note by Wing Commander Henry Pearson Rogers at the foot of the page stated that the Deputy Chief of Air Staff would take the matter up with Fighter Command. They no doubt recommended the two other pilots who were subsequently posted.

Fg Off Norman William Lee
Plt Off Kenric Newton Lathrop Murray

Pilot Officer Blackburn did in fact travel out on the Cape Hawke but asked, for personal reasons, not to be one of the pilots flying off. As for the two rejected pilots Sergeant Murray Irving Gass was eventually posted to Malta in June 1942 flying off HMS Eagle. Four months later on October 4th he was shot down into the sea, his body was never recovered. On May 9th 1942 Harry Fox, an American with the Royal Canadian Air Force, flew into Malta from the USS Wasp. Within a week he had also been shot down and killed, again his body was lost to the sea.

Pilot Officer Peter Nash kept a diary, which mentioned that on January 30th he was informed by his commanding officer that he was to be posted, he was told the destination as being Malta, but first he had to report to Portreath, Cornwall. The following day having spent sometime with his parents in London he began the train journey to Cornwall, arriving on Sunday February 1st. RAF Portreath was used as the last stage from which ferrying aircraft would leave England on their journey to North Africa and the Middle East. Several other pilots had also arrived at that time. The pilots were all later vaccinated, and then had the chance to fly a Spitfire II borrowed from 66 Squadron, which had a long-range fuel tank. This additional tank was fitted permanently to the port wing of the aircraft, providing an extra 40 gallons of fuel. It was not the jettisonable 90-gallon tank fitted under the central fuselage that would actually be used later on the delivery to Malta. Peter Nash described the Spitfire used as **"Very ropey."** Flt Sgt David Ferraby recalled later that, because of misty flying conditions, they had to come in to land from the sea and over the cliff. One of the pilots came in so low that he tore off the Pitot Tube from the wing, (this provided the aircrafts air speed readings), but he was still able to make a safe landing.

On February 1st the Air Ministry sent a coded telegram to RAF Headquarters, Malta, informing them that Spitfires and their carefully selected pilots would be sent out that month and that because of the restricted space on the carrier, only 15 could be sent. Their advice given below showed perhaps a lack of appreciation of the desperate situation in Malta:

'You will therefore have to conserve these aircraft as much as possible and restrict their use to essential high flying operations over Malta for which their performance makes them especially suitable. We have found here Spitfires are generally not as robust as Hurricanes and require good surfaced runways. Anything you can do to improve surfaces of selected aerodrome will prolong their serviceable life.'

Enquiries were also made on the availability of Browning Machine guns for the aircraft if they were to be delivered without then. The reply was received the next day confirming that good stocks were available on Malta. Also on February 2nd the pilots received both their tropical and flying kit, this included a .38 revolver and 50 rounds of ammunition. Some of the pilots then left to begin their leave, only to be called back for a meeting the following morning with Wg Cdr McLean who advised them more details of the forthcoming operation. The pilots were then dismissed for their short period of leave. Peter Nash noted in his diary:

'I guess we are in for a pretty sticky time'

On February 6th a coded telegram was sent to Gibraltar advising of the forthcoming delivery of Spitfires and that this time, unlike the Hurricane deliveries, the aircraft would be assembled on the quay and then craned on to the aircraft carrier. It was stated that the group consisted of 12 Officers and 145 other ranks, plus an expert from Supermarine who would also embark on the carrier. It was confirmed that the aircraft were to be loaded with cannon only and the machine guns were to be removed and retained. The RAF staff at Gibraltar were also made aware of the arrival of the escorting Blenheims due on the 12th.

The eight Blenheim crews, who were to navigate and lead the Spitfires, had been advised that they were, prior to leaving in addition to their normal training, to carry out practice flights leading formations of aircraft working in liaison with 131 Squadron, who would provide the aircraft for the formation flying.

The fighter pilots reported to RAF Kirkham, near Blackpool at 16:00 on February 8th and were all billeted together in a single hut. Four more pilots joined the group the next day. Checks were made to ensure all were properly kitted out and had received their inoculations and vaccinations, a further inoculation was given against Yellow Fever. They were also paid up to date and given an advance of the next 28 days pay. The officer pilots were given a kit limit of 224 lbs and the airmen of two kitbags. Only 30lb of kit, excluding flying gear, could be taken to embarkation, of which 20 lb had to be left at Gibraltar to follow later with the remainder of their kit when possible. This left 10lbs of kit, which was to be stowed within the Spitfire. The pilots travelled in their blue uniforms and were granted an allowance of £20.00 each to purchase any kit that could not be fitted in to their 30lb quota. All baggage was marked with the pilots name, rank, number, the code word 'Quarter' and 'Middle East' only.

David Ferraby said that the Spotter pilots never actually saw their kit again as it was sent to Malta from Gibraltar by a submarine that was sunk by enemy action. This was probably HMS Pandora (N42) a type 'P' submarine that had left Gibraltar with supplies bound for Malta. She was hit on April 1st 1942 by two bombs from Italian aircraft and sank in under 4 minutes whilst in the Grand Harbour before unloading had been completed. Twenty-five out of the crew of 53 were killed. The submarine was later raised in September 1943 but was subsequently scrapped.

The Vice Chief of Naval Staff approved the Navy's part of the forthcoming delivery operation on February 7th. The aircraft were to take off from the carrier in daylight around 600 miles from Malta and, flying at a speed of 155mph, would have sufficient range with the additional fuel tanks for 890 miles. The Spitfires would be stowed below deck for protection against both weather and the sea, with the Eagles own two Sea Hurricanes being stored on deck in the shelter of the island command centre.

The Air Ministry on February 7th advised Gibraltar and Malta of the two code names that would be used during the operation. The first phase up until embarkation on the aircraft carrier was completed would be **'Quarter,'** which had been referred to earlier, the second phase, the delivery of the aircraft to Malta would be code named **'Spotter'**.

On the 9th February the Air Ministry advised Air Vice Marshall Hugh Pugh Lloyd, the senior Air Officer Commanding on Malta that the intention was to have five Spitfire squadrons when possible based on Malta, and the first of these Spitfires were now on the way to the island.

At 4:00am on Tuesday February 10th the pilots boarded several lorries, along with their baggage, and were driven down to the docks at Liverpool, one of the baggage lorries suffered a burst radiator on the way and had to be towed in by one of the other vehicles. By 10:00 all were aboard the M.V.Cape Hawke, the ship chosen for the operation, with the Spitfires packed in individual crates below deck in the cargo hold.

The M.V.Cape Hawke at the time was a relatively new cargo vessel built by Lithgows Ltd of Glasgow. She was launched in 1940 and completed in 1941, she was owned by the Lyle Shipping Company, Glasgow. Powered by diesel engines she was 447 feet long with a breadth of 56 feet and a gross tonnage of 6,884. She would survive her wartime service and was eventually broken up for scrap in 1967.

The cargo ship M V Cape Hawke owned by the Lyle Shipping Company
(www.clydebuiltships.co.uk)

Peter Nash wrote of her in his diary:

'Carpenters have done a good job in four days- four berth bunks for officers- tier bunks for troops. We mess in wardroom. Shove off at 14:00pm. Sea calm but ship lightly laden and will roll pretty bad in bad weather'.

Flt Lt John Yarra was not very impressed with the ship describing her as a

'**Dirty little 5,000-tonner**' and wrote:

'**The conditions are not fit for animals to live in. The beds are lousy and all the condensation from the roof falls on us when we sleep**'.

Leading Aircraftman George Revell was one of the fitters who were part of the Special Operations Maintenance Party, the men who would erect the Spitfires, although he was unaware of that at this stage. He had been told by Station Headquarters that he was to go to RAF Kirkham for a special aircraft course, and that he would then get 28 days leave before embarking overseas. Having had 48-hours leave, he reported to Kirkham on February 8th. George, as the pilots previously had done, under went the various medicals, vaccinations and inoculations, prior to collecting overseas kit. The men were then informed that there was in fact no special aircraft course and no leave, and they would be embarking for service overseas two days later on the 10th. It would be a week later at sea on the Cape Hawke before George and his colleagues found out from Squadron Leader Hughes, the Senior Engineering Officer, and Wg Cdr John McLean what their destination, and mission were to be.

Pilot Officer Peter Nash continued his diary whilst on-board the MV Cape Hawke:

Peter Nash Diary: Wednesday 11th February
'**Passed a very good night. Weather still OK although cloudy. We are escorted by two corvettes and accompanied by another ship like ours, evidently for rescue purposes. We rounded north coast of Ireland today. Whisky 6/- per bottle, Gin 4/-, cigarettes 3/4d per 100. Played cards all day. Ship rocks a lot even in our calm seas, heaven help my stomach if we strike a bad patch. We logged 204 miles today.**'
(Malta Aviation Museum)

Peter Nash Diary: Thursday 12th February
'**Weather still holding but swell increasing with the result that she rolls more and more. All pilots OK but 50% of the troops down with sickness. There is a U-Boat 100 miles behind us and chasing us. We shall possibly hear from him anonymously. We logged 209 miles today. We are about 150 miles off the west coast of Ireland, course 218 degrees.**'

'**Our two escorting corvettes are making very rough weather in these seas. The food is pretty grim. 21:00 enemy aircraft reported in vicinity.**'

Leading Aircraftman George Revell on the contrary seemed to like the food:

'The food has been exceptionally good and better than any RAF cooking. The story goes that the cook was brought out of retirement for this trip. He works miracles in a tiny cramped room that rejoices in the name of a galley, partly open to the weather. Many hours have I spent there 'spud bashing' but it was quite pleasant'.

'We take it in turn to be Mess Orderly and this means carrying the food from the galley to your messmates. This is an heroic task when she is performing that 'corkscrew' movement and many a medal has been won by lads carrying egg and bacon, porridge and coffee across a slippery deck in the poor light of early morning so that the lads could have their breakfast.

'A canteen aboard does a roaring trade with cigarettes at 50 for 1/8d and biscuits, chocolate and sweets. Among those sharing our accommodation are some Sergeant pilots-2 of them share a wind up gramophone and play a record of 'Stop beating around the mulberry bush' At frequent intervals. One is an Aussie (Jack Yarra) and his pal is from New Zealand.

Diary of an 'Erk' with S.O.M.P. (RAF Museum London)

Peter Nash Diary: Friday 13th February

'Sea calm. We logged 246 miles today. I got up this morning a bit late to find I'd missed the washing water. Felt pretty grubby all day. The Wing-Co gave us another gen session this morning. Had a light party this evening. I didn't drink much. U-Boat scare tonight. Nothing serious.

'Incidentally P/O Blackburn shot a seagull this morning. That combined with the date has given the crew a bit of the blues. We should reach Gibraltar about Wednesday. My God, I hope so. We heard about the Scharnhorst and Co. getting away. Pretty bad show. All the Swordfish that went out were shot down.'

On this day the Air Ministry advised Gibraltar to pass on to Wg Cdr John McLean of the changing of the Spitfires radio call sign from **LYGON,** which had been used several times previously, to **EXILE.** The ground station on Malta would be call sign **GONDAR.**

Peter Nash Diary: Saturday 14th February

'Weather deteriorating. We only logged 178 miles today. Everyone pretty cheesed. Phoney air raid alarm this morning. We now reckon another 6 days before we reach Gibraltar. Holy smoke! Played cards tonight and won £1. Not much else to say. I have only two thoughts-one for my girl (the biggest one) and one for when the hell we get off the bloody ship. We also had a spot of bother in the engine room this evening. A bolt sheered somewhere. So we hove to and lay wallowing and rolling frightfully for about half an hour.'

The Air Ministry sent on this day (14th) a secret Cypher to the RAF Shipper, Gibraltar advising of the handling required for the crated Spitfires that were on the way:

16 Spitfires left U.K. 10/2 name of ship follows, Care in off loading is required as swinging irons have been found to be defective. Desireable that supplementary sling wires round each end be used during discharge. Steady lifts to be made and all jerking avoided.

Peter Nash Diary: Sunday 15th February
'I slept in and missed breakfast and lunch this morning. Weather pretty grim. Everything pretty rough. Our cabins are streaming water and they stink to high heaven of paint, sweat and general rancidness. Our progress is getting slower, only 120 miles today. We may reach Gibraltar by Friday. We are all damp and filthy dirty.'

A Naval secret cipher was sent on the 15th from the Director of Sea Transport stating:

British ship CAPE HAWKE speed 10 knots sailed U.K. 10th February with following for discharge at Gibraltar.
1 Launch weighing 16 tons. 8 tons baggage, 22 tons mail, 3 tons ammunition. 14 tons stores, 19 Spitfires and 1 fulmar aircraft. Also on-board 13 officers and 131 other ranks R.A.F. and 1 civilian passenger.

The civilian was almost certainly the representative from Supermarine the Spitfire manufacturers who was travelling with the party. The number of Spitfires listed as 19 was incorrect, as only sixteen is referred to in all further reports.

Peter Nash Diary: Monday 16th February
'Slept through breakfast again today. Weather abated today. Excitement this evening. We know we were due to pass a north bound convoy that

was being attacked by U-Boats about 19:00 hours. We did not see convoy but a U-Boat alarm went out and the corvettes dashed around and lobbed a couple of depth charges out. It has quietened down now but evidently we are being followed by several of the bastards. We may see some fun tonight. 'The old ship is going absolutely flat out now.'

In the early hours of the 16th February a Sunderland aircraft waited north of Malta to avoid an ongoing air raid before attempting to land. On-board were a group of eight pilots, all with previous experience of flying the Spitfire; they were to boost the number of pilots available when the new fighters arrived. They were led by a Canadian, Squadron Leader Stanley Turner DFC, nicknamed 'Bull' who took over command of 249 Squadron on Malta. He was a seasoned pilot who had seen extensive action over France and Britain, with 10 victories already to his name. Accompanying him were two pilots from 66 Squadron Flight Lieutenant Percy 'Laddie' Lucas and the Channel Islander Pilot Officer Raoul Daddo-Langlois. Three other Pilot Officers, Harry Fox from Liverpool, Bob Sergeant and an American, Tex Putnam, were also on-board, along with two Australians, Sergeant Tim Goldsmith and Tom Freeman. Another small group of pilots would follow later on in the month.

Peter Nash Diary: Tuesday 17th February
'The night passed quietly. A Spanish ship has been bombed 100 miles away. Sea not too bad, making a good speed. Heavy sea mist rolled up towards evening. The chaps who have top bunks are beginning to give them up and sleep in the wardroom to dodge the water that cascades down on them in multitudinous droplets from metal ceiling of the cabin. I'm damn glad I have a lower bunk! Logged 180 miles today.'

Peter Nash Diary: Wednesday 18th February
'Weather fine. Turned east today. Logged 230 miles. Not much to write about, all quiet, we now know who is not coming. They are P/O Blackburn (at his own request owing to his wife, don't blame him), Sgt Jack 'Slim' Yarra RAAF and another Sergeant.'

Yarra was on the eventual list to fly off but was prevented from doing so as his Spitfire had been used to provide parts for the other aircraft, and so was not flyable. It is not clear who the sergeant pilot referred to was, possibly Sgt Harry Fox, (not to be confused with the Plt Off Harry Fox who had flown to Malta on the Sunderland two days earlier).

Peter Nash Diary: Thursday 19th February

'Making good progress in good weather and good calm sea. We were met by a Sunderland. The destroyer that we expected has not turned up. Work has started by getting jigs etc out of hold and erecting on deck.

'The Chief Steward caught his second (who is very far gone in the nut) stealing. He beat him up by hitting, first with his right and followed up with his head. The second steward's face is pretty battered!'

Prime Minister Winston Churchill received a telegram this day (19th) from the Middle East Commander in Chief expressing his serious concern at the air situation on Malta. The Chiefs of Staff were consequently tasked with reviewing the position and informing Churchill of their intentions. Later, with the agreement of the Prime Minister a cable was sent back to the Middle East advising that assistance would be provided to Malta as a priority and stating:

'Our view is that Malta is of such importance both as an air staging point and as an impediment to the enemy reinforcement route that the most drastic steps are justifiable to sustain it. Even if the Axis maintain their present scale of attack on Malta thus reducing its value it will continue to be of great importance to war as a whole by containing important enemy air forces during critical months.'

An encrypted telegram was also sent on the 19th to Gibraltar confirming that the Cape Hawke was on her way with sixteen crated Spitfires, twelve cases of lubricating oil and 283 cases of Aero parts. To ease the unloading the cases were marked to show that they contained either maintenance equipment, erection equipment, or equipment to be carried in the Spitfires on their delivery flight. Also included were what was termed Accoutrements, no doubt the pilots and others airmen's personal kit.

The cargo ship also carried a variety of stores for Gibraltar including 196 cases of bedding, a 45-foot refuelling launch, a Fulmar aircraft, 25 petrol tanks, 251 cases of oil and a replacement gun turret for aircraft A6109. In addition there was an eagerly awaited 847 bags of mail.

Peter Nash Diary: Friday 20th February

'While writing this I am sitting up on the forward deck sunning myself. The weather is lovely and the sea calm. A plane (I think a Hudson) has just appeared to port. It has disappeared for the time being but no doubt he will be back. A destroyer has added herself to our escort today. We are due at Gibraltar early tomorrow morning. Work is progressing on getting the jigs rigged on the forward deck but the pilots this afternoon are taking tea and biscuits in this glorious sun.

'At about 7:30pm there was some excitement when one of the corvettes raced about dropping depth charges. Plenty of noise!! All quiet in an hour, however. We sighted Cape St Vincent light this evening.'

Peter Nash Diary: Saturday 21st February

'We docked this morning in Gibraltar. Raining in buckets full. The top of the rock is completely obscured by thick white mist that drifts about in the wind eddies. Leggo, Plagis and I went ashore and had lunch at the Bristol. Very good food. Bags of fruit- oranges, tangerines, bananas, grapefruit. We came back to the ship for tea and a small general talk by the Wing-Co. Later we went to the Embassy where we all met and got pretty tight. The band consists of one Spaniard of doubtful origin and 8 'calientes' who alternately blow their lungs out and eat innumerable chocolates. Got pretty lively. All pubs close at 9:30pm so we went to a joint called Casino Calpe where you drink out of cups. Met army officers (Devon's). They took us to their mess where stayed till 1:30am (curfew) Talked our way back through police. Visiting them Tuesday. Leggo and Plagis squiffy.'

In the early morning of the 21st a Sunderland flying boat arrived on Malta after an 11-hour flight from Gibraltar, carrying Squadron Leader Ronald Chaffe who would take over as commanding officer of 185 Squadron. Accompanying him were ten more Spitfire pilots, including New Zealander Keith Lawrence who already had a number of victories to his name from the Battle of Britain, along with fellow New Zealander Plt Off Jeff West. There were also three Canadians, Flt Lt Bud Connell, Fg Off Buck McNair and Buck Buchanan. Plt Off Jimmy James was from Rhodesia and Plt Off Sandy McHan was American. The group also included the Australian Flt Sgt Gordon Tweedale, plus Sergeant Charlie Broad, Plt Off D'Arcy Milburn and Plt Off Dennis Kelly.

After twelve days at sea the Cape Hawke finally docked at the Inner Harbour of Gibraltar with the airmen pleased to be finally back on dry land, if only temporarily. The men had time to explore their new surroundings, David Ferraby was amazed whilst out walking to bump in to his barber from his home town of Hornsea, and found that he had been part of the crew on-board one of their escorting corvettes.

Also tied to the quay was the aircraft carrier HMS Eagle, a ship that had started out as a battleship. Ordered by the Chilean government to be called Almirante Cochrane, she was purchased whilst still under construction by Armstrong Whitworth from the Chileans in 1918 and converted into an aircraft carrier. It was not, however, until 1924 she was commissioned for use and even then she still had her engine room instruments written in metric and Spanish. She was easily identifiable, as she was the only British carrier to have two funnels. Displacing 27,000 tonnes with a length of 667 feet and a breadth of 92 feet, she was powered by steam turbines fed from 32 boilers that allowed her to reach a speed of 24 knots. Her own complement of aircraft in 1942 were the torpedo carrying Fairey Swordfish biplanes and Hawker Sea Hurricanes, with their squadron members making up a total of around 835 men on-board.

HMS Eagle in a prewar visit to the Grand Harbour, Malta.

The sixteen large crates from Cape Hawke were unloaded and lined up on the quay, but for security reasons work would not start until after dark. German spies were suspected to be in the area, and a daily work force of Spanish labourers, who might have had German sympathies, also worked in the docks. They would cross from Spain at dawn to work in the harbour, but had to return back across the frontier by dusk.

Peter Nash Diary: Sunday 22nd February
'When we got back last night Plt Off Ken Murray RAAF (very drunk

and objectionable) cleared up. Everyone feeling pretty liverish especially Guerin. We went over to drome to see Blenheim boys. Lunched at Bristol. Flg Off Norman Lee, Murray and Heppell still drinking but Heppell does control himself! Looked at the sub in afternoon very interesting. The Lieutenant then took us (Leggo and I) aboard the parent ship Maidstone and we had a couple of drinks. I went to bed at a reasonable hour but got up in my pyjamas because corvette officers were aboard in a party, very lively. Eventually in bed about 3:30am.'

At 8:00pm on the 22nd the men of the Special Erection Party began to open the crates. The crates were substantial wooden units having steel straps around them leading to slinging points at the top. The crate ends were secured by a number of coach bolts accessed from behind wooden covers nailed to the crates. Once the covers had been carefully removed they were retained. The end of the crate was then removed to allow access into the crate, where various aircraft parts had to be removed first before access could be made to the bolts on the floor that secured a cradle on which the fuselage was mounted.

A Coles Crane lorry operated by an RAF driver was then positioned to pick up the slings attached to the lifting points on the roof of the crate at the opened end. A careful lift by the crane then allowed access to the underside of the crate to which a brave and trusting airman then went beneath, in order to help slacken the bolts of the cradle, which could then be removed from inside the crate. Any items not required immediately were then placed back in the crate, which was then resealed with the access covers being replaced. Any debris or signs of activity were then removed, so that by the next morning when the Spanish labourers returned to the area, it looked just the same as it had done the day before. The night's work, which had been hampered by heavy rain, finally finished at 2:00am.

Peter Nash Diary: Monday 23rd February
'Got up pretty late this morning. Had lunch on the ship regretted it. Leggo, Plagis Guerin and I went ashore about 1:30pm and booked rooms at the Rock Hotel for tonight. Dropped in at the Bristol during our very impromptu shopping tour. Had a damn fine haircut. Booked seats at the RN cinema then back to Rock for dinner. Went to flicks and saw 'Virginia City' Quite good. Before entering cinema everyone buys fruit and nuts from the stall outside. It makes quite a succulent show!!'

After dark on the 23rd work recommenced on the harbour quay, beginning with the removal of the ends of the crates previously worked on. The Coles Crane was used to lift the crate at the far end to help slide the fuselage attached to its cradle out of the crate. The bolts securing the two together were then removed. Next, the fuselage was lifted by the crane via a sling and pivoted on its tail wheel, until a trestle could be positioned just behind the engine bulkhead, allowing the fuselage to be lowered on to the trestle.

Having removed the fuselage, the wings, in their protective frames, were then carried from the crate and positioned adjacent to the fuselage. The supporting framework was removed and then the wing was manhandled into position to allow a minimum number of rootend bolts to be inserted, securing the wing to the fuselage. Once this had been done the undercarriage could be lowered and locked down. No attempt was made to connect any of the other systems at this stage. The crane then lifted the Spitfire in order that the trestle could be removed, and the aircraft was then positioned to a point adjacent to HMS Eagle where her flight deck crane could hoist the aircraft aboard.

The lighting on the flight deck was reduced to a bare minimum so that any curious Spanish or German eyes could not easily see the work going on. To create a diversion during the lifting of the Spitfires or their additional equipment, the Fleet Air Arm crews arranged some activity on the flight deck including running up the engines of the Sea Hurricanes to attract attention their way. Work continued until 7:00am, by which time 12 of the 16 Spitfires had been removed from their crates part assembled and craned onto the Eagle. Once on-board, the Spitfires were pushed on to the lift and taken below deck to the hangar, along with a large pallet on wheels which contained items still to be fitted to the aircraft including propeller, tailplane, rudder, elevators, armaments, fairings and the 90 gallon fuselage fuel tank. At the end of the work the crates were once again restored to look as though they had not been touched.

Peter Nash Diary: Tuesday 24th February
'Passed a very pleasant night at the Rock. Arose around 8:30am. After breakfast back to Cape Hawke. Had lunch at Rock and checked out. Got kit out of ship and went aboard aircraft carrier Eagle. Very good cabins. Had a quiet session in the evening in the wardroom with a sub name Smedding who lives at Rye and knows Ramsden. Shot a few lines to each other and bed around 12:00 midnight. Very good weather today. They got 12 Spitfires aboard the Eagle. The troops are working wonderfully well.'

On Malta, Squadron Leader Stan Turner, the commanding officer of 249 Squadron, led Laddie Lucas out on to the balcony of the Xara Palace in Mdina, which served as the officers' quarters. Lucas was told he would be one of the new flight commanders and Turner wanted him to change the manner of flying from the vic formation, of 3 aircraft in an arrow head formation, to line abreast, similar to that flown successfully by the Germans. The two pilots together later flew a Hurricane each for 35 minutes to practise the new style, which would be flown from then onwards on Malta.

During the 24th the RAF members of the Special Operations Maintenance Party moved on to the HMS Eagle. In the evening the remaining four Spitfires were unloaded from their containers and an hour after midnight were also aboard the Eagle. The now empty crates, in which the Spitfires had been delivered, were retained to be used for the construction of buildings at North Front which was to be the new assembly area for the Special Operations Maintenance Party on Gibraltar. The tired assembly crews slept on the lower hangar deck beneath the wings of the Spitfires on canvas and metal framed folding beds with a couple of blankets supplied by the Navy.

The accommodation for the pilots was not ideal either David Ferraby noted:

'At least on Cape Hawke we had our wooden bunks, but on Eagle the crew and us had to doss down wherever we weren't in the way. The spot I picked for my bedding was on top of a wire mesh lock-up store in the hangar, with blokes assembling Spits all night long.'
Malta: The Spitfire Year 1942. Christopher Shores, Brian Cull with Nicola Malizia (Grub Street 1991)

Peter Nash Diary: Wednesday 25th February
'Weather holding fine. Work progressing on aircraft. Last aboard last night. Stayed in hangar most of day with the kite. All the boys working on it were on the echelon at Biggin Hill and know me. I vaguely remember a few of them but not very well!! However, my plane is further forward and giving the least trouble of the lot. Expected to sail tonight.'

Despite their late night the RAF assembly workers were woken at 6:30 the next day for breakfast before starting the further fitting out of the aircraft from around 8:00am. Squadron Leader 'Shorty' Hughes, the Senior Engineering Officer in charge, had divided the assembly workers into work parties, each having two Spitfires to continue building. Propellers were fitted, radiator systems assembled and filled with glycol coolant, instruments and radios were fitted, hydraulics and airlines were coupled, along with countless other tasks

29

both big and small.

When the aircraft were completed they were taken up on deck to be fuelled and to have their engines run. The aircraft were not test flown, not only for secrecy, but also because they could not be landed back on the carrier. There was considerable difficulty experienced during these engine tests in getting a reliable transfer of fuel from the external fuselage tanks, a problem that would reoccur later.

LAC George Revell noted that both cannons and machine guns were fitted to the aircraft despite the earlier instructions that machine guns would not be carried in order to reduce weight, and therefore increase the aircrafts endurance. The guns were also harmonised to converge the shells to one point, this task being carried out under the cover of darkness. The gun harmonisation may not have been carried out on all the Spitfires, as prior to going into action on Malta on March 10th the cannons of some aircraft still required this work to be completed.

A secret cypher sent from Gibraltar to Malta on the 26th stated that the Browning machine guns from the Spitfires had been retained at Gibraltar. David Ferraby also remembered that the empty machine gun ammunition boxes in the wing were used as storage areas for their kit, so only the cannons must have been fitted for the flight.

On the 25th a Naval cypher was sent to Malta confirming HMS Eagle and her escort would leave Gibraltar on the 27th and on the second day out the Spitfires would be flown off in two flights of eight, one hour apart starting at approximately 7:20am, each flight would be led by two Blenheims, with four other Blenheims following in reserve. The first group of Spitfires was ordered to land at Takali, the second group and the Blenheims at Luqa.

Peter Nash Diary: Thursday 26th February
'We sailed at 02:00 this morning (27th). Weather glorious. Some of the planes on deck running up. Owing to the difficulty of manoeuvring the aircraft, a slight reallocation has taken place. 'Owing to the fact that I have altered the oxygen fittings on 366 I am keeping it (cheers) and flying in the first party. Engines going beautifully. Air Arm boys shaken by the guts in our engines!'

The work on the Spitfires continued again on the 26th until around midnight. Then in the early hours of the 27th HMS Eagle set sail for Malta along with her escort from Force H, a naval formation that had been created in 1940 to replace the presence of the French fleet in the western Mediterranean. HMS Eagle was also escorted by the aircraft carrier HMS Argus, carrying nine Fulmar aircraft to provide fighter protection. In the convoy were the Battleship HMS Malaya and the light cruiser HMS Hermione, plus ten destroyers: Active, Anthony, Blankney, Croome, Duncan, Exmoor, Laforey, Lightning, Whitehall and Wishart. During the trip precautionary depth charges were deployed although there was no sign of enemy activity.

This first attempted delivery of Spitfires to Malta was, however, to end as a dismal failure. After around 20 hours at sea the continued problems with the fuel transfer from the external tanks was to bring a postponement of the delivery. Flight Lieutenant Stanley Grant described the problem:

'The next day when we were well clear of land Hughes brought the aircraft up on deck to run the engines and, above all, to test the functioning of the long-range tanks without which the operation was not on. These first 90-gallon tanks had evidently been produced in a great hurry and were 'a bit of a lash up'. The fuel was drawn up into the main tanks by suction and if there was the slightest air leak in the seal between the tank and the fuselage, there was no transfer.

'Hughes soon found that the seals were not satisfactory and although he and his team strove hard all that day and well into the night he could not make them work properly. Accordingly, around midnight, with our take off due the next morning, Hughes sent a message to the Admiral via Wing Commander Maclean, saying that the aircraft could not be allowed to take off without further extensive tests. And since his men had now been working for over twenty hours without rest they could not continue without some sleep. We heard later that the Admiral nearly exploded, and sent back the message that under no circumstances could his ships hang around in daylight in the middle of the Mediterranean, within easy reach of enemy bombers. The Spitfires had to take off the next morning – at all costs. But Hughes was adamant. The aircraft were not, in his view, serviceable and he could not agree to their take off until he was certain that the tanks would work. So the Admiral had to give in, and the whole fleet turned around and steamed back to Gibraltar.'

Skies Of Fire: Dramatic Air Combat. Alfred Price. (Cassell & Co. 2002)

The 90-gallon fuel tanks that caused so many problems were made from a light alloy and located underneath the centre of the aircraft fuselage, between the undercarriage legs. They attached to the aircraft by a spigot on top of the tank engaging in a housing beneath the underside of the aircraft, and were retained by a locking mechanism that could be released from the cockpit. Two hooks under the aircraft prevented the tank falling backwards and possibly damaging the aircraft when it was jettisoned.

The front upper part of the tank had a filler cap, and a vent pipe ran along the top venting at the rear. The fuel was transferred by suction via a spring-loaded connection on top of the tank to the fuselage. Washers and grease were used to try and create an airtight seal between the tank and the fuselage.

The tanks were subsequently removed to be examined having been drained by using the Eagles refuelling equipment to suck out the contents, with a screwed plug in the bottom being removed from the tank to drain off the remaining fuel that could not be reached. The problem was thought to be from an air leak as fuel was being vented out, so various attempts were made to improve the connection. Although some minor improvement was made, it was not enough to risk going ahead with the mission.

Peter Nash Diary: Friday 27th February
'Back at Gibraltar 10:00 last night. We could not have gone anyway, the weather was bad at Malta. Work going on in hangar.'

Peter Nash Diary: Saturday 28th February
'Very little to enter here. Still at Gibraltar. Aircraft gradually becoming serviceable.'

A secret Naval Cypher was sent from Gibraltar advising of the postponement of the delivery due to the problems with the tanks, which at this stage, they believed that they could resolve without assistance from the UK.

Another secret cypher from Gibraltar made the following points:

1) Long-range tanks had not been fitted nor tested with petrol in before aircraft left UK.

2) Assembly parties had no experience with long-range tanks and had no reason to expect that tanks crated in individual aircraft would not fit.

3) A large number of parts were missing which entailed stripping 16th aircraft to make 15 serviceable.

4) I do not intend to leave Gibraltar until Air Commodore reports all aircraft are ready to take to the air.

5) In all respects other than long-range tanks I am informed parts of aircraft were serviceable and erection satisfactory.

6) Urge most strongly that in future operations aircraft are assembled

and tested with all components in place in UK before being crated.

7) After consulting Air Commodore consider advisable expert in fitting tanks should be flown out.

At RAF Odiham late on the evening of February 28th an urgent investigation was begun to discover the likely problem with the additional fuel tanks. Under Wing Commander MacDiarmid, an attempt was made to replicate the problems in Gibraltar. Fighter Command, made a crated Spitfire (AB502) available with an erection crew to unpack and assemble it, including the fitting of a similar 90-gallon fuel tank. Work was started at 8:00am on the following morning March 1st and was completed by 1:00pm.

The first attempt by the fitters to connect the fuel tank resulted in a severe leak at the spring-loaded junction between the tank and fuselage. It was decided to drain and remove the tank and try again to refit the unit. Having reassembled the tank, the next connection attempt worked without fault. Mr Auxtel of the Supermarine Design Department, who was in attendance, noted that special precautions were necessary to align the spring-loaded connection on fitting. To test his theories were correct, the spring-loaded junction was disturbed, and, as expected, this produced a substantial fuel leak.

The same day (March 1st) the recommendations were sent from the Air Ministry in London to Gibraltar outlining the special precautions required:

Part 1) Similar defects recently experienced here proved due to mal-alignment of spring-loaded connection to tank. Following is correct sequence of assembly.

(a) Confirm rubber-seating washer is correctly located in top of tank outlet connection and that it is clean and lightly smeared with anti-freeze grease.

(b) Confirm spherical cone of spring joint is free from burrs and clean.

Part 2) Correct assembly of tank to aircraft most important, five men are required.

(a) Four men to support tank until jettison mechanism is engaged.

(b) One man in cockpit to engage jettison mechanism and to confirm correct alignment of spring loaded connection, this must be checked as follows. Grip the elbow at top end of spring loaded connection pull it up and release sharply. This elbow is situated on floor of cockpit immediately in front of port rudder pedal.

Part 3) Prove assembly by ground test of engine with main petrol tank

cock in OFF position. Jettison tank cock only in ON position.

The last part of the message also advised that Flight Lieutenant Oatey was on his way to Gibraltar. He was listed as being an expert on the operation of the Hispano cannons, if as it seems there was also a problem with the Spitfires cannons, no doubt this was due to the cannons jamming and not firing, as this problem continued to affect the aircraft later on, even when they were on Malta.

The additional time provided by the delay allowed other work to continue on the Spitfires, including on March 1st and 2nd daily inspections being carried out. The additional equipment that was to be carried within the Spitfires along with the pilot's personal equipment was also packed at this stage into the aircraft.

Not all of the aircraft assembly crew would be required to go on-board Eagle for the fly off, and those who were to go were notified on March 3rd. When first advised that they were going for service overseas the men were told it would be for a period of six weeks, but, with other Spitfire deliveries imminent after Operation Spotter, it would be July 12th before the first of these men returned to the UK.

Peter Nash Diary: Wednesday 4th March
'Still at Gibraltar awaiting the experts. Everybody frightfully cheesed off.'

A secret Naval cypher sent from Gibraltar to the Air Ministry on the 4th stated that the Spitfires were now all serviceable. The problem had been rectified by the **'interchange of tanks and spring loaded ball valve, and also packing up the tank outlet pipe with flat rubber washers 1/6 to 1/8 inches under moulded washer in order to raise rubber washer making more positive contact with spring-loaded union on aircraft'.**

The aircraft had been run up and were considered airworthy by the engineering officers. They then requested going on with the delivery with out waiting for the arrival of the experts from the UK. The Air Ministry at Whitehall advised that they could go ahead if confident with their modifications, but that the two experts due would arrive very early the following morning. In view of this update the decision to wait was made.

The flight, now reduced to 15 aircraft with the other one having being used to supply parts, would now fly as one group of eight aircraft followed by another of 7 one hour later, each escorted by two Blenheims as previously arranged, with four in reserve following in pairs at half hour intervals. However all aircraft were now ordered to land at Luqa.

The expected experts did arrive on the 5th. The representative to inspect the tanks was Arthur Black a metallurgist who had worked with Supermarine since 1926, including involvement with the Schneider Trophy winning aircraft. It was rumoured that his departure for Gibraltar had been so sudden that he was still wearing evening dress from a previous engagement when he landed. A fuel tank had been left on the hangar floor for him to examine. He soon identified what he believed was the cause of the problem. Underneath the tank there was a small bulbous protrusion in the bottom of the tank that was a sump. The fuel transfer pipe reached within a short distance of this area, and any damage, particularly dents, to this part of the tank would obstruct the fuel flow. The solution was to cut away a part of the damaged area and then to solder on a new metal patch. Having been tested successfully, this was carried out on all the fuel tanks.

Peter Nash Diary: Thursday 5th March

'The experts arrived this morning. Leggo, Guerin and I went to the Embassy at about 2:00 this afternoon and stayed till 9:30pm. Met some good guys. Also met the girl drummer from the Universal downstairs. She caused great amusement with an English expression she has picked up. "Poor as piss". Back on the ship about 10:00pm. We sail tonight. (Cheers).'

In the early morning of March 6th Operation Spotter was back on once again with the Eagle setting sail for Malta, along with her accompanying protective escort from Force H. When at sea the aircraft were, in turn, aligned on the flight deck facing safely out to sea to have their cannons test fired, the majority of which still had problems that required adjustments to be carried out. The engines were also successfully run up and, after all the problems the 15 Spitfires were now ready to go. Apart from the photo-reconnaissance version, these would be the first Spitfires to be based beyond the shores of the United Kingdom.

At around 3:45pm a flight of what were identified as French aircraft appeared to be commencing a bombing run towards the Eagle and Force H. Several of the escorting vessels began to open fire at them, forcing the intruders to promptly turn away from the convoy without further incident.

Peter Nash Diary: Friday 6th March

'We sailed at 3:00am. Harmonised and tested cannons. (Nearly got a destroyer!) E/A approached this afternoon. Malaya opened fire and we

followed with a few rounds. Poor shooting. All set to go tomorrow.'

The pilots were up early on March 7th no doubt excited and apprehensive about what would happen later on that morning, it would be the first time that any Spitfire had been flown from an aircraft carrier. All the pilots would also be making their first take off from an aircraft carrier, in Spitfires that had only recently been assembled, and which had not even been test flown.

The first flight of eight were due to take off around 7:20am led by Squadron Leader Stanley Grant, but the two escorting Blenheims did not arrive on time. The Blenheims were required to provide navigation to Malta, as it was not possible to accurately set the Spitfires newly installed compasses whilst on the Eagle. The take off time was put back two hours to 9:15, but still there was no sign of the escort.

HMS Eagle with the Operation Spotter Spitfires on her stern.

The intention had been for the Blenheims to take off before first light from Gibraltar in order to rendezvous with the Eagle, but the pilots from 1442 Flight were not experienced enough to take off in the dark, and, due to adverse weather conditions, they postponed until after daybreak. Consequently the rendezvous was not until around 10:20am. Then HMS Eagle was steered into the wind, with her speed increased to over 15 knots to allow the Spitfires sufficient lift to take off from the short 400-foot long flight deck.

The pilots had waited nervously for the time to take off. They had sat in their Spitfires cockpits for 30 minutes before the Blenheims arrived, the engines were fully run up, with the radiator flaps set to open to prevent the aircraft from overheating. The main fuel tanks were selected as 'on', the additional fuel tank would not be used until 2,000 feet had been gained, and the other tanks then turned off till required again. As the Spitfires in turn roared down and off the deck at full throttle, they all sank unnervingly below the level of the ship's bow before the Merlin engines pulled them up in to the sky. Flt Lt Philip Heppell noted **"There were some exciting moments and the sea was very close for some."** The prevailing weather conditions were described as only just possible for the take offs, with a force 7 westerly wind and a moderating sea.

The seven aircraft of 'B' Flight, to be led by Flt Lt Norman Macqueen, waited on the Eagle for their escorting Blenheims to arrive. One Blenheim had had to turn back and return to Gibraltar with an engine problem, the other

An Operation Spotter Spitfire begins its flight to Malta (F Galea)

continued on to the Eagle, with the Spitfires taking off at around 11:50am. Fifteen minutes later the four shadowing reserve Blenheims arrived together, instead of 30 minutes apart, and they also continued on to Malta.

The Spitfires after take off, were initially to fly straight ahead until at least a height of 400 feet had been reached, with the undercarriage brought up as soon as possible to reduce drag. The radio was turned on to receive any messages but radio silence would be maintained unless there was an emergency. The cockpit canopy, which had been left open to aid escape should the aircraft have crashed off the ship into the sea, was slid shut. It was unlikely that any pilot plunging into the sea would have survived, as the aircraft carrier would have ploughed straight over the top of both pilot and aircraft.

The departure point was given as 50 miles north east of Algiers which left a flight of around four hours to cover approximately 650 miles to Malta, during which the pilots anxiously listened out for any change in the note of their Spitfires engine that might indicate a problem. If their single engine failed and they went into the sea their chances of rescue were virtually nil.

Once the altitude of 400 feet had been achieved the pilots reduced engine revs to 2,400 and climbed to join the Blenheim escort in their predetermined positions and then further reduced revs to 2,050 rpm and maintained the speed of the Blenheim. At this stage the external fuel tank would be used, and when it had been run dry it could be jettisoned if deemed necessary to further reduce drag, although Plt Off Peter Nash was the only pilot to do so. Thirty minutes before their estimated time of arrival the pilots turned on their I.F.F. (Identification Friend or Foe) transmitters to identify them as allied aircraft to the island's radar.

It had been arranged that the Spitfire pilots would check the accuracy of their compasses in conjunction with the Blenheims. If they became lost or separated, their pilot's notes, received beforehand and carried with them, gave instructions on what to do, ending on a patriotic note:

'On last leg head north. Turn east on reaching land (Sicily) Follow coast to easternmost end and then set compass to 222 degrees for Malta.
Don't flap or worry-------There'll always be an England'

Enemy aircraft had reported several sightings of the Force H convoy from around 10:25 on the first day out and onwards; the ships in turn also plotted several radar contacts of enemy aircraft. Fighters were launched from HMS Argus on the afternoon of the second day when the weather conditions had improved, but no interceptions were made.

The Spitfires were also not intercepted on the flight to Malta, the second flight of aircraft did however spot some Axis aircraft as Flt Lt Philip Heppell recalled:

'As we flew between the isle of Pantelleria and Tunisia, I spotted three tri-engined transports- clearly sitting ducks. Calling my No.2 I went in for the attack, only to discover the guns were unloaded. Some anti-climax- so we resumed our course to Malta.'

Approaching Malta the Spitfires were called by Group Captain 'Woody'

Woodhall welcoming them and warning of Me109s in the area, but the aircraft all landed at Takali airfield under the protection of Hurricanes patrolling overhead. Flight Lieutenant Philip Heppell noted:

'Landing at Takali I noticed a lack of life and indicated to my flight to disperse the Spits. When an airman popped out of a slit trench and told me in haste that there was an air raid in progress. Taking cover, I asked why the Hurricanes were flying around in formation at deck level. The answer was they have had appalling losses and they are trying to keep out of the way of the Huns until the Spits are able to help them. Although this took some believing, it was true and was a preface to what was to come and how demoralised the air raids had made the defenders.'

The rumour of Spitfires coming to Malta had been around the island for sometime, with the deeply religious Maltese praying that the 'Speedfires' as many referred to them as, would be received before the food supplies ran out, or worse before an invasion. On March 7th at around 3:00pm local time the sound of aircraft approaching was heard, their shape spotted by some coming in low and fast over the sea, then rising to clear the buildings. Some thought it was yet another air raid, which was coming in undetected, but others were cheering and counting their numbers as they flashed past rocking their wings in salute.

Sergeant Tim Goldsmith was in the Mess in Mdina when the Spitfires arrived:

"A familiar whistling brought us tumbling out, and it was true, they were here! The pilots, and the rest of the population, felt a great surge of elation as the new sleek fighters slipped in to land. The last one seemed to be having trouble with his undercarriage, and the watchers in the Mess observed professionally as the pilot finally put the Spitfire down.

Later half a dozen sergeants, looking pretty tired and with bloodshot eyes, trundled in to the Mess and threw down their kit. I was very pleased to welcome another Australian whom I had known in England, Paul Brennan from Brisbane. The man who had undercarriage trouble turned out to be Ray Hesselyn."

BLENHEIM.   PILOT'S DRILL. FLT. HEPPELL
STEHEA. BLUE.!   EXILE. BLUE.
TAKE OFF   "R"

   FLAPS - UP
RUDDER TRIM   - FULLY WOUND FORWARD
TAIL TRIM   - ONE AND HALF NOTCHES DOWN FROM CENTRAL.
RADIATOR   - FULLY OPEN AS FROM START UP.
FUEL COCK   - BOTH MAIN GRAVITY TANKS ON.
PITCH   - FULLY FORWARD.
CLIMB   - OPEN THROTTLE FULLY FORWARD AND CLIMB
                 TO AT LEAST 400 FEET STRAIGHT AHEAD. A.
WIRELESS   - SWITCH ON TO RECEIVE ON BUTTON........

AIRBOURNE   -

UNDERCARRIAGE - RETRACT AS SOON AS POSSIBLE.
CLIMB   - AFTER 400 FEET REDUCE REVS TO 2400
                 AT + 2 BOOST AT 170 M. P.H.
TRIM   - CLOSE HOOD AND TRIM AIRCRAFT TO
                 CLIMB "HANDS AND FEET OFF" TO HEIGHT
                 OF ESCORT.
FUEL   - SWITCH ON TO EXTRA TANKS AT 2,000 FT
                 THEN SWITCH OFF MAIN TANKS.
FORMATION   - JOIN-UP AS SOON AS POSSIBLE IN PRE-
                 DETERMINED POSITIONS.
CRUISING
REVS &   - ONCE IN FORMATION REDUCE TO 2050 REVS
FUEL   USE THROTTLE TO GET 160 M.P.H. OR
                 SPEED OF ESCORT. FLY ON EXTRA TANK
                 UNTIL IT RUNS DRY, SWITCH ON MAIN
                 TANKS. N. B. JETTISON EXTRA TANKS
                 IF THOUGHT NECESSARY WHEN EMPTY,
                 EXTRA 50 MILES ENDURANCE.
COMPASS   - CHECK COMPASSES WITH ESCORT AS
                 ARRANGED.
WIRELESS   - MAINTAIN R/T SILENCE, IN EMERGENCY
                 USE FOLLOWING BUTTONS AND CALL-SIGNS
                 AIRCRAFT CALL-SIGN.... EXILE....
                 BUTTON A....... FULGEL....
                 BUTTON B...........................
                 BUTTON C ....
                 BUTTON D .... FIXER...STATION.
                 N.B CALL UP IF NEAR BASE AND HAVE TO
                 ABANDON AIRCRAFT BUTTON "A"
                 CALL.............................
                 OTHER AIRCRAFT TAKE AIR SEA RESCUE
                 DRILL ON R/T
NOTE   - NOTE CHARGE ON AMMETER AND INCREASE
                 REVS IF NECESSARY, TO KEEP IT CHARG-
                 ING WHILE ON EXTRA TANK.
I.F.F.   - ON AT E.T.A. MINUS 30 MINUTES.
E.T.A.   - COURSE.............
                 DISTANCE....... 168. MILES..
                 TIME........... HOUR...
IF SEPARATED   ON LAST LEG HEAD NORTH. TURN EAST
OR LOST   - ON REACHING LAND (SICILY) FOLLOW
                 COAST TO EASTERNMOST END THEN SET
                 COMPASS TO 222 DEGREES FOR MALTA
                 DON'T FLAP OR WORRY--------THERE'LL
                 ALWAYS BE AN ENGLAND.

Flt Lt Heppell's Operation Spotter pilot notes.

Malta: No Place For Beginners

In early March 1942 16 pilots left the shores of England on their long journey to the besieged island of Malta, they were no doubt excited but apprehensive about what the future there might hold for them. The men, all had some experience of flying the Spitfire, some already had scored victories, but most had not. Paul Brennan states in the book that he had not even fired his guns in anger before Malta. They hoped that they would play their part, and be able to make a difference on Malta. Four of the pilots would certainly do more than that; out of the ten highest scoring pilots on Malta during the war, four of them were Operation Spotter pilots, John Plagis, John Yarra and Ray Hesselyn had twelve confirmed victories each, and Paul Brennan would go on to get ten.

At the end of April, a month after the arrival of the Spotter pilots, a signal was sent from Malta to the Air Ministry in London stating that the calibre of the Spitfire pilots recently sent as part of Operation Calendar (46 Spitfires delivered April 20th) needed to be improved, the men had not been up to the standard of the more experienced pilots previously flown out. Too many like Paul Brennan earlier had not yet fired their guns in action. Malta was described as **'No place for beginners. Casualties up to now the beginners.. Hope Malta can be treated as a special case.'**

The sixteen pilots of Operation Spotter originated from several different Commonwealth countries. The group were made up of six who had been born in England, plus one who had been born in India but raised in England, a Scotsman, four Australians, two New Zealanders, a South African and a Greek national, the latter two both having been raised in Southern Rhodesia.

The oldest amongst them was 28-year-old James Guerin with the youngest being nineteen-year-old John 'Junior' Tayleur; the average age was 22. Six of the pilots would be killed within three months of their arrival on Malta. One of them Ian Cormack's body was lost to the sea between the small island of Filfla and Malta. The other five who were killed lie buried in shared graves in the Capuccini Naval Cemetery.

The Capuccini Naval Cemetery is located on the southern outskirts of the village of Kalkara, approximately 2 kilometres south east of the hamlet of Rinella. In 1915 during the First World War the wounded and sick from the campaigns in Salonika and Gallipoli were brought to Malta to recover, those injured or wounded that did not survive were buried in the cemetery. The bodies of many First World War sailors, from ships either torpedoed or sunk by mine, were also interred there. On Malta the earth is shallow with hard rock beneath, making graves difficult to dig. The limited ground available required that many graves would be dug as communal or shared tombs during the two World Wars.

Three of the pilots who did survive their time on Malta did not live to see the final victory. John Yarra was killed before the end of 1942, whilst Paul Brennan and Robert Sim were both killed the following year, on opposite sides of the world, and within two days of each other. Paul Brennan lost his life in Australia, the only one of the pilots to be buried within his home country.

In all, nine out of the sixteen Operation Spotter pilots made the ultimate sacrifice during the war. Three of those nine killed were lost to the sea and have no known grave. They are remembered either on the Malta Memorial in Floriana, which lists 2,298 airmen lost through enemy action or accident, flying to or from Mediterranean bases, or on the Air Forces Memorial at Runnymede, Surrey, which bears the names of over 20,000 airmen lost in operations from the United Kingdom, and North and Western Europe. All the graves and memorials are respectfully cared for by the Commonwealth War Graves Commission, which had been set up originally in May 1917 as the Imperial War Graves Commission, an official organisation concerned with the fate of the graves during and after the end of the First World War. The Second World war saw a further 559 cemeteries and 36 new memorials added to those of the first great conflict. Today the names of over 1.7 million men and women, with or without a known grave, are recorded and commemorated.

Capuccini Navel Cemetery, the final resting place of five Operation Spotter pilots.

Of the seven Operation Spotter pilots who survived Malta and the rest of the war, two sadly died very young of cancer; John Tayleur aged 33, and Ray Hesselyn aged 42. John Plagis died at his own hand aged just 56. The three remaining lived into their sixties with David Ferraby reaching the fine old age of 87.

In late July 1942 Ray Hesselyn and his good friend Paul Brennan left Malta at the end of their tour to start a period of rest and recuperation, before going on to a new posting in the UK. With three weeks leave granted to them, one of their first calls was to replace their tatty and worn out uniforms. Having smartened themselves up they made their way to London, where for a few days they enjoyed the luxury of a stay at the Savoy Hotel.

Whilst in London the two pilots met with the journalist Henry Bateson along with Eric Baume the editor of the Truth, a weekly tabloid newspaper published in Melbourne, Australia. After some coaxing the two pilots agreed to write a book about their time on Malta. This was published the following year as Spitfires Over Malta. The book with around 50,000 words across 96 pages had been written in conjunction with Henry Bateson in under two weeks. The foreword for the book was written by the Anglo-Irish Peer Lord Londonderry (Charles Vane-Tempest-Stewart) a pilot himself, who had been the Secretary of State for Air during the 1930s. He also spent a large sum of money on a party for the two; his daughter Lady Margaret Stewart also later regaled them with another party. The two pilots mixed freely amongst the aristocracy and within the prominent social circles of London. An invitation was also accepted to visit the Houses of Parliament where they met with Prime Minister Winston Churchill and high-ranking members of his government. The Germans later reminded Paul Brennan when he became a prisoner of war of the parties and the social occasions, impressing him by how much they knew of this period, probably gleaned at the time from newspaper articles.

Raymond Hesselyn had decided to keep the book when it was published as a surprise for his parents, but the editor Eric Baume not knowing this had cabled them telling them of it beforehand, so Raymond wrote a letter to his parents telling them first about his Malta experiences prior to the books publication.

Paul and Ray dedicated Spitfires over Malta **"To the Fighter Pilots of MALTA past, present and future"**. The book is believed to have sold over 50,000 copies across the three editions British, New Zealand and Australian. The two pilots had made an agreement that if either one of them was killed, then the books royalties would all go to the surviving pilot

The Times Literary Supplement reviewed Spitfires over Malta in April 1943 and described it as an:

'…Interesting first hand account of the defence of Malta, Britain's "fixed aircraft carrier" in the Mediterranean, and in so doing to shed new light on a feat which has won the admiration of the whole world

'The story covers a period of only just over four months-from the begin-

ning of March to the middle of July 1942…

'Two of the authors played a brilliant part in the battle: Hesselyn, a New Zealander destroying 12 enemy aircraft, and Brennan, an Australian accounting for 10. They dictated their story to Mr Bateson who prepared it for publication. "Spitfires Over Malta" not only gives details of the air struggle but provides a splendid picture of the suffering and heroism of the island people. It makes a heartening story.'

The Malta Memorial located in Floriana commemorating
2,298 airmen with no known grave.

30th Thousand

"Spitfires" OVER MALTA

By
PILOT-OFFICER
PAUL BRENNAN D.F.C., D.F.M.

PILOT-OFFICER
RAY HESSELYN D.F.M. & BAR

and **HENRY BATESON**

ILLUSTRATED
2/- NET

FOREWORD

I have been invited by the authors of Spitfires Over Malta to write a Foreword and am very glad to do what I can to introduce this book to the public.

The authors are two fighter pilots who have been on continuous service in Malta for four and a half months and have been awarded the D.F.C. and D.F.M. in one case, and the D.F.M. and bar in another, for distinguished services. The full story of Malta and its heroic defence has yet to be told, but this enthralling narrative gives some idea of what has been done to maintain British traditions and prestige in this, the greatest war of all-time.

I had the great pleasure of meeting these two officers and two of their friends when they had just returned from Malta and, naturally, I was very anxious to hear of all they had done. I had the greatest difficulty in extracting from them anything but the barest details of the splendid parts which they had obviously played, and perhaps my interminable questionings, obviously showing a desire for information, prompted them to write this story to give the public—who certainly have been subjected to bombing and hardships here—some idea of what the R.A.F. has done and the manner in which the pilots carry out their duties.

It may be contended that we in this country become complacent and look on war as something outside our ordinary lives. This stirring tale shows us that it is our solemn duty never to forget that whilst we are living in comparative peace here our young men from every corner of the Empire are fighting night and day in different parts of the world to preserve us from danger and at the same time to win a war which has clearly developed into a life—and—death struggle for the establishment of those doctrines and the maintenance of those principles which make life worthwhile.

LONDONDERRY.

INTRODUCTION

The writing of this book was made possible on December 16, 1939. On that date the Empire Air Training Scheme, which has never received the publicity it deserves, was ratified by Great Britain, Australia, Canada and New Zealand. Henceforth the sun was never to set upon training operations for Democracy's air armada of the future. An elaborate network of aerodromes and flying training Schools of various types were constructed in many parts of the world. Once this preparatory work was well under way, thousands upon thousands of eager, keen eyed youngsters began to enter the recruiting and receiving depots and to pass on to initial and elementary flying taining schools. Men from all parts of the British Isles journeyed to Canada, the United States and Rhodesia; Australians and New Zealanders crossed the seas to Canada, Rhodesia and the Mother Country; Canadians, Americans and Rhodesians voyaged to Great Britain.

Together with the subsidiary schemes adopted by South Africa, Southern Rhodesia and India, and, on a more modified scale, the cooperation of the United States, the Empire Air Training Scheme ensured an ever increasing flow of trained air crews and skilled ground personnel to man and maintain the steadily mounting total of the Empire's fleet of reconnaissance, fighting, bombing, torpedo carrying and mine laying aircraft.

Months later, as the British air offensive developed in weight and intensity, and the war spread to new theatres of operations, the rich harvest of the Empire Air Training Scheme was garnered. From the rugged Highlands of Scotland and the heat-dazed towns of Australia's vast outback, from the purlieus of Whitechapel and the sweeping prairies of Canada, from the crowded cities and rich farmlands of America and the dense bush country of New Zealand, from the tropical jungles of New Guinea and the open veldt of South Africa, from shop and office, factory and warehouse, farm and field, there, came a rising torrent of pilots, navigators, observers, wireless operators, air gunners, mechanics, engineers, riggers, fitters. And like a flood driver that has crashed its banks, they swept forward in innumerable streams to operational squadrons the world over—to Great Britain, Gibraltar, Egypt, Libya, Syria, Iraq, Iceland, Burma, India, Malaya, Singapore, even Russia, and a dozen other places besides. Wherever the enemy had to be repelled, wherever a blow might be struck at him, there young men trained under the Empire Air Training Scheme were, and are, to be found.

So it was that, from thousands of miles across the Seven Seas, the Crusaders of the Skies journeyed to ancient Malta, island fortress of the

Mediterranean. Britishers and Americans, Australians and New Zealanders, Canadians and Rhodesians gathered there as the Knights of St. John had gathered centuries before. Many of these young men, even in their wildest dreams, had never imagined that Ta-Kali and Luqa, Halfar and M'dina, Valetta and Mosta would become names as familiar to them as those of their own homelands. But the cold reality of war banded them together in this small, sun lit isle, not merely as its defenders, but as its saviours; for if it is the Navy which has garrisoned and provisioned Malta, it is the Air Force which has held it inviolate for the Democratic Powers.

Covering a period of slightly over four months, from the beginning of March until the middle of July 1942, this book tells, simply but graphically, the story of these Crusaders of the Skies. Their ordeals and triumphs are related against the sombre background of the Luftwaffe's attempts to reduce Malta to impotency. It was in these four months that the island lived through the grimmest and most stirring chapter of its long history. The battle for supremacy in its deep blue skies opened on a quiet note rose rapidly to a crescendo as the fighters and bombers from Sicily overbore, but did not wholly conquer, the defences, died down for a brief period, and then swelled to a thunderous chorus as the Spitfires and Hurricanes finally routed and subdued the German and Italian air invaders. The story of this initial defeat and final triumph, of merciless bombing raids and fierce dogfights, is the book's main theme. It is essentially a book about Fighter pilots. It relates in simple, unadorned prose their exploits and adventures in the air and their experiences on the ground. The plain, matter-of-fact accounts of air combats are thrilling because of their very simplicity of language and detailed accuracy. They recapture for the reader something of the dazzling speed and quickness of manoeuvre which characterize dogfights today. Interwoven with this account of the air fighting are sharp, unforgettable pictures of the sufferings and heroism of the people of Malta, and of the ground organization which enabled the British aircraft to be kept in the air. Yet it is not merely a stirring chronicle, a narrative of daring deeds, of dauntless courage, of patient endurance. Through its pages there runs a rich psychological vein. It provides a glimpse of the intimate thoughts and fears of those who battle thousands of feet above the earth, and it reveals the gradual evolution of a successful air fighter and capable section leader from a raw untested pilot.

The book is the work of two fighter pilots who went to Malta as sergeants with comparatively little operational experience, and, in view of the diversity of nationalities constituting the Royal Air Force squadrons in Malta, it is peculiarly appropriate that they should be two who travelled furthest to play their part in Malta's defence two, moreover, who came to the ancient headquarters of the Knights of St. John from the new countries "Down Under".

Paul Brennan is an Australian from Brisbane, capital of the northern state of Queensland; Ray Hesselyn, a New Zealander from the far southern city of Invercargill. Both boys of twenty two, Paul was an articled law clerk when he enlisted, and Hess a clerk in a New Zealand Government department. Possessing that originality of thought and fertility of resource and initiative which rightly are the prerogatives of new countries, both are keen, shrewd observers of all that goes on around them, and their memories are impressionable and retentive. If it were not so, this book could not have been written.

Cheery, high spirited, happy-go-lucky, yet coldly determined and courageous when determination and courage are most needed, Paul and Hess became known throughout the island as "The Problem Children of Malta". It was an apt description. On the ground, with their independence of thought and impish sense of humour, they were a problem to their officers, whose outlook was more traditional, less original. In the air, where their resourcefulness and eagleness of eye found unrestricted scope, they were a problem for the Hun and Italian fighters. Hess shot down 12, and Paul 10, enemy aircraft. Each won the D.F.M., Hess adding a bar to his, and Paul also being awarded the D.F.C., and both gained promotion to commissioned rank.

My own part in the writing of this book has been small. I did not share the adventures it records, and that my name is on the title page is due wholly to the insistence of Paul and Hess that, as their cobber, it should be coupled with theirs. But it is their book, not mine. They dictated it to me while they were in London on three weeks leave. Each described, in response to my prompting questions, his own adventures in the air, and both combined to provide the material which does not relate to personal flying experiences. At first we tried dictating it to a stenographer, but the words came haltingly and the language was stilted and unreal. Then I started to type it to the boys' dictation, and, freed of their self-consciousness, able to swear and to natter in Air Force language, as they would have done had they been in the mess, the story came alive. As a New Zealander by birth and an Australian by virtue of many years' residence, I was able to speak their language and understand their minds, and if I have construction, it has been in my ability to help them translate into words what they, and their fellows, went through in Malta. I have altered as little as possible of what they dictated, preferring to retain their own language and methods of expression. I have added even less. There has been no embellishment of their story, my alterations being concerned mainly with securing continuity and clarity. The adoption of this method has made it necessary to add a glossary of Air Force terms and Australian expressions, which may not be known to the average reader.

Throughout the book the first person is used, and this requires a word of explanation. Paul is the narrator, but except when he is describing his own individual exploits when flying, he speaks for Hess as well as for himself. They were great cobbers, and were seldom out of each other's company save when on readiness or in the air. They shared the adventures and incidents which Paul relates, and the thoughts and feelings attributed to Paul are in fact a composite picture to which each has contributed. Whenever Hesselyn takes up the narrative to describe his own flying experience, the first person has been retained, but for the sake of clarity, Hesselyn's name has been put in the margin and the text has been set in italic type. At the same time, to avoid needless repetition, the thoughts and reactions common to both boys have been combined in Paul's personal accounts of his first flights over Malta and of his early leading of subsections and sections. They were so nearly identical with those of Hess that it did not seem desirable to distinguish between them. It would have meant covering the same ground twice. We would all three like to express our sincere thanks to the many friends who have assisted and encouraged us in the writing of this book. To Truth and Sportsman Ltd., of Australia and New Zealand, and to that company's European editor, Mr. Eric Baume, we are under a deep debt of gratitude. Without the facilities which Mr. Baume and the progressive company, which he represents, extended to us, and without the constant encouragement they gave us, the book could not have been written. We are grateful also to the officials of the Royal Air Force, the Royal Australian Air Force, and the Royal New Zealand Air Force for their friendly co-operation and for the permission which they granted so readily for the book's publication. Our thanks are due also to Daphne Jackson, whose fingers grew numb with the work we gave her in typing the manuscript.

HENRY BATESON.

August 30, 1942

Postscript: Since the completion of the book, events in the Mediterranean have moved swiftly. In Libya, the Eighth Army's great offensive has driven Rommel as far back, at the moment, as El Agheila in North Africa, the United Nations have launched their offensive, and the decisive battle for Tunisia approaches. These events have brought a transformation to Malta, and have proved, if proof was ever needed, that the heroic defence of the island as narrated in these pages has not been in vain. For today Malta is the advanced air base of the United Nations in their Mediterranean offensive a base from which the R.A.F. is striking, not only at Axis convoys, but at the aerodromes of Sicily and the ports and airfields of Tunisia. The importance of its offensive role in the North African operations cannot be over stressed, and infuses into the vivid story of how it was defended and held for the Allies in the first half of this year, an added interest. We know now that the cost and the sacrifices have been worthwhile and will not go unavenged. In the interval between completion of the MS. and publication, several of those mentioned in these pages have been awarded decorations. It has not been possible to draw attention to these in every case, and we ask the recipients to accept our sincere apologies for this unavoidable omission.

December 8, 1942.   HENRY BATESON.

CHAPTER I

March 1942

We saw Malta for the first time on the morning of March 7, 1942. Some hours earlier, in perfect weather, we had flown our Spitfires—the first Spits for Malta—from the flight deck of an aircraft carrier. The island appeared first as a tiny speck against the horizon, still many miles out, but the visibility was tremendous. As we drew closer, the island's features became more distinct. Soon we could see the brown cliffs of the rocky coastline; the huddled, white stone buildings; the narrow, twisting streets; the small, vivid green fields, intersected by white stonewalls. Inshore, the sea changed colour abruptly. The light, clear green of the shallows, fringed by white foam where the waves gently washed the shore, replaced the dark blueness of the deeper waters.

We were still ten miles out, flying at 3000 feet, when we had our first experience of the ground control station and our introduction to Group Captain Woodhall, senior Fighter Controller. His calm voice came to us clearly over the R/T "Hullo, Exile boys! Keep on your present course. Watch out for a few 109's below." Not knowing what to expect, we felt nervous and apprehensive, and immediately started to weave, keeping a sharp lookout. We saw nothing of the Hun fighters. Flight Lieutenant Norman MacQueen, an Englishman, called for a homing. Chasing some Ju.52's we had seen some distance from Malta, he had become separated from the squadron.

We dropped down lower, rather fearfully wondering where the 109's could be, but still seeing nothing of them. The Grand Harbour now stood out very sharply, as also did the yellow sand stoned Mosta Dome. Third largest in the world, it dominated the huddle of white buildings. Away to the north, 60 miles off, we could see Sicily, the base from which all air operations against Malta are conducted.

It was faintly outlined as a flat beach, with a bank of cumulus cloud above it. Further north still, the snow-capped cone of Mount Etna was more clearly visible.

From amid the patchwork of small, bright fields we picked out Ta-Kali aerodrome, and prepared to land. Hess could not get his undercart down. He burnt up the R/T telling everybody of his predicament, but finally decided to use his emergency equipment, and came in last, after the rest of us had landed. Ta-Kali seemed very small and rough, and not as well equipped as the aerodromes to which we had become accustomed in Britain. It bore unmistakable scars of bombing. The dispersal to which we walked was a mass of rubble, and we were told that a pilot had been killed there a few days previously.

No transport was waiting for us. Petrol is scarce in Malta and worth almost its weight in gold. Very tired and brassed off, we bundled our kit on our shoulders, and climbed the hill to our mess. The Maltese gave us a warm welcome. They shouted cheery greetings, while the children followed closely behind us, calling "Spitfire! Spitfire!" The owner of the house in which the sergeant pilots had their mess greeted us at the door, and told us how honoured the Maltese people felt at receiving from England the first Spitfires to operate outside that country.

Some of the pilots of 249 Squadron had arrived previously aboard a Sunderland. That night we met them in the officers' mess in Rabat. Also present were many of the Hurriboys who, against terrific odds, had been providing Malta with its fighter defence for many months. It was a pretty scruffy untidy lot, mostly with beards, who gathered in the mess. The boys came from all over the world. Englishmen, Scots, Welshmen, Australians, Canadians, New Zealanders, Rhodesians, and Americans jostled one another as they replenished glasses. Some were old friends. I had trained with Sergeant Pilot John Livingstone ("Tony") Boyd, both in Australia and Canada, but until I saw him in the mess did not know that this tall, blue-eyed jackeroo from Byrnestown, in outback Queensland, had become a Hurriboy in Malta. Sergeant Pilot Tim Goldsmith, an Australian from Sydney, was another old cobber well—known to both Hess and myself. He had flown a great deal with Hess in England and had come to Malta aboard the Sunderland. Hess ran across another friend in a fellow New Zealander, Sergeant Pilot Sole, who shortly was destined to go on to Egypt.

In the mess, too, we met Woody for the first time in the flesh. Hearing his calm, unhurried voice on the R/T I had pictured him as a big, broad shouldered, obviously capable fellow. I found him a man of about 45, of medium build and with greying hair. There was a merry twinkle in his eye, and he spoke quietly, calmly, giving one an instant feeling of confidence in his ability and judgment. He had served in the Battle of Britain as a fighter controller, and before going to Malta had been stationmaster at Tangmere. He told us briefly what was expected of us. The Spitfires were to operate four or eight at a time. We were to cover the Hurris on their climb up, engaging and keeping the 109's busy while the Hurriboys dealt with the bombers. Since their arrival in Malta the Hurris had been doing brilliant work, but latterly they had been taking considerable punishment from the 109's. Hence the reason why we were to cover them. The suggested strategy seemed sound enough in theory, but it was to prove unworkable in practice. The Huns' fighter escorts were generally so heavy that the Spits and Hurris together could not cope with them, and not infrequently the 109's were able to break through us.

Next morning we had our first experience of the 88's. We were standing on Ta-Kali when the sirens went. As we arrived at Eastern dispersal the airman of the watch, maintaining liaison between Fighter Control and the pilots by telephone, ran from the hut, fired a Very light and jumped into a slit trench. In reply to our questions he told us the light was the signal for "Danger imminent; take cover." The ground staff had disappeared from view, and except for ourselves the aerodrome appeared deserted.

We decided to stay above ground and watch proceedings. The heavy ack-ack guns provided our first pointer to the bombers. They began firing when the 88's were still out at sea. Soon we could see the bombers, with strong fighter escort, coming in over the Grand Harbour at about 15,000 feet. There were six of them, accompanied by 20 fighters. Luckily for us the 88's did not attack Ta-Kali but, leaving their escort, passed over our heads at heights varying from 6000 to 10,000 feet, made straight for Luqa aerodrome, four miles away, and released their bombs. In a few minutes the attack was over, and as the bombers joined up again with their escort out to sea the Hurris attacked. Many dogfights developed, but we were disappointed to see nothing shot down. Gradually, as the raiders disappeared out of range on the other side of the island, the ack-ack guns quietened.

There was no wind that morning, and tall columns of smoke and dust from the bombing hung above Luqa for some hours. But, not having ourselves been bombed, we could see nothing in these raids to worry about, and could not understand people taking cover.

Next day we explored Valetta. We set out early on the seven-mile journey to the city, the weather, though not the scenery, reminding me of early autumn in Australia. Hess, Bob Sim, another New Zealander, Ian Cormack, a Scot, and Junior Tayleur, an Englishman, were the four sergeant pilots who accompanied me, and we walked as far as the Fleur de Lys archway, on the outskirts of the small town of Hamrun, before we secured transport. We succeeded then in hiring a gharri horse drawn, four wheeled carriage with two very narrow seats facing each other. It was driven by an incredibly old and incredibly dirty Maltese. We squeezed our way into the gharri, and, cooped up tightly, with nowhere to put our knees, we jolted and bounced the rest of the way to Valetta.

The city had not yet been severely bombed. Heavy damage had been done not far away, particularly in the dockyard districts where the Illustrious had been repaired late the year before, and towns close to aerodromes had suffered considerably. Valetta itself, however, was still comparatively intact. Bombs had fallen in it and buildings had been demolished or damaged, but we found they were the exception rather than the rule. The Opera House, a fine building with Corinthian columns, still stood and few of the many churches, most of which had been built by the people in their spare time, had been hit. They were constructed of locally cut sandstone, beautifully ornamented by some of the finest Spanish and Italian masters.

As we wandered through Valetta we noticed that on many of the walls the Maltese had scrawled, "Bomb Rome!" This surprised us, as the Maltese are deeply Roman Catholic, but it was characteristic of the people's morale. Everybody was pleased to see us. A crowd of children quickly gathered on our heels. They followed us everywhere, and it was impossible to get rid of them. They made buzzing noises to represent aeroplanes, tried to loop the loop, fell over constantly, and generally indulged in every kind of antic. We had expected to find the Maltese looking lean and hungry, and with their nerves shaken. We thought they would be rather anti-British. Instead the people looked well fed, were cheerful, and were markedly pro-British. Food seemed plentiful enough, and after a drink of very bad beer we had an excellent meal of a pork chop, sausages and chips, with two eggs each. About four o'clock, rather to our surprise, some buses started to run, and we caught one to M'dina.

That evening we attended our first picture show. The cinema at Rabat looked as if it had been a house from which the interior walls had been removed in order to convert it into one large hall. The screen was grimy, and the house half full with the dirtiest, rowdiest children I have ever seen or heard. Every now and then the film would break, the manager would step on the stage to announce that the show would resume in a few minutes, and the children would stamp their feet, whistle, and yell at the top of their voices. It reminded me of a bush cinema in an outback Queensland town.

They were busy days that followed. There was much for us to see and learn. We had to acquaint ourselves thoroughly with the topography of the island, so that, flying at any height, we could visualize it without the aid of maps. We also had to learn all we could regarding the Huns' methods and tricks. The knowledge we gained in those days proved invaluable later on. The Hun bombers from the various Sicilian aerodromes joined up with their lighter escort over Comiso aerodrome, the principal fighter base on Sicily, and then moved south for Malta. They would cross the coast at one of half a dozen places St. Paul's Bay, slightly northwest of Ta-Kali; the Grand Harbour; Zonkor Point, most south easterly point; Kalafrana Bay, south of Zonkor Point; Halfar, near Delimara, or the Dingli Cliffs, south of Ta-Kali. After an attack on the Grand Harbour, Luqa or Halfar, at both of which latter places there were aerodromes, the bombers mostly went out over Filfla, a small, uninhabited island three miles south of Malta, or Kalafrana Bay. The 109's would circle above Filfla while waiting for the bombers to do their work, and would then escort them back to Sicily.

The Hun bombers generally came over three, six or sometimes eight at a time, with an escort of 109's ranging in numbers from 12 to 20. Their principal targets were our aerodromes. The bombers and their lighter escort were met by the Hurricanes and a fierce ack-ack barrage. The Hurris had been consistently attacking them, but had neither the speed nor the firepower to make much impression on the raiders. One morning shortly after our arrival we watched six Hurricanes trying to engage the 88's.

The Hurris were at about 5000 feet over M'dina, and they were being attacked from above by 109's. So menaced were they by the latter that they could not get within range of the bombers. We realized then what a stiff task the Hurriboys had been facing.

On March 11 I made my first flight. The signal to scramble came at about eleven o'clock, after an uneventful morning at dispersal. Eight or nine Hurricanes were already airborne. We rushed to our aircraft, and in less than two minutes were off the ground. Squadron Leader Stan Grant, of the R.A.F., was leading, and I was flying number two to Flight Lieutenant Bud Connell, a Canadian, being Red four in the section. Climbing at a steady 140 m.p.h. we joined the Hurriboys from Halfar above St. Paul's Bay, and orbited the island, gaining still more height. Woody, who, as usual, was controlling, told us some big jobs, with fighter escort, were coming south about 30 miles north of St. Paul's Bay. We were at 12,000 feet when my reflector sight, which I had already switched on, began to dim, and the various cockpit and under-carriage lights commenced to fade. My electrical system had packed up. It was not a pleasant start to my flying career over Malta. I realized that I had no R/T and should have returned to base, but I decided to remain aloft and see what happened.

We climbed out to meet the Huns. Three 109's came towards us at about our height. Bud Connell and I saw them at the same time, and pulled round together. With a quick deflection shot Bud damaged one. I fired at another, without reflector sight, pointing my nose in his general direction. I am sure I did not hit him. The Huns climbed above us, and we started turning inside them in an effort to get on their tails. They obviously had a healthy respect for the Spitfire for although we gave them plenty of invitations they refused to come down and engage. Stan Grant and his number two, who were ahead of us, had a similar experience. They mixed it with a number of 109's, but without result. We landed at Ta-Kali after having been 40 minutes in the air, and although we had merely exchanged shots with the Hun we thought the flight had been a good pipe-opener.

The most vivid impression I gained that morning concerned the 109. It struck me as a very sinister and lethal looking aircraft. It flew over Malta with a brownish-bluish camouflage, and its big airscrew revolved very slowly. The spinner was painted yellow, and in its centre was a single cannon with a high rate of fire. The 109, smaller than the Spitfire, had remarkably clean, clear-cut lines. We were to discover later that these aircraft were being flown by pilots from the crack Moelders group in the Luftwaffe.

There was plenty of nattering in dispersal after we landed. The four of us could talk of nothing but our sortie. Stan Grant said the 109's were fairly fast and nippy. He had had a squirt, but didn't know if he had scored any hits. Bud felt certain he had hit one, and I also was convinced he had. We found a bullet hole about two feet behind Bud's cockpit, on a level with his head, and spent the rest of the morning wondering whether in my excitement and inexperience I had put it there.

Never before had I fired my guns at the enemy. My feelings were curious and mixed, as I suppose are those of all pilots who go into action for the first time. On the climb up I knew I did not have the score weighed up. I was extremely nervous and excited, but the thought flashed across my mind that if the worst came to the worst my leader was bound to look after me. I had complete confidence in him, and tried to create a favourable impression on him by maintaining good formation. Once the Hun was sighted, however, all nervousness and excitement left me. I was surprised to find myself cool and calm, my mind being occupied solely with the business of shooting him down and not getting shot down myself. When I first fired my guns I had a remarkable feeling of aloof detachment. I felt no personal animosity, no anger. My sole thought was whether I was in range and shooting straight. Once the engagement was over, and we were bound for our base, my thoughts were concerned again with flying correctly and with landing without being jumped by 109's from above. I threw many apprehensive glances over my shoulders, searching the sky behind and above me. As I was later to learn, it was a wise precaution which one could not take too often. Oddly enough, although I had many flights over Malta subsequently, my reactions were invariably the same. Always I was nervous and excited until I encountered the enemy, and then became icily calm.

During the next few days we all felt our way. More and more of the boys went up on scrambles. Pilot Officer Pete Nash, a slightly built Englishman of medium height, with penetrating blue eyes, shot down the first enemy aircraft to be destroyed by a Spitfire over Malta. His quick success did not surprise us. He was one of the most accurate shots of the first Spitfire boys, and had had some experience in sweeps over France, where he had shot down two Focke Wulf 190's and a Me.109. A Rhodesian, Pilot Officer Duggie Leggo, also had one confirmed, but his fellow Rhodesian and cobber, Pilot Officer Johnnie Plagis, the son of a Greek, was very disappointed at being credited with only a probable. Yet another Rhodesian, Flying Officer Buck Buchanan, was also given a probable. Tall and good looking, he had been in the Rhodesian police force, and was certain his109 had gone into the drink.

I saw a good deal of my fellow Australian, Tony Boyd, and picked up many wrinkles from him. He had been posted to Malta on Hurricanes after completing his operational training and allowed me to go through his logbook. The Hurris had eight machine guns for armament, and were not only considerably inferior to the Spitfire, but were also no match for the best German aircraft used over Malta. Yet from the time the Germans first arrived in Sicily, about December1941, until we brought in the first Spitfires, the Hurris had been holding the fort. They had done a magnificent job against great and often overwhelming odds. Tony told me a great deal about German methods and tactics knowledge which was to help me greatly. The Hurris had been meeting some three German raids daily. Three or six Ju.88's, strongly escorted by fighters, would come over at a time. Sometimes there would be10 or 12 Hurris serviceable, at other times only two or three, but no matter what the number, whether 12 or two, the Hurriboys would take off each time. Constantly they intercepted the incoming bombers and fighters, and although they did not destroy many of them, they repeatedly spoilt the aim of the bombers and kept the 109's flying high. Tony, one of the keenest, most determined of the Hurriboys, had fought about 15 combats, destroying one enemy aircraft and probably destroying three others. When I commented on the large number of enemy aircraft he had damaged, compared with the number he had destroyed, he explained the difficulty of shooting them down. He would chase the 88's, finally catch them, and, getting into range, would open fire with his machine guns. The recoil of his guns, however, would push him out of range again, and before he could recover position, to get in another squirt, the 88's had escaped. Nevertheless, Tony loved his Hurricane. He admitted its inferior armament as compared with the cannon-firing Spitfire, but maintained stoutly that he could out-turn any enemy aircraft that liked to turn up with him. He contended also that his tactics enabled him to interfere with the Hun bombers, spoiling their aim, and to keep the fighters flying high. Our discussions in the mess, over a pint of unpalatable Maltese beer, were long, animated and profitable. We learnt a great deal about the Huns' tricks. I listened attentively, and somewhat enviously, to these chaps who knew it all. In later weeks, when flying, I often recalled something Tony or one of the others had told me, and tried to apply it myself. A real knowledge of Hun tactics, of course, comes only with personal experience, but many lessons may be learnt in the mess. It was there, for example, that I began to appreciate the prime necessity for maintaining a careful lookout at all times, so as to guard against being jumped from behind. Those talks in the mess taught us all, I think, how little we did know and how much we had to learn. But each of us, in the busy months ahead, had to learn the hard way. Luck and the splendid leaders we had helped me a great deal, and yet I feel that the fact that I survived to return to England was due in no small measure to what I was told during these early March days by the boys with experience. After much complaining about getting no flying I made my second trip on March 17. Bud Connell, my usual section leader, was not on readiness that morning, and his place was taken by Flight Lieutenant Heppell, D.F.C., a tall, languid, apparently indifferent Englishman who had proved himself in air battles over France. Four Spitfires were on readiness, and we were so determined and eager to have everything on the top line by dawn that we walked down to the aerodrome far earlier than necessary. It was another typical Malta day. The sky was clear and blue, and the rising sun very red. Towards Sicily, where we looked so often, light, misty cloud at about 500 feet enshrouded the coastline. We were keen to be off, but as we nattered desultorily in dispersal, trying to hide our nervous eagerness, the minutes dragged by wearily, and each seemed an eternity. We had begun to think there would be no early show, when the 'phone rang. It was no scramble; the Fighter Controller merely wished to speak to Hep. We were curious to know what it was about, but we got no clue from Hep's terse affirmatives. As he hung up, he turned and said: "All right, boys, out to your kites and see they're running well. We may get off soon."

My aircraft was 400 yards from dispersal, and I ran all the way in case I should be late. I strapped on my parachute, and in my eagerness and excitement could not find the right place for the straps. Eventually, however, I was ready in my aircraft, teed up for the Very light from dispersal the signal to scramble. The other boys were also in their cockpits, and waiting. It was 6.30. The sun had risen, but was still very low, and the thought crossed my mind that at any rate the Hun would not be up in the sun that morning. I looked over my cockpit, checked and rechecked my trim, switched on my reflector sight, and set the graticule bars on my sights for 109's at 250yards, the range at which I hoped to engage. Even at that very early stage I put my gun button from "Safe" to "Fire". I primed my motor, tested my R/T and turned on my oxygen. I was strung right up, and as the minutes sped by I felt very, very nervous. Repeatedly my thoughts reverted to the mess and the many stories of combats told there, and I felt sharply depressed with the knowledge of my own inexperience.

Suddenly the big moment came. My ground crew did not wait for the light. As the airman of the watch rushed from the dispersal hut with the Very pistol in his hand, they shouted, "Scramble! Scramble!" I pressed my starter button and pushed open my throttle. My airscrew turned over once, and the motor roared. Before I had collected my thoughts, I was alongside Hep, and saw him wave us forward to the take off.

We climbed straight ahead towards the southeast. Hep's matter of fact voice came over the R/T as he reported.

"Hullo, Gondar. Pinto Red section airborne. Are you receiving me? Over."

Woody's clear, steady voice replied.

"Hullo, Pinto Red leader. Receiving you loud and clear. This party is about 40 miles north, coming south. Gain your angels quickly."

Nothing more was said. We continued to climb. I was trying hard to fly good formation, something which later became automatic. We were at 10,000 feet before Woody called up again.

"Hullo, boys. The party is now 20 miles north of St. Paul's Bay, moving south. There are some big jobs, with fighter escort."

I looked towards the north. The sky was clear and cloudless. The coast of Sicily and the outline of Mount Etna, farther north, stood out sharply, but I could see nothing of the enemy. Up we went still higher. I was horribly nervous. The period of the climb up is, I think, the most nerve racking for a fighter pilot. You are never certain that you have climbed high enough, and there is always the fear that the enemy may be above you. Neither do you know, or at least are not sure, that you have gained the right tactical position. At this time, of course, these things did not mean a great deal to me. It was not until some weeks later, when leading my own section, that I appreciated the cardinal principles of air leadership, and realized the strain under which Hep, who had possessed no experience of defensive fighter warfare, but only of offensive sweeps over France, must have been under on this occasion.

We were six miles east of Zonkor Point, and at 17,000 feet, with the sun, now well up, behind us, when Woody told us the enemy was approaching the harbour and warned us to keep a sharp lookout. Two seconds later Hep spotted them. "O.K., boys," he told us. "They're at ten o'clock, slightly above us. Break into them." I turned. I could see some 109's, but no bombers, and I started towards them. As I did so, Hep reported that there were more behind us. I could not see these either, but, nervous and confused, broke left and found myself on my own. Nothing fired at me, and I myself did not find a target. After a few minutes Junior Tayleur, who was flying Red four in the section joined me. I felt better at having somebody with me, and started to climb, with Junior right behind. Having gained some height we turned back east to Zonkor Point again. There was a lot of chatter on the R/T, but it did not convey very much to me. We were six miles east of Zonkor Point when, looking down, I saw six 88's, with their close fighter escort, silhouetted against the sunlit sea. I told Junior the enemy was at nine o'clock below us and we would go up sun to attack.

We went up sun. Two other aircraft appeared on my starboard quarter. I thought they were the other two Spitfires that were airborne. I was quickly disillusioned. As the distance between us lessened, I recognized the long nose and clean-cut fuselage of the 109. I warned Junior that they were 109's and about to attack. At that instant his aircraft, much to my dismay, dived straight down. He told me over the R/T that his seat had fallen off its hinges and jammed his control column fully forward.

I felt very lonely as the Huns started to turn above me, one acting as a decoy and the other trying to get on my tail. I tried hard to think of all I had learned at the discussions in the mess, but the paramount thought in my mind was: "If I can shoot down one, or damage it, I'll be able to get home." I was certain that if I left without doing so the 109's would overtake me on the way back and shoot me down.

I started turning with them. One was in front, the other behind. Round and round we went. Suddenly the one in front decided to go up sun. Luckily for me, he was not quite certain where I was. As he straightened up, I was 100 feet below and 200 yards behind him, dead astern. I pulled a bead on him at once, tracer from the other 109 whipping past my port wingtip as I did so. I could see my explosive cannon shells and machine gun bullets bursting along the front 109's fuselage, behind his cockpit and on his port wing-root. I gave him six seconds - a long burst. For a moment or two the 109 seemed to hang, then it dived straight down. I had no time to watch it crash into the sea 20,000 feet below. The second 109 was still firing, although his bullets were not hitting me. I glanced over my shoulder, and saw that he was breaking away. At this moment Hep called up, saying he was being attacked by five 109's and asking if anybody could help him. I told him I was having a good fight with two myself, and that I would see him later, but not then.

As he broke away, the 109 behind me followed his friend towards the sea. I was 300 yards behind him. Deciding to give chase, and convinced I could not get closer, I gave him a short burst at that range. In my excitement I pressed the wrong gun button and fired only my machine guns. I did not notice my mistake, and imagined my cannon ammunition must be exhausted. I broke away to return to base, but first called up Hep and asked him how he was doing. He replied: "These Huns think they can shoot me down. Not bloody likely!"

Ten minutes later I landed, and was screaming to all and sundry about my terrible battle. Everybody must have been bored to tears during the next few days with my oft-repeated story of my first Hun.

When I landed I felt I had been flying for hours, and was surprised to find I had been airborne for only 40 minutes. The actual engagement could not have lasted more than 15 minutes, of which only two or three were spent in close contact. My impressions and reactions stood out with a clarity, which amazed me. I recalled every detail, every thought, with astonishing vividness. Nothing was blurred.

Hep, Junior and Flight Sergeant Ian Cormack, the fourth member of the section, landed. All three were disgusted. I was the only one who had scored a victory. Hep had had a squirt or two, but without inflicting any damage. I asked him how he had managed to get away from the five 109's which had attacked him. Rather nonchalantly he replied, "We did a bit of turning round for a bit. They had the odd squirt at me. I had a squirt at them. Then they just wandered back to Sicily." I wondered if, when I escaped from five, I would treat the matter so coolly. Junior, after dropping about 8000 feet, had managed to get his seat back into position, and had then returned to base. Cormack after the first break when we went into attack, had not encountered any Huns.

Indeed the luck was dead against Mac that day. He took off with the three of us after about an hour. We scrambled too late, and the Huns were above us as we started to climb up. Woody kept issuing warnings that there were many 109's over the island. I was feeling very worried. We were trying to get height quickly, and were climbing with a low air speed. We were at about 8000 feet over Filfla when Mac's attractive Scotch accent came over the R/T, reporting 109's above us. There were four of them, two in front of us and two behind. The pair in front were acting as decoys, seeking to distract our attention while the other two attacked from behind. Hep, of course, did not fall for these tactics. We broke left to shake the Huns from our tails, and at that instant, looking towards the sun, I spotted a big formation of at least 10 enemy fighters coming down at us. It was an ugly moment, for our tactical position was bad. I warned Hep, but he also had seen them, and, with good judgment, called to us: "I think it's time we went home, boys. On your backs, and out of it!" I half rolled my aircraft and went into a vertical dive, skidding as violently as I could, with my throttle fully open. Cormack, slightly ahead of me, was doing the same thing. I was diving at such a terrific pace that my airspeed indicator went off the clock. My controls were heavy and I could not move them. I had to fly on the trim. As I eased out of the dive at about 4000 feet I heard Woody call up Hep and ask if we were O.K. Hep replied that we were returning to base, but he feared some one was missing. I looked down, and about two miles south of Filfla saw the splash of an aircraft crashing into the sea. I wondered whether it was Junior or Mac, and decided it was probably the former, as he was less experienced than Cormack. When we landed, however, I found it was Mac who was missing. We were convinced he had not been hit, and decided that his aircraft must have started to pull out of the dive of its own accord. When this happens at high speed the pilot is not strong enough to do anything about it. Mac probably blacked out, and was still unconscious when he hit the sea. He was the first of the 249 Squadron Spitfire boys to lose his life in the defence of Malta, and his death was a great blow to us all.

I finished my readiness at midday. Stan Grant and his boys, who included Johnny Plagis and, I think, Flying Officer Ron West, Mac's cousin, took over. After the indecisive skirmishes of the previous few days the Spitfires really came into their own that afternoon. Without loss to themselves, the boys shot down four confirmed, with others probably destroyed and damaged.

The German bombers continued to come in, three or six at a time. They were bombing the harbour and the aerodromes by day, but, rather to my disappointment, Ta-Kali itself had not been attacked. I was intrigued about the bombing, and wanted to see what it felt like. I was very soon to know only too well. Rumours were afoot that a heavy blitz was about to develop against Malta.

Our reconnaissance aircraft, engaged in photographing the Sicilian aerodromes, reported a big increase in Luftwaffe fighter and bomber strength. All sorts of figures were being given for the number of 88's in Sicily, but the most reliable estimate appeared to be about 200. Reports of the presence of 87's had also been received. We hailed these with delight, believing the 87's would prove our piece of cake. A big increase was also reported in the number of 109's. Indeed, for a couple of days after the 17th it was noticeable that the Hun fighter escort was larger. We did not receive this news with the same enthusiasm as the reports of the presence of 87's. We had a considerable number of Spitfires, and we did not object to fighting the 109's at odds, but with the reports that well over 100 German fighters were in Sicily it seemed as if those odds would be too great. There was much speculation as to when the blitz would start, but, apart from the increase in the number of fighters accompanying the bombers, nothing developed during the next couple of days.

The squadron's score, however, was slowly mounting-the beginning of a score, which later was to eclipse even that of the top-notch squadron in the Battle of Britain. By March 20 it consisted mainly of fighters, but although it was principally the task of the Hurris to go for the bombers, we had got a few healthy squirts at 88's, and had brought some down.

I did not go on readiness again until the afternoon of March 20. Bud Connell was leading, with me as his number two. Junior was flying as number two to Pilot Officer Buck McNair, a Canadian from Montreal and a great friend of Bud's. The morning had been uneventful, and the early part of the afternoon also passed without incident. The calm seemed artificial. We felt that something was due to break any minute, and as we nattered outside dispersal, enjoying the warm sunshine, we decided we had picked a good afternoon to go on readiness. We were sure the Hun before long would be over in full force. It was a perfect day for interception. Light cumulus cloud was above the island at about 3000 feet, and high above it light cirrus cloud formed a perfect background against which aircraft would show up. The telephone rang at half past three, and Bud was summoned to it. I got up, tied the straps of my Mae West, and began to wander over to my aircraft, thinking, "Here it comes." I felt the same tightening of the chest, the same feeling of nervous excitement, that I always experienced at this stage of proceedings. I was halfway to my Spitfire when I was called back. "It's all off for this afternoon," announced Bud, "but there are big things doing. We're stood down. They expect the Hun in big force soon, and want maximum serviceability for tomorrow." He added that our section would take readiness in the morning, and so would be in on the party.

So far there had been only three raids against the harbour. We decided the Hun also must be concentrating on securing maximum serviceability. But shortly after the sunset, the sirens went. The signals in Malta are different from those in Britain. Three wails, each of 15 seconds duration, announce the Alert, and so accustomed to raids are the people of Malta that more are unnecessary. All Clear is signalled by a single long wail, lasting for perhaps 30 seconds. In Britain, both for the Alert and the All Clear, the sirens sound for much longer.

With several other sergeant pilots, including Tim Goldsmith and Bob Sim, I walked up to the bastions at M'dina. We were mostly new boys. Old hands like Sergeant Pilots Ted Kopp, a Canadian, and Tim Woods, an Englishman, both of whom had been flying Hurris for sometime, were wiser, and prudently sought a rock shelter as soon as they saw what was coming along. Several officers joined us on the bastions. They included Flight Lieutenant (later Squadron Leader) P. B. ("Laddie") Lucas, an Englishman with whom we Australians and New Zealanders got on uncommonly well; Pilot Officer Geoff West, D.F.M., from New Zealand; Johnny Plagis, Duggie Leggo, Bud Connell, and a number of others. The officers had heard from Fighter Control that a big plot was coming in, and we hazarded the guess that the blitz of which we had heard so many rumours was at last about to begin.

The sun, although low down, had not yet set, and the sky was clear except for some light whispy cloud above Ta-Kali, when the guns at Naxxur began engaging. The first wave of bombers, with their escort of 109's, was coming in a little north of the harbour; heading straight for Ta-Kali. I picked them up when they were crossing the coast. They were flying at about 14,000 feet, with the puffs of our flak dotted all round them. The 12 bombers, flying in two sections of six, showed up as the rays of the dying sun caught them. They were straggled out, so as to reduce the target presented to our ack-ack guns. In the face of the heavy barrage, they dived straight for Ta-Kali, a mile from where we stood, and released their bombs at from 6000 to 8000 feet. Each carried about 10 bombs, one big one and the rest smaller, and they laid their eggs dead across the runway and our dispersal area. As the second wave of 15 came in, all the heavy guns on this part of the island were firing furiously. The new arrivals also put their noses down for Ta-Kali. They were carrying very big bombs, and M'dina literally shook as these burst on the aerodrome below. The bombers in the second wave came much lower than those in the first, and as they went out the rear-gunners strafed the aerodrome with incendiary bullets.

The light was now beginning to fail, and the flashes from the heavy guns and the bursting bombs were growing brighter. The Bofors guns, engaging the low flying bombers, were setting up a brilliant fireworks display. The stench of burning cordite drifted with the gentle breeze towards us. The din was appalling. There was a continuous roar of gunfire, and almost as continuously a whistle of bombs. The bombers kept coming, as more waves crossed the coast and dived on Ta-Kali. Some of them dropped loads of incendiaries around eastern dispersal and these, burning with a very bright white light, served to illuminate the target for still further waves of bombers. A petrol bowser on the perimeter track caught fire and, like an aircraft at western dispersal, blazed fiercely. The flames were reflected in the cloud above the aerodrome.

It grew appreciably darker, but still the bombers came. The flashes of the guns became more vivid, and the bursting bombs threw up great showers of sparks. A pall of dust and smoke, hanging like a low cloud, drifted slowly towards M'dina. It blanketed the Bofors guns, but they were still firing as hard as ever, using their predictors to get on their targets. Suddenly a great column of flame shot hundreds of feet into the air. A bomb had burst beneath a petrol bowser, but the next instant it stopped burning. The blast from the bomb had blown it out. One 88, hit by flak on its dive down, never pulled out. It crashed not far from the aerodrome and burnt itself out. We cheered wildly as we saw it hit the ground. Another went into the sea, half a mile from shore.

The attack lasted three-quarters of an hour and I witnessed 80 bombers dive bomb the aerodrome. An old Maltese stood beside me throughout. He was as nervous and excited as I was, but he never took cover, and watched the whole spectacular scene until its end. I myself was neither bomb nor raid conscious. It was my first experience of a mass raid, and I found it novel and interesting. Indeed, I was so intrigued that I was not conscious of the danger of our position. Shrapnel was tinkling down all around us, while, though I did not realize it at the time; there was always the possibility of a loaded bomber crashing near us or of a bomb falling short of its target. The determination of the German pilots impressed me forcibly. They pressed home their attacks despite the heavy and accurate barrage.

When the last bomb had burst and the guns had fallen silent, we descended to the aerodrome to see if we could help sort things out. As we went down, we decided that casualties on the 'drome must have been very heavy, and we were amazed when we discovered that the total casualties in personnel comprised one airman wounded. Ta-Kali it self however had suffered severely, and the aerodrome was badly cratered. A petrol bowser, situated some distance from where the fires were raging, had been hit in 50 different places by shrapnel, and we seized the opportunity to fill our cigarette lighters.

As we crossed the aerodrome we bumped into two bomb disposal men from the Army-an officer and a sergeant. They were searching for delayed action bombs. The sergeant had been hit on his tin hat by a piece of shrapnel, and proudly showed us the dent. We stumbled over a piece of bomb case about four feet high. It must have come from at least a thousand pounder, and we had it picked up later as a souvenir for our dispersal. There was nothing we could do on the aerodrome, and we returned to the mess to discuss the raid over a beer.

Hess was convinced that invasion was imminent. We knew the Hun had been preparing something for us, but we had not expected it to be so heavy. The raid, designed to put our Spitfires out of action, savoured of true blitzkrieg tactics, and we were all inclined to agree with Hess that it was the prelude to invasion. We took our revolvers from out kit bags, cleaned and oiled them, and strapped them on, determined at least to knock off a few parachutists. While we were doing this, I advanced the view that the raid indicated how greatly the Hun feared our Spits, and that we should feel it rather a compliment to the squadron. I was promptly told by one of the others that he thought it a compliment we could do without. Invasion, despite our fears, did not come, but the raid heralded the heaviest, most concentrated air attack of the war a blitz paralleled only in the story of the assault on Sebastopol.

I did not get up for readiness next morning, as I knew the aerodrome would be unserviceable. Shortly after breakfast, however, Hess, Sim and myself went down to see how things looked. We found a scene of incredible and indescribable confusion. The aerodrome was thickly cratered all over. Not far from western dispersal a water main had been blown up, and a miniature lake had formed. The dispersals themselves had been hit, and all our flying kit destroyed. The blackened remains of burnt out buildings fringed the aerodrome. The smashed and twisted wreckage of destroyed and damaged aircraft littered the ground. It seemed impossible that any of our aircraft could have survived, or, if they had, that they could be flown from Ta-Kali for weeks to come.

For the first time I realized the supreme importance of the ground organization and of the excellence of the co-operation between the Services.

The ground crews had been at work since dawn. They were salvaging damaged aircraft, and getting ready for take off those that were still serviceable. Men from the Army were clearing away wreckage, seeking out delayed action bombs, and filling in the bomb holes. Twice that day they were subjected to mass dive-bombing attacks, carried out on each occasion by more than, 50 aircraft. Those working on the aerodrome took shelter only at the last moment, diving for the inadequate cover of the slit trenches a few seconds before the bombs began to burst. These trenches, only five or six feet deep, were completely exposed overhead, but provided the only shelter available.

As I watched these fresh attacks I felt certain our Spitfires were finished. Yet that afternoon about six of them took off from Ta-Kali and were flown to Luqa. It was a remarkable achievement. The ingenuity and improvisation of the ground staff was startling. Two of the aircraft had new wings taken from bombed aircraft, a third had a new motor, fitted that day, and the others were all patched in one way or another. The Army, working ceaselessly, had filled in sufficient bomb holes to provide a serviceable runway along which the aircraft took off. The work so efficiently carried out that day, however, was to prove typical of the maintenance throughout the ensuing battle. Conditions at all times were very difficult, but no obstacle proved insurmountable. The ground crews, who had not previously worked on Spitfires and many of whom had not even seen a Spit until our arrival, contributed as substantially to our subsequent victory as did the pilots. At first their knowledge of the Spit was so slight that the pilots had to show them how to change oxygen bottles, but the erks learnt quickly and completely justified everybody's confidence in them.

With the raids against Ta-Kali continuing, it was obviously unprofitable to operate from there, and we moved to Luqa. I still thought, despite the afternoon's success in getting off six aircraft, that my pessimism would be justified, and that Ta-Kali would be off the map for several weeks at least. I was wrong. Within a couple of days of the heavy initial attack Ta-Kali was once again serviceable. The erks and the Army, not the pilots, had licked the Hun bombers.

The Hurriboys, operating from Halfar, which had not been heavily bombed, did valiant work on the 21st. They were up against tough opposition. The 109 boys were not only very determined, but they were also courageous and skilful. They used every trick they had learnt in Spain, Poland, France, Britain and Russia. They resolutely attacked our fighters, seeking to beat down our fighter defence, so as to give their bombers an open go. Yet neither the overwhelming odds nor the enemy's determination deterred the Hurri-boys. They went in every time with rare dash and courage, and scored more than one notable success.

Hess was on the aerodrome shortly after noon, nattering to an Army Bren gunner who reckoned he had shot down a 109 earlier that morning. While they were chattering eight Me. 110's came out of the sun in a shallow dive. Hess and the gunner flung themselves flat on the ground, but all the bombs fell short and none hit the aerodrome. The 110's machine-gunned the aerodrome as they passed over, some of their bullets striking within a few feet of Hess and his friend. As the pair stood up they saw four Hurris diving out of the sun on to the tails of the bombers, which were straggled out line abreast. The Hurricanes opened fire as the bombers crossed the coast, apparently taking the 110's by surprise. It was point blank range, and almost simultaneously four of the110's dived seawards. Two of them burst into flames, flicked over and fell straight into the drink. The other two lazily rolled on their backs and then dropped straight into the sea. The remaining four 110's at once broke, and began weaving, each steering a different course for home. Splitting up, the Hurricanes each gave chase to a 110, shooting down two more before returning to base. Two of these Me's fell to Flight Lieutenant (later Squadron Leader) Mortimer Rose, D.F.C. and bar.

Following a raid in the afternoon, I went up on the bastions at M'dina. The Hurriboys were returning to the aerodrome. The 109's, following them in, were trying to shoot them down as they sought to land. Every time the Hurriboys, twisting and turning, out manoeuvred the 109's, which were using their tactics of diving, taking a quick squirt, and climbing away again. A Hurri would put its wheels and flaps down, and start an approach to the landing path, but four 109's would come screaming down out of sun. The Hurri would immediately turn straight into them, and the 109's, being less manoeuvrable, could not get sufficient deflection to secure hits. Using their superior speed they would pull up their noses and go climbing out to sea. Most of the Hurriboys had no ammunition left, and the firing was all on one side. The Hurris had no option but to wait until the109's were forced by shortage of petrol to return to base. Then they came in and landed quickly one after the other. The Huns had lost at least 19 aircraft that day.

During the next few days the raids continued. Not so many bombers came over at once as on the first big do, but they came over more often, Luqa and Halfar were both attacked several times, as also were the dock installations at the Grand Harbour. Valetta was not yet a target, but a few stray bombs fell in the town, and some damage was caused.

The first raid occurred generally about eight o'clock in the morning. Twenty to 30 bombers, rarely escorted by fewer than 50 109's, would come in. A lull followed until about midday, when the second raid usually managed to interrupt our lunch. The third raid came sometimes about four, sometimes as late as six o'clock. Both the midday and afternoon raids were of about the same strength as the morning blitz. All the bombers at this time were 88's. We saw no Italians, and the 87's did not put in an appearance until about the 25th.

Casualties among the civilian population were remarkably light. They totalled only 231 killed during the whole of March, with double that number injured. There were adequate shelters, tunnelled into the solid sandstone, 40 feet underground. Some of them comprised long shafts driven horizontally into the rock, with numerous rooms, cut out by individual families, running off them. Others consisted of a fairly steep, vertical passage which gave access, 40 or 50 feet below ground, to a single large chamber hewn from the rock. These shelters, impregnable even to direct hits, were primarily responsible for the lightness of the casualties.

At first the people were rather frightened and disorganized by the severity of the blitz. After the first few days, however, their attitude noticeably changed. They became well disciplined and determined, and grew very angry. They did not complain, but went about chalking on the remaining walls, "Bomb Rome!" The 109's were maintaining a constant patrol near the island. This meant all day alerts. The sirens sounded first shortly after dawn, and very often the All Clear did not come until nearly dusk. The Maltese, however, did not remain in the shelters throughout the day. A considerable number of Maltese workmen had augmented the ranks of the Army working on the aerodromes, and they behaved very well.

I quickly lost my indifference to bombing. Lying in a slit trench, seeing the wrong end of an 88 pointing at one and his bombs coming one's way, quickly changes one's point of view. I have never been so frightened and scared as when I was first dive-bombed. In the air one can at least do something when attacked. On the ground, however, one experienced a feeling of complete helplessness. There is nothing one can do, except hope and pray that this lot is not for you. We soon learnt how to distinguish between near misses and bombs falling a safe distance away. If all you heard was a faint scream, followed by a screech, you knew you were fairly safe. When you could hear the bombs slither, you knew they would fall very close indeed.

This period is very confused in memory. I think we were all rather shocked by the sustained intensity of the attack and by the comparative weakness of the island's defences. The guns did a damned good job of work, but they were rather swamped by the mass attacks, and had not the accuracy which they later attained. They destroyed a number of enemy aircraft, principally bombers, but did not notch the big scores which subsequently came their way. The Hurris, although slower than the 109's, repeatedly broke through the heavy fighter escort and attacked the 88's. Tony Boyd's description of his experiences was not only amusing, but also typical. "I manage after a lot of hard work to get within range," he told me. "I give him a squirt with the scatter guns, and the recoil pushes my aircraft out of range again. If I happen to hit him, I see the bullets bounce off." The vital parts of the 88's were protected by bulletproof armour plating, and the Hurricane, with eight machine-guns and no cannons, was not powerfully enough armed to be deadly. The pilot had to be very lucky to shoot down an 88, but a few of them succeeded. An Australian, Sergeant Pilot G. E. Tweedale, of Brisbane, Queensland, was one. Tweedie, who had just come out of hospital after an argument with a 109, got on the tail of an 88 and brought it down with his machine-guns. We were suffering heavier losses than the enemy at this stage, and the ranks of the indomitable Hurriboys were being thinned. Forced to accept overwhelming odds, some of our best pilots were shot down. Sergeant Pilot Jackie Mayall, another Australian, was among them. He had won a great reputation in Malta for skill and courage. On this particular day the Hurris were split up by 109's, and Mayall found himself alone with about six enemy fighters. He kept turning with them, but apparently did not see one behind him, and crashed into the sea off Filfla.

While the excitement was at its height, we received small but welcome Spitfire reinforcements. A squadron under the command of Squadron Leader (later Wing Commander) E. J. Gracie, D.F.C., reached Malta. Gracie, a veteran of the Battle of Britain, had eight Huns to his credit, all but one being bombers. "During this war," he told me, "I have seen only three fighters—the one I shot down and two others - so I just imagine the fighters aren't there." He was a rather stocky, slightly bald Englishman, and although he told us he had joined the R.A.F. because it was the only service in which he could do his fighting sitting down, he seemed always to be going somewhere with short, rapid strides and a very businesslike air. With him came a number of other pilots who were to play distinguished parts in the Subsequent battles. Flight Lieutenant Johnny Johnston was an Englishman, Pilot Officers Jimmie Peek and MacLeod were Eagle Squadron boys; Flight Lieutenant Barton, whom we nicknamed "The Admiral", had been in the Fleet Air Arm, and Sergeant Pilot Jack ("Slim") Yarra, an Australian from Grafton, New South Wales, was an old friend from my squadron in England.

In the face of the Huns' huge fighter escorts, the Spitfires, instead of being called upon to take care of the 109's, were directed against the bombers. "The 88's must be destroyed at all costs," was the new ruling issued.

On the 24th I flew again. A convoy, under the command of Admiral Vian, had reached Malta despite continuous air and sea attack. One ship had been damaged and was being towed into Kalafrana Bay. Two Spitfires were required to patrol above it, and Geoff West and I were assigned to the job. We expected plenty of excitement, but were disappointed. Nothing happened, and we came back very brassed off, not having seen a sausage. Bud Connell flew later in the morning, but also saw nothing. It was the same story next day. I flew, but again without result. It was sheer bad luck. Plenty of 109's and 88's were over Malta, but I simply was not flying at the right time.

On the afternoon of the 26th I took off again. Bud Connell, Buck McNair, and Junior Tayleur were with me. We climbed south of the island and went up sun, being joined by Johnny Johnston and another Spit from 126 Squadron. We were at about 18,000 feet when a big bunch of 88's, heavily escorted, arrived over the harbour. As Connell led us in, Woody called up: "Take it quietly, boys. I have a lovely party for you. There are some 87's on the way." Bud, however, decided to attack the 88's. They seemed to be everywhere, and there were so many I could not decide which to attack. After a few seconds hesitation, however, I turned on one, opening fire when well out of range. It was the first 88 I had attacked, and it seemed much closer to me than it was. I was still out of range when I fired again. I pressed the wrong gun-button and fired my machine-guns only. The 88's rear-gunner also opened fire, but for a moment I did not realize that the white tracer coming from his guns was return fire. I thought I had hit him.

Just then I had a quick look behind. Two 109's were coming down on me. I had to leave the 88 and turn towards the fighters, but instead of engaging they rolled on their backs and went down. I turned back to my 88, which, travelling parallel with the coast, was streaking over Filfla. Buck McNair also gave chase. He was about 200, yards ahead of me and 500 yards from the bomber. The 88's throttles were wide open, and a streak of brown smoke was pouring from each exhaust, due to the pilot's heavy demand on his motors. Buck caught the bomber south of Gozo, and gave him a short burst. I could see the spent cannon shells falling out of Buck's wings and the black smoke coming from his guns. He gave the fleeing bomber a second and longer burst. Its starboard wing root and motor caught fire. The 88 commenced to disintegrate and, as Buck broke off his attack, crashed into the sea. Buck and I joined up and, without further incident, returned to base.

Bud and Junior had landed. The former had found the 87's, shooting down one. Johnny, who was with him, had got another. He was shot up by a 109 in the process, but managed to bring his aircraft back to base. Junior had fired the odd squirt, but without any luck. The Hurriboys had also found the 87's, and had done well.

I felt I had made a complete mess of it. The other boys were putting them in the bag, but I seemed to be doing no good at all, and was very annoyed.

An hour later we took off again, Pilot Officer Sandy McHan, one of the newly arrived boys from an Eagle Squadron, flying in place of Junior. It was another big party, but this time they were after the ship in Kalafrana Bay. We were at 22,000 feet before they arrived, and Woody, who had kept us posted about their movements, brought us in at the right moment. We found a big formation of

88's below us, diving on the ship. This time I did not hesitate, but picking one out went straight for him. I was 600 yards behind, and closing, when I looked back for 109's. I could not see any, but 200 feet above me was another 88. As I looked up, it released its bombs. They whistled past me, twenty feet from my wing tip, and gave me a most unpleasant shock. I closed on the 88 in front and, holding my fire until well within range, concentrated on his starboard motor. I could see large pieces falling off the 88 as my explosive cannon-shells went in. The bomber's rear-gunner was blazing away at me, so I gave him a short burst. He stopped firing. Probably I had killed him. Flak was bursting all around us, as I had delivered my attack while we were flying through the barrage. In Malta the guns do not cease firing under any circumstances, and although the Spits were supposed to attack outside the barrage, we went in amongst the flak if the Huns were there.

I kept up my attack until my ammunition was exhausted, and then broke away. I knew the 88 was badly damaged and probably would not reach its base. When I landed I found McHan had experienced a bad break. He was flying through the barrage, and about to open fire on an 88, when a Bofors shell ripped through his wing. He had to land straight away. Bud and Buck, however, had each set an 88 on fire, but as neither theirs nor mine was seen to crash we were credited with probables only.

These two dos were my first experience of mass enemy attacks. I was still very inexperienced, and my first feeling, in finding so many targets offering was one of complete confusion. All preconceived ideas of formation flying went by the board. It was every man for himself. Selecting a target, you told your leader you were going in, and in you went, keeping a sharp look out behind in case you were jumped by 109's.

We held a post-mortem after we landed, frankly swopping our impressions. The mass raids promised to be a piece of cake, and we anticipated taking heavy toll of the raiders. The German fighters, determined and skilful when attacked, did not display the same efficiency in their escort work. Most of them had come from Northern France. There they had been engaged on defensive fighter tactics, and over Malta their early offensive bomber escorts showed unmistakable traces of their inexperience. They were to learn rapidly, but at the moment their escort work was inferior. Bud Connell, I think, aptly summed up our impressions at seeing the big formations of 88's diving across the island when he remarked: "I'm glad I was above, and not underneath, them." The others felt Malta would prove a fighter's paradise, but I was depressed at my inexperience. I felt I had not done well, and told Bud so. He cheered me up, and gave me some worthwhile tips for the future, "Make your decisions quickly," he advised me. "Don't be confused` by numbers. You can't shoot them all down. Pick one out, and give him everything you've got. If you hang about up there the 109's will certainly get you." It was good advice.

For a quarter of an hour after I landed from both these flights I felt much as I had when in the air—worked up to fever pitch, excited, elated. I was restless. I couldn't sit still. I had to walk about continuously. I picked up a pencil, drew a couple of lines, tossed it aside again. I turned to a book, glanced at a few lines, flung it down. I talked all the time, puffing the while at a cigarette. Every little incident, no matter how trivial, served as a subject for natter. I related how my aircraft had been flying a bit left wing low. I told how my motor had bags of guts just when I needed it most. I described how the Hun had reacted to my attack, and gave my impression of the flak through which we had flown. They were immaterial, inconsequential things, but my tongue was loosened, and I just had to talk. Nobody listened to me. The other pilots were doing the same things themselves. Gradually this feeling of restlessness wore off. Extreme weariness, mental rather than physical, overtook me, and I sat down, exhausted. I noticed the same reaction in the others. Yet had we scrambled again, as I found on later occasions, these feelings would have vanished, and one would have become fresh and alert again.

I did not fly during the remainder of March. I beetled about the mess and the bastions, studying the form of the 109's. They began towards the end of the month to vary their tactics from day to day. Sometimes they would send in a fighter sweep first to engage our fighters and keep them off the bombers. At other times the 109's would do very close escort on the bombers, with from half a dozen to as many as 25 or 30 fighters on either flank. All of us learnt a lot from this sky gazing, and after each raid we would work out tactics among ourselves. The scene in the mess was the same every night. Grouped round the small room, sipping beer as we sat on chairs and tables, there would be a discussion, with everybody joining in.

Sometimes the Air Officer Commanding, Air Vice Marshal (later Sir) Hugh Pugh-Lloyd visited us at dispersal. He dropped in on us at Luqa on one occasion, and the sirens sounded as he arrived. He decided to stay and watch, and so that he could get a good view he walked out on to the aerodrome. Johnny Plagis was with him. As the 88's started to come down on the aerodrome, Johnny thought the place to be was in the shelter, and he tugged rather urgently at Lloyd's arm. "Point these devils out to me, Plagis," was the only reply Johnny received. "I must study their tactics." Johnny retorted, "They're right above our heads, dropping their bombs." Lloyd was as cool as ever. He took no notice of the bursting bombs, but continued to scan the skies, watching, eagle eyed, every move of the Huns. It was not until Johnny insisted upon going to shelter that Lloyd agreed to take cover. This incident was typical of the A.O.C., who's personal courage and confidence in his men made him a very popular personality in Malta. On another occasion, when he was at an aerodrome which also was being bombed, he refused to take cover while the bombs were dropping all around, and had to be ordered to shelter by the stationmaster. It was not bravado. Lloyd wanted to know how the Hun was doing, and believed in seeing for himself.

I began at this time to dream a great deal, and always my dreams were associated with the mass formations of bombers. They were confused and disjointed. Sometimes I would be in the air, attacking the bombers; at other times I would be on the ground, being bombed. These dreams persisted throughout my stay in Malta, occurring almost every night. All the boys, in greater or lesser degree, had a similar experience.

The fairly heavy, consistent attacks against the harbour continued during the last few days of the month. We were keeping up the pressure on the Huns and were knocking a few down, but, although he lost 52 bombers and 7 fighters for certain in March, we were not sufficiently strong numerically to make a very big impression on the large number of aircraft coming over. We had our victories and our losses. Duggie Leggo, Johnny Plagis's great cobber, was one of those to go. He was lagging slightly from formation when a 109 came down out of sun. Getting dead astern of Duggie, he let him have it from 50 yards. Duggie rolled on his back, and went into the sea.

Late in the month cheery Tony Boyd learnt that he had been awarded the D.F.M. He had earned it. Boyd stood out among the Hurriboys, all of whom had done an exceptionally fine job. After receiving our congratulations in the mess, he remarked that he thought it high time he went out and earned his decoration. That was typical of Tony, who invariably deprecated his own deeds. Later that evening Hesselyn and I were sitting in our billet. The Hun had bombed the power line to M'dina, and we were without lights. "Well, Bren," remarked Hess, "I think we'd better have one of those each," referring to Tony's gong. "Right, we'll get one," I replied. It was a pact we kept later.

CHAPTER II

APRIL 1942

I flew again on April 1. We took off only once, and although we saw some 109's they were too far away to attack. Other than that, the flip was without incident. Completely browned off, we handed over at lunch time.

HESSELYN

Stan Grant, Pete Nash, Johnny Plagis, Buck Buchanan, Flying Officer Norman Lee, an Englishman, and I arrived at the aerodrome on the dot at one o'clock. I had done some half dozen scrambles in March, but beyond an occasional squirt at 109's and 88's, these dos had been uneventful. However, they had given me good experience, and although still very much a novice I was feeling more confident than when I had gone up over Malta for the first few times.

We scrambled immediately, leaving in such a hurry that I was caught unprepared and had to borrow Bob Sim's parachute and helmet. A Hun fighter sweep was reported to be on its way, but when we engaged the 109's at 14,000 feet there were only four of them, apparently over on reconnaissance. One broke away as we turned towards them. Johnny at once gave chase, caught it, and shot it down in flames. The rest of us turned with the 109's, but we could not get on their tails, and after a few minutes they headed for home, out distancing our pursuit.

Ten minutes after landing, Grant, Nash, Lee and Plagis again scrambled. Buck and I watched from the ground as all four went in to attack 30 88's, which had come over to bomb the harbour. The boys flew right through the flak to get at the bombers. We could hear the staccato barking of the aircraft cannons above the roar of the ack-ack guns, and were able to distinguish our own from the enemy's fire, that of the Spits being louder and more irregular than that of the 109's. Stan, Johnny and Pete shot down an 88 each. We saw Pete's burst into flames and head straight for the sea, sending up a column of water as it crashed. The other two also fell into the sea, but from where we stood we could not follow them all the way down. Norman was unlucky. He was attacking an 88 when he was shot up by 109's. He forced landed on the aerodrome with a cannon shell hole in his wing. A shell-splinter had entered his ankle and he had to be packed off to hospital.

An hour later Stan, Johnny, Buck and I went up. Fighter Control sent us to 10,000 feet to patrol, and we were there when Woody told us a Dornier 24, with heavy fighter escort, was coming in. The Huns were about 10 miles out to sea when Stan sighted them and told us they were at four o'clock below and on the deck. I could see the flying boat, with its escort all round it like a swarm of bees. From the height at which we were flying, the Hun machines looked like small silvery specks on the water. Stan led us down until we were directly behind the enemy and about 5000 feet above. Then he told us to go in and take our pick. I chose the one on the extreme right, and as I dived on him I could see the rest of the boys going in, line abreast. I quickly caught my 109, but I was coming in too fast, and overshot him. However, I got a good bead on the one ahead. It was a lucky break. This 109 was turning at the time, and I had him dead in my sights. Opening fire from about 50 yards, I gave him a four-second burst. He flipped on his back immediately and went straight into the drink. I was as excited as hell. I told everybody, including Woody that I had shot down my first, screaming over the R./ T : "I've got one! I 've got one!" My number one, Buck, called up. "Shut up, Hess. We all know you've got one."

So elated was I at my success that, foolishly, I began circling round the 109 in the drink, laughing at him. Suddenly Johnny's urgent voice reached me over the R/T "For Christ's sake turn, Hess. You've got two on your tail," he shouted. His

75

words sobered me abruptly. I became aware of two streams of explosive cannon shell passing my port wing. I never worked so hard in all my life as in the next few seconds. I swung my aircraft round, and turned into the two Huns. They broke away immediately and started for home, and I gave chase. Buck, busily engaged with three 109's, called up, "Spits, for God's sake come and help me," but I called him back, telling him I was too busy myself and couldn't come. Stan and Johnny, apparently having run out of ammunition, were on their way home. I chased my two 109's, but couldn't catch them, and, having run out of ammo and being about 40 miles out, I decided to return to base. Fortunately I was not molested on the way home.

When I landed I found I had pressed the wrong gun button, and had shot down my first Hun with machine-guns alone. I was thrilled and elated and told everybody who would listen about my feat, but Stan Grant took some of the wind out of my sails when he ticked me off good and proper for getting so excited and burning up the R/T Johnny had also got one, but Stan and Buck had managed only to damage one apiece. Buck told me he had seen two machines coming towards him, but thinking they were Spits, had not worried. When they turned out to be 109's, he had found more work than enough getting away from them, and at one stage had as many as five enemy fighters round him.

Ninety minutes later we scrambled again, Pete Nash taking off with us as an extra. A heavy plot of bombers, all 87's this time, was coming in. We left the ground over late, and as we were getting height were jumped by 20 or 30 enemy fighters. The 109's broke us up completely and forced us down to 1000 feet. Pete and I, having eventually evaded the 109's, watched the 87's finish their dive, and then went straight after them through the flak. We each got on a bomber's tail. Pete was slightly ahead of me, and I could see him firing before I opened up. His shells were striking, and suddenly his 87 blew up in the air. I had no time to see any more. I was within 100 yards of my 87, and, pressing the right gun button this time, I gave him everything I had. In a couple of seconds he burst into flames and dived straight into the drink. The 109's came at us both from all directions, but, evading them by turning and twisting, we shot off for home. As I was coming in to land, with wheels and flaps down, I was jumped by a 109. I could see his tracer whipping past my wing, and, giving the engine everything it had, I pulled up wheels and flaps and turned steeply. The 109 overshot me and climbed away. I continued with my landing, and he did not interfere again.

It had been a most successful party. Stan, Johnny and Buck had each shot down an 87, so we had destroyed five for the scramble.

This was the second occasion on which our Spitfires had engaged the 87's, and we had scored a notable success. Fifteen 87's had come over, and we had bagged a third of them with only five Spits operating. The Stukas had flown in a staggered vic formation, which resembles a V with the tops of the letter very widely spaced, and they had been very heavily escorted by 109's. The fighters were not only on the flanks and above the bombers, but also weaving below, so as to protect them from belly attack.

The public has a wholly exaggerated opinion of the Stuka and its capabilities, due, no doubt, to all that has been written concerning dive-bombing in France and Crete. I myself at one stage believed the 87's were a valuable and efficient weapon, but the day's operations convinced me that the Spitfire was the Stuka's master. Later experiences in Malta merely confirmed that opinion and, to my mind, proved conclusively that dive-bombing by 87's is only practicable and profitable when the attacking force has absolute local air superiority.

At all times the Stuka is very vulnerable to fighter attack. Before it has dropped its bombs it is not manoeuvrable. If you can bounce it then it cannot get away. You can always out manoeuvre it, and, closing in to your range, you can send it down with a two or three second burst. Even when making its steep vertical dive it is a piece of cake for a fighter. Its speed is not nearly fast enough to carry it away from a Spitfire, and when following down an 87 I have misjudged my speed and overshot it. The Stuka becomes more manoeuvrable once it has dropped its bombs, but it is still no match for the fighter. We could always turn our Spits inside the 87's, hopelessly out manoeuvring them and placing them at our mercy. At no time, however, is the Stuka more vulnerable to fighter attack than when pulling out of its dive. For a few seconds it literally becomes helpless. As soon as the pilot presses the bomb release it is automatically pulled out of its dive by a device which takes control of the aircraft. This device is necessary because the suddenness of the pullout causes both pilot and rear-gunner to blackout. The manoeuvre is so violent that on occasions I believe the pilot loses consciousness. In any event, during these few seconds, he is certain to be crouched in his cockpit with his head between his knees, seeking to avoid blackout. If a fighter jumps him at this moment, he is powerless to manoeuvre away, while the rear-gunner is equally powerless to open fire. The 87 is then the fighter's meat.

We quickly developed an effective attack against the 87's, and consistently we took heavy toll of them throughout my stay in Malta. Flying a parallel course, we would follow them down outside the flak. Immediately they cleared the barrage, and started to pull out of their dive, we would whip on to their tails. The rear-gunner would get the first squirt from our guns, the motor or the pilot the second. Rarely did the 87 survive. Incidentally, it was the most satisfactory of all German aircraft to shoot down. A couple of our cannon-shells had only to crash into it, and often it would explode with a vivid red flash, disintegrating in mid-air.

Such is my view of the Stuka from the air. I have little better opinion of it when on the ground beneath it. On several days during the first weeks of April

I was dive bombed on the aerodrome by as many as 20 Stukas at a time. I would watch them come over in their staggered formation at about 15,000 feet. As they approached the coast, they invariably went into a gentle dive to gain speed, and then, when above their objective, put their noses straight down. They dived at an incidence of 80 to 85 degrees. At 5000 feet their bombs, clearly visible on the wings, were released. When I was standing fairly well underneath the diving 87's, it seemed as if the bombs suddenly drifted slightly away from the aircraft. At first they appeared to float a little behind, then quickly overtake, the 'plane. Both the aircraft and the bombs appeared to be coming straight at me, but a little experience of dive-bombing rapidly taught me to judge accurately where the Stuka's bombs would fall. I knew whether I was likely to be hit or not. I often watched the 87's from the open, and always had time in which to reach a slit trench if I judged the bombs were addressed to me.

I would rather be dive-bombed by 87's than by 88's, and we had plenty of experience of the latter at this time. Approaching the coast at about the same height and in the same formation as the 87's, they also dived gently to gather speed. Then, as they neared the target, they lowered their diving brakes, and came down on their objective at an incidence of from 45 to 50 degrees. They looked much bigger and more ponderous than the 87's, and carried a far heavier bomb load about 3000 lb. As against 1000 lb. They had no bomb aimer aboard, the bomb release being in charge of the pilot. He depended on the bombs following the course of the aircraft to hit the target. Over Malta, the 88's sometimes carried a couple of 1000 pounders and a number of smaller bombs, or their cargo was composed of about a dozen 250 pounders. Occasionally they came over carrying only a single 3000 pounder. When I was not too far away, I could always see this large bomb, which rather resembled the fuselage of a 109, turning in the air as it descended. Its blast effect was tremendous. One day, standing on the bastions at M'dina, I watched 20 88's drop a 3000 pounder each on Ta-Kali. The bombs fell all around eastern dispersal, a mile from where I was standing with my body sheltered by the bastions but my head exposed. Even at that distance I could feel the blast. It was just as if someone had struck me a sharp blow on the face. The bombing of the 88's was almost as accurate as that of the 87's, and because of the heavier bomb load naturally inflicted greater damage. I never stood in the open when the 88's were dive-bombing, but always took shelter at once. They released their bombs all together, and a stick from an 88 would cover a wide area.

Both the 87's and the 88's dropped bombs with whistles and screamers attached to them. My first experience of them was terrifying. I thought every bomb was coming straight at me, although some of them were falling more than half a mile away. It was sometime before I got used to these nerve-racking devices. Once my ears became attuned to the bombing, however, I was able to judge pretty accurately how close they were. The only difficulty with this method was that by the time I knew whether I was going to get it, I would have had it unless I was in a slit trench. I therefore took no risks.

Heavy bomb-loads were dropped daily on Malta throughout the early part of April. The aerodromes continued to be bombed heavily, and there were frequent raids against the Grand Harbour. But the Hun, pressing home his attacks and exploiting his mastery of the air to the full, was increasing the number of his targets. Bombs began to fall over a wider area. Valetta started to cop it, and as the days went by, more and more of the city was blasted into ruin. Mosta, near Ta-Kali, Floriana, and other places which had escaped all but a few stray bombs suffered considerable damage.

Life steadily became more hazardous and difficult. The transport, water supply, electric power and telephone systems were disorganized. We were forced to take refuge in the slit trenches more frequently, and to remain in them for longer periods. Our daily rations were often delayed in reaching us, and we had to fall back on our reserve stocks. Meals appeared at irregular hours, and the quality of the food deteriorated. In the sergeant's mess, which had been one of the best on the island, bully beef appeared more frequently. Often there was no bread. Breakfast in particular was much disorganized. The sirens which heralded the early morning raid generally sent the cooks and waiters scurrying to shelter, and the mess would be deserted when we arrived. Each pilot cooked his own breakfast, scrounging round the kitchen and selecting whatever he could find. Frequently there were no lights, and the radio was silenced. We missed the daily news bulletins of the B.B.C. The news sheet, printed in English and published daily, sometimes got through to us, but more often arrived several days late. We began to feel almost completely out of touch with events outside Malta. Both cinemas in Rabat closed down.

Even worse was the plight of the civilian population. The Maltese were in and out of the shelters throughout the day and, although the bombers were not yet coming over at night, slept in them each evening. Food distribution was erratic, and the problem of cooking acute. Hot meals made an ever less frequent appearance. Casualties, although still light, were mounting. The schools, however, were not closed. I often watched the children being marched to shelter when danger was imminent. They seemed cheerful and unworried, and whenever they spotted a pilot would break ranks and run across to him, crying at the top of their youthful voices, "Spitfire! Spitfire! Pilot! Pilot!" They seemed to be able to stand up to the nerve-racking strain of the bombing better than the older people. The latter looked tired, nervy.

Watching their churches, monuments and homes being destroyed, it must have been obvious to them that the Hun was on top, at least for the moment. Their morale, however, was unshaken. I spoke to many of them, and discovered that their paramount feeling was a bitter hatred against the Germans and Italians. Their confidence in victory was unshaken. Again and again they told me that the Hun would be beaten in the end, and whenever they saw one shot down they cheered wildly.

The Hun also had plenty of respect for our aircraft and pilots. I talked for some time with a 109 pilot Norman MacQueen had shot down. His sole interest in life seemed to be to fly a 109 and have plenty of squirts. Indeed, flying was in his blood, and outside flying he had little interest in the war. He told me he did not think it would make much difference who won the war. I asked him what he and his fellow pilots thought of the Spit, and he answered unhesitatingly that it was a very good aircraft. He considered the 109 faster, but admitted it did not have the Spit's manoeuvrability. Then we became engaged in a technical argument on the relative merits of the Spitfire and the109.

The Hun admitted the proficiency of our pilots, but boasted a great deal about his section leader, Neuhoff, declaring he had 38 victories in the air to his credit. Neuhoff, he told me, had fought in Spain, Poland, France, and the Battle of Britain. He said we would never get Neuhoff. Yet when the Hun, his broken leg mended, arrived at his prisoner-of-war camp it was to find Neuhoff already there. He had been shot down by Buck Buchanan, who, coming out of sun, had set the German's aircraft on fire. Neuhoff had baled out and was taken prisoner.

The same day I spoke to the rear-gunner of an 87, which had been shot down by flak while attacking the harbour. He also had broken his leg when he baled out. He said the 87 was very vulnerable to fighter aircraft, especially as it was pulling out of its dive. He could speak little English, and this made his opinion, which confirmed my view of he 87, all the more valuable. He did not know what I thought of the 87, and was not merely agreeing for the sake of politeness.

Between the 1st and the 21st I flew only once. The rest of the boys were also doing little flying. I had no success when I went up on the 6th, but the other boys, when they did fly, were shooting down the Huns consistently. An Australian, Pilot Officer John Bisley, had destroyed five Huns. On the 5th he had chased some enemy bombers all the way back to Sicily, shooting down two of them. The Hun fighter escort attacked him, but although he received severe wounds Bis got back to his base and crash-landed. Later he was awarded the D.F.C. for this action. The squadron's score was mounting. Norman Macqueen had shot down about five, and Pete Nash and Johnny Plagis had each got four. Several of the others had two or three to their credit. By April 10 the squadron's total was about 35 destroyed, with others probably destroyed or damaged. It was not a large tally considering the number of Huns coming over, but it was a decent bag having regard to the small total of our operational flying hours.

If we did little flying during this period we were by no means entirely idle. We were expecting Spitfire reinforcements, and there was much activity on the aerodrome. The Army, assisted by the Malta auxiliary police, was busily building sandbag dispersal pens for aircraft, and as we would not be doing much flying until the new Spits arrived Stan Grant decided we should lend a hand. We were to build a pen which was to be known as the Pilot's Pen. We embarked on an ambitious scheme with much energy. On and off for a fortnight we worked at the construction of a double pen. It provided us with a lot of fun, but half-way through our interest waned and our energy flagged, and the Army had to finish it for us. The bungers-up of bomb-holes, who were drawn from the ranks of the Army, were doing a really good job. On every aerodrome, no matter how frequently the bombers came over, they kept a landing-path clear for us. Ta-Kali was again in use, and we were operating also from every other aerodrome in Malta. For that, the bungers-up of bomb-holes were primarily responsible.

Our ack-ack defences steadily improved in accuracy. The gunners were obtaining plenty of practice, but they had to conserve ammunition and the number of guns was fewer than in later days. Yet by the end of April they had destroyed 101 enemy aircraft during that month. As the total mounted during the month, and the Hun began to realize the increasing accuracy of the ack-ack barrage, the bombers opened up on the gun positions. There were several posts of heavies dotted along the coastline at Naxxur. Coming from the north to bomb the harbour, Luqa or Ta-Kali, the German bombers generally crossed the coast here, and the Naxxur guns were beginning to get results. On practically every raid for a week, from about the 10th to the 17th, three 88's made these gun positions their only target. They dropped many bombs in the area, but never succeeded in silencing the guns. These attacks were typical of those which later developed against gun positions all over the island.

There was very close co-operation between the guns and the fighters, but it was a standing rule that once the barrage started it stopped for no one. Fighters went through it at their peril. I was on the aerodrome one afternoon when the boys were scrambled. Thirty 88's came in and dive-bombed the harbour. We were watching them coming in when suddenly our fighters appeared. The four Spits swooped down on the bombers. One, getting on the tail of an 88, followed it into the barrage. Flak was bursting all around both it and the bomber, and suddenly we saw the Spit disintegrate in mid air. We saw nobody bale out. When the other three Spits landed we found that Flight Lieutenant Hepple was missing.

81

We felt depressed, being certain that he had bought it. Suddenly the 'phone rang in dispersal, and the airman of the watch, answering it, announced that it was Hep. We gave a cheer, and Ronnie West took the receiver. He told us afterwards that Hep had baled out at 500 feet, and was in Imtafa hospital, having slightly injured a leg. He had been hit by a Bofors shell aimed at the 88. I saw Hep in hospital next day, and his own account of the adventure was terse. "I remember my aircraft exploding," he told me, "and I don't remember another bloody thing until I was floating down in my 'chute." Hep must have got out of his smashed Spit and, without conscious thought, pulled the rip cord of his parachute.

Another curious, and, I think, unique, incident occurred a day or two later. Johnny Johnston took part in a scramble, and became engaged with a 109. He was so intent on attacking this fellow that he did not see another 109 jump him from behind. The second Hun fired a short burst before Johnny slipped away from him. The Spitfire was not badly damaged, but Johnny had to return to his base at Luqa. At this moment a bombing attack was developing on Luqa. Unfortunately Johnny did not notice the 88's coming down, and continued his landing approach. One moment he was flying over Luqa at about 50 feet. The next he was upside down with very little aircraft left at 1000 feet. He pulled his harness release, dropped out, and came home by parachute. He had been blown up by a bomb exploding on the aerodrome. The blast had carried his aircraft up to 1000 feet and wrecked it. "I was quietly flying over Luqa in a Spitfire at 50 feet one minute," Johnny told us when he landed. "The next I was on my back at 1000, with only a seat left."

As soon as our fighter defence weakened, as it had weakened soon after the beginning of April, enemy activity decreased, but only very slightly. The Hun came over as regularly and as often, but with rather fewer aircraft on each occasion. The mass bombing, although still intense and severe, was not quite as heavy as it had been when the month opened. Then the Swordfish boys made a successful anti-shipping strike. It was directed at a convoy carrying supplies to Rommel, and it seemed to annoy the Hun no end. On the 7th he launched a tremendous effort. His bombing, possibly because he wanted to run further convoys to Rommel, was directed obviously at neutralizing Malta. The frequency and times of the raids remained much the same, although sometimes a fourth was added to the day's quota. But they were made in far greater strength. Each time three or four waves of bombers would come in, and there would be as many as 40 bombers to each wave.

Valetta was attacked consistently and indiscriminately. The Opera House, one of the island's most beautiful monuments, was destroyed. Churches and hospitals were hit, and dwelling houses and business premises blasted with increasing frequency. The Army camps were dive-bombed incessantly, and attempts were made all over the island to silence gun positions. At the same time, there was no relaxation of the bombing of the aerodromes. Between the 7th and 15th, when the attack slackened at last, the Huns dropped the greater part of the 6000 tons of bombs which fell on Malta during April.

Conditions throughout the island grew worse. They had been bad enough at the beginning of the month, but they were now much worse. Housing was acutely short. Our ground staff, who had been living in and near Mosta, had to be found accommodation elsewhere. The majority of the civilians had no homes but the rock shelters. The difficulties of transport, water supply, food distribution and communications, acute enough earlier in the month, were intensified almost a hundredfold. The schools closed down.

Among the pilots a wave of depression set in. We felt impotent and helpless. There were so many targets and practically no aircraft with which to shoot at them. Most of us had to watch from the ground instead of fighting in the air, and we did not like it. The 126 Squadron boys, operating from Luqa, had a few Spitfires left, and scrambled on every possible occasion. So also did the Hurriboys from Halfar, but again it was the same story of too few aircraft. Whenever the boys flew, they spent at least half an hour getting beaten up on the circuit by the 109's while attempting to land. The numerical odds against our fighters were overwhelming. They could only nibble, when what was needed was a large sized bite. Yet Malta, between the 1st and 21st, had destroyed for certain 117 enemy aircraft.

But shortly after this intensified blitz broke over Malta we received cheering news. All the pilots were summoned to a meeting at the officers' mess. Woody told us that the Air Officer Commanding (Air Vice Marshal Pugh-Lloyd) would speak to us later. While we were waiting for him we discussed the position, and decided that it was a hell of a business when fighter pilots were sitting on the ground while the Hun was doing what he liked above our heads. Lloyd arrived about nine o'clock. He spoke very briefly, but he gave us what we needed most, hope. "It's as hard for me not to be able to give you aircraft as it is for you not to have them," he declared, "but, believe me, you will have them soon. When you get them, I know what you'll do to those devils."

Nobody could tell us when the new Spits were due, but a whisper went round that the 20th was the day. By nine o'clock that morning Hess and I, with a number of others, had walked up to the bastions at M'dina and were eagerly looking westward. It was ten o'clock before we saw the new Spits sweep across Imtafa Hill and come into the circuit at Ta-Kali. As they passed above our heads, someone yelled excitedly, "Look, they've got four cannons!" Sure enough, they had. They were a later Mark Spitfire than those engaged in sweeps over the Channel. When we realized this, we were greatly bucked.

We felt that in England they must understand something of our difficulties. Squadron Leader Gracie, who had gone to lead them in, was in command of the new arrivals. Some of them clearly did not know the form, and had some difficulty in landing. There was a clear landing-path, but on either side there were bomb-holes, and some of the boys had difficulty in deciding exactly where to alight.

As they were touching down, we raced for the aerodrome. The boys, with all their kit, were in a bus by the time we arrived. We had time only to glance round for familiar faces. I knew one of the new arrivals an Englishman, Pilot Officer Jack Slade. He was from my old squadron in England, and had taught me a lot when I first arrived there. There were a number of New Zealanders known to Hess, including Pilot Officer Mitchell and Sergeant Pilots Jack Rae and Reg Dickson, the latter from Invercargill, Hess's home town.

An hour after the Spits had landed, some 87's and 88's came over and bombed Ta-Kali. Many of the new Spits had not been serviced, but some of them, flown by the old hands, went up. They did fairly well, but the raid had come too soon after the Spitfires had landed for us to be able to get sufficient aircraft into the air. It was inevitable that we should lose some of the four cannon Spits which remained on the ground, and some were destroyed and damaged.

HESSELYN

The Hun bombers were trying to get rid of the new Spits before they could commence flying, and they came over several times during the afternoon. With Buck Buchanan, my number one, I went on readiness at one o'clock. Laddie Lucas, Flying Officer Raoul Daddo-Langlois, Buck McNair, and Junior Tayleur scrambled a few minutes later. Buck and I were outside dispersal, and we watched the Spits climb up to 15,000 feet. A dozen 88's came in at 12,000 feet, while some 7000 feet below them eight Hurris, trying to gain height, were mixing it with a lot of 109's. The bombers, instead of attacking Ta-Kali, dive-bombed the harbour. The Spitfires started to come down on the bombers, but were forced to engage 109's coming down behind them. One, evading the 109's, got on the tail of an 88, which, after a few seconds, burst into flames. It failed to pull out of its dive, and headed straight into the drink.

At this moment eight 87's swept in over Ta-Kali, and Buck and I dived for a shelter. With the Spits fully engaged with the 109's, the 87's had matters all their own way, and they gave the aerodrome a pasting. By the time the Spits had shaken off the 109's the 87's were well on their way home, and only one Spit managed to get within even long range of them.

When Buck and I came out of the shelter we found some 15 109's in the circuit. The Hurris were trying to hold them off so that the Spits could land. I noticed one Spit with its wing-tip sheered off. He was flying low down, with a bunch of 109's above, and was whistling round the circuit, waiting a favourable moment to come in and land. His damaged wing was plainly visible from the ground. About 18 inches of it was missing, and instead of the usual elliptical section of a Spit wing, it looked rather like the square-cut wing of a 109e. Eventually the Spit came in to land, but overshot. It was running past dispersal when the pilot whipped up his undercart, and skidded the aircraft along on its belly, the only way in which he could prevent the Spit from turning over on its nose on the rough ground at the end of the aerodrome or crashing into the brick houses in the field beyond. The Spitfire can be landed with perfect safety on its belly, and the damage to the aircraft is never great. It was so with this one. It came to rest in a light cloud of dust. Brennan ran towards it, but the 109's swooped down and started to beat up the aerodrome. Brennan dodged behind some sandbags, and Buck and I ran towards a slit trench. Before we could reach it, the 109's were overhead and we had to fling ourselves on the ground. As we did so I saw Raoul Daddo-Langlois leap from the cockpit of the Spitfire and make a beeline for dispersal. Machine-gun bullets ploughed into the ground all around us, and a cannon-shell burst within a few yards of Buck, but luckily we were not hit. Curious to know what had happened to clip off the Spit's wing tip, I joined Raoul as soon as the 109's had passed over. "I was doing a head-on on a 109, and he was doing a head-on on me," he explained. "He wouldn't break, and I wouldn't break, so we collided. The only difference is that I knocked of his whole wing." This incident confirmed our view that the Spitfire was a much tougher and better constructed aircraft than the 109.

After beetling around the circuit for about 20 minutes the rest of the boys were able to land. Junior Tayleur had been unlucky. In a head-on attack, a 109 put an explosive shell through his hood, lacerating his face and eyes. He was bleeding profusely, but courageously carried on, attacking and probably destroying an 87. When he landed he taxied his aircraft right up to its pen, and was then taken to hospital. After his discharge he returned to England.

About four o'clock a plot of 88's was reported, and a dozen Spits scrambled at once. Buck and I were very brassed off. We had been put on aerodrome defence, and took off a quarter of an hour after the boys had scrambled. Our job was to go out to sea, and wait there to give the boys cover when they came in to land. There were a lot of 109's about, but they gave us no trouble until we had got up to about 10,000 feet. We were by then some distance from the island, and could see neither the bombers nor the Spitfires. Four 109's began making passes at us. Being on a specific job, we were supposed to ignore them, and to avoid getting into a mix-up. They were very persistent, however, and Buck finally decided that we would have to mix it, whether we liked it or not. We turned into them, and for perhaps five minutes all six aircraft went round and round in tight circles, the 109's trying to get on our tails and we on theirs. We drifted steadily closer to the island, and eventually two of the 109's climbed away. We concentrated on the remaining two. I got on the tail of one, and almost simultaneously Buck got behind the other. We were almost over

Filfla by now, and the two 109's headed for Sicily, putting their noses down to gain speed. We chased them across Malta, and caught them as they crossed the coast at St. Paul's Bay. I gave mine a four-second burst. Very gently, his nose starting to dip down, he hung poised for a second; then suddenly went into a vertical dive, crashing straight into the drink. A few seconds later I saw Buck's 109 also crash into the sea.

We started to turn, intending to regain our position south of the island so as to cover the boys when they returned to land, but were jumped by four 109's. They succeeded in separating us. I dived and turned towards the ground, and when I pulled out at 1000 feet the two 109's which had attacked me were no longer on my tail. Hardly had I made certain of this when I found myself in amongst some 88's going out over Filfla. I got a quick, two-second deflection shot at one before my cannons jammed, but although I could see some strikes along his fuselage, he kept going and was only damaged. Buck had already landed when I came in. He had got in a few squirts at the other 109's, but had done no damage.

Sitting in the sergeants' mess that night, we were shooting a line to the new boys when word came that everybody was required at the officers' mess for a conference. As we set out, the sirens sounded. We warned the new boys to be careful, as it was probably a big plot coming in and they would be certain to bomb Ta-Kali. However, we reached the officers' mess without incident, and fixed ourselves up with a drink. The A.O.C. arrived shortly afterwards—and so did the bombers. We were all standing up. Lloyd, a whisky and soda in one hand, a cigarette in the other, was looking very pleased. "Well, boys, you've got your Spitfires," he announced. "Tomorrow you'll have a big battle. Pop'em all in the bag." At that moment the 88's dived straight across the M'dina mess for Ta-Kali, and the bombs began to scream. Unceremoniously, the old hands dived under the billiard table or ducked quietly into corners. Stan Grant, standing in front of a window quickly edged away. The new boys looked nervous and bewildered. But Lloyd sipped his whisky imperturbably and, addressing the new boys, remarked: "I would have liked to give you new boys a warm welcome. The Hun has given you a warmer one. Do the same to him tomorrow." The bombs fell very close, and the mess rocked. A few pieces of plaster fell to the floor. Then the bombers had gone. The rest of the evening was uneventful. I think the new boys were surprised by the manner in which we went under the billiard table, and probably thought we were unduly nervous. They soon learned about bombing, as we had learned after our arrival. Before we broke up, Stan Grant told me I would not be flying until the following afternoon. I felt brassed off, as I was anxious to get cracking.

HESSELYN

I was on dawn readiness on the 21st, but it was ten o'clock before we had our first scramble. It was a disappointing show. A Hun fighter sweep came over, and Stan Grant, Johnny Plagis, Buck Buchanan and myself went up. We saw little of the Hun aircraft and, apart from damaging a 109, had no joy.

About noon we scrambled again. A big plot of bombers was reported. We climbed to 20,000 feet, and there the 109's tried to break us up, so as to prevent us going for the incoming bombers. We refused to mix it with them for a while, but eventually I was compelled to turn into two 109's. I turned to what I imagined was the rear enemy fighter, but it proved to be the leading 109. I was surprised to find him in my sights, as I had turned very quickly, but had the presence of mind to press my gun-button. I caught him with a lucky climbing deflection shot. The Hun disintegrated in the air. Pieces of the 109 flew in all directions, and the pilot, literally blown out of his aircraft, shot out on the right-hand side and hurtled towards the earth. His parachute did not open. I had fired all four cannons, and although it was only a snap shot, 30 to 40 of my cannon shells must have ripped into his fuselage.

The fact that I had turned into the leader by mistake gave the other Hun his opportunity. He got on my tail, and in my mirror I could see him behind me, firing for all he was worth. I broke down promptly, and aileron turned to about 2000 feet, with the Hun following all the way. Johnny Plagis was on the 109's tail, but we were all so close together that he could not fire for fear of hitting me. At 2000 feet, however, the Hun gave up the chase, and climbed away out to sea. Johnny followed him, and probably destroyed him. I began to climb to regain height, and was over Gozo when I spotted six to eight 87's diving on Ta-Kali. I waited until they came out of their dive, by which time I had gained a good tactical position, 4000 feet above them. Making the most of this advantage I dived on the rear 87, opening up on him from dead astern. I gave him a four-second burst, and he went down in flames, straight into the drink. A bunch of 109's jumped me, but I evaded them by diving and turning, and by the time I was over M'dina I had shaken them off. A 109, low down, was shooting up Ta-Kali. I dived on him and followed him as far, as Kalafrana Bay, but could not get closer than 300 yards. I fired all the way, but could only see strikes near his tail plane. He climbed away, shaking me off without difficulty. I returned to Ta-Kali and landed.

Knowing that I was not to fly until the afternoon I made no haste to get up that morning. I was in the middle of breakfast when a message reached me that Stan Grant wanted me to go down and fly immediately. A small, bald-headed New Zealander, Sergeant Pilot "Dusty" Miller, decided to come along with me. We collected our flying-kit, and set out for western dispersal. Then the sirens went. I was inclined to wait until after the raid before proceeding, as no cover was available on the road to the aerodrome, However, after a few minutes' hesitation, we decided to carry on. We were within 500 yards of western dispersal when the 87's and 88's arrived and dived on Ta-Kali. There were about 50 of them, heavily escorted, as usual, by 109's. Dusty and I jumped into a narrow ditch which, although we did not notice it at the time, was full of stinging nettles. For a quarter of an hour we crouched in it, listening to the scream and bursting of bombs. Then the raiders passed over and we resumed our journey.

Stan Grant, much to my annoyance, told me he had not sent for me, and Miller and I returned to the mess for lunch. Norman MacQueen, who was leading the flight that afternoon as Bud Connell had gone to the Middle East to bring in some Hurricanes, Buck Mcnair, Laddie Lucas, and Raoul Daddo-Langlois set off with me for the aerodrome after lunch. The sirens sounded before we left M'dina, and we were halfway to dispersal when thirty 87's began diving on Ta-Kali. We waited in a gun-post until the bombers had departed. Dozens of 109's were over the aerodrome, waiting for our boys to come in and land. We arrived at western dispersal to find that we should have reported to eastern. We started to walk across the aerodrome, and as we did so the 109 boys decided to beat it up. I got a hell of a fright. We were wearing our Mae Wests. They were bright yellow, and easily seen from the air. I felt sure that the 109's could not miss us, and for the first time was grateful that there were bomb-holes on the 'drome. I dived into the nearest as the 109's came down with guns blazing. They shot up both dispersals, as well as the pens around the aerodrome, The Bofors guns engaged them, and the small arms on Ta-Kali opened up. The din was terrific, and the 10 minutes I spent in the bomb hole seemed much longer. Some of the boys had been caught in the open, and as I clambered out of my bomb hole I wondered what had happened to them. I found them shaken, but, fortunately, uninjured. They had had a lucky escape. Two 109's coming over Imtafa Hill had already selected their targets before they saw the boys, and then it was too late for them to change. Had they sighted the boys a few seconds' earlier they would almost certainly have sprayed them. As it was, there were no casualties.

We scrambled at three o'clock, climbing south of the island and getting to 26,000 feet, with the sun behind us. Woody called up and said: "Hullo, Mac. There's a big plot building up, but it's taking a long time to come south. Keep your present angels, and save your gravy. I'll tell you when to come in." We stooged round until Woody gave us the word. Then we sailed in. Buck and I went to Comino Channel, between Gozo and Malta. Buck reported 20 109's and told me to break left, but to stay with him. I could not see the 109's, and when I asked where they were Buck told me they were all around us. We had lost some height, and suddenly, glancing behind me, I saw four 109's coming down on me.

I pulled round, and blacked out. When my vision cleared I saw them again, and also another bunch about 2000 feet above me. Three of the four 109's overshot me. The fourth made his turn too wide, and I got inside him. I was slightly below him when I attacked from 200 yards. I allowed some deflection, firing perhaps 20 feet ahead of him in the hope that his aircraft and my bullets would arrive at that spot simultaneously. They did. The 109 and my shells met. He spurted glycol. I kept on firing, as I was determined to make certain of him. He caught fire. Black smoke poured out of him. He rolled on his back, and went into a vertical dive. I followed him down in case he was foxing, but he went straight into the drink.

As he crashed, it struck me suddenly that there might be something on my tail. In my excitement I had forgotten to look, but luckily, none of the other 109's had dived down on me. Woody reported that the 88's were diving on Ta-Kali, and I pulled up to 10,000 feet. The next instant the 88's were diving past my nose, with Mac and the other boys coming down from above to attack them. I picked out one 88, and went for him. MacQueen, 100 yards to my left, was also attacking an 88, and I could see his guns firing. Indeed, for a moment I thought the black smoke from his cannon meant he was on fire, and it gave me a sudden shock until I realized he was firing. I got within 200 yards of my 88, and as I pressed my gun button his rear-gunner opened fire, Although I was flying one of the new four-cannon Spits, only one cannon on each wing was loaded. I had fired for about a second when my port cannon packed up. Luckily I was travelling fast. This prevented my aircraft from slewing from the recoil of my starboard cannon, as I was able to correct with rudder. I concentrated my fire on the 88's starboard motor and wing-root, and I could see my shells hitting. After perhaps six seconds, by which time I had fired all my ammunition, the 88 caught fire. Bits were flying off him, and the flames were spreading as he continued in his dive, and he was well ablaze when he crashed. Buck's 88 also went down, crashing into the sea.

Returning to land, I had my first experience of being beaten up in the circuit. A great pall of smoke and dust from the bombing was hanging over Ta-Kali. I made a couple of dummy runs over the aerodrome, and could see that the landing-path was well cratered. Just then I sighted six 109's at 5000 feet, waiting to pounce. I was flying very low, and could see the other boys kicking about the circuit, waiting to try and get in. I beetled up Imtafa Valley, between Imtafa and M'Dina Hills, skipped around some windmills at the top of the valley, and swung down a valley on the other side. For 30 minutes I kept this up. Again and again the 109's dived down from above and attacked me. Again and again I thanked my stars that the Spit was such a manoeuvrable aircraft. Each time I was attacked, I turned violently. The 109's were not sufficiently manoeuvrable to get a deflection shot at me, and their shells and bullets whipped past behind me. But it was a nerve-racking business. With all the violent turning and twisting I was compelled to undertake, I began to feel very sick. I wanted to vomit, but somehow managed to choke it back. My neck ached from constantly twisting it from side to side, looking back, and from holding it up, while doing tight turns, against the extra gravity force. The constant fear that a 109 would get me kept me nervous and strung right up. I was flying automatically, devoting my whole attention to watching the skies above. At the end of half an hour, when I was feeling exhausted and ill, Laddie called up: "Look, Mac, this is a hell of a bloody do. We must get in. We'll cover each other in." Mac replied that we were to go in, and he would cover us.

I started a normal circuit, about 300 feet above the aerodrome, put my wheels and flaps down, did a weaving approach, and as my wheels touched ground felt a sigh of relief. I taxied to my pen, forgetting to put up my flaps. All I could do when I got there was to lie back in the cockpit and gasp for breath. The ground crew had to help me out of my aircraft, and, dazed and dizzy, I groped my way along the wing out of my pen. I met Laddie as I was wandering over to dispersal. He was taking off his Mae West. I noticed his tunic was soaked with perspiration. I pulled off my Mae West, and was surprised to find my tunic in the same condition. We both looked up to see how Mac was getting on. He was making his approach, about 50 feet up. Suddenly two 109's darted out of sun. I said to Laddie, "Mac's had it." The 109's were dead astern of him, firing at a range of 50 yards. Their shooting, however, was poor, and they had not hit him. Whipping up his wheels, Mac turned sharply into them. The 109's overshot him, carried on, and beat up the aerodrome. Mac made a quick dart, put down his wheels, and managed to get in. He landed with two gallons of petrol, at the pace we were using it, sufficient fuel for only another two minutes in the air. I had had five gallons, the others about the same.

On the 22nd there was no cessation of the attacks. In fact, they increased in intensity. From early morning the 87's and 88's came over. I went on readiness in the afternoon, and, with Mac again leading, we soon scrambled. We were at 25,000 feet south of the island when the 88's came in. It was one of the biggest raids on Malta, over 150 bombers and fighters crossing the coast. The first wave attacked the harbour, but we left them alone. The second lot raided Luqa, and Woody brought us in. They were below me, moving towards Filfla at between 8000 and 10,000 feet. With the others, I dived down on them. As I started to close on one, I looked behind and saw two 109's on my tail. I judged them to be too far away to open fire, and I decided I had a good chance of getting my 88 before the 109's could get properly on my tail. I did not break away, but continued my dive, and at 300 yards opened fire. I gave him a three seconds burst, but my port cannon then packed up. I stopped firing and took a quick look behind. The 109's were closing fast faster than I had expected. I decided to risk another squirt at the 88, as I was very close to him. I gave him two seconds. The 109's were now firing. Their tracers were whipping past my starboard wing, and their shells exploding five or six feet away from me. I broke violently left, and as I did so saw six more 109's coming down at me from above. I pulled up and fired at one. My speed was too low, however, to fire with only one cannon, and my aircraft slewed violently away, sending my shots wide. I decided Filfla was too hot a spot. I dived away.

Woody reported more 88's diving on Ta-Kali and, believing I had shaken off all the 109's, I headed for there. I picked out an 88 that was diving, intending to follow him down to get some speed, so that I could attack him with my one gun. I had a quick look behind, and could see nothing. I started a stall turn down with the bomber. Suddenly there was a flash between my legs and a loud bang in the cockpit. A cannon-shell from a 109 had joined me in the cockpit. I was paralysed with fear. For a few seconds I just sat there, doing nothing. I was fascinated by my flying boots, which had been ripped to ribbons. Then, as I looked down, I became aware of a big hole in my aircraft, close to my right foot. It struck me that I had better do something. Automatically, without conscious thought, I worked it out that I must break right, as he must be doing a starboard quarter attack on me. I did so. I did not see the 109 at any stage, either which way he came or which way he went. As I broke right I asked myself, "Will I have to bale out?" I tried my ailerons. They were working. So were my elevators. I decided that as I had them I could force land anywhere, and that I would not have to bale out. I dived down to land, but owing to the haze of smoke and dust from the bombing I could not see the aerodrome. I was very low when at last I picked it up.

I had another session in the circuit. Round and round I went on my usual beat up the valleys. Each time I swung round the windmills to enter the second valley the 109's came down out of sun and had a crack at me. It was as nerve-racking as on the first occasion, and I felt exactly the same as on the previous day. I thought I would be up there forever, and would never be able to land. The smoke was clearing slowly from the aerodrome. Craters seemed to be everywhere. I decided Ta-Kali was unhealthy, and that if I was to land I would have to go elsewhere. I flew down to within five or 10 feet of the water, shielded from attack on the port side by the Dingli Cliffs, which are about 100 feet high. I imagined nobody would spot me there, and I began to feel less depressed. My optimism was premature. A great streak of tracer flashed past me. I realized that 109's had seen me trying to creep off, and, coming down sun, had got on my tail. I could not turn in towards the cliffs and had to swing out to sea. I did so, and managed to evade the 109's.

I rejoined the rest of the boys at Ta-Kali. I was feeling right down in the dumps, and anxiously pressed my petrol gauge every few minutes as I went round the circuit several times. I knew my gravy was running short, and that I must get down quickly. I decided to go in. I was determined to stay down, no matter what happened, whether I ended up in a bomb-hole or with a broken undercart. At 100 feet I put my wheels and flaps down, did a violent steep turn over the fence, side-slipped my height away, fish-tailed my speed off, and popped my aircraft down right between two bomb holes. I stopped my landing run within a few feet of a third crater. An airman had to come out and guide me to my pen through the maze of bomb-holes. I felt exhausted and dead tired, both physically and mentally. The strain, particularly in the circuit, had played me right out.

During the last few days things had hotted up very considerably. Both bombing and air fighting had grown more intense. In my opinion, the Hun had imagined that Malta had been neutralized by his previous attacks. He had now realized that this had not been the case. Our activity, both on the ground and in the air, had increased. His initial heavy bombing had failed to knock out Malta. We had more fighters in the air than at the beginning of the month. Our barrage was heavier and more accurate. The Hun was losing more bombers and fighters than he had been. We were far from being on top, but Malta was hitting back more strongly than before the intense bombing commenced. The Hun began to hit harder also, seeking to achieve what his first attacks had failed to do. He sent over more bombers, and made more sorties. His fighters showed renewed determination. The pilots appeared to have been gingered up by their command. Methodically, the Hun still came over at breakfast and lunch, and again late in the afternoon. The number of bombers in each wave, however, increased. On a single day more than 300 bombers crossed the coast. More fighters than ever came over with each wave of bombers, and the task of the Spit boys became increasingly difficult. Always the odds were against us, and often they were overwhelming odds.

The Hurricanes, forced to fend more and more for themselves, faced an even more difficult job. Every time they went up they had to face a swarm of 109's from the time they were airborne. Slower and with a less powerful armament, they could not hit back to the same extent as the Spits. Nevertheless they continued to go in against these heavy odds, disturbing the aim of the bombers and occasionally shooting down the odd one. Their losses were heavy. A squadron of pilots who had arrived in Malta during the blitz had been almost wiped out, and only a handful of these boys remained.

The Spits helped the Hurriboys whenever they could. Frequently we went over to Halfar with very little gravy and no ammo in order to cover them in.

I talked to Tony Boyd, "Slim" Yarra, who had come to Malta as a Spit pilot but had been posted to Hurris shortly after his arrival because of his previous experience on this aircraft, Tweedale, and many of the other Hurriboys. They were all brassed off at flying Hurricanes when the Spit boys were shooting down the Huns, and they would have liked to have converted to Spits. They felt they could have done a better job then. Oddly enough, they did not feel they were more likely to be shot down than we. Every Hurriboy I spoke to considered the Hurri more manoeuvrable even than a Spit, and was convinced that he could dodge any single 109 which tried to bounce him. Their one complaint was that while we were destroying Hun fighters and bombers, they were merely damaging them; Tony and Tweedie had each shot down an 88 with machine guns, and were very elated at having performed this unusual feat.

During the first moon period of April the Hun commenced night bombing in earnest. The 88's and 87's came over singly, but on some nights as many as 30 or 40 would make the trip from Sicily. These bombers mainly operated against the aerodromes, and the 88's, in an effort to confuse the ack-ack predictors generally came over with motors out of synchronization. We had the answer to the night bombing raids. Some Beaufighters had arrived at the same time as the first Spits, and they were very active and successful against the night raiders. At first it was difficult for us to distinguish the noise of a Beaufighter on patrol from that of an 88 with its motors out of synchronization, but we soon learned. The 88 had a whining, high-pitched hum the Beaufighter had a rather deeper and steadier note.

It was in these night raids that we had our first experience of Italians over Malta. Both their fighters and bombers had operated from Sicily the previous year, but since our arrival with the first Spits we had not seen an Italian aircraft. Now, however, their bombers began to put in an appearance again. They were mostly Breda 20's and Savoia Marchetti 84's. Both these aircraft were much larger than the 88, but in bomb-carrying capacity and performance they were decidedly inferior. The Italian pilots did not impress us. They showed little determination, and they had the wind up at anything that looked at all hostile. The Beaufighters worried them badly, while the barrage and searchlights also scared them. Frequently they would drop their bombs in the sea without attempting to cross the coast. Knowing this, we nearly always got a good laugh out of the Italian communiqués, which were broadcast by Rome Radio and were often reproduced in the Malta Times. They were always grossly exaggerated. Even the civilians commented scathingly on their falsity.

We took heavy toll both of the German and Italian night-bombers. An

Englishman, Pilot Officer (later Flying Officer) Tubby Daniels, shot down three in one flip. Sergeant Pilot "Dusty" Miller, not the New Zealander, but a small dark Welshman, one night shot down a Breda 20. He gave it a 23-second burst with the powerful Beaufighter armament, and it crashed on Malta. As it was spinning earthwards some of the crew baled out, and they were later captured. Miller spoke to the rear-gunner. The latter told "Dusty" that when the Beaufighter opened fire his pilot had rung him up on the intercom and asked if he were testing his guns. Next moment the port motor burst into flames, and the rear-gunner was baling out. The second rear-gunner we found next morning in the crashed machine, with 18 cannon shell wounds on various parts of his body. "If that bloke had tried to bale out, he had so much lead aboard his parachute wouldn't have held him up anyway," was "Dusty's" terse comment.

The heavy and consistent day and night bombing inevitably did much damage to our aerodromes. They were always the most popular target with the Hun bombers, and were pounded without respite. Yet even at the end of the month we were still operating aircraft from every one of Malta's aerodromes. For this the technical and maintenance services were primarily responsible. Our administrative buildings at Ta-Kali had been flattened, and our headquarters staff had moved to a cave. These changes did not affect the manner in which the ground organization was carried out. Squadron Leader Gracie, now promoted to Wing Commander, became stationmaster at Ta-Kali. He was not only popular, but remarkably efficient, and was responsible for many improvements in our organization. He appreciated the importance of the morale of the ground personnel. He knew that if they could be made to feel that they were hitting back at the Hun, they would be much happier. Accordingly he set up a number of light machine-gun posts around the aerodrome, and when ever raiders came over these were manned by the ground crews. He also gave every airman who wanted one a rifle and ammunition with which to blaze away at the 109's strafing the aerodrome or beating up the boys in the circuit. Needless to say, every airman took one. The damage which they inflicted may not have been great, but these measures had a wonderfully tonic effect, and the spirits of the ground crews soared. Another innovation of Gracie's was the provision of a heading for daily routine orders. "It is the duty of every airman to kill the enemy" appeared at the top of the orders from the time Gracie took over. It captured the imagination of both pilots and ground crews. It seemed to breathe a new spirit of determination. We felt, and Gracie often hinted, that big things were coming. It seemed to all of us that the time was drawing closer when we should win the battle of Malta.

On the 25th I scrambled late in the afternoon. Buck Mcnair was leading, with Squadron Leader Lord David Hamilton, the brother of the Duke of Hamilton, as his number two. He had arrived with the last Spitfire reinforcements, and was flying number two to learn the Malta form. I was leading the sub-section, and had another new boy, Pilot Officer Linton, a Canadian, as my number two. A big plot was on the way. As we climbed up south of the island I found my airspeed indicator was not working. Some bees had been building a nest in the air vent to the instrument, and the ground staff had not noticed them. Although it handicapped me I decided to carry on. We got into position up sun.

The first wave of bombers made Ta-Kali their target, but, on Woody's instructions, we left them alone and did not go in until the second wave attacked Naxxur. The air was very crowded. Flak bursts, 88's and 109's seemed to be everywhere. Well below me, going out to sea over the Dingli cliffs, I could see the bombers, which had raided Ta-Kali. Also below me were the 88's diving on Naxxur. I selected one and dived down to attack him. At the same moment six 109's, doing close escort on the port side of the formation of 88's came down on me. I had to leave my bomber and pull up into the 109's. All but the last overshot me. I pulled up 30 or 40 feet underneath him. It was point-blank range, and every detail of his machine stood out vividly. I could see his markings, his twin radiators, his retracted wheels, even the rivet heads on his fuselage. I gave him a second and a half with all four cannon. The result gave me a terrible fright. His starboard wing snapped off near the fuselage. It folded back, and banged against his fuselage. For a moment I thought it was going to tear away from his machine and come hurtling into my aircraft. I broke down very violently so as to avoid it.

Five hundred yards away, and dead in front of me, was an 88. I started to close, taking a quick look behind me. More 109's were coming down on me, but they were still out of range. I decided to take a chance, and try to deal with my 88 before the 109's were on me. As I closed in the 88's rear gunner opened fire. This meant nothing to me; it never did. In the heat of action it does not occur to you that you are running any risks yourself from the two machine-guns of an 88's rear turret. You do not visualize yourself being hit, but merely think you must knock off the rear gunner in case he damages your aircraft and forces you to bale out. I was so excited, and so keen to get the 88 before the 109's forced me to break away, that I was unaware his bullets were hitting my aircraft. I continued diving straight at him until I was only 250 yards behind him. Then I opened fire with all four cannon. The rear gunner stopped firing. I concentrated my fire now against the 88's two motors and the pilot's glasshouse. I could see my shells crashing into him, and in a few seconds he started to smoke. I was acutely conscious of the 109's diving on me, and knew that if I waited to check my aim I would be cold meat for them. The thought went through my mind that I must get my 88 quickly. I kept on firing. It was only for a matter of seconds, but seconds in air combat seem like minutes. He caught fire and started to disintegrate.

That was enough for me. I turned on my side and skidded violently sidewards. I flew straight into the slipstream from the 88. For a moment I thought I had been hit by the 109's behind me. My Spit flicked over on its back. I could exercise no control over it. For a couple of seconds, although it seemed far longer, I was flying upside down. Then I regained control, righted the machine, and looked round, rather apprehensively, for the 109's. Two of them had over-shot me. The others were milling about above the bombers.

Buck McNair's voice, inquiring where I was and if I was all right, came to me over the R/T I replied that I was O.K., but right in amongst them. Indeed, I seemed to be surrounded by 88's and 109's. Buck told me he was going to have a crack at some 87's. I could see them dive-bombing the harbour, with 109's covering them in every direction, but I could not see Buck. I told him to watch the fighter escort. I had expended all my ammunition on the 88, and to get away from the Hun machines which seemed on every side of me I dived down into the Ta-Kali circuit. There our light flak guns, which had been strengthened, were keeping the 109's higher than usual, providing us with a rather better chance of landing safely. I beetled round for about ten minutes, and then Buck joined me, having also run out of ammunition. The 109's kept making passes at us through the flak, and, deciding that things were getting a little too hot, we set off for the other end of the island. On the way down we flew over Luqa as some more 88's began to give it a pounding. We nearly had the same experience as Johnny Johnston. As we broke away from the aerodrome my aircraft was rocked violently by the explosion of bombs below. The blast did not hurtle me high into the air, as it had done with Johnny, but I had to work like hell to keep control. I was pitched everywhere before I eventually got clear.

Buck and I climbed up, intending to do dummy attacks on the 109's in an effort to scare them off. We had just started off when Woody called up and, telling us that the Hurriboys were very short of gravy and must get in, asked if we could help them. We flew down to Halfar. The Hurricanes were twisting and turning at zero feet, with the 109's beating them up. The Huns spotted us from a distance, and promptly made out to sea, where they climbed to 5000 feet and settled down to watch. Buck called Woody to tell the Hurriboys to pancake while we covered them. They came into land, but several times as one Hurri did an approach, with wheels and flaps down, another, a couple of hundred yards behind, would do a dummy run over the aerodrome, looking for a landing path between the bomb holes. Almost invariably the first Hurriboy, mistaking the second for a 109, would break violently left, and pull up his wheels and flaps. Some of the Hurriboys even mistook us for 109's.

Buck's language over the R/T was lurid, and he kept telling the Hurriboys that if they didn't get down he'd shoot them down. We were running short of gravy and were thoroughly annoyed. The Hurriboys hurled back some affable abuse, but eventually all got in and we beetled off back to Ta-Kali.

I still had no airspeed indicator, and Buck had to formate me in. I got into position in echelon starboard on Buck, and we started a circuit. The upwind end of the landing-path was a maze of bomb-holes, and I realized I would have to land very short. As we approached Buck called, "You're doing 120 now," and, a few seconds later, "Now you're down to 100, but I think you're too high. Go round again." I was too brassed off to worry whether I pranged or not. I decided to go on in. I touched down, and swung my aircraft away from the pitted landing-path, breaking violently. I stopped inches away from a bomb-hole. When I examined my aircraft I found 10 bullet holes. They must have come from the rear gunner of the 88.One was through the prop, some six inches above my head. I was amazed to find that the 88 had hit me, as at the time I had neither heard nor felt any of his bullets strike my aircraft.

We were all rather anxious about the new boys, but they landed shortly afterwards. Neither had got anything, but both Buck and I had each shot down two confirmed. We celebrated in front of dispersal with a war dance- a cross between a Maori haka and an Australian corroboree. Buck, a Canadian, knew neither of these native dances, and couldn't do it very well, but that didn't worry us.

This was the first time I had led a sub-section. It brought back memories of my initial trips over Malta, when I was a raw hand. I knew that Linny would be counting on me to the same extent as I had counted on my leaders when I first flew in Malta. I found this responsibility improved my flying and increased my vigilance. My formation flying had become automatic, but the knowledge that I was leading made me pay a good deal more attention to it. I recalled how much easier it had been for me in my early flights if the sub-section leader maintained position without violent alterations in throttle setting. This caused me to make it as easy as possible for Linny. I remembered also how little I had seen of what was happening around me, and I guessed Linny would be in the same position. Therefore I kept a sharper lookout than ever, so that I might give him ample warning. Yet although leading meant added responsibilities, I found it stimulating. I had greater confidence in myself, and was determined, not only to do well myself, but also that Linny should do well.

Before we went up Mac had called me aside and talked to me on the question of leading. He told me there were three paramount rules- firstly, get your section into a good tactical position to start; secondly, lead your men into attack with decision and without hesitation once you sight the enemy, and, thirdly, use your judgment when to get them out. I tried to act on these rules when leading sub-sections, and later when promoted to lead sections. They are rules which every leader should follow.

I was beginning to realize that I was an old hand. This was not due alone to the fact that I had become a sub-section leader. Several of the new boys, some of whom had had a lot of experience in sweeps over Northern France, had been flying during the last few days. After they had been up on a scramble these fellows would come and speak to me about the form in Malta. They had many questions to ask, and looked to me for help and advice. I realized that these boys were going through the same experience, and indeed a more difficult experience, than I had six weeks earlier. Even fellows who had been in the Battle of Britain found they had problems they wished to discuss with an old hand. They told me frankly they found things much tougher in Malta. Some of those who had been sweeping over Northern France and the Channel found themselves quite at sea. They were confused by the entirely different conditions. New Zealander Jack Rae, who had done some 50 sweeps and shot down two FW 190's before coming to Malta, had a bad time at first. He told me he had never been more terrified than on his first couple of flights over Malta. His electrical system packed up on his first trip, and he had no R/T He decided to land, but as he was approaching, with wheels and flaps down, the 88's started dive-bombing. "I was convinced I'd be dead at any tick of the clock," he told me. He survived that trip only to be shot up on his next. He baled out and spent about a month in Imtafa hospital with cannon wounds in a leg. Like most of us, he learnt the hard way, but he became one of the outstanding pilots in the squadron.

Another new chap was Squadron Leader Bisdee, D.F.C. This Englishman had his first Malta flip with Gracie and another new boy. It was an unlucky day for them. Bisdee had to swim home, making his landfall on the Dingli cliffs. These were too steep and rough for him to scale unaided, and he was rescued at some peril by two Maltese fishermen. The other new boy unfortunately was killed. Only Gracie got home with his aircraft.

Still the scoreboard arithmetic was excellent. The squadron had about 10 to one confirmed victories in its favour. Squadron 126 had not quite as good a record, but it had shot down far more than it had lost. New Spitfire squadrons were beginning to form, and already they were starting their tallies of confirmed victories.

HESSELYN

About noon on the 26th Buck Buchanan told me we were to go on readiness at one o'clock. Pete Nash, Buck, Pilot Officer Jimmy James, a young Rhodesian, and myself walked down to the aerodrome together. It was a pretty ugly walk. We tramped over debris, skirted bomb-holes, and dodged delayed action bombs, which were marked by warning red flags. Here and there we could see one of these bombs suddenly exploding. At dispersal the hut, which had been hit by a bomb, was a mass of wreckage. The flight sergeant in charge of the ground crew reported that Buck's machine was unserviceable. Buck was as mad as a hatter, but there was nothing he could do about it. No other aircraft was available for him, and he told Pete to lead if we were scrambled.

We sat round in the sun, waiting for something to happen. A big plot was soon reported coming in, and we climbed into our cockpits and were strapped in, ready to take off Thirty-five 109's were already over the island when we received word to scramble. I was pretty worried, expecting to be jumped by the 109's before we gained much height. I was worried still more after we had taken off Pete's electrical system packed up. With his R/T useless, he signalled me to take over by waggling his wings and pointing downwards. As he went down to land, I called up Jimmy and told him to come in closer and stay with me.

Woody told us to get as much height as we could and wait, so we climbed up into sun. We could see the 109's above us. Some were behind, some in front, some on either side. I counted 20 in all. Woody kept calling up, telling us to watch the small jobs. We managed to get up to 16,000 feet without trouble. Then four 109's began making a pass at us, with others following in behind them. I felt bloody awful, and wondered what I should do. I was afraid that if we attacked these109's we should be separated, and would not then have the same chance against the bombers, even if we were able to escape from the 109's. However, I decided that if we attacked we might bluff our way out of it. It seemed to be the only thing to do. I told Jimmy we were going in at the four in front and that he was to take the rear one while I took the leader. I tackled the leader at about 200 yards from the port quarter, and I could see Jimmy going in from the same angle on the rear 109.

I had a chance for only a snap shot, but even so I saw one of my shells strike on the 109's starboard wing. The others were too high and missed.

Even in these few seconds other 109's had closed in, and I could see more coming. It was as if the German leader had called in all the Hun fighters over the island. I at once went into a tight turn, and stayed there, with my head looking backwards half the time. I lost sight of Jimmy, but called him up and told him to keep turning and not lose his head.

Straightening out for a second to take a squirt at a 109 in front, I was attacked head-on by about six others. I could see the shells and bullets coming from their noses and wings. One bullet hit my aircraft and flicked it over slightly, so that I was flying half on my side and half on my back. I straightened up, and the 109`s came at me again, some head on and others from astern. I felt scared stiff and thought that I was for it. I called up Jimmy, telling him to go on his back and down. I could see it was hopeless for us to face such odds. I also went on my back and, by diving and turning to about 4000 feet, managed to shake off what had happened to him. Woody called up to say the bombers were diving on the harbour. I tried several times to reach them, but the109's *were everywhere, like so many swarms of bees. Each time I was pushed back by them.*

I climbed up and away from them to about 8000 feet. Then Woody announced that 87's were diving on Ta-Kali. I caught one as he was going down in his dive, and went down after him, trying to get a bead on him. Not until he was pulling out of his dive did I finally get him in my sights. The rear-gunner was firing, but he didn't worry me, as I knew he could not hit me. I opened fire at 300 yards, but could see only a few shells strike him on the starboard wing. I straightened my aircraft after this two seconds' burst, and let him have four seconds. This time I hit him fairly. He burst into vivid flames, and a second or two later two' chutes came out. Both opened, and I could see them drifting lazily downwards. As I was watching them I was attacked by four 109's. They came, two on either side of me, from astern. I turned into those on the port side and used up all my ammunition on them. I then went into a steep turn, and kept turning until the 109's finally left me.

By this time I was over St. Paul's Bay. I went towards Ta-Kali, looking for Jimmy. A Spit was over the aerodrome, and I recognized it by its markings as Jimmy's aircraft it jettisoned its hood and, realizing that he was in trouble, I covered him while he landed. He force-landed on the aerodrome, landing on his belly with his wheels up. More109's were coming in and strafing the 'drome. I saw Jimmy get out of his aircraft and run towards a bomb hole, into which he slithered. I beetled off round the valleys and played hide and seek with the 109's staying there until Woody said most of the small jobs had gone home. By this time I had very little gravy, and simply had to land. I did a dummy run over the aerodrome, and could see that the landing path was damaged badly by bombs. The craters seemed to be everywhere, but using my brakes to steer my Spit between the bomb holes I eventually got in safely.

This was the most hectic hour of fighting I had ever had over Malta. Five minutes after I landed I was shaking like a leaf. I smoked one cigarette after another, drawing at them without stopping. Not until half an hour later did I begin to feel normal again. Then I punished Buck's ears for at least an hour, recounting my experiences in every detail and telling him how I wished he had been there to lead. It was the first time I had led over Malta, and although I enjoyed it, and got a great kick out of it, I found it was a tougher job than I had imagined.

Jimmy, after we had been separated, had shaken off the first batch of 109's, but was later caught by a second bunch as he was going into the 88's over the harbour. His aircraft was badly shot about, while he himself was wounded in the left leg and neck by cannon splinters. He had escaped further injuries when he force landed, however, and was quite cheerful as he was taken away to hospital. He flew again in Spits over Malta, and survived to return to England.

As the month of April ended, German tactics were again changing. The number of Hun bombers coming over in each raid began to fall once more. The attack had lost something of its impetus. The fighter escort for the 87's and 88's, which had been large enough in the middle of the month, increased still further. On each raid the 30 or 40 bombers were escorted by as many as 80 fighters. The Huns also began to send over a fighter sweep to engage our Spits and Hurris before the bombers came in. While this engagement was taking place the bombers would orbit with their close escort, waiting until we had been forced down or driven into a position from which it was unlikely we would be able to attack them. If the fighter sweep succeeded in this object the Hun bombers were free to attack their target unmolested. If it failed the bombers still attacked, depending for cover upon their close fighter escort. I have no doubt these new tactics were forced upon the Huns through the success of the Spits.

April 29 was a remarkably tense day. The ack-ack boys were on their toes. They had shot down 99 Huns since April 1. They wanted badly to get their century. We were as keenly interested and wished to see them succeed. After each raid there was a rush to find out whether the guns had clicked their hundredth Hun. The 29th ended, and they had not. Somebody, I don't know who, had promised every ack-ack gunner on the island a bottle of beer if the guns obtained their century, and the only thing worrying the ack-ack boys on the night of the 29th was that the Huns might not come over next day. They need not have worried. It was just another Malta day. There were perhaps rather fewer bombers in the sky, but there were bags of 109's. About five o'clock in the afternoon we heard that the ack-ack boys had won their beer. They had topped their century, and had one to boot as well. They had shot down a 109 and an 88.

CHAPTER III

MAY 1942

On May 2 we saw our first Italian fighters. I flew in the morning, going up with Norman MacQueen, Linny, and a new boy, Pilot Officer Watts, an Englishman. Watty was flying number two to Mac, and Linny number two to me. My aircraft required an air test. I took off tested it, and found it still required attention. By nine o'clock it was ready for a second test, and I again took off. Mac and Watty came up with me, as they wished to test their cannons. They went down to fire them on an uninhabited island, while I stooged around Gozo, testing my motor. I did not see any enemy aircraft, but Mac and Watty found four 109's and, instead of firing at Filfla, did their cannon test on the Hun machines. It was successful. Between them they shot down one. We had no other joy that morning.

HESSELYN

Buck Buchanan, two new boys and myself began our afternoons readiness by chasing away a reconnaissance 88 without getting as much as a squirt at him. It was an uneventful do. An hour after we returned from this flip Buck and I scrambled again. This time a fairly big party was reported coming in. We climbed up due south of the island until, at 20,000 feet, we reached the base of the thick cloud, and Woody gave us several courses to steer to bring us on to the plot. After flying in the cloud for what seemed ages we came down fast. As we broke cloud we saw six 88's about 1000 feet below us. They had a heavy escort of 109's, and on the starboard of the bombers was what was to us a new type of machine and formation. At first glance we did not know what they were, but later recognized them as Italian fighters—Macchi 202's. There were 13, and they were flying tightly packed in echelon starboard formation. This was the first time we had seen such a formation over Malta, and we wondered if the Huns were trying something new. Almost invariably their fighters flew in fours or sixes, widely spaced inline abreast. Our interest quickened still further when we saw that the Macchis, like the bombers, were heavily escorted by 109's. However, we had little time to devote to them, and started to go in at the 88's.

I chose the rear one, which was lagging slightly. I was getting nicely within range, and considered I had him dead to rights, when I was attacked head on by four 109's. At the same moment other 109's, which I had not previously seen, broke cloud behind me and came down, trying to get on my tail. I saw I had no chance of getting my 88, and would have to leave him. I turned and climbed for the cover of the cloud. As I went up I saw Buck doing precisely the same thing, and judged that he also had been jumped by 109's. A game of hide-and-seek with the Hun followed. Every time we broke cloud to come down to take a squirt at the 88's we were chased back promptly by the 109's. This game lasted for something like 10 minutes, and then Woody told us 88's were diving on Luqa. Buck and I simultaneously broke cloud some distance from the bombers and their escort. We started diving on the 88's, believing we could out distance the 109's. We were wrong. They came down after us in a swarm, but as they did so I noticed that the Macchis, still flying their tight echelon starboard formation, remained put. We were given no chance of getting near the bombers, and continually had to turn into the 109's. Both of us had plenty of squirts at the Hun fighters, but as far as I was concerned without effect. We were beginning to run short of ammo, and Buck decided the only thing to do was to return home. Over Ta-Kali we found more 109's, and for what seemed hours, though it could not have been more than 20 minutes; we were beaten up in the circuit. At last, however, the majority of the 109's cleared out and headed for Sicily. A few were still left up high, but they did not trouble us, and we were able to come in and land. I had not scored a hit, but Buck believed he had damaged a 109.

During the next few days the Italians came over regularly. The Macchis were not very numerous, and, escorted by 109's, always flew the same formation as on the 2nd. Whenever any of our boys went anywhere near them they headed promptly for home. We decided they were coming over simply to gain experience of Malta, and, by sitting aloft and watching, to learn the form.

On May 4 I flew again. Norman MacQueen was leading, and had a new American boy, Pilot Officer Almos, of the Eagle Squadron, as his number two. Sitting in dispersal, we discussed the Huns' new tactics. We were after bombers, and that being the case we could not afford to engage the fighter sweep or to mix it with the escorting109's. Mac decided we should get well clear of the island, gain plenty of height, go well up sun, and avoid contact until the bombers arrived. Having gained this tactical position, we were to come in with plenty of speed, using it to try to break through the fighter screen, and take to the bombers.

We scrambled late in the afternoon. Almos and Linny were rather slow getting off the ground, and when the fighter sweep came in we were only at 8000 feet. The Huns caught us as we headed up sun, a little south of Gozo. The 109's were everywhere. Linny and I were at once separated from Mac and Almos. The two of us mixed it with eight 109's in a hell of a dogfight. We went into violent steep turns, dived down, and pulled up again at them. But the Hun fighters came at us from every direction, from the beam, underneath, astern and head on. We were separated in a twinkling. The last I saw of Linny was when he was in a vertical dive, skidding and twisting like blazes, with four 109's hotly pursuing him. It seemed to me as if I had been throwing my aircraft about for an hour, although probably it was less than five minutes, when a Hun blundered. He made a belly attack on me, missed and overshot. He pulled straight up ahead of me. He was a sitting target. I gave him four seconds. He went into a spin, pouring glycol. During the next few minutes, by manoeuvring violently, I succeeded in shaking off the other 109's.

I called up Linny, and learning he was over Ta-Kali I joined him there. Woody reported that some 109's, low down, were off the harbour, and we went out to meet them. As we crossed the coast, however, Almos called up that Mac was in trouble and wanted to land. Followed by Linny, I turned back to give Mac cover. We were approaching Ta-Kali when I saw him. He was gliding across the aerodrome at 5000 feet, and seemed to be under control. As I watched his aircraft gave a sudden lurch, side slipped about 1000 feet, and then seemed to come under control again. I did not like the look of things. I called up: "Mac, if you're not O.K., for God's sake bale out. I will cover you." There was no reply. A couple of seconds later his aircraft gave another lurch, went into a vertical dive, and crashed at Naxxur, a mile from the aerodrome. Almos and Linny landed while I covered them in, but it was some time before I was able to get in myself.

Everybody was down in the dumps over Mac. We felt his loss very keenly. He was one of our finest pilots, and had shot down at least eight Huns. He had been one of the first Spitfire pilots awarded the D.F.C. for operations over Malta, and he had richly earned his gong. At the time of his death he was acting as C.O. of the squadron, but neither that nor the fact that I was merely a sergeant pilot had prevented us from being the best of good cobbers. We had made many plans against our return to England.

Mac's death had a sobering effect on me. I had begun to think I knew all there was to know about air fighting. I had shot down my sixth Hun that very day. In addition, the deferential attitude of the new boys, who constantly sought my advice, had strengthened my confidence in myself. The death of such an experienced and capable fighter pilot as Mac brought me to a realization that I did not know as much as I had thought I did. I saw that I could not hope to continue taking the risks I had been taking, and stay alive. I recalled some of my recent flips, and shuddered as I thought how close I had been to disaster when attacking the 88's I had destroyed. I had held a poor opinion of the shooting prowess of the Hun fighter pilots. On every occasion but one they had missed me. I had thought that it must follow that they would always miss me. Now I knew I was wrong, and that I had, rather foolishly, underrated the Hun. I was still as determined as ever to win the gong which Hess and I had each decided should be ours, but Mac's death convinced me I must not impatiently attack the 88's and chance the attacks of the 109's.

Almos was the first American I had flown with, although I had met most of those who had reached Malta in April and came to know quite a number of those who arrived in May. They were a good bunch of boys. One of the most amusing was Pilot Officer Macleod, from Connecticut. His backchat to the Maltese waiters was a feature of the mess, and often raised a laugh when we badly wanted something to laugh over. He would ask if there was a sweet, and when told that there was, would at once demand strawberry shortcake, with not too much cream on it. To those who have not fought in Malta this may sound a very weak joke, but it appealed to us as being extremely funny. Not only did the Maltese waiters understand hardly a word he was saying, but strawberry shortcake, piled with cream, was to us merely an unattainable dream. Malta food was Malta food. Bully beef gave us most of our meals. Served hot, it provided our breakfast cold, it gave us our lunch; camouflaged, it served us for dinner. Sweets there were, but nobody ever recognized them. Apart from goats' milk, which did not agree with any of us, the only milk we saw came out of tins.

An immense fellow, at least 6 ft. 3 in. tall and weighing about 16 stone, MacLeod was the heaviest fighter pilot on Malta. He had plenty of bad luck, but it never interfered with his cheerfulness. On one occasion a 109 caught him unawares, and he had to bale out. How a fellow of his height and bulk managed to bale out at all was always a mystery to us, but his explanation was simple. He declared that if a 109 did to us what this particular one had done to him, we would bale out of a matchbox. He landed in the drink about two miles from shore, and swam home. When he gained the shore he said it was the best swim he had ever had, and that the water was perfect. Over the R/T, as might be expected, MacLeod was frequently amusing. He gave us many a laugh when we were aloft. Once Woody told us that Italian bombers were coming in at 20,000 feet. Mac's comment came promptly. "They must be keeping their ice cream cold," he told everybody who was airborne at the time. Mac did his term in Malta, and returned to England.

Jimmy Peck, who won the D.F.C., was another American Pilot Officer with whom we served in Malta. When it was decided to form an American flight in 126 Squadron, it was Jimmy who was selected as its Flight Commander. He was promoted Flight Lieutenant, and proved his worth. He and MacLeod were the first American Spitfire pilots to destroy a 109 over Malta. Each shot down his 109 on the same day, March 24, and in the same flight. A quiet, unassuming little fellow, Jimmy was a direct contrast to MacLeod physically, and he lacked the latter's ready wit. Yet, although they were an incongruous pair, they were great buddies, and were always to be seen in each other's company.

Another American to win the D.F.C. in Malta was Pilot Officer Tilley. He was the third of the trio around which the American flight was formed, the other pair, of course, being MacLeod and Jimmy. He was not only a skilful and courageous pilot, but he was also perhaps the most striking looking of all the Americans I met in Malta. He was tall, well built, and invariably smart.

Pilot Officer McHan, another American in our squadron, Almos, and several other Eagle Squadron boys were posted to this flight from other squadrons. They gave a good account of themselves in the battles that followed, but as they were in a different squadron we did not fly with them. We saw them at occasional dos in the mess or when wandering round different parts of Malta, and knew more about their personalities than we did of their exploits in the air.

Shortly after the commencement of May the Hun bombers, although they made their appearances as regularly as ever, were not so numerous. The different waves contained fewer machines. The fighter escorts, however, were as big as ever, and we found it harder to get in among the bombers. The 109 pilots were showing greater determination, and experience had enabled them to improve their air tactics considerably. Moreover, they always outnumbered us. We were fighting a stern, uphill battle, and were coming off second best. Many of our best pilots were away. Among those who remained, Malta dog, almost like gastric influenza, was going the rounds. We were feeling the strain, not only of the continuous air fighting, but also of the bombing and the general living conditions of Malta. Our barrage also was falling away. The gunners were growing tired, and many of the gun barrels were becoming worn. All of us were getting less sleep, for the Hun and Italian bombers were coming over in greater numbers at night. When the moon was favourable they were pressing home these attacks more determinedly than previously, and were coming down much lower. We had insufficient night fighters to hold them all back. With the lengthening days we were doing longer periods of readiness, and the night bombing prevented us from obtaining a proper measure of sleep. We were becoming irritable and on edge. Even Hess and I, firm cobbers as we were, started to snap and snarl at each other, and much the same occurred with the rest of the boys.

The civilian population was showing the effects of the strain in somewhat similar fashion. The Maltese appeared to have aged and looked more haggard and nervous. Less and less of Valetta was standing. Half the streets were blocked with debris, and the interiors of the houses were everywhere spewing out of the doorways. Practically every civilian was living in one of the rock shelters. Food distribution was becoming more difficult than ever, and the authorities had been forced to set up communal feeding centres. I think that at this time the Maltese must have been more apprehensive of a Hun victory than at any time during the drawn out battle for Malta. Yet whenever we ventured into Valetta or visited one of the island's other towns we invariably received a warm welcome. Haggard faces would break into a smile, and a cheery word would greet us. They never failed to show the admiration they felt for the fighter pilots defending the island.

This was how things were when Gracie called us together. A feeling of grimness seemed to hang over the meeting. Gracie told us what every one of us knew in his own heart, that the position in Malta was critical. "We must stop the Hun or we have had Malta," he told us. "You haven't had the aircraft, I know. You're getting them now. There is no secret about when they're coming. They'll be here on the 9th. We are turning on a big organization at Ta-Kali and the other aerodromes to receive them. With your help I want to see every aircraft in the air, if necessary, within 15 minutes after they land." Gracie's news cheered us enormously. We forgot our depression. The old hands drew together, and for hours nattered about tactics, the make up of sections, and methods of interception. All our old keenness and buoyant optimism returned. The new boys, who were holding their own informal gathering, showed plainly that they were equally bucked. Everybody was more determined. We believed that at last we would really have a chance to stop the Hun.

HESSELYN

On the 5th Buck and I scrambled in the morning to cover one of our reconnaissance aircraft, which had been over Sicily taking photographs. It was being chased by Italian fighters. No sooner were we airborne than Woody reported two 109's low down over Halfar. Widening our formation until we were 500 yards apart, we began to search. There was low, misty cloud, and visibility was very bad. We failed to find the two 109s' over Halfar, and continued our search elsewhere over the island. We were going towards Ta–Kali when, looking behind, I saw flak bursting by the Grand Harbour. I could see the guns were firing at two 109's, probably the same pair we were seeking. Buck and I turned round towards them. The leader, evidently alert, went into cloud immediately, but his number two acted too slowly. So did Buck. Turning more steeply than Buck, I got in ahead of him, and, getting my sights on the109, fired for two seconds before my cannons packed up. The 109 went into a steep dive towards Ta-Kali. Thinking I had got him, and as pleased as hell, I followed him down, calling up Buck and telling him I had shot down the 109. But the Hun suddenly pulled out of his dive and climbed straight up into cloud, getting away.

When we landed Buck was very brassed off "You bastard!" he said. "I lead you all round the sky, and you won't even let me get a, crack at them." As he was speaking the erks came running up to tell us that as the 109 had been diving down, a bus, loaded with Maltese civilians, had been going towards Rabat from Ta-Kali. The civilians had imagined the 109 was going to shoot them up, and they had piled out of the bus. One man, diving out of a window, had cracked his skull on the road and died shortly afterwards.

The 8th was a very busy day. There was a full dress rehearsal of the arrangements for the arrival of the Spits the following morning. Each pilot had been assigned to a pen. It was his responsibility to see that there was ample fuel, oil, coolant and ammunition for the aircraft when it landed. Every detail of the organization was tested thoroughly. The Army was there in full force. Bungers-up of bomb-holes, stretcher-bearers, despatch-riders, who were to maintain communications if telephone or signalling arrangements were interrupted, and Bren- gun carriers, which were to be used for hauling out of the way any aircraft that might crash, were instructed fully in their duties. The arrangements for meals, which were to be served on the aerodrome, were also tried out. During the morning Gracie, inspecting the arrangements, told Hess and myself that we had each been awarded the D.F.M.

That afternoon, while a crowd of us were walking up from our rehearsal, the 87's and 88's came over. We ran for shelter, and when we reached it we noticed that each 87 released three bombs. These were chained together, so that they fell together within a small area. Bud Connell, who had returned from the Middle East with some new Hurris, and Buck Buchanan were unlucky. They failed to reach shelter, and had to lie out in the open. Buck escaped injury, but Bud was wounded. He was taken to hospital. The rest of us escaped with a shaking.

In the evening there was another conference. Gracie declared everything was set for the morning. He said he had inspected the arrangements, detected the flaws, and rectified them. He handed each pilot typewritten instructions in duplicate, one copy being for the new pilot arriving in the aircraft. Gracie warned us that we would be on readiness from dawn to dusk until such time as the Hun was beaten. He made it clear that this was to be a supreme effort, and that we must get on top, no matter what casualties it cost us.

At dawn next morning Gracie again addressed us. He stood on the roof of a utility truck, with pilots, ground crew, and soldiers lined-up on the aerodrome in front of him. He spoke in the same strain as on the previous evening, and wished us all good luck. Oddly enough, on this crucial 9th, the 88's omitted their usual morning do. They did not come over, and neither did any 109's. Between nine and ten o'clock four boys scrambled. The rest of us knew they had gone up to cover the arrival of the new Spitfires. Everybody was happy and excited, keyed up with expectation.

In a few minutes the new boys started coming in over Imtafa Hill. At the same moment the 109's also arrived over Malta. The first bunch of Spits landed. I led an aircraft into my pen. The waiting ground crew pounced on it eagerly, and began to rearm and refuel it. Its pilot, Pilot Officer Barnefather, an Englishman, climbed out of the cockpit, and I handed him his written instructions. More Spits were coming over the hill. They arrived in the circuit at the same time as a number of 109's. One of my erks, a big, wild looking fellow who had not shaved for three days, kept changing tools every few minutes. One minute he would have a rifle in his hands and be pot shooting at the 109's; the next he would grab a tool and be undoing some screws on the Spit's panel. Barnefather and I watched the Spits circling. "That one will get it in a moment," I remarked. It did. A 109 blew a large piece out of the Spit's port side near the cockpit. The Spit made hurriedly for the aerodrome, and after three attempts successfully force-landed. By this time there was a terrific din going on. The ground defences were engaging heavily, and there was a lot of cannon-fire going on between the opposing aircraft. On the aerodrome, newly arrived Spits were being shepherded to their pens. They were refuelled and rearmed quickly, and pilots clambered into the cockpits, ready to take off immediately the order came. Within ten minutes of landing, many of the new Spits were going up again. It was a triumph of organization.

Hurricanes had by now put in an appearance and, in the absence of bombers, were having a crack at the 109's. Tony Boyd, very much in a hurry, came whistling over the fence and put his Hurri down wheels up. He made the most perfect forced-landing I have ever witnessed. From 300 feet, where a 109 had let him have it, he whipped his Hurri round, slipped off his height, nipped in over the fence, and put down his aircraft in front of dispersal. He was covered in glycol, but uninjured, and his machine was not badly damaged. A newly arrived Spit taxied up to my pen, and the pilot, Flight Sergeant Williams, a Canadian who was to become well known to us as Willy the Kid, asked what he was to do. At that moment the Huns elected to comedown and strafe the aerodrome. I told him to hop out and follow me. We took cover, the Huns missing both us and the aircraft. When they had passed over we found a pen for Willy the Kid's machine. One 109, which went over the aerodrome in a gentle glide at 500 feet, failed to pull out. It crashed into the drink a few hundred yards off St. Paul's Bay. Every erk who had fired a rifle that morning claimed to have brought down this Hun.

More Spits came in, the last touching down shortly before eleven o'clock. One Australian, Flight Lieutenant Ray Sly, who had been a member of the famous Australian Spitfire Squadron led by Paddy Finucane, misjudged his approach at Halfar and crashed into a pen on the edge of the aerodrome. He received fatal injuries. Three other Aussies, Sergeant Pilots Eric Maher, Ken Mitchell and Len Reid, landed safely. Not long afterwards a big plot of 88's was reported. I was flying with Johnny Plagis and Watty. Stan Grant, who had arrived with the new Spits, was leading us. We went up, but my electrical system failed, and I landed just in time to be dive-bombed by twenty 88's. Throughout the afternoon the 87's and 88's came over. It was the most nerve-racking experience I have ever been through. Twice I started to take off as they came in. A flat tyre kept me on the ground the first time. Of course, the 88's would do up our end of the aerodrome. I flung myself into a slit trench. The bombs fell all round us, and some of them were big ones. We were covered with rubble and debris, and the breath was just about knocked out of us. On the second occasion I was standing by in my aircraft. I was strapped in ready to take off, waiting for the green light which was the signal to go. As I waited I saw the erks on the starter battery look up, give a wave, and run for their lives. For a moment I did not realize what was happening. Then I looked up. Some 30 88's were coming down on our end of the aerodrome. I ripped off my straps, but in my hurry forgot all about my dinghy cord. This jerked me back, and for a few seconds I was poised on the wing-root. As I got rid of the cord I looked up and saw the 88's release their bombs. I ran as hard as I could for the slit trench, beating the bombs by the narrowest of short heads. Everything rocked again, and the air vibrated with the appalling din of bursting bombs and snapping guns, After the 88's passed over we started to climb out of the slit trenches but the 109's came down and ground strafed the aerodrome. I ducked back into the trench. Not so my big erk. Unconcernedly, he sat on the side of the trench, and blazed away at the Huns with his rifle.

This proved the last raid of the day. It ended between five and six o'clock, but it was not until 9.30 that we were free to leave the aerodrome. By then we were dog tired and covered with dust. We had inflicted considerable losses on the enemy. Between them, our fighters and ack-ack guns had destroyed 13 aircraft for certain, had probably destroyed 11 others and had damaged at least another 20. Our squadron had lost only one pilot and a solitary machine. He was a short, quiet spoken Englishman who had been jumped by 109's at 1000 feet. Diving away from them, he failed to pull out of his dive, and crashed into the drink. We collapsed into bed immediately we reached our quarters, but we were destined to get but little sleep. Throughout the night 87's and 88's continuously dive bombed Ta-Kali.

We went on readiness about five o'clock on the morning of the 10th. All of us felt tired out, but the fact that we believed the battle was going in our favour cheered us tremendously. To our surprise, comparatively little damage had been done by the night raiders. They had dropped a large number of delayed action bombs. These made the journey to the aerodrome, never very pleasant at the best of times, damned uncomfortable. It was still dark, and we could not see the bombs. A crowd of bomb disposal boys, searching for them, had dealt with a number, but there were plenty still unrecovered, and we had any number of shocks. Every now and then one would explode with a terrific roar. In fact, as the morning wore on, there were so many of these explosions that we grew accustomed to them and took little notice.

The day broke fine and clear, and as the darkness lifted we could see Sicily as a faint blue on the horizon, with Mount Etna showing up clearly. To our disappointment, however, there was no early morning blitz. We had bags of Spitfires serviceable, and we were all eager to get into the air. It was not until nearly ten o'clock that the Very lights started going up. Aircraft began taking off immediately, sweeping over our heads in fours, line abreast. Stan Grant, Watty, and two others got off. Johnny Plagis and I were to be next. We were waiting only for the signal. Then the Alert sounded. I cursed heartily, thinking my day was going to prove a repetition of the previous one, when every time I was ready to leave the ground something had happened to prevent me getting airborne. But at last the signal came. Johnny and I took off, closely followed by Buck Buchanan and two aircraft of his section. The fourth member of Buck's quartet, Hess, had a flat tyre taxi-ing out, and could not leave the ground.

We climbed steeply, endeavouring to gain height rapidly. There were already many 109's above the island, and the bombers were due to arrive any minute. We managed to reach 14,000 feet when 109's attacked us over Filfla. As they came in I could see more 109's above, waiting the opportunity to jump us. All five of us started turning with the 109's attacking us. Woody called up and told us the 87's were diving the harbour. While Buck and his pair held off the Hun fighters, Johnny and I beetled over the harbour. The barrage was the heaviest I had seen so far in Malta. The flak puffs were so numerous that they formed a great wall of cloud, contrasting oddly with the Bofors shells shooting up like huge, glowing match heads. We dived through the barrage to get at the 87's on the other side. I looked down as we went through the flak, and the ground seemed to be on fire with the blaze of guns. My aircraft was not hit, but it rolled and yawed, and almost got out of control. I came out of the barrage suddenly. The sky seemed to be filled with aircraft. The first thought that struck me, so numerous were the aircraft, was that there was great risk of collision, and that I would have to watch out carefully. Spitfires were coming in from all points of the compass, and there were plenty of 109's about as well. Three thousand feet below me, sharply silhouetted against the blue sea, a couple of fellows in parachutes were floating downwards. The thought occurred to me that I might be joining them shortly. As I watched a 109 crash into the sea I thought that at any rate there was one less with which to contend. Tracers started to whip past my port wing. I turned to starboard. An 87 was right in front of me. It was in the act of pulling out of its dive. I gave it a quick squirt, but overshot it, and found a 109 dead ahead of me. I had a quick squirt at him, but again overshot. Buck was yelling: "Spits over the harbour, for Christ's sake climb! They're up here." I pulled up my nose to gain height, giving the motor all she had. As I shot up, climbing 5000 feet in a few seconds, I had another quick squirt this time into the belly of an 87. I saw cannon shells go into his motor, but had no time to see what effect they had on him. Then I was above the 87's, and went into a steep climbing turn, waiting to pick out one.

Spits seemed to be everywhere, weaving beside the barrage, ready to pounce on the 87's as they pulled out of their dive. It was not long before the Spits were getting on the tails of the 87's. Wherever I looked I could see only 87's with Spits already on their tails. It was several seconds before I saw one which I reckoned was my meat. Diving on to his tail, I opened fire, noticing an 87 crash into the sea and start to burn as I did so. My fellow went into a hell of a steep turn, and I followed him round, firing all the time. I had given him three seconds when the thought flashed through my mind, "This damn'87 should blow up." But, to my surprise, he didn't, so I kept firing. There came no return fire: either the barrage or my fire had got the rear gunner. The 87 continued in his steep turn, climbing all the time. I hung to him grimly, and kept on firing. I could see all my stuff going into his cockpit and motor. Suddenly he went to pieces. He literally flew apart, an awesome but satisfying sight for a fighter pilot. His radiator fell off, the air scoop broke away, the pilot's hood whirled off in one piece, and bits of fuselage scattered in every direction. Black smoke poured from him. Rather dumbfounded, I was watching him spinning down when Johnny called up: "Spit attacking 87, there's something firing at you." I looked round quickly; I saw the big yellow spinner of a 109 about 50 yards from my tail. Flashes were coming from his guns. I got a hell of a fright, and pulled the stick back to turn. By this time my speed had fallen away. My aircraft gave a hell of a shudder, flicked over on its back, and started to spin. The suddenness of events so confused me that I did not realize I was spinning. I imagined the 109 had got me, and I prepared to bale out. Subconsciously I must have applied corrective control. My Spit stopped spinning to the left, and I was so surprised that I almost let it go into a spin to the right. The 109, probably deciding that he had shot me down, had left. Johnny told me later that the Hun had been firing at me for about 10 seconds.

I put my nose down to gather speed. Right beneath me, about 100 yards from the bomber I had seen crash earlier, my 87 was plunging into the sea. Having no ammunition left, I went home. I was very excited and elated when I landed, and told everybody how we were pasting hell out of the Hun over the harbour. Stan Grant, who had landed before me, was very brassed off. He had been up to 30,000 feet turning with 109's, and had not been able to have a crack at the 87's. I did not take off again. I was so tired out that, despite all the noise and excitement, I slept throughout the afternoon.

HESSELYN

Because of my flat tyre, I missed the morning do. From Ta-Kali the barrage over the harbour looked like an immense black umbrella. Aircraft seemed to be everywhere, and every 87 appeared to have a Spit hard on its tail. Indeed, Johnny Plagis, when he landed, told me that so many 87's had Spits on their tails that he had been forced to go seven miles out to sea to find one to shoot down. Even over St. Paul's Bay, three miles from the harbour, Spits were chasing 87's going out seawards on their return journey to Sicily. Few of them reached their base. It was a remarkable sight. The 87 's were going down in flames or crashing in spins. Sometimes only one was hurtling downwards, sometimes two or three together. It was strange and uncanny to see the blazing aircraft going through the thick barrage like miniature comets. Over Halfar, Luqa and Ta-Kali innumerable dogfights were going on between Spits and 109's. Aircraft were turning and twisting, climbing and diving in every direction, and we could hear their cannons above the heavy roar of the ack-ack guns. There seemed a hell of a lot of 109's, but there were more Spits, and from the ground, looking at the whole panorama, we could see plainly that our boys were definitely on top. The Hun was getting a hiding. I counted 12 opened parachutes drifting towards the sea. They were floating down lazily, presenting a curious contrast to the diving, twisting and turning aircraft. I watched two 109's crash, one by St. Paul's Bay, the second at Naxxur. The latter burst into flames as it hit the ground. I lost all count of time. It seemed as though the battle lasted for hours, although in reality it was all over in from 20 to 30 minutes. I was completely fascinated by the scene, and could do nothing but watch in silence. Not so the ground crews. They went berserk with excitement. They cheered madly, and threw into the air their tools, tin hats, rifles, and everything they could lay their hands on. They realized, as we all did, that at last we had gained air superiority.

About 2.30 in the afternoon, Stan Grant, Buck Buchanan, Watty and myself took off we climbed into sun, Woody advising us to get as much angels as possible. At 25,000 feet he told us a big plot of 88's was coming in, with plenty of small jobs high up. We stooged round for five or ten minutes before Woody called us in, telling us to come down fast over the harbour. At that moment Stan Grant saw them, and called that they were at nine o'clock, below. I picked them up quickly enough. There were 20 bombers, strung out in a great gaggle. We started to go down. I waited for a couple of seconds to take a good look behind, and then went down to cover Buck's tail. I could see Stan getting on to the tail of an 88. He was 5000 feet below me, but I could see plainly the white stuff coming from his wings as he fired. A few seconds later his 88 was crashing in flames. I took another hurried look behind, but could still see nothing. Buck went in on the tail of an 88. I was preparing to go down on to the tail of another when there was a terrific explosion in my cockpit. Simultaneously I felt a slight jerk at my helmet. An explosive bullet had hit the hood and, nicking my helmet, had exploded against the instrument panel. At the same time a cannon shell burst near the port wing-root. I knew instinctively I had been jumped. I skidded to starboard. The 109 overshot me, and pulled up just in front. He seemed to fill the whole of my view, blotting out everything else. I could see the pilot clearly as he sat in his cockpit, looking back. The range could not have been more than 20 yards. I fired. My shells struck first on his starboard wing, and, as he flew across my line of fire, travelled right across his cockpit and then crashed into his port wing. Pieces flew off him in all directions. He seemed to be cut in half. His machine literally collapsed, and went down in bits of varying size. I blacked out momentarily. When I came to I was over the sea at about 2000 feet, and my aircraft was in a vertical dive. I felt dazed and weak. I knew my aircraft had been hit badly, and from the cockpit could see a gaping hole in my port wing. I glanced in the mirror and could see a tear in my helmet. I nosed my Spit gently out of the dive and tested *my controls. They responded, and I headed for Ta-Kali, landing without mishap.*

Stan, Buck and Watty landed shortly afterwards. Stan and Buck had each shot one down, and Watty had probably destroyed a third. At four o'clock, as I was suffering shock, I was packed off to bed. At that time, during the day's engagements, we had destroyed 16 enemy aircraft for certain, and probably destroyed an additional 14, and were known to have damaged 12 others.

By evening we felt that we had won our most important battle. Fifteen 87's had come over in the morning, and only two had managed to limp home. We had destroyed the remaining 13. In the afternoon we had shot down a number of 88's, while, throughout the day, we had also taken toll of the 109's. Our total bag for the 10th was 23 destroyed, 20 probably destroyed, and 20 damaged. Even Rome Radio, never given to exaggerating Hun losses, admitted that 37 Axis aircraft failed to return to base that day. To minimize the effect of such a heavy loss, it claimed that 47 Spitfires had been destroyed, but in actual fact we lost only two aircraft and one pilot. It was the heaviest defeat the Germans had suffered over Malta. Our morale skyrocketed. The new boys who had come in with the last Spits were keen to get into the air. They had not yet gone up, as on the 9th and 10th all the flying had been done by the experienced boys. I could not help noticing how different was the outlook of these new boys as compared with those who had brought in the previous reinforcements. Everybody, new boys as well as old, was riding on the crest of the wave. Most of us who had been in Malta for some time were feeling strained and nervy, but Woody wanted the old hands to keep flying, and we were determined to do so.

The day's operations had an enormous effect on the civilian population. I heard that thousands of people had stood, with bombs and shrapnel falling all round them, to watch the spectacular battle over the Grand Harbour. They cheered and cheered every time a Hun crashed. When evening came the Maltese knew that we had won a great victory. The gloom and depression which had hung over Malta for so long lifted and vanished.

We were convinced we were well on the way to licking the Hun. We were well organized on the ground, and we had an ample supply of confident, experienced pilots. We did not care how long the battle lasted. We were determined to win it, and we felt certain that we would win. Every time the Hun came near Malta we intended to keep every Spitfire in the air until he was driven off. The ground crews worked 18 hours a day, ensuring that our aircraft were on the top line. Their morale was higher than it had ever been. My crew was typical. On the night of the 9th, after we had been dive bombed all day, I had promised them I would shoot down a bomber next day. When I landed on the 10th and told them I had got an 87, everyone of them wanted to buy me a drink.

Our victory on the 9th and 10th was reflected quickly by changed conditions in the air. There was little bombing during the night of the 10th, and on the 11th Johnny Plagis, Willie the Kid, another new boy and myself took off in a sweep towards Sicily. A week or so earlier, with bags of 109's over Malta, an offensive sweep towards the enemy's base would have been an impossibility. We would never have considered it seriously. Now, however, we felt confident that we could carry out such sweeps successfully.

My motor gave trouble, and I was compelled to force-land on Luqa. The other boys carried on. The new boy became separated from the formation, and had to call for homings in order to get back to base. Johnny and Willie the Kid located eight Macchi 202's. They became separated as they attacked. Johnny singled out one Macchi, and gave chase to it. The Italian was steep turning near the sea. Johnny, ignoring the Macchis on his own tail, got into position to draw bead on the one in front of him. He was about to open fire when it crashed into the sea. The Italian pilot, possibly in fright at having a Spit on his tail, apparently had made his turn too tight. He stalled his aircraft and lost control. Johnny, turning into the Macchis behind him, had an odd poop at them, but without effect. Neither did Willie the Kid have any luck, and the Macchis made off homewards.

Only a few Hun aircraft came over Malta during the early part of the morning. They were mostly reconnaissance aircraft, and they did not stay long. No bombs were dropped. It was clear that the Hun was licking his wounds from the previous day. I waited at Luqa until my motor had been overhauled, and then flew back to Ta-Kali. Johnny had already landed. He had formed a good opinion of the Macchis. He told me they were pretty good aircraft, and that their pilots, with the exception of the one who had crashed, had handled their machines well. He admitted he had found it more difficult than he had expected to get away from them, but had no doubt whatever that the Spitfire was far superior to the Italian fighters. This was the first time any pilots from our squadron had been engaged with them. Some of the boys from other squadrons on the island had encountered them previously, but we were all eager to know what one of our own pilots thought of them.

About seven o'clock we scrambled again. Woody told us some bombers were coming in. They did not follow their usual course, but went southeast of the island, and there started to orbit. We were at 18,000 feet when we asked for a vector to intercept the bombers. Woody told us they were 10 miles southeast of Kalafrana Bay, adding that there were three of them, with a heavy fighter escort. We had just flown over Filfla when Woody called up again to say that one of the bombers was diving on Halfar. Johnny and I saw this bomber simultaneously, but Johnny left me behind on the turn. Willie the Kid followed him down to attack the 88. I looked up and saw eight 109's going down to attack Johnny and Willie. Since I was far behind the bomber, and Johnny and Willie were closing it fast, I warned Johnny about the 109's, telling him to go in and leave me to attack the fighters. I was quickly involved in a fierce dogfight. The 109`s would come down behind, shoot at me, pull up ahead, turn round, come at me again head on. I did everything I could with my Spitfire, but I was soon yelling for help over the R/T I heard Woody call up, "Boys, go to Kalafrana and help Paul. He is in trouble." I certainly was.

I had lost all my speed in my turns. My aircraft was shuddering and on the point of stalling. Once or twice it did flick, but I managed, somehow or other, to maintain control. At last, after an agony of waiting, Pete Nash and another Spitfire arrived and chased away the 109's. By this time I was feeling pretty shaky. It was the most determined attack the 109's had made on me. I soon recovered, and while Pete and the other Spit were still chasing the 109's I climbed in an effort to gain height. Woody announced that some 109's were off the harbour, and I turned in that direction. It was not long before I saw two 109's about three miles out to sea, off the harbour. They were lowdown, and had just turned, leaving their tails to the sun. I dived on them, calling up other Spits that were milling about to come and lend a hand. The 109's were going faster than I had thought, and I had a long chase. It was not until we were 20 miles north of Gozo, roughly a third of the way to Sicily, that I caught up with them. I gave the rear one a short burst, but saw no result. He began to turn. I turned inside him, and gave him another very short burst. He could not have been more than 10 feet from the water, and suddenly his right wing hit the sea. He Catherine-wheeled on his wing tips and tail once or twice, and then blew up. The leading 109 escaped. I found Pete Nash right behind me. He covered me back to Malta, since I was down so low.

Johnny and Willie had landed when I came in. They had probably destroyed an 88 the only one of the trio of bombers to cross the coast. The other two dropped their bombs in the sea, and fled for Sicily. This was in sharp distinction to the normal Hun form. Only a few days earlier the 87's and 88's had been doing as they pleased. They had been pressing home their attacks, and showing the greatest determination. But now that the Spits had won the mastery of the air over Malta they were already displaying far more caution. It was heartening, after all we had gone through, to feel that we had the Hun bombers badly shaken. The 109's, however, constituted a different proposition. They were showing greater determination than ever, as I had discovered that morning. We had little doubt they had received instructions to destroy the Spitfires at all costs.

The remainder of the 11th was uneventful. We saw no more bombers. A few reconnaissance aircraft were all that came over, and they were chased away promptly by Spits. During the 72 hours preceding 10.45 p.m. on the 11th, we had destroyed 36 enemy aircraft, probably destroyed 31, and damaged at least 45. The ack-ack boys had shot down a number of these, but the majority had been destroyed or probably destroyed in air combat. Most of them had fallen to the boys of the squadron. Indeed, the squadron tally was now pushing up around the 80 mark, a figure well in excess of that of any other Spitfire squadron in Malta.

Things had been so strenuous on the 9th and 10th, and we had been so weary when we were at last free to leave the aerodrome, that we had been able to hold few natters. The quiet day of the 11th enabled us to post ourselves with various odd items of news. I learnt that Tweedie was among the missing. He had taken off on the 9th, and had not been heard of again. We presumed he had been shot down in the hectic fighting, and had crashed into the drink. He was later awarded a posthumous D.F.M. An Englishman, Pilot Officer Mike Graves, from 126 Squadron, was leading eight Spitfires on the same day when five Eyetye bombers came over. They were strongly escorted, but, led by Mike, the Spits broke through the fighters and shot down every one of the five bombers. It was for his part in this affair that Graves was later awarded the D.F.C.

On the 12th both Hess and I were on dawn readiness. We were feeling tired and worn out after the strenuous work of the last few days, but were as keen as ever to get into the air. For several hours there was nothing to do but hang about the aerodrome. Things were quiet, and it was not until 10.30 that the Hun put in an appearance. We scrambled, with Stan Grant leading. Hess and I were delayed in taking off and we were no sooner airborne than Hess discovered he had no oxygen. This meant he could not go over 10,000 feet. I knew the others would climb much higher than this, and I told Hess to join up with me and we would have some fun together, low down. We climbed to 8000 feet and stayed there. A few bombers, heavily escorted, were on the way. While we waited for them to put in an appearance we cruised up and down the island. They were soon reported over Comino channel. We beetled over there at once, but could find no trace of them.

More Huns were now reported over Halfar, and we turned in that direction. As we approached I could see a beehive a mile southeast of Filfla and at about our height. I told Hess we would hop in. I turned steeply. Before me there were literally dozens of 109's, with a Spitfire pulling up at them. The Spit had a squirt, pulled round, and dived towards the island. As he did so a 109 pounced on him from behind. I warned the Spit that he was being attacked. He did not seem to hear me, but kept a straight dive. The 109 was 100 yards behind, and firing all the time. The Spit continued diving until he was 30 or 40 feet above the sea. Then the pilot called up : "Good-bye, Woody. I've had it." I recognized the voice as that of a New Zealander, Pilot Officer Mitchell. A couple of seconds later his aircraft hit the sea, and a column of water shot into the air. He must have been doing 300 m.p.h. when he crashed.

In the meantime, trying to get at the 109 on Mitch's tail, I had lost a good deal of height. Hess was also on his way down, and got to the 109 first. I saw him open fire at a range of 150 yards. I looked up. Some 109's were circling above us. I did not want to see Hess get it like Mitch, so I weaved above him to cover his tail. He was still following the 109 out to sea, giving him a squirt at every opportunity, when the 109's above came down on me. I went into a violent steep turn to the right, and saw tracer from the first Hun miss me, passing my port wing. His bullets must have been very close. I could hear the explosion of his self-destroying ammunition above the roar of my motor as the greyish black puffs appeared beside my cockpit, like a miniature barrage. The 109 overshot me. I pulled round to fire at him, but before I could line him up another 109 attacked me from behind. Again I turned violently right. More tracer went past my right wing tip. More explosive shells burst beside my cockpit. This 109 also overshot me. I tried to get a shot at him as he flew past. A third 109 attacked me from the rear. I pulled away again as his tracer whistled past me. My aircraft was becoming unmanoeuvrable. I had lost my speed, and the controls were sluggish. I began to think I would never get out of this lot, and with that thought came a feeling that I had been a bloody fool in biting off more than I could chew.

As these thoughts flitted through my brain the first 109 came down on me again, this time in a head on attack. I could see the flashes of his guns firing from the centre of his slow revving spinner and the leading edges of his wings. His shells and bullets tore past the top of the cockpit. I believed that they would all miss me, but to make sure, as I thought, that they did, I trod on bottom rudder. There was a sharp crack as though somebody had hit my cockpit with a sledgehammer. Something hit my left arm and knocked it off the throttle quadrant. A tingling pain shot through it, but I found I was still able to use it. For a few seconds, expecting a row of bullets straight across my body, I did nothing. But the bullets did not come. The 109 had stopped firing and pulled away above my head, compelled to do so apparently in order to avoid a collision. I tested my controls. They were still working, but at that instant my aircraft flicked over and went into a spin. I worked strenuously, the pain in my arm giving me hell. My aircraft had fallen 2000 feet before I got it out of the spin. It was in the nick of time. I was only a few hundred feet above the water.

Fortunately the 109's, doubtless thinking they had shot me down, did not follow. I had recovered my speed, and my aircraft seemed to be flying normally. I cleared the cliffs, and made for home. Blood had seeped through my sleeve, and my arm ached dully. I landed at Ta-Kali, feeling dazed and shaken. An examination of my aircraft showed that only one cannon-shell had hit it. It had struck the portside of the bulletproof windscreen, which had splintered. Some of the splinters had come through and hit my arm. An erk gave me a good stiff whisky, and I was taken to hospital.

HESSELYN

I saw Mitch diving with the 109 on his tail at the same time as Paul. I broke away from Paul at once and dived after the 109. It was about 1000 yards away and slightly below me. I closed on it rapidly, and when I had got within 500 yards he broke away from following Mitch and shot out seawards. I knew then that he was my piece of cake. At 150 yards I gave him the first squirt. I was by this time wholly occupied with the 109, and had lost sight of both Mitch and Paul. I saw my shells striking the water behind the fleeing 109. I realized I was firing too low. I pulled up the nose of my aircraft, and gave him another quick squirt. This time my shells must have hit him, although I did not see them do so. His speed slackened perceptibly. After that it was just like training days all over again. I throttled back to avoid overshooting him. His speed continued to slacken as we skimmed the sea at about 50 feet. I fired another burst, checked for skid, and gave him another and longer burst. This time I hit him squarely. He flicked over on his back, hung poised for a moment, and dropped straight into the drink. I circled round to see if the pilot would get out. He didn't.

By this time I was 20 miles south of the island. There were no other aircraft near me, but I could hear a lot of nattering on the R/T about 109's being over Kalafrana Bay. I headed for there, climbing all the way. I was at 5000 feet when I arrived over Kalafrana. I could see some Spits milling round 2000 feet below me. The 109's were 2000 to 3000 feet above me. I called up the Spits and told them to climb up and give me a hand. Then I pulled up at the 109's. I got a quick snap shot at one. I blew half his tail off but, with two others covering him, he was able to dive away in the direction of Sicily. I could only claim him as damaged. At this moment my aircraft stalled owing to loss of speed. I spun down for about 2000 feet before I recovered control. The Spits were still milling round, low down on the deck. Apparently they had not heard my earlier call. As I started to regain height, Woody announced that more 109's were over Grand Harbour at about 8000 feet. I could already see them above me. There were four, and I climbed into them. I went into a tight turn, and held it, managing to get a two second squirt at one of the 109's. My ammunition ran out. There was nothing for it but to get away as quickly as I could. I rolled on my back, and dived and turned towards the ground, pulling out at about 1000 feet. The 109's did not follow, and I landed without further trouble.

119

My ground crew were waiting with a bit of chalk to see if they could mark up another swastika on my aircraft, and when I told them they could they cheered loudly.

I did not fly again on the 12th, and in the afternoon visited Imtafa hospital to see Paul. He was brassed off at being there, and was making no bones about telling off all and sundry. Even the cigarettes I had brought him failed to improve his temper. There was a gaggle of pilots in the hospital, and I had to go the rounds. Junior Tayleur, Jack Rae, Bud Connell, Jimmie James, Junior Crist, who was a Canadian flight sergeant, and a couple of Hurriboys with broken legs were anxious to know how the Spits were getting on, and bombarded me with eager questions.

I was sitting talking to Paul when the sirens went. We took no notice, imagining that it was merely another fighter sweep. Ten minutes later, however, the guns started to go to town. I went outside to see what was going on. Nurses, orderlies, out patients, and visitors lined the verandahs and pathways. They were pointing up at the flak and shouting. I looked up, too, and saw an amazing sight. Five bombers were stooging along in tightly packed vic formation, with flak bursting all round them. Everybody near me was shouting "Italians!" I could not recognize the aircraft, however, as they were 20,000 feet up. Some Spitfires went into attack, and I could hear their cannon fire above the noise of the guns. Suddenly one of the bombers caught fire. It started to spin down, with a Spit still on its tail. A mass of smoke and flame poured from the bomber. The Spit, which, I think, was piloted by Tim Goldsmith, an Australian sergeant pilot, began passing in wide circles round the bomber. Tim was no longer firing, but obviously watching the spectacle, which his marksmanship had created. At 10,000 feet four 'chutes came out from the blazing bomber. Two of them opened. The other pair streamed, but did not fill. Going faster than the stricken bomber, these latter 'chutes contrasted oddly with those which had already opened and which were floating gently earthwards. Burning pieces were hurtling off the bomber now and falling like a shower of fireworks. The crowd was cheering, shouting itself hoarse. There came a stampede as Maltese rushed in all directions in an effort to be first to reach the bomber. It crashed on land, between Halfar and Luqa, and when it hit the ground a great sheet of flame and smoke shot skywards.

This was the first Italian bomber I had seen shot down over Malta by a Spitfire. They had not been doing very much day raiding, and when they had come over in daylight they had generally been intercepted before reaching the coast. Mostly the Italian bombers had been coming over singly under cover of darkness. Perhaps the salutary lesson given by Mike Graves and his crowd to the five Eyetyes on the 9th had had its effect on the morale of the Italian crews. At any rate, the remaining four Italians dropped their bombs wide of their target, Luqa, and turned for Sicily, still maintaining their tight formation. That was the last raid of the day. During the night a few raiders crossed the coast, but, generally speaking, it was quiet.

The comparative lull was maintained throughout the 13th. The Hun had taken a bad beating, and our fighter defence was definitely on top. The Germans had probably realized that mass raids were no longer a practicable proposition unless heavy losses were to be incurred. Few bombers came over, and when they did cross the coast they were very heavily escorted. As many as 50 or 60 fighters would come in with six bombers. The 109's were active and showed plenty of determination. They seemed to be probing for a weak spot in our fighter defences. Their tactics varied. Sometimes the 109's would sweep for as long as twenty minutes before the half dozen bombers would come in. Next time they would remain in one big bunch, coming straight in and going straight out again with the bombers. It did not matter what tricks they tried they could not get on top of the Spits. We had more evidence this day that the morale of the crews of the 88's had been rudely shaken. More than once, so fearful were they of the Spits, they jettisoned their bombs in the sea. I felt the battle of Malta had been won, but I realized that if we were to maintain our superiority there was still a lot of work to be done.

Stan Grant's section was the first off in the morning. Then the sirens went, and our section, with Ronnie West leading, stood by. We climbed into our aircraft, strapped ourselves in, and waited for the signal. The 109's, some of them low down, were over the island already, and no sooner had we got the signal to scramble than they began beating up the aerodrome. We were taxi-ing along the runway as the 109's were passing over, but their cannon and machine gun fire fortunately missed us. No sooner were we off the ground, however, than more 109's jumped us. In a twinkling our section was split up. I had just pulled up my wheels, trimmed my aircraft and was passing over Imtafa Hospital when a 109 whipped across in front of me. I turned on him. I got no more than a hasty snap shot. I could see no results, and he climbed away. As I was on my own, I joined up with a section from another squadron which was climbing up. Ronnie West, Linny and Willie the Kid, the three other members of my own section, had already joined up with other sections.

We climbed up west of Gozo, reaching 12,000 feet without being molested. Eight of us were now together. I saw two 109's on my starboard beam and at about my height. I told the rest of the formation, and turned towards them. The leader of the pair began climbing away, but his number two failed to follow, apparently not having seen me. I was able to get on his tail without trouble, and opened fire at about 100 yards. He was obviously a new hand, and kept going straight and level, enabling me to get a good bead on him. I gave him two seconds. He dived straight down with smoke and glycol pouring from him. I watched him crash into the drink.

The rest of the formation had continued to climb, and as they were now about 6000 feet above me I realized I would have to carry on on my own. I heard over the R./T. that there was something doing over Kalafrana Bay, and I beetled across there. I found a real mix up. Spits and 109's were everywhere at about 5000 feet. As I arrived on the scene

I saw a 109 diving on a Spit's tail. I went in at once, attacking him from the starboard quarter. I could see my shells striking his fuselage. He turned on his back. I turned on mine, firing all the time. He started to go down in a gentle dive, and I kept firing at him to make sure of him. He crashed into the bay, and as he hit the water Ronnie West's voice came to me over the R./T. "Spit that just shot down that 109, thanks a hell of a lot."

I joined up with another Spit, the pilot of which turned out to be Willie the Kid. We flew round for some time, but could get no more joy. Most of the 109's low down had streaked for home. Only those high up remained. Both Willie and I had exhausted our ammo, and we returned to base. When I landed I was told our squadron had enjoyed a good morning, shooting down several enemy aircraft and damaging many others.

The afternoon was quiet, so was the evening, and I was able to pay another visit to the boys in hospital. Even during the night there was little activity. The Hun was keeping away.

I was on dawn readiness on the 14th. No Huns came over early, but about 10.30, shortly after the sirens had gone, we scrambled. Ronnie West, Linny, Willie the Kid and myself had no sooner run out to our aircraft than a number of 109's, coming out of sun, bombed the aerodrome. They were occasionally in the habit of doing this, each 109 carrying about 500 lb. of bombs. This lot did little or no damage, and failed to get our aircraft. We were able to take off and climbed to 5000 feet. Woody then instructed us to operate as an independent section, telling us to climb to about 20,000 feet and to go 20 miles southeast of the island. We were not attacked on our climb up. As we patrolled at the appointed spot, cruising round for about five minutes, we could hear the rest of the boys going in at the first wave of bombers. We could see the flak bursting, but we could not see any aircraft. We might have gone over, but Woody told us to wait, as more Huns were on their way. It was evident the Jerries were a good deal more active than they had been for several days.

A few minutes later, after I had seen the vapour trails of 109's high above us, Woody gave us a vector to intercept another plot coming in, telling us there had been a second wave already. We steered north, and after a few minutes sighted three 88's flying in vic formation. They were about 1000 feet below and out to our right. They had no close fighter escort. We turned, and went in to attack. I took the right hand one, Ronnie the centre, and Linny the one on the left. Willie the Kid must have blacked out on the turn round. He lost contact, and later followed me down. I got on the tail of my 88, closed to about 50 yards, and opened fire. I could see three members of the 88's crew in the glasshouse, as well as the rear-gunner, who had already opened fire. I gave it everything I had. I saw my shells strike along the 88's fuselage and smack into the glasshouse. It was carrying a bomb load, and blew up. Pieces flew in all directions, being so widely scattered that I had to go into a violent turn to avoid the fragments. I could see Ronnie firing at his 88, and in a few seconds it went down in flames. By now the 109's whose smoke trails I had *seen above were coming down on us. I broke down and headed for the coast, so as to get away from them. Willie followed close behind me. As I went down I saw the remaining Hun bomber. He was headed towards Sicily, and smoke was pouring from one of his engines. Linny, apparently having used up all his ammunition, had given up chasing it, and was following us down. It seemed to take us an age to reach the coast. The 109's, however, failed to catch us and eventually broke off the pursuit.*

When we landed we learnt that the first wave of bombers had consisted of three 88's. All three had been shot down by the Spits. Two of the second wave of six had also been shot down. The remainder, having jettisoned their bombs in the sea, had headed for home, hotly pursued by Spitfires. We had got two of our three, and badly damaged the third 88. A fourth wave, also comprised of only three 88's, came in after we had landed, but they dropped their bombs 10 miles from the coast, and then hurriedly turned back for Sicily.

From the hospital verandahs I watched the morning dos. I saw the three 88's in the first bombing wave shot down. An Englishman in another squadron, Sergeant Pilot Johnny Hurst, got on to the first of these three 88's as they dived on Ta-Kali. I saw him open fire, and a few seconds later one bomber's starboard motor flew out. The 88 rolled on its back, went into a flat, sluggish, inverted spin, and crashed on the edge of the aerodrome, bursting into flames. Other Spits shot down the two remaining bombers. They crashed into the sea.

It was during this morning that I witnessed the only collision between Spitfires which occurred over Malta while we were there. A 109 flew across at about 8000 feet. He was pouring glycol, having been hit badly by Bob Sim. There were four Spitfires on his tail, and he was skidding violently to avoid them. Hardly had he passed over our heads than two of the Spits collided and disintegrated. Both pilots baled out and landed safely. The 109 boy had to follow suit, and was taken prisoner.

From what I saw during the morning I realized the Hun was employing new tactics. I was discharged from the hospital at lunchtime, and strolled across to the mess, where I found Hess telling the other boys of the Huns' new methods. We talked things over, and agreed that it was a good sign. Indeed, we felt very happy. The fact that the Hun was sending over his bombers in such small numbers, and staggered so far apart, convinced us that we had the Battle of Malta in the bag. The Hun's object was clear. By sending over one wave, and then others spaced at intervals, he was trying to get all our aircraft into the air at once, and then, when the Spits were forced to land to refuel, to do his main bombing with his final wave of 88's. Undoubtedly, this last wave would have made the aerodrome their target. The109's were shooting down so few of our fighters that the Hun considered his only chance of getting rid of the Spits was to bomb them as they were refuelling. This plan miscarried hopelessly. It proved an absolute flop. We played havoc with the early waves, and still had plenty of Spits aloft when the fourth plot came over. Indeed, I doubt if the final wave of Hun bombers ever left Sicily. In my opinion the enemy recognized after the fourth wave that we could do to this form of attack exactly what we had done to his mass attacks on the 10th, and called the whole plan off.

Nattering in the mess, I learnt that many of the Hurriboys had converted to Spitfires; Slim Yarra, Bob Sim and Flight Sergeant Nick Ferraby, a Yorkshire man with a broad accent, all three of whom had been posted to Hurris from our squadron, were now back on Spits. Tony Boyd was another who had converted, while I learnt that Tweedale had been piloting a Spitfire when he had failed to return to base on the 9th. Sergeant Pilot Dodds, a Canadian who had shot down three Huns while on Hurris, was another who had become a Spit boy.

During the afternoon word reached us that Tony Boyd had been killed. He had scrambled early in the afternoon, and with Nick Ferraby attacked eight Macchi 202's, going at them from underneath. Tony apparently was hit. His aircraft spun out from the mix up like a corkscrew, and he crashed close to Ta-Kali. I had known Tony well. He was not only one of the most capable, determined and courageous pilots on Malta, but he was also an outstanding personality. He was cheery and happy at all times, and throughout the depressing periods of April and early May he had been an inspiration to every one of us. We felt Tony's death keenly, and it cast a gloom over his fellow Australians.

With Bud Connell, who had also been discharged from hospital, I went into Valetta late in the afternoon. The Maltese were immensely happy, and the changed outlook was reflected even in the streets. While we had been making no impression on the Hun, the debris which had spilled across the roadways had been left there. Everybody had felt it was no use attempting to clear it away, since after the next raid it would be as bad as ever. Now, however, gangs of men were everywhere clearing away the debris, and making Valetta's narrow streets passable again. The general air of relief was most noticeable. I wandered round the shops, trying to buy some D.F.M. ribbon, so that Hess and myself might put up our gongs. None was obtainable, but each time I entered a shop and asked for some D.F.M. ribbon I was asked, "Spitfire pilot?" When I replied, "Yes," the shopkeeper wanted to pile gifts on me, and I had the greatest difficulty in refusing them. I believe that had I accepted they would have presented me with the whole of their stock and the shop as well.

Things were very quiet during the remainder of May. I flew on the 17th, when the Hun sent over a small number of fighter sweeps. I exchanged shots with some 109's, but without result on either side. On the way up I felt extremely nervous, and this nervousness, which was much more acute than at any time since my initial trips over Malta, did not leave me until we got into holts with some 109's. Then it vanished like a flash. When I went up next day, the 18th, most of my old confidence had returned.

On this occasion four Spitfires were ordered to take off, but at the last moment Stan Grant, who was to have led, found that his aircraft was unserviceable. He ran across to my pen as I was taxiing out, and told me to lead the others, flying as a three. This was the first time I had led a flight, and I got a hell of a kick out of it. We took off, but a few seconds later Ronnie West followed us up, and joined us as a fourth. He told me to keep on leading, and that he would take over the sub-section. Woody was resting, and we had a new controller, Squadron Leader Birtwhistle. We had been scrambled to look for some 109's. They had come over in search of one of their pilots who had baled out into the drink on the 17th. We went 15 miles south of the island without finding them, and were then directed to the east in search of more 109's which had been reported. It was early morning, with the rays of the rising sun reflected on the sea. About 10 miles east of Zonkor Point I spotted four aircraft silhouetted against the sea. They were three miles east of us, and about 2000 feet below. Having reported them to Ronnie, I headed straight for them. We circled above them. I think they must have mistaken us for 109's, and imagined we were those which had been south of the island come to join up with them. They were flying in two pairs, and were obviously Italians. I put them down as Macchis.

I told Ronnie to take the pair on the left, and, followed by my number two, Sergeant Pilot Johnny Gilbert, an Englishman whose home was in the Argentine, I dived on the right hand pair. I gave one a short burst from dead astern. I saw some of my shells hit his port wing. He pulled away sharply, cutting right across Johnny's nose. I saw Johnny give him a squirt, and he went away pouring glycol. Meanwhile I had pulled on to the second one. He promptly went into a vertical dive. I followed him, caught him as he was pulling out of his dive at 2000 feet and, getting dead behind him, gave him a long burst. He hung there for a second, rolled on his back, and hit the sea. As he crashed I saw another aircraft spin into the sea half a mile away. As I thought it might be one of our boys, I called up the others, and Ronnie told me he had just shot down one of the Eyetyes. As the other two Spits also answered my call, I knew the second aircraft to crash must also have been an Italian. I told the section to return to base independently.

When we landed we reported the enemy aircraft as Macchis. We had destroyed three out of four without getting a bullet-hole in any of our aircraft. The one Johnny had hit force landed at Zonkor Point, and it was then we learnt that the Eyetyes had not been Macchis, but Reggiane 2001's, the latest Italian fighter.

It was on this day that Jack Yarra won his D.F.M. He had gone up with a

New Zealander from his squadron, Sergeant Pilot Shaw, shortly before the first wave of 88's came over. They were jumped by four 109's, but succeeded in shaking them off after having mixed it with them for a few minutes. Woody then called up, and, saying a Hun pilot had baled out into the drink, ordered them to cover the rescue launch. Shaw, whose aircraft had been shot up rather badly, was compelled to return to base, and Yarra found himself alone over the launch with at least 13 109's. Sitting on top of the launch, he held off the Huns. Each time the 109's came down to attack, Slim turned into them and drove them off. He shot down one for certain and probably destroyed a second in the process. He got the first 109 right above the launch, and its pilot baled out, hitting the water about 50 yards away. The launch altered its course to pick up the Hun, and as it reached him one of the 109's came down on it. Slim hopped on its tail promptly, but before he forced it to climb away, it had sprayed the water round the launch and the Hun pilot with machine gun bullets, fortunately without injuring anybody. At the pace at which he was firing, Yarra quickly ran out of ammo. Nevertheless, he continued to sit on top of the launch, and each time the 109's came down, turned on them and delivered dummy attacks. In this way he kept the enemy at bay for three-quarters of an hour, and did not leave the launch until it was safely back in port. As he was flying back to Ta-Kali to land, Slim was tackled by four 109's, and he had to turn into them. The few minutes involved in this action almost made all the difference to Yarra. It practically exhausted his gravy, and as he entered the Ta-Kali circuit his motor cut out. He glided down to the aerodrome and landed safely, but it had been a narrow squeak. Not a drop of petrol was left in his tanks.

Yarra returned to England, and later became a flight lieutenant in an R.A.F. Spitfire squadron. With five other Australians, he was attacking a convoy in the Channel when his aircraft was hit by flak. Yarra baled out and his parachute streamed, but unfortunately it caught in his tail plane and when it tore loose it failed to open. He went into the drink.

There was great excitement in the mess in the evening. Hess had been awarded a bar to his D.F.M. He had shot down 11, the last five of which he had destroyed between the 10th and 14th.

The Hun obviously felt very annoyed over his whacking. The 109 boys often loaded up with hand grenades, which they dropped over the side as they flew across the island, while the Italians began dropping all kinds of booby-traps. These took various forms, and presented some odd problems for the bomb disposal boys. One of the latter was cycling along the road near Halfar one day when he saw a fountain pen lying in the dust. "One of their new tricks," he thought, dismounting. He pulled out his handkerchief and, making a sling, gingerly placed the fountain pen in it. Leaving his bicycle behind him, so that he could devote his whole attention to preventing the fountain pen being jolted, he trudged the rest of the way to his workshop. There he set up some blast-proof screens, very carefully locked the fountain pen in a vice, and prepared to deal with it. Working from behind the screens, he gently unscrewed the top. When he had completed this task with meticulous care, he found that, sure enough, it was a fountain pen that he had retrieved.

I had the highest admiration for these bomb disposal boys. They performed a dangerous task with remarkable courage. This was not a job which appealed to me. It was altogether too risky and dangerous for my liking, and I take off my hat to every member of Malta's bomb disposal squads.

The civilians, of course, were warned consistently about the Italian booby traps. Unfortunately all did not heed these repeated warnings, and casualties, particularly among children, occurred. On one occasion a small boy was walking 20 or 30 yards behind his family when he found what we used to call a butterfly bomb. It is an innocuous looking affair, made of metal and shaped rather like a butterfly. He called out to his parents to look at what he had found, and threw it over to them. It hit a wall where they were standing and a second later the boy was an orphan.

Sometimes small anti-personnel bombs, with a delayed action, were dropped. One day some Maltese workmen employed on the aerodrome found one of these. They tried to knock off the top by banging it against the side of a utility truck. An armament sergeant, noticing their action, rushed over and warned them it was a bomb. Possibly because it had not gone off they refused to believe him. They kept trying to knock off the top. The sergeant, realizing the futility of further protest, moved away smartly. By this time quite a crowd of workmen had gathered, but fortunately only four of them were killed when the bomb exploded.

We scrambled often after the 18th to intercept 109's. But even the Hun fighters were now chary of us. They flew so high and were so wary that we could not catch them. There was little bombing, and it was done mostly by the 109's. They were simply hit-and-run raids. The 109's would dive on Ta-Kali from 25,000 to 10,000 feet, drop their bombs, and make back north at full speed. Occasionally some Italian bombers, Savoia Marchetti 84's, came over. Flying either as a three or a five, they would stay very high, and were heavily escorted by both Italian and Hun fighters. At the height at which they would come in, these S.M.84's looked almost transparent against the blue sky, and their course would be marked clearly for a long time afterwards by the drifting white puffs of the flak. Their bombing was most inaccurate. They rarely hit the target, and did little damage. We brought down one or two of these machines.

About this time we lost Pete Nash, whose score was 13 destroyed. He took off with a young New Zealander, Sergeant Pilot Lorry Verrol. They attacked five 109's, and a bitter dogfight developed. Lorry landed safely, having shot down one, but Pete crashed at the same time as a 109, both pilots being killed.

The last few days of May were so quiet that we could afford to send off sections on practice flying, and many of the more recent arrivals went up with the old hands. For those of us who had been in Malta from the time the Spits first arrived, it presented a striking contrast to the conditions which had existed. Indeed, had anybody told us a few weeks' earlier that we would be practice flying at the end of May, we would have told them they were crazy. But it happened, and it happened because the Spits had won a great victory.

CHAPTER IV

JUNE 1942

June opened on the same quiet note. Twice or thrice daily, the109's would come over, flying very high. Sometimes they would dive down and drop bombs on Ta-Kali, but mostly they were engaged on reconnaissance and would simply stooge over the island, high up. We scrambled often to intercept them, but nearly always they avoided combat. They were hard to catch, and only occasionally did we exchange shots with them. The Italian bombers, however, came over fairly consistently. They were heavily escorted by their own fighters, principally Macchi 202's and Reggiane 2001's, and invariably flew the same tightly packed formation. Their bombing was as inaccurate as ever, and despite their numerous escort we shot down many of them. On one occasion Laddie Lucas and his section scrambled when three Italian bombers came over. They accounted for all three.

We also took heavy toll of the Italian fighters. They were powered with the German Daimler-Benz 1350 h.p. motor, and were slower, but much more manoeuvrable, than the 109. The Italian pilots were game enough and ready to mix it with us, but once in a dogfight they showed little knowledge of combat tactics. Their pet habit was to perform aerobatics as a means of evasive action. Their loops, flick rolls, and rolls off the top were never effective, and we had little difficulty in shooting down a considerable number. Rome Radio, of course, claimed that the Italian fighters destroyed many Spitfires, but in actual fact they got very few of our boys.

On the 6th Johnny Plagis earned a bar to his D.F.C. He led four Spits against more than 10 Italian fighters, which fled for home. The Spits gave chase, and Johnny himself shot down two of the Re.2001's some 40 miles out to sea. On the 11th I was promoted to pilot officer and two days later Hess also received his commission.

Night bombing became consistent and grew heavier, particularly with the first moon period of June. The Huns had found day bombing too expensive, whether carried out by large or small formations, and they began now to concentrate upon night attacks. These were delivered by 87's, 88's and Italian aircraft, between 20 and 30 bomber crossing the coast each night. During moon periods the attacks increased in severity, culminating in moderately heavy dive-bombing at the full moon. As many as 50 aircraft would then come over. These night raids were carried out to a pattern. The bombers would come in one at a time, with five or ten minute intervals between them, and usually the first arrived shortly after we had gone to bed. No matter how the attacks were delivered, the first aircraft to arrive generally dropped about eight parachute flares. These burned with a bright yellow light, and as they drifted down burning pieces would break off reminding me of a lighted candle from which the wax was dripping. The flares left a wavy white wake which formed curious patterns in the light cast by the flares themselves. The principal targets of the night bombers were the aerodromes, but damage was surprisingly small.

Both the Hun and Italian bombers were scared of our night fighters, and their losses were heavy. This was particularly so towards the end of June, after we had received a reinforcement of night fighter pilots. Among these was a Canadian, Flying Officer Moose Fumerton, D.F.C. In two successive nights he shot down four bombers, getting two on each night. Even Rome Radio admitted the efficiency of our night defences, describing how their pilots "were pursued and ambushed by night fighters, blinded by searchlights, and shot at by anti-aircraft fire". The commentator ended up by saying that the lot of the Axis pilots over Malta was a hard one. It certainly was. The ack-ack boys did fairly well at night, and steadily built up their tally of destroyed aircraft.

Although enemy activity over Malta during June was much less than it had been in May, living conditions had deteriorated further. We were feeling the strain of the exacting months through which we had passed. There was a shortage of almost all foodstuffs, although locally grown tomatoes, figs, peaches, plums and other fruit somewhat eased the position. Rationing, both of food and water, was severe and stringently enforced, and was accepted by the Maltese without a murmur. There was less and less camouflage on the bully beef. All extra messing was abolished, and the officers lived on the same rations as the airmen. To conserve fuel, no lights were permitted in the mess. For the civilians conditions were more difficult still. Emergency measures in the way of communal cooking and feeding were intensified and were organized exceptionally well. The cheerful manner in which all privations were accepted was remarkable. There was plenty of good-natured grousing, but it was not directed against the restrictions themselves so much as the methods of enforcement. Everybody knew the position, and willingly faced it. Indeed, the cooperation which the authorities received from all sections of the community impressed us very favourably, and I often heard it commented upon in the mess.

Rommel's offensive in Libya had begun late in May and at the beginning of June was meeting with success. He had to look to Naples for the bulk of his reinforcements and supplies, and whenever one of his convoys was making the passage enemy activity over Malta flared up. This was the signal for our Beauforts. We Spitfire boys had the job of covering them out of Malta, and then handed over to the long-range day Beaufighters. Covering the Beauforts was our happiest job. We were always glad to see them go out, for we knew that Malta's primary purpose was an offensive one directed at enemy shipping. It was also an easy job. I cannot remember any occasion when we were attacked by 109's while escorting the Beauforts, and the latter always cleared the island without any difficulty. Their torpedoes sank many ships in the convoys bound for Rommel. One of the Beaufort captains was Pilot Officer Jimmy McSharry, an Australian from Mount Morgan, Queensland. He made his first operational flight from Malta, and it proved an eventful flip. He went in to 1000 yards, let go his fish, and turned round for home. As he was doing so an ack-ack shell exploded in front of his aircraft. He was wounded in the face, but brought his aircraft back to base despite his injuries. He spent three weeks in hospital, but what annoyed hindmost was that owing to being wounded he had been unable to observe whether his fish had found its mark.

On the 15th a convoy reached Malta. It was a big day for everybody. We had prepared thoroughly for its arrival. Our reconnaissance aircraft had been on the job for several days, shadowing the Italian Fleet. Bombers based on Malta attacked, not only the Italian ships, but also the aerodromes in Sicily. It was current gossip in Malta that after one heavy raid on the Italian Fleet, at Taranto, the Italian crews took their hammocks ashore the following night and did not return to their ships until daylight. It was for his work in keeping tab on the Italian ships that Sergeant Pilot Colquhoun, of the R.A.F. was awarded his D.F.M. Another pilot who did fine work at this time was Pilot Officer Harry Colbeck, a New Zealander. He flew a reconnaissance aircraft, and carried out many sorties.

The Spits did not go into action until the morning the convoy was due, but then they made over 300 sorties. From first light we went out on continuous patrol. It was an impressive sight. From Ta-Kali we could see the Spits from Luqa disappearing over Imtafa Hill in sections of four, spread out wide. Dawn was just breaking, and in a few minutes the Spits merged with the dark western sky. Throughout the day there was a continuous hum of aircraft over Malta, and they were all our own. Spits came and went with monotonous regularity. The majority of them were on patrol above the convoy, but a few escorted torpedo carrying Swordfish on their sorties against the Italian warships.

All day long reports came in of our successes. The convoy was being heavily attacked by German and Italian bombers, escorted by Me.110's and a few Macchi 200's, and the Spits did good work against them. Tim Goldsmith, who had been awarded the D.F.M. on the 5th, at which time he had destroyed at least five enemy aircraft, had a most successful day. Within 10 minutes he shot down two and probably destroyed a third, bringing his tally to 11 confirmed victories. It was for this feat that he later received the D.F.C. Slim Yarra was another Australian to do well, and bagged a couple.

One of the last sorties of the day was carried out by Laddie Lucas and his section, comprising Raoul Daddo-Langlois, Linny, and a Canadian, Pilot officer Jones. They took off as the sun was setting and, going west of the island, climbed to 17,000 feet. There they got into position, and were told by Fighter Control to orbit and look out for enemy aircraft which were approaching the convoy. By this time the sun had set and dusk was closing in. Control called them up and advised them they were very near the bombers. Laddie realized that from above he would not see them against the dark sea. Diving down, he sighted the enemy bombers silhouetted against the light western sky. There were 12 88's, without fighter escort. Laddie himself shot down one, Raoul got another, Jonesy a third, and Linny a probable. Two of the 88's burst into flames, and in the half-light they looked like meteors as they dived blazing towards the sea. Laddie later was awarded the D.F.C. for this day's work.

We had our umbrella ready at first light on the 16th, the convoy having arrived during the night. Six 88's attacked fairly early. The heavy and accurate barrage put them off their aim and the majority of the bombs fell harmlessly into the sea. They got nowhere near the ships. The naval boys who had come in with the convoy went to town, and their anti aircraft guns added substantial weight to the harbour defences.

About the 20th our squadron bagged its hundredth Hun with Spitfires. Originally equipped with Hurricanes, 249 Squadron had destroyed 27 enemy aircraft when it converted to Spitfires, and, including this initial total, it shot down its hundredth aircraft during the big do in May. The century for Spits, however, did not come up until about June 20. The previous day I was on readiness in the afternoon. We 'phoned Flight Lieutenant Keith Aitken, our intelligence officer to find out our exact tally, and he told us it stood at 99 2/3rds confirmed. All that afternoon we prayed for sight of the Eyeties, but they did not come. Next day the enemy put in an appearance, and one of the new boys did the trick. So far as Hess and I were concerned, it was too late. We had gone on leave that morning, and missed the very fine party in the mess in the evening. The champagne was on the A.O.C.

Bombing activity stepped up during the last half of June. Daylight attacks, which had recommenced about the 10th, though still on a light scale compared with the previous months, grew more numerous. We began to expect the Italians over every day, and sometimes they put in an appearance both in the morning and evening. We scrambled more frequently than for some time, but neither Hess nor I had any luck. Some of the other boys did well, however. Slim Yarra, going in to attack some Italian bombers, was jumped by about a dozen Italian fighters. He turned round on them and shot down two in a few seconds. Jack Rae, who had come out of hospital a few weeks earlier, Lorry Verrol, and a Canadian, Flight Sergeant Middlemiss, intercepted a Do.24 about 40 miles from Malta. The flying boat was escorted by 12 Macchis, with some 109's up higher. Rae, Verrol and Middlemiss each shot down one. Ronnie West and Johnny Plagis, each of whom had been promoted flight lieutenant, were two others who were prominent.

Our victory in May had placed us on top of the Hun, and the comparatively quiet June we had experienced proved how far reaching had been that victory.

CHAPTER V

JULY 1942

With the beginning of July, the German daylight attacks were again in full swing. Their methods had changed radically. Six or, at the most, eight bombers, with a large fighter escort, often totalling as many as 50 aircraft, would come over at a time. Instead of their usual dive to about 8000 feet or lower to release their bombs, they would do high level bombing from 18,000 feet. Once or twice they tried their low diving tactics, but on such occasions we inflicted such heavy losses on them that they reverted promptly to their high level attacks. Their fighter escort was well planned, and, on the whole, proved most skilful, revealing something of its old determination. Whenever we attacked the bombers we would find a 109 on our tail within a couple of minutes.

I had nine confirmed victories, and was most anxious to reach double figures in Malta. On the 7th I went on readiness, knowing that my term in Malta was nearing its end. I was determined to get my tenth that morning. Laddie Lucas was leading. He had taken over command of the squadron from Stan Grant, who had been promoted wing commander. We had 12 aircraft at readiness. Raoul Daddo-Langlois was leading four aircraft in blue section, and I four in green section. We planned to operate as a squadron, so we could tackle the Hun no matter what the height at which he came in. Our 12 aircraft took off and joined up, climbing up east of the island into the sun.

At 15,000 feet we left Raoul and his section to deal with the bombers if they dived, and Laddie and I took our sections up to 20,000feet. There Laddie reported aircraft dead ahead at the same level as ourselves. I could see six 88's, but at first could not pick out their fighter escorts. However, as we got closer, I could see that the bombers had fighters swarming all round them. They tried to head up sun. Telling Laddie I would head them off I manoeuvred into position, and then led my section in, head on. The 88's were flying line abreast, and as we got into range all six of them opened fire with their two forward guns. These are in the wings of the 88, and at first their black smoke made me think for a moment that all the bombers had inexplicably caught fire. Then I realized they were firing. I pressed my own gun-button when the range was about 450 yards, aiming at the extreme starboard 88. I gave him a couple of seconds. As I grew rapidly closer to him his tracer whipped by me, but without hitting my aircraft. I went in until I was only 50 yards from him, and then I had to break down to avoid a collision. At the same instant he pulled up away from me. I had no time to observe results. The 109's started coming down on me and, having learnt my lesson the day I had been shot up, I dived down immediately and gathered speed. Three 109's followed me. As soon as I had gained sufficient speed, I whipped my aircraft out of their line of fire, turned slightly and skidded away to the left. Their leader shot past under my starboard wing. I slipped back on his tail, 50 yards behind him, and gave him three seconds. I saw my shells travel up his fuselage and hit the motor and cockpit. A streak of oil appeared on his port fuselage and he went into a vicious spiral towards the sea. He was out of control, and crashed into the drink.

Seeing their leader go, the other two pulled up at once. I followed, got about 200 yards behind one, and started to fire. Three or four of my shells hit his starboard wing. Then my port cannon packed up, and my aircraft slewed away. It was no use staying. I told my boys to pancake as soon as they had finished engaging, and dived down. I had forgotten my aircraft was trimmed for the climb, the effect of which is to maintain a back pressure on the control column. In consequence, I skidded violently as I went down, and as my speed increased the aircraft decided to pull out of the dive itself. It did this so violently that I lost consciousness. When I came to I was on my back, pointing straight at the sun. It was an uncanny feeling coming to again. For a couple of seconds I did not even realize that I was in an aircraft. Instead I believed I was sitting in dispersal. I could not understand the noise of the motor and wondered what it could be. Then I remembered where I was. I righted my aircraft and went down to sea level, passing over the spot where my 109 had crashed. The machine itself had vanished completely, but a great patch of white foam was still bubbling up.

When I landed I found that Raoul's aircraft had been hit by 109's, while one of his boys, Bob Middlemiss, the Canadian, was missing. We thought he might have baled out and be in the drink. Laddie and Jack Rae took off to look for him, but after an hour they returned without having sighted him. I took off with Flight Sergeant Delara, who had been a test pilot in the R.A.F. before being posted to Malta, and we made a series of S turns across the path of our engagement. After about an hour we located Middlemiss sitting in his dinghy in the middle of a patch of florescence. He was waving a red flag, and appeared to be all right. Delara called up Fighter Control, gave them a fix, and the rescue launch soon had Middlemiss ashore.

Later that day there was another raid. Some of our boys went up, and in trying to break through the heavy fighter escort to get at the bombers, three of them had to bale out and ended up in the drink. Two of them, Nick Ferraby and a Canadian, Flight Sergeant DeNancreed, were from our squadron. I was assigned the job of escorting the rescue launch to the scene, but we saw no enemy aircraft, and the three boys were picked up without incident. This was the last operational flight I made over Malta.

HESSELYN

On the 6th I flew again. I was told to use my section independently of the rest of the squadron, and I decided to try out some new tactics. I took my section to 15,000 feet and five miles east of the island, intending to wait there for the 88's while the remainder of the squadron engaged the fighters. I am sure this plan would have worked had there been any 88's, but the incoming bombers proved to be Italians, and they were flying at 22,000 feet. The other sections, which had climbed above us, attacked them, and had some joy. Flying Officers Norman Lee, leading Red section, and Smith, leading Blue section, each shot down a Cant 2007, while a Canadian, Sergeant Pilot "Screwball" Buerling, destroyed two Italian fighters, both Re. 2001's, and damaged a bomber. We were far too low and never engaged, but we covered the rescue launch while it picked up two Italians who had baled out into the drink. It was Buerling who, after we left the island, became Malta's ace fighter, gaining promotion to pilot officer, receiving the D.S.O., D.F.C. and D.F.M., and shooting down 28 enemy aircraft.

Later in the day I tried out these tactics again, and this time the bombers were 88's, We got in amongst them, but before we could engage we had to mix it with 109's and my section was broken up. Pilot Officer Barclay-Hill, who came from India, and Buerling each bagged a 109. Before we landed we again covered the rescue launch, which was sent out to pick up the crew of an 88.

I had better luck on the 7th. When the signal to scramble came, my ground crew were changing an oxygen bottle, and as a result I took off a couple of minutes after the other boys. I caught up with the rest of my section at about 8000 feet. We were then south-east of the island, and we turned to come in towards Filfla. Woody advised that 88's were dive-bombing Luqa. We were a fair distance out, and I put down my nose to pick up speed in the hope of reaching Luqa before the bombers left. We arrived too late, the bombers having already turned for home over Halfar. Willie the Kid and I stooged back to Filfla, and there we mixed it with a number of 109's at 2000 feet. I saw Willie get on the tail of one. It went into a spin after a few seconds, and crashed into the drink. Four 109's passed right across in front of me, and I attacked the rear one from starboard. I gave him about four seconds before my cannons packed up. I could not see my shells strike, and as he kept on flying, I thought I had missed him. But a few seconds later he flicked on his back and dived straight into the drink. More Spits arrived, and while they were engaging the 109's Willie and I went home. This was the first aircraft I had shot down since May 14, and I felt so pleased about it that I punished everybody's ears with my story of how I had got it.

After this scramble I was told to stand down. Orders had been issued that the old hands were not to fly. It was considered that they were operationally tired and needed a rest. However, I went up again about midday, when we intercepted seven 88's just before they began to dive. The bombers had a heavy fighter escort on either side, but I called up Woody, told him it was a piece of cake, and that I would cut him off a slice. Instead of going in one after the other we went down in pairs and got on the tails of the bombers as they were diving. We flew right through the flak and, at the speed at which we were travelling, rapidly overhauled the 88's. I singled out one, and opened fire at about 50 yards. After about three seconds, my cannons packed up, but I had set the 88's starboard engine on fire. He started to dive towards the drink, and I thought I had got him. He pulled out, however, and the last I saw of him he was heading out to sea, low down. I saw Willie on the tail of another. He set its port engine on fire. It turned seawards, with Willie still on its tail, and then, apparently badly damaged, doubled back towards Malta. Willie stayed on its tail and gave it another long burst. It went down in flames of Filfla. Johnny Gilbert, coming down with Pilot Officer Chuck McLean behind him was jumped by 109's. None of us saw what happened to him, but Gilbert failed to return to base, and we circled the island, searching the drink. We found a Hun pilot near Filfla, but when the rescue launch reached him he was dead, and all three of us came in and landed.

I had my last operational night On the 15th, when we went up to intercept a Hun fighter sweep. We climbed to 25,000 feet, and then my motor cut. It picked up again at 15,000 feet, and I stooged round at that height for about a quarter of an hour without encountering any 109's, so came in and landed.

By this time Hess and I had received our postings to England, whither we were to return for a rest. While we waited to get away we took things quietly at Sliema, doing a spot of swimming and plenty of sunbathing. At last we were told to report to Luqa, and learnt that we were to leave that night. We were hanging about waiting when the 88's came over. Neither of us had any intention of getting blown up on our last night in Malta, and immediately the barrage went up we raced for the shelters. The aerodrome was the target of the bombers, but they missed it. From the door of the shelter we watched the first three 88's get knocked down by flak. Things quietened down then, although enemy aircraft were still over the island. We hung round until 2 a.m. when, much to our disgust, we were told our departure had been postponed.

Forty-eight hours later we left the island. Moose Fumerton was the last person to whom I said goodbye. As I climbed into the aircraft that was to take us on the first stage of our journey, he told me he had shot down his eleventh that night. A few minutes later we took off, and as we headed out to sea I pulled back the window curtain.

Malta was bathed in moonlight. The white roads and buildings of M'dina showed up sharply, and the detail of the rest of the island stood out almost as clearly. Gradually the island faded into the distance. I leaned over to Hess. "There's another chapter closed, and we're still alive," I remarked. We shook hands on it.

GLOSSARY

Angels.... Height.

Bags of gut . . . Plenty of power.

Beehive.... Swarm of aircraft manoeuvring in combat.

Beetled off . . . Flew away.

Big jobs .... Bombers. •

Brassed off . . . Fed up. .

Bungers-up of bomb-holes. Army men engaged in filling up bomb-holes on aerodromes.

Clock .... Air-speed indicator.

Cobber.... Friend; pal; buddie.

Dispersal.... Hut in which pilots wait to take off.

Drink .... Sea.

Erk .... Member of ground crew below the rank of corporal.

Fly on the trim . . . Manoeuvring aircraft without using control column or rudder bars.

Gaggle.... Large number of aircraft.

Glasshouse . . . Pilot's cockpit.

Glycol . . . . . Coolant.

Gong.... Decoration.

Gravy .... Petrol.

Natter.... Chatter; discussion.

Never saw a sausage . . Did not see anything.

Orbit .... To circle.

Packed up . . . Jammed; stopped.

Pancake .... To land.

Piece of cake . . . Easy victim, easily defeated.

Plot..... Formation of enemy aircraft.

Pranged .... To damage aircraft in landing.

Scatter guns . . . Machine-guns.

Scramble .... Take off; operational flight.

Scrounging . . . Secure additional rations by looking round for oneself.

Sergeant-pielo . . . Sergeant-pilot.

Skidding.... To move aircraft crabwise in air.

Small jobs . . . Fighters.

Stooge .... Fly about—hang around.

Teed up .... All ready; prepared.

Undercart . . . Under carriage.

Vector … Course to steer.

Wing root . . . Part of aircraft's wing immediate adjacent to the fuselage.

SPITFIRES OVER MALTA

Pilot-Officer PAUL BRENNAN,
D.F.C., D.F.M.
(ROYAL AUSTRALIAN AIR FORCE)

Pilot-Officer RAY HESSELYN,
D.F.M. and Bar
(ROYAL NEW ZEALAND AIR FORCE)

AND

HENRY BATESON

With a Foreword by LORD LONDONDERRY

Malta—yesterday the most blitzed island in the world; today, the United Nations' offensive base in the Mediterranean. Simply but vividly, *Spitfires Over Malta* tells how that change in Malta's role —from the defensive to the offensive—was made possible. Written by three young men from the Empire's southernmost Dominions, Australia and New Zealand, it gives the most graphic and comprehensive picture of Malta's ordeal under the Luftwaffe's remorseless hammering, and of how the R.A.F., equipped with the latest type of Spitfires, finally routed the German and Italian air forces.

Two of the authors were Spitfire pilots who shot down twelve and ten enemy aircraft respectively, each earning two decorations. They relate their own experiences in the air, and their own thrilling stories of their air combats constitute the best descriptions of air fighting which this war has produced. Their thoughts, their reactions, even the mistakes they made are recorded with graphic simplicity. But the book is much more than a record of dog-fights. It reveals the tactics with which the Luftwaffe attempted to knock out Malta; it relates the hardships which the civilian population suffered; it tells how the pilots lived when on the ground, and it portrays the splendid organization and *esprit de corps* of all three Services which enabled Malta to survive.

Malta's victory was a United Nations' victory. The pilots who finally swept the Luftwaffe from the island's clear blue skies came from all over the world—from Scotland and England, Australia and New Zealand, Canada and America, Rhodesia and South Africa. *Spitfires Over Malta* tells the story of many of their individual exploits, recording their names and deeds for posterity.

Illustrated 2/- net
JARROLDS PUBLISHERS (London) LIMITED.

Pilot Officer Paul Brennan DFC DFM
(Royal Australian Air Force)

Pilot Officer Ray Hesselyn DFC and Bar
(Royal New Zealand Air Force)

The Spitfire Pilots Of Operation Spotter:

Flt Sgt Virgil Paul Brennan
Flt Sgt Ian Maxwell Cormack
Flt Sgt David Ferraby
Sqd Ldr Stanley Bernard Grant
Plt Off James Joseph Guerin
Flt Lt Philip Whaley Ellis Heppell
Sgt Raymond Brown Hesselyn
Fg Off Norman William Lee
Plt Off Douglas Cecil Leggo
Flt Lt Norman Carter Macqueen
Plt Off Kenric Newton Lathrop Murray
Plt Off Peter Alfred Nash
Plt Off 'John' Ioannis Agorastos Plagis
Sgt Robert James Sim
Sgt John Lovett Tayleur
Flt Lt John William Yarra

Virgil Paul Brennan

Paul was born on March 6th 1920 in the town of Warwick, Queensland, in the north east of Australia. Born into a large family he was the fifth child of Edgar James Brennan and his wife Katherine. The young Paul was Nicknamed 'Digger' as a child due to his outgoing and adventuresome nature. In 1930 he began his education at St Joseph's College, Nudgee, an all boys Roman Catholic school located in Boondall a suburb of Brisbane, followed by attendance at Brisbane High School and then Downlands College, in Toowoomba. Later he studied part time at the University Of Queensland. Paul's father was a solicitor and he followed him in to the profession by becoming a Law Clerk with Neil O'Sullivan, a Solicitor in Queen Street, Brisbane.

On June 11th 1940, Paul aged 20, enrolled with the Royal Australian Air Force, at the No.3 Recruiting Centre in Brisbane. Like all the other Australians at that time he was listed as a British Subject and swore an oath to serve the King. In his application, when asked about any criminal convictions, he confessed to a car parking traffic offence in 1938 for which he had received a fine. On November 8th he was formerly enlisted in to the RAAF

Paul in a Miles Master training aircraft in 1942 (L McAulay)

and signed up **'For the duration of the war plus twelve months thereafter.'** He passed the medical and his physical characteristics were written on his file:

Height: 5 feet 9 and half inches. Weight: 154 pounds (11 Stone). Chest:

32 to 36 inches. Complexion: Olive. Eyes: Brown. Hair: Black.

Having been accepted, Paul was appointed three days later to No.2 Initial Training School at Lindfield New South Wales (NSW) where he was taught the basics of military life.

After four weeks at Lindfield, on January 9th 1941 Paul, now a Leading Aircraftman (service number 404692) joined No.8 Elementary Flying Training School at Narrandera, NSW, where he received around fifty hours of basic aviation tuition under the Empire Air Training Scheme. This scheme had been set up to train aircrew in Commonwealth countries during the war and was more commonly known as the British Commonwealth Air Training Plan. Paul experienced the controls of an aircraft for the first time in a dual controlled de Havilland DH82 Tiger Moth Bi-plane. He was one of 3,800 student pilots who commenced their flying training at Narrandera during the war.

On March 6th Paul reported to No.2 Embarkation Depot at RAAF Bradfield Park, where he received a final medical and was then supplied with the uniform and kit required for his next destination, which would be overseas. Paul was posted to Canada to continue his flying training on attachment to the Royal Canadian Air Force. On March 21st he left Sydney Harbour for the 4-week sea voyage, finally docking at Vancouver, British Columbia, on April 17th 1941. Paul then travelled by train to No.1 Service Flying Training School at Camp Borden near Ontario. At this site the Royal Canadian Air Force took on the training of aircrew in skies safe from the threat of an attack by enemy aircraft. There were 93 similar training schools that operated throughout Canada from over 230 sites, and at its peak over 3,000 trainees graduated each month, with a total of 131,000 pilots trained during the war, Camp Borden itself produced 2,728 of these.

At Service Flying Training Schools the pilots were, according to their ability, trained on either twin engined aircraft such as the Avro Anson, if they were destined to fly with Bomber or Coastal Command, or if they had the aptitude for fighters they were trained on the single engined North American Harvard. The Harvard was a more powerful two-seat monoplane with an enclosed cockpit and retractable undercarriage, the reduced drag making it faster than the Tiger Moth. Student pilots also faced the dangers of night and instrument flying, formation flying and long cross country navigation exercises.

Paul's course, number 26, lasted for ten weeks and during that time he completed 64 hours of dual flying with an instructor, 66 hours solo, plus 10 hours night flying. Time was also spent in the Link trainer, an early type of flight simulator. Out of a class of 53 student pilots he passed the course as 12th highest with a pass rate of 73%.

Of his flying training the Squadron Commander wrote:

'Has progressed steadily, learns quickly and has no outstanding faults,' and on his ground training **'Very satisfactory, although somewhat inclined to take things for granted.'**

As an Operational pilot he was listed as **'Above Average. Well disciplined. Confident, aggressive and self-reliant'** His overall assessment was given as **'Average,'** with the recommendation that he be commissioned as a Pilot Officer.

At the end of the course on July 3rd 1941 Paul qualified as a pilot and gained his 'Wings,' but was only promoted to the rank of Sergeant. The following day he travelled to 'M' depot Halifax, Nova Scotia, to await onward travel by ship to England. He left Canada on July 16th and arrived in the UK exactly one month later on August 16th.

Having attended No.3 Personnel Reception Centre in Bournemouth, Paul received a weeks leave before joining No.53 Operational Training Unit on August 23rd. He stayed with 53 OTU based at Llandow in Glamorganshire, Wales, for around six weeks, where he experienced his first flight in a 360mph Supermarine Spitfire.

The two great friends Paul and Ray together in Malta 1942 (P Lee)

On October 7th 1941 Paul joined his first operational squadron, No.64, based at Drem, East Lothian in Scotland, the squadron were flying the Spitfire MkII defending the surrounding area, and carrying out coastal patrols.

In mid November the squadron were sent south to Hornchurch in Essex and began to take on the new Spitfire MkVb, in which they flew aggressive fighter sweeps over occupied France. During November Paul also spent two days with the Air Fighting Development Unit probably at RAF Duxford. The unit held several captured front line enemy aircraft, which were flown and evaluated in order to devise tactics. The pilots were then taught the best approach to attack and destroy the different types of German aircraft.

On January 4th 1942, whilst still with 64 Squadron, Paul was promoted to the rank of Flight Sergeant. He was also, later that month, advised of his next posting which would take him over seas, after a period of leave, to Malta. On February 9th he reported to RAF Kirkham where he would meet for the first time the other pilots due to go to Malta, one of whom was Ray Hesselyn who would become a particularly close friend of Paul's.

Paul has described his own experiences on Malta in his book Spitfires Over Malta. His exploits earned him on May 22nd the award of the Distinguished Flying Medal (DFM), which was confirmed in the Supplement to the London Gazette:

'This airman is a most determined and courageous pilot. An exceptional shot, he always presses home his attacks with vigour. In two combats, he has destroyed at least 4 enemy aircraft and damaged others.'

The DFM was awarded to non commissioned officers for **'An Act or acts of valour, courage or devotion performed whilst flying in active operations against the enemy.'**

Laddie Lucas one of his flight Commanders in 249 Squadron described Paul as follows:

'He did not compromise in the air or on the ground. He was splendidly aggressive, but he tempered his aggression with an engaging brand of humour which saw the funny side of things when our fortunes were at there lowest ebb. He was a marvellous Squadron member.

'It took him some little while to determine what his judgement was of a colleague. He sniffed around a character rather as a dog gives a doubtful dinner the once over, but when once he has made his mind up about a guy and that person measured up to his requirements, then he would offer 250 per cent support. Paul was solid and loyal to a point in his friendships.

'I fancy he looked at me to begin with and said to himself: "Wait a moment! This looks like a stuck up Pom. Better watch him" But after a week or so in the flight we had sorted one another out and there never was a pilot who gave me, on the ground or in the air, finer or more devoted service.'

Malta: The Thorn In Rommel's Side. Laddie Lucas (Stanley Paul 1992)

Paul's excellent sense of humour can be seen in the following three episodes.

Before his Malta posting Paul had told another pilot that during his time with 64 Squadron in England, at the Meteorological briefings held before they flew, reference was made to 'the odd spot of precipitation.' He confessed that he had not realised that this meant rain until a long time after he had left the UK.

One evening in Malta, Paul and his good friend Ray Hesselyn decided to go for a drink at The Union Club in Strada Reale, in Valletta. This was a club for officers only for which they, as lowly sergeants did not qualify to enter. However, they both put on fake shoulder epaulettes to look like officers and casually strolled in. Once in the 'Snake Pit' bar they had the misfortune to come across Group Captain 'Woody' Woodhall the Senior Controller. Concerned that they had committed a Court Martial Offence by impersonating an officer, they were horrified as to what might happen next. They were very relieved when Woody played along, bought them each a whisky, but then recommended that they both get out, and fast.

In late April New Zealander Flt Sgt Jack Rae flew from the U.S.S. Wasp as part of Operation Calendar, which supplied a contingent of 46 reinforcing Spitfires to the island. Fellow Kiwi Ray Hesselyn and Paul managed to get him allocated to join them at 249 Squadron. On May 1st Flt Sgt Jack Rae whilst flying a Spitfire, was shot up by an Me109 with several cannon shells striking his aircraft. He was injured in the foot and leg and by small metal fragments embedded in his forehead. He was forced to bale out of his damaged and uncontrollable aircraft. Having landed safely, he was rescued by some British army soldiers from a local Maltese man, who, thought him German and was threatening him with a shotgun. Jack was then taken to Mtarfa hospital where his wounds were treated and his leg put into a plaster cast. He was able to get around with the aid of a crutch and hoped to leave to join the other pilots, but the medical staff insisted that he stayed longer at the hospital.

Paul was also in the hospital recovering from a wounded arm, the result of a cannon shell striking his cockpit. He had become tired of the monotony of the days spent there and the over authoritarian excesses of one of the senior nurses. The two pilots therefore decided to abscond together for a day out.

They knew where their clothes were and, with the help of two nurses, they sneaked out of the building and set off in a hired horse and carriage. They spent the day enjoying their time with the local Maltese, laughing together and drinking wine, although the wine seemed not to mix to well with their antibiotics.

Whilst sat outside a shop they were suddenly confronted by a platoon of soldiers, a Sergeant marched up and said he was there to arrest them. The soldiers had apparently been searching for hours around Mtarfa and Mdina for the two escapees. Jack and Paul politely thanked the men for their concern,

and for providing them with an escort and transport back to the hospital. They believed that would be the end of the matter, with the ongoing war continuing all around them, but they were both charged with escaping from a military hospital and summoned before the commanding officer. He went through the motions of a reprimand for the benefit of the army sergeant before dismissing him; he then invited both pilots to his office for a friendly chat. Not long after this incident Paul was awarded, on May 15th, another promotion to Pilot Officer, the rank he had been recommended for when he completed his training.

Paul flew his last operational flight on July 7th having flown over 35 hours in the skies above Malta, taking part in 47 sorties, 22 of these involving combat

Jack Rae revisiting Malta in 2005.

with the Axis forces. When he left at the end of July he had ten confirmed kills against German and Italian aircraft, with one probable, plus six others damaged.

At the end of a period of leave, recovering from the harsh living conditions of Malta, Paul, on August 22nd was posted as an instructor to join No.52 OTU based at Aston Down in Gloucestershire. Here he passed on the knowledge and skills he had gained to recently qualified pilots. Whilst to a degree this was seen as a rest away from daily fighting action, it could also be a very dangerous

146

time teaching pupils in the units dual controlled Miles Masters and Harvards; accidents were not uncommon, and many proved to be fatal.

Paul would however have felt at home at his new unit, as many of the other instructors were also former Malta pilots. Flight Sergeant Robert Sim, and Sergeant John Tayleur who had both flown off the Eagle with Paul were there, along with later arrivals Flt. Lt. Raoul Daddo-Langlois, Plt Off Robert 'Barney' Barnfather and Fg Off Michael Graves. For his actions against Axis aircraft on Malta Paul was awarded, the Distinguished Flying Cross (DFC) confirmed in the London Gazette on October 6th 1942. This medal was conferred on the same basis as the DFM but was bestowed on Officers. On November 3rd Paul, along with his instructor colleague Michael Graves from 52 OTU, attended Buckingham Palace in London to receive their medals. His majesty King George VI presented a proud Paul with both his DFM and the DFC.

Paul proudly wearing the medal ribbons for the DFC and DFM (F Galea)

Soon after this Paul received two promotions- on November 15th he was promoted to Flying Officer, and on December 1st to acting Flight Lieutenant.

On January 17th 1943 Paul's time with 52 OTU came to an end when he was posted to join 452 Squadron Royal Australian Air Force, he was going back to his home country of Australia to defend it against attacks by the Japanese. The Operational Records Book noted on his leaving:

'A successful pilot from Malta and a keen and interesting personality, Paul Brennan quickly made his mark at this station, and has done a good job here particularly as the Officer commanding Night Flying Flight.'

Prior to his departure Paul was sent on January 17th 1943 to No.2 Personnel Despatch Centre at Wilmslow in Cheshire. He left England on January 22nd for the long voyage home, his ship reaching Brisbane on 17th April 1943.

147

On the other side of the world the threat from the Japanese forces saw the formation of No.79 Squadron RAAF, which was formed on 26th April 1943 at Woolloomanata Homestead, near Geelong, Victoria. Squadron Leader Alan Rawlinson, a two-tour veteran with six victories, commanded the pilots. The squadron came under the jurisdiction of RAAF Laverton, Near Melbourne. Newly equipped with Spitfires, the squadron were deployed to New Guinea for the defence of that area. Paul was posted to this new squadron on the 1st May, and probably did not spend any time with 452 the squadron to which he had originally been posted to join.

Sqd Ldr Rawlinson said of Paul:

'Paul Brennan was posted in about 14 days before we left for New Guinea. I was delighted to have such an experienced Spitfire pilot with us. He had an easy nature, and he fitted in with the rest of the chaps. He was still strained, a bit taut. I had the feeling he was marshalling his reserves for the tour he was about to undertake; a bit tired.'

Against All Odds. Lex McAulay. (Hutchinson Australia 1989)

No.79 Squadron left Laverton fitted with 90 gallon under fuselage slipper tanks. They were led by a Lodestar aircraft to perform navigation duties for them as some of the Spitfires were new and had not had their compasses correctly calibrated. The squadron flew north via Richmond and Amberley, with the next leg on June 13th to Garbutt in Townsville northern Australia.

As the Spitfires came into land at Garbutt airfield, a tragic collision occurred between two aircraft, during which Paul lost his life. He did not die in action, as had so many of his contemporaries, but in an accident, at the end of a long transit ferry flight. Sqn Ldr Rawlinson described what he witnessed:

'We were landing in stream, Paul was running towards the south end of the strip, and the aircraft behind him, tail down, did not see Brennan's Spitfire in front and overran it, cutting it to pieces half way down the runway. I was parked in a dispersal about 70 metres away and saw the whole thing. I was so cramped after 4½ hours in the cockpit that I couldn't move, couldn't walk let alone run.'

Against All Odds. Lex McAulay. (Hutchinson Australia 1989)

The Squadron Record Book described the events:

'F/O Brennan (JG954) and Sgt Gardner (JG897) came into collision

148

on landing at Townsville. JG954 burst into flames and was completely destroyed and JG897 was so extensively damaged it was written off.'

Another witness Flt Sgt P.F. Turner of 79 Squadron gave further details in a statement on August 13th 1943:

'At approximately 14:00 hours on the 13th June 1943, at Garbutt aerodrome, Townsville, F/O V.P. Brennan cut in on Sgt Gardner, whilst landing. Sgt Gardner notified F/O Brennan of the aircraft following. He received no reply. F/O Brennan touched down on the left of the runway. Sgt Gardner approached on right of runway. F/O Brennan landed very short and at the conclusion of his landing run, turned across the path of Sgt Gardner's aircraft, and they collided.'

Although he was still alive when carried from the wreckage he died on his way to the General Hospital at Townsville. Whilst no doubt greatly shocked, the other pilot involved, Sgt Leslie Henry Gardner was not injured in the collision.

On the same day a telegram was sent to Paul's brother, John Patrick Brennan, listed as his next of kin, which Paul had specifically requested on his records, so that his mother would, in the case of his death, hear of it through John and not in a telegram. A confirmation letter with condolences was sent to his mother Katherine Brennan a week later.

The family of his good friend Ray Hesselyn wrote to Paul's mother and received the following reply back from Paul's brother.

'Mother has asked me to write to you and thank you most sincerely for your kind letter which reached us yesterday.

It is most thoughtful and kind of you and Mrs Hesselyn to write to mother at a time when every kind thought is appreciated.

'Paul's death was really most tragic, but we have comfort in the thought that we had him home with us for a little while to tell us of the gallant exploits of himself and that other "problem child of Malta."

'Their photograph together shows that they indeed have a likeness in that look of daredevil courage which took both of them to the top of the tree.'
Hess. James Sutherland. (Regal Books 2000)

The term 'Problem child' is a reference to their Malta days when close friends, Paul and Ray Hesselyn, who were always together, were referred to as the '**Problem**

children of Malta' because of their antics together. They were also referred to by their commanding officer Laddie Lucas as the **'Twins.'**

During the Second World War Sir William Rothenstein one of several official war artists toured aerodromes all over Britain producing a series of portraits of RAF personnel. The War Artists Advisory Committee purchased some of these and commissioned one other.

Although Paul was the subject of one of these drawings, forty of which were eventually published in a book called Men Of The RAF published in 1942 by Oxford University Press, Paul's picture does not feature in the book.

Sometime after Paul's death Ray Hesselyn saw a copy of the picture of Paul in the office of Eric Baume, the chief Editor of the Truth newspaper. Ray, looking at the picture, and in a rare show of emotion said **'He makes the old cow too fat'** and suddenly burst in to tears at the loss of his great friend.

In August a version of this portrait, possibly Paul's own, was sent from RAAF Head Quarters in London, to Australia, and in early August this was handed to Paul's mother by a public relations officer to whom she expressed her **'sincere appreciation of this official recognition'**

A former Malta pilot and colleague Flt Lt Raoul Daddo-Langlois wrote of Paul:

'Paul had fought against overwhelming odds for four months in Malta, and had taken heavy toll of the Germans sent against the island. Paul, always cheerful a good natured chap full of talk, (he could get himself anything by talking) and always ready for a fight.

'Paul was in my flight and we fought side by side during the dark days of March and April. How well I knew the always present grin, the lock of black hair which hung over his eye and the never ending flow of talk, smooth and persuasive or harsh and assertive if the occasion demanded.

'Paul's outlook on life was sharp and realistic. He had done well in private enterprise before the war and would doubtless have continued so afterwards. He had a quick grasp of world affairs and all that went on around him, and was never slow to express an opinion in a blunt and open manner.

'There will be many who will mourn the loss of so fine a character.'

Flight Lieutenant Virgil Paul Brennan DFM DFC was buried at the Townsville War Cemetery, Queensland, Australia. Grave A.D.12. He was aged just 23. His name is also listed on the Australian War Memorial, Campbell, Canberra. Panel 104 in the Commemorative Area.

Ian Maxwell Cormack

The city of Elgin is located within the county of Morayshire in the north east of Scotland. It is one of few cities that has a cathedral which has been preserved as a ruin, the building having been destroyed by fire and neglect over many years, with much of what remains today dating back to the 13th century.

In Institution Road, Elgin, Avenue House was to play a large part in the life of the Cormack family, both as a family home and as a place for their profession as Dentists. John Cormack Snr. had three sons, one of whom Sidney, was lost in an accident at sea in 1900, the other two sons Alexander and John both followed in their father's footsteps by becoming licensed Dental Surgeons.

On October 1st 1910 John, aged 32, married Constance Maxwell Christie the daughter of local hotelier William Christie at St Geradine's church in Lossiemouth. The married couple had two children both born at the family home, Avenue House. Their first child, Muriel, was born two years after their marriage in September 1912, followed eight years later by Ian born at 5:45 on the morning of June 2nd 1920.

Ian poses nonchalantly on his motorbike, circa 1940 (I Boraston)

Ian's education began at the Springfield Junior School in Elgin, a fee-paying primary school. He then went on to the Elgin Academy in Moray Street, Elgin (now the Moray College), and then his education continued at the Aberdeen Grammar School where, between 1936 and 1938, he stayed in the School Boarding House, going home only at weekends. His parents were at the time living around 30 miles away at the Station Hotel, which they owned and ran in Mintlaw, whilst John's uncle Alexander Cormack continued his work as a dentist at Avenue House.

Ian was an enthusiastic rugby player and proudly played for the Aberdeen School Rugby XV during the 1938 – 1939 season. Also at school with Ian, at both Springfield and Elgin academy, was his cousin Ronald West, whose father was the renowned local artist David West. Both boys fulfilled their ambition to join the RAF and coincidently would serve together on Malta in 1942.

On May 20th 1940 Ian travelled to the No.3 Recruitment Centre at RAF Padgate, near Warrington in England to join the RAF Volunteer Reserve, where he was issued with his service number of 998452 becoming an Aircraftman Second Class.

It was on July 1st that Ian was called to No.54 Group Flying Training, then based at the Norcliffe Hotel on the coast at Babbacombe, Torquay, Devon.

Several of the other seaside hotels had also been requisitioned and were being used as accommodation for the airmen during their training period. On July 15th Ian was posted to No.4 Initial Training Wing at RAF Paignton in

Ian (on the right) during training with an unknown colleague (I Boraston)

Devon, where he began his basic ground training. This included drill, physical exercises and plenty of classroom work on flight theory, navigation and meteorology, culminating with an examination at the end of the course.

On completion of this first course on August 24th 1940, Ian was promoted from Aircraftman Second Class to Leading Aircraftman. He was then sent on to 50 Group of Flying Training Command based at RAF Yatesbury in Wiltshire. Here he would take to the air for the first time as a pilot under training in a de Havilland Tiger Moth bi-plane. After successful completion of this course Ian was then posted on October 5th to join No.15 Service Flying Training School based at RAF Kidlington in Oxford, where his training would continue on the faster North American Harvard aircraft. At the end of the course on January 13th 1941 Ian had gained his 'Wings' having passed the flying and other examinations with a mark of 66.4%. This brought him another promotion to the rank of Sergeant.

After a period of leave Ian's next posting was to 56 Operational Training Unit on January 31st 1941. 56 OTU were stationed at RAF Sutton Bridge in Lincolnshire, where his instruction would continue in Miles Master aircraft and the Hawker Hurricane MkI, the other current front line fighter along with the Supermarine Spitfire.

On March 3rd 1941 Ian was posted to 213, his first operational Squadron, which was based at RAF Castletown, Caithness, Scotland equipped with the Hurricane MkI as a part of 13 Group Fighter Command. The role of 213 Squadron was the defence of the far north of Scotland including the Naval anchorage of Scapa Flow. No doubt pleased to be back in the country of his birth, his stay would not prove to be very long, as two months later in early May, 213 Squadron boarded HMS Furious for service in Egypt. Ian, perhaps not being an experienced enough pilot, did not travel with them but was transferred to 222 Squadron.

At the time 222 were based at RAF Matlaske in Norfolk as part of 12 Group Fighter Command flying the Supermarine Spitfire MkI and MkII. They then became part of 11 Group in July 1941 and were based at Manston in Kent. In August 1941 they moved again to North Weald, and were then equipped with the more powerful Spitfire MkV. During this period Ian would have been involved in the interception of enemy fighters and bombers, and carrying out offensive sweeps across the English channel and into occupied Northern France. On October 1st Ian was promoted again to the rank of Flight Sergeant.

In late January 1942 Ian would have been told of his posting to Malta and he met with his other Operation Spotter pilots at RAF Portreath in Cornwall, to begin the journey to Malta where he became part of 249 Squadron based at Takali.

The Spitfires first went into action on March 10th 1942, it is not known if Ian had flown between then and March 17th when he flew possibly for the first time over Malta. Early on the morning of the 17th 23 Ju88s attacked the airfield at Luqa, destroying several Wellington bombers and a petrol bowser.

The bombing also damaged several of the nearby towns, which resulted in many civilian deaths. Eleven Hurricanes and four Spitfires led by Flt Lt Philip Heppell were scrambled to intercept the raid; Flt Sgt Paul Brennan, Sgt Junior Tayleur and Ian flew the other three Spitfires. In this engagement Paul Brennan was the only one who was successfully able to shoot down one of the Me109 fighters, he described the others as feeling **"disgusted"** that they had not been able to destroy any of the enemy aircraft.

Just before 10:00 another raid of seven Ju88s with an escort of four Me109 fighters approached the island. Flt Lt Heppell once again led off four Spitfires to intercept, including Ian. Unable to gain a position of advantage over the enemy aircraft Heppell ordered the Spitfires to dive back down to the airfield to land, which they did. But Ian's aircraft (AB300 GN-C) did not pull out of the dive and plunged into the sea close to the small island of Filfla. The other pilots believed that Ian might have been rendered unconscious by the violent diving manoeuvre. Alternatively his controls may have locked solid as the aircraft plunged down at great speed. Flt Sgt Ferraby wrote:

'Why they didn't just turn towards the 109s. I don't know. Cormack blacked out and spun in.'

It seems more likely that he was actually shot down by Obl Gerhard Michalski of 4/JG53 who made a claim for a Spitfire destroyed at the time. Ian's cousin Fg Off Ronald West, who had been flown in a Sunderland to the island during February, made several sweeps over the area around Filfla in search of Ian, but his body was never found.

The Scottish newspaper the Northern Scot carried an article on Ronald West announcing:

'Moray fighter pilot, Flying Officer Ronald West, (from) Lossiemouth, who has been awarded the D.F.C. for gallant service, vowed a few months ago to avenge the death of his cousin and boyhood chum Sergeant Pilot Ian Cormack, son of Mr and Mrs Cormack (of the) Mintlaw Station Hotel, and formerly of Elgin. Sergeant Pilot Cormack lost his life in the defence of Malta.

'Flying Officer West, who has been in the Middle East for some months, has already amply fulfilled his vow. He has destroyed at least six enemy aircraft and damaged others.'

Ronald West later lost his life on May 24th 1944 in an accident whilst attempting to land an aircraft with a defective undercarriage.

Plt Off Peter Nash Wrote in his diary for Tuesday March 17th 1942:

'...More Raids. Flt Sgt Ian Cormack killed this afternoon. Ops are pinning too much faith in the Spits. They sent four against fifteen 109s and five 88s. Crazy.'

Ian had been described by Flt Sgt David Ferraby as a **"Slightly built chap"** his RAF records show him to have been five feet seven tall with black hair and brown eyes, and noted to be of very good character. David Ferraby also described him as **'Another good buddy.'** At school he had been described as showing **'keenness in everything he did, and popular with everyone who knew him.'**

The family headstone in Elgin cemetery (The War Graves Photographic Project)

His Squadron leader Stanley Grant wrote of him:

'He was conspicuous for his courage and cheerfulness.'

The body of 21-year-old Flight Sergeant Ian Maxwell Cormack was never recovered; his name is remembered on several memorials. The Commonwealth Air Forces Memorial in Floriana, Malta, where Ian's name is on Panel 3 Column 1. His name is also listed on the village war memorial in Maud, near Mintlaw, Scotland. In addition, the Elgin City War Memorial in the High Street, outside St Giles Church bears his name.

Ian is also remembered on the family headstone of his parents John and Constance Cormack who are buried together in Elgin Cemetery, Linkwood Road, New Elgin; Headstone reference NE(E)806.

He is also mentioned in the Roll Of Honour for both Elgin Academy and the Aberdeen Grammar School.

The Scottish National War Memorial consists of many books that comprise the Roll Of Honour, these are held in the Hall Of Honour in Crown Square, within Edinburgh Castle, Scotland. Ian's name is listed along with the names of over 200,000 other Scottish casualties of both the First and Second World Wars, and other subsequent military campaigns

Ian's name on the Malta Memorial in Floriana. Below also is the name of Murray Gass, who was withdrawn from the original list of Operation Spotter pilots.

David Lake Ferraby

David Ferraby was born on August 30th 1920 to parents David and Florence and their two daughters Joan and Margaret in Hornsea, East Yorkshire, a small seaside resort on the north east coast of England.

David's education began at St Bede's Preparatory School in Hornsea, followed by becoming a boarder of Bridlington School, Bridlington. Having completed his education he spent a short while working for a company of accountants in Hull before joining the family firm of Ferraby and Hare.

Ferraby and Hare based at Waterhouse Lane, Hull, were wholesale horticulturists and makers of traditional Chinese style matting bass bags, these bags were designed to carry fish and game whilst keeping the contents cool. In 1938 David tried to join the RAF Volunteer Reserve but at that pre war stage there were more volunteers than places and his application was unsuccessful. He was however able to enlist the following year as an airman under training with the service number 748048.

The town of Brough is located on the northern side of the river Humber approximately 12 miles from the city of Hull. In 1916 the Blackburn Aeroplane and Motor Company Ltd established a factory and an airfield there, changing their name later in 1939 to Blackburn Aircraft Ltd. It was here that David experienced his first flying training on June 3rd 1939, in a Blackburn B.2 biplane (G-ACBK). These were single engined biplanes with an all-metal fuselage, having fabric covered wings and tail, with a fixed undercarriage. The main difference from the other training aircraft of that period, the Tiger Moth, was that the pupil and instructor sat side by side, as opposed to tandem style, one behind the other.

'I joined the happy band of weekend flying blokes in May 1939 and started flying soon afterwards. I soon learned the elementary rudiments of controlling an aircraft, but am sorry to say there was too much time between flights, so only knocked up 20 hours before the "present emergency."

'When it started there were to many aircrews for the schools to absorb quickly so I amongst many others was given 3 months "holiday at home" on full pay. Then on December 6th 1939 we got moving at last, but to what a job. Almost 6 months of square bashing and ground school at I.T.W. Cambridge.'

David's 'square bashing' as he called it, started at No.1 Initial Training Wing in Cambridge on December 6th and continued until the end of May 1940. He then transferred to No.18 Elementary Flying Training School at Fair Oaks, Surrey. There his training to fly continued in de Havilland 82A Tiger Moths, with his first solo flight taking place during June. At this stage David was one of six on the course chosen to train as a fighter pilot, and he spent 10 days on a pre fighter course with No.10 Elementary Flying Training School at Yatesbury, Wiltshire. On July 20th he moved to No.15 Service Flying Training School, which at the time was flying North American Harvard training aircraft from airfields in South Cerney, Gloucestershire, and Chipping Norton, Oxfordshire, the latter being an Advanced Training Station. At the end of this period in October, David's Log Book was stamped with his proficiency as a pilot with his grade given as '**Average.**' Having been awarded his 'Wings' as a pilot, David was promoted to the rank of Sergeant.

On the 4th October David moved to No.7 Operational Training Unit based at Hawarden, Flintshire. Wales, or the '**land of mud and mist**' as David and his colleagues called it. Here the operational knowledge of established pilots with combat experience could be passed on to the pupils. One of these instructors, although he was only aged 19 at the time, was Fg Off Peter Ayerst. Peter had taken part in the Battle of France and the Battle of Britain and continued to fly operationally throughout the war. On October 8th Peter was the instructor pilot in a Miles Master dual trainer giving tuition to David, this flight was followed later the same day by David's first solo in a Spitfire (L1017). Weather conditions restricted flying hours during this training period, which continued until the end of October, so David was only able to get in six and a half hours flying in Spitfires before he was posted to join his first operational squadron.

David and three of his fellow 7 OTU trainees were posted to 611 Squadron at Digby, Lincolnshire, where they became operational with the squadron when they had amassed 20 hours of flying on Spitfires. David enjoyed his time with 611 noting that nearly all the pilots had cars and plenty of petrol for them. In December, 611 was moved further south where there would be more contact with the enemy but David was not considered experienced enough, so on December 2nd 1940 he was transferred to 222 Squadron based at Coltishall, near Norwich in Norfolk.

No.222 Squadron was still flying the MkI Spitfire and were predominantly involved in intercepting German aircraft and patrolling the coast. They also performed what was known as 'kipper patrols', which were the protection of fishing boats in the North Sea. David was in 'B' flight under the command of South African and former Battle of Britain pilot Flt Lt Brian Van Mentz DFC.

On February 17th whilst flying Spitfire MkI X4676, David claimed his first victory, which was shared with Sgt P. Davis. They had left Coltishall at 2:00pm to patrol the area around the coastal town of Sheringham. Ten minutes into the patrol a lone Junkers Ju88 bomber was spotted below them at 6,000 feet. The section dived down, led by Sgt Davis as Black One. Closing to 200 metres he open fired, which silenced the rear gunner. Sgt Davis continued firing until he ran out of ammunition. Although he believed he had hit the aircraft, there was no visible effect. He then swung off to fly parallel to the enemy aircraft, this allowed David flying as Black Two to start his attack. The Ju88 was trying to make evasive turns to the left and right to shake off the attackers. David fired a four second burst from 250 metres, followed by a two 2 second burst from 150 metres. At this point accurate return fire was once again returned from the rear gunner's position, striking David's aircraft. David expended the rest of his ammunition on the Ju88 and then both Black One and Black Two followed the aircraft out to sea for a further 3 minutes, by then the starboard engine was on fire. The German pilot was forced down into the sea, where the aircraft remained on the surface for around six seconds before sinking, only one crew member was seen swimming away near the tail. On returning safely to base David discovered that the return fire from the Ju88 that had struck his aircraft had put a bullet through each wing, one of which punctured the port tyre, the other had damaged the starboard rear elevator.

The rest of February and March 1941 continued with further patrols and scrambles to intercept intruding German aircraft, plus practise flights to include some dusk and night flying sessions.

Whilst at 222 David had a 1934 Singer car, a coupe, which, as most of the pilots did at the time, he was running in part on 100-octane aviation fuel, with the addition of some used oil to attempt to disguise the distinctive colour. One day in Newmarket the police stopped him and a sample of his petrol was taken which showed him to be using unauthorised fuel. Realising he could be in a lot of trouble later on when charged, the following day he put his name forward on a list of those wishing to serve overseas. He was just too late though, as the names had already been forwarded on. When the summons did come through it was mistakenly in the name of the passenger, another RAF pilot who had been with David in the car at the time, and because of this confusion David was never charged. However, his Commanding Officer was aware that he had got away with this misdemeanour, and ordered him to keep his car 10 miles away from their base for the next three months. David promptly sold the car for £30.00, the same price he had bought it for.

On April 26th 'B' Flights leader Flt Lt Brian Van Mentz DFC, was killed, when, just before closing time a bomb landed on the Ferry Inn public house at

Horning, Norfolk. This was one of the popular pubs frequented by the pilots of 222 Squadron, a member of its medical staff was also amongst the twenty people killed in the raid.

The following day David was on an early morning patrol having taken off from Coltishall at 6:50am with Fg Off John Burgess. Thirty minutes later they encountered a Ju88 approaching Great Yarmouth at around 8,000 feet. When the German crew spotted the Spitfires they dived their aircraft into the cover of clouds below at 5,000ft, pursued by the Spitfires, which were now closing in on them despite the defensive fire coming from the Ju88. At 400 metres Burgess began firing, but lost the bomber in the cloud. Emerging from the other side, and now at 350 metres, Burgess fired the rest of his ammunition. There was this time no reply from the rear gunner. With the port engine, on fire David continued the attack with a one second burst from 450 metres, then a one and half second burst from 250 closing to 150 metres, he observed strikes on the aircraft before it was lost in the cloud once more. As they were around sixty miles out to sea, operations called them to return back to base, so a 'damaged only' was all that they were able to claim.

Twenty-year-old Plt Off Bernard Klee was made commanding officer of 'B' flight and he signed off David's entries in his log book. Sadly, he was also killed a few weeks later on May 4th when, in the early hours, a Ju88 dropped seven bombs onto the airfield at RAF Coltishall. Fg Off Burgess and Plt Off Klee both set off in pursuit, but on catching the intruder, Klee's aircraft was struck by return fire from the Ju88 that sent it crashing down to the ground.

The role of 222 was becoming more varied with shipping convoy patrols, fighter sweeps in to occupied France and escort support to bombers attacking enemy targets. David noted that several times he returned from these sorties with bullet holes in his aircraft but he was never injured. On July 1st they were posted to the forward airfield of Manston on the south east coast for twenty days. This was followed by a period at Southend, before transferring to North Weald in Essex during the middle of August where they began receiving the new MkV Spitfire. Flight magazine in September 1941 lists that David was amongst serving RAF crew who had recently been wounded in action. It is not known how he was wounded or the extent of his injuries.

David stayed with 222 Squadron until the end of January 1942. He had made some good friends whilst with the squadron, and 40 years later they held a reunion but only 12 were still alive to attend, many of whom he remained in touch with thereafter.

Having previously volunteered for service abroad, in February David found out he was due to be posted to Malta and travelled to Portreath, Cornwall where he met the other pilots due to be posted overseas.

David flew Spitfire AB331 off the aircraft carrier HMS Eagle on March 7th 1942, a flight noted in his logbook as being of three hours forty-five minutes duration to Malta.

'Don't know how we were chosen for take off order, but I know I was the eighth. There was only room on deck for eight Spitfires at a time, to leave sufficient take-off run, so we went off in two lots.'
249 At War: Brian Cull, Frederick Galea (Grub Street 1997)

David flew for the first time on Malta on March 11th in Spitfire AB341/ GN-E when, along with three others Spitfires and sixteen Hurricanes, they intercepted an approaching raid by two Ju88s with an escort of six Me109s. The bombers turned away without attacking their targets but several dogfights broke out between the opposing fighters. David fired at a Me109 but no result was observed.

The following day David was scrambled twice, the first time no enemy was seen and on the second sortie he had to return to Luqa after fifteen minutes when oil from his engine obliterated the windscreen. He made two more flights during March but made no contact. April continued in the same manner with a scramble on the first day with Sgt Robert Sim, but again nothing was seen during the hour they were in the air together.

A further sixteen Spitfires had been flown off HMS Eagle in two deliveries to Malta. In Operation Picket I, nine Spitfires were flown off on March 21st. Eight days later seven Spitfires were successfully launched in Operation Picket II. With losses and unserviceable aircraft, there were by now more experienced Spitfire pilots than available aircraft on Malta. The Hurricane squadron 185 was, however, short of pilots so it was decided in mid April that some pilots with Hurricane experience would transfer from 249 to 185 squadron based at Hal Far under the command off Acting Squadron Leader Rhys Lloyd.

David did not have any prior experience on the Hurricane, yet he still transferred, possibly to stay with his fellow Operation Spotter pilot and good friend Sgt Robert Sim who joined 185, along with Flt Lt John Plagis. On April 13th David flew his first solo in a Hurricane MkII for 50 minutes, to gain experience of the aircrafts handling, with a further familiarity flight on April 28th. The same day he was scrambled as part of 'A' flight to intercept a raid but was not able to get into a position to fire his guns.

On May 2nd David flew two test flights in a Hurricane. A week later, on the 9th a second delivery of 60 Spitfires (46 had arrived on April 20th) flew off the USS Wasp and HMS Eagle to the island. David, now with 'B' flight, flew cover whilst they landed. This allowed 185 Squadron to replace their war weary Hurricanes for new Spitfires which all took on the squadron code of GL. On May 13th David tested BR294, one of the new fighters, followed later by a scramble in the same aircraft in pursuit of a reconnaissance aircraft, but he was unable to catch it.

Close to Hal Far airfield, where David was based, was an anti aircraft position manned by soldiers. One of them, David was surprised to find, was also called the fairly rare surname of Ferraby, but was no relation. The pilots spent quite a bit of time off duty with the soldiers and sometimes sheltered during raids in a cave that the soldiers used as a cookhouse. The gun post was later targeted by a Ju87 dive-bomber, which accurately unleashed its bomb killing many of the soldiers although no pilots were there at the time of the attack.

May 14th was to be a hard day for David with the loss of two of his colleagues from 185 Squadron. Around 9:00am the first raid came over the island, three Ju88s with a large escort of Me109 fighters. 28 Spitfires were scrambled to intercept, 5 were from 185 Squadron, led by Flt Lt Keith Lawrence, and included David, Sgt Tony Boyd and Sgt Colin Finlay. In the many dogfights that followed the meeting of the two opposing sides, David fired at six different Me109s but was unable to observe any results in the confusion. Colin Finlay was seen to be attacked by several Me109s setting his aircraft on fire, forcing him to bale out, but his parachute did not open and he plunged into the sea 400 metres off shore from Wied iz-Zurrieq. Two Maltese soldiers quickly launched a small boat undaunted by the German fighters still overhead and, after around ten minutes reached Colin, but he was found to be dead when brought ashore. The twenty-year-old pilot nicknamed "Ginger" from Sutton Valance, Kent, was buried in the Capuccini Naval Cemetery, Malta.

Within three hours another larger raid appeared, again a small group of Ju88 and Ju87 bombers protected by a large group of both German and Italian fighters. The bombers attacked Takali airfield, seventeen Spitfires and four Hurricanes were sent to intercept them. David, again flying with the Australian Tony Boyd, attacked the Macchi 202 fighters. David fired a five second burst of fire at one, which turned away pouring black smoke; this was claimed as probably destroyed. The Spitfire of Tony Boyd had been struck by the cannons of a German fighter, witnessed by Plt Off Tilley who was on the ground having his aircraft refuelled.

'A dogfight started overhead- some three Ju88s came in with 109 escort, ack-ack going like mad, bursts all over the sky - then I saw a 109 sit on

a Spitfire's tail and I heard the brr of cannon. The Spit rolled over and dived vertically in what appeared to be a controlled evasive manoeuvre, doing a series of aileron turns: there was no smoke trail and apparently he was OK but for some reason I felt he'd had it. Sure enough, he started to pull out to late, at 100 feet, then, when it looked as if he would make it, the pilot either died or lost consciousness and ploughed into the deck on the far side of the drome at 300mph. So at 13.05 hours the career of Sgt Pilot Tony Boyd came to an abrupt and spectacular end - just a terrific explosion and a long sheet of flame.'

Spitfires Over Malta: Brian Cull, Frederick Galea. (Grub Street 2005)

Tragically, both Colin Finlay and twenty-two year old Tony Boyd (whose first name was John, but he preferred to be known as Tony rather than that of his second Christian name, Livingstone), were tour expired and were due to leave the island on the next available flight to Gibraltar.

David provided details of his own combat in a report to the Station Intelligence Officer:

'I was Attire Yellow 2 and we were scrambled at 12:35 and told to gain angels as fast as possible. This we did with the information of 12 or so Ju87s coming in over the island. I first saw these when we were climbing hard and flying west over Hal Far. The E/A were then between St Paul's and Grand Harbour. We climbed towards them and passed 150-200 feet beneath going in opposite directions, we turned round behind them to their level and a general melee followed. During this, one of them, which we now saw were Macchis, slid down from the port side right into my sights about 150 yards range. I gave him a burst of 4-5 seconds, noticing pieces fall from him and black smoke. He then went into a spin which I observed for a couple of turns and then broke away, my guns still firing as they jammed. I did not see him again so I joined up with Red Section a few moments later, after all E/A disappeared.'

David flew several times during the next week but either, did not meet the enemy or, no result was observed from his firing after an engagement. On May 26th he was scrambled against a group of approximately 20 fighters and bombers and noted he was '**jumped**' three times in the dogfight but managed to evade them all successfully. 185 Squadron's sometimes-irreverent Operations book noted:

'During the afternoon the boys had two scrambles and were unfortunate to be jumped twice. F/Sgt Ferraby did some quick thinking when he discovered some Me 109s coming down, and found the rest of the formation unable to receive him on the R/T. He immediately turned into his number two, who did a quick break to avoid collision, causing the sky to become littered with Spitfires doing amazing evoloutions. However the Hun was foxed completely and beetled off home, muttering threats.'

May 28th saw Sqd Ldr Lloyd tour expired and command of 185 Squadron was passed to the newly promoted Sqd Ldr Keith Lawrence, a former Battle of Britain pilot.

At approximately 6:00pm David took off along with 3 other pilots from 185 Squadron plus four pilots from 126 Squadron. The Spitfires intercepted three Italian SM84 bombers intent on bombing Luqa airfield, with a large escort of RE2001 and Me109 fighters. David attacked and damaged one of the RE2001 fighters; he also had a quarter share in the destruction of a bomber, identification being difficult during the fast moving action within the dogfight. He believed it was a Cant 1007, a three-engined aircraft, one of the other pilots involved thought it was a Fiat BR20 bomber. Whichever it was, it was later confirmed as destroyed.

David wrote in his Logbook:

'Had a wizard time beating up the Eye-ties'

On June 11th David was promoted from Flight Sergeant to Pilot Officer (125759) but was unable to buy any new uniform due to shortages on the besieged island. He was, therefore, unable to show his new rank as an officer, so his Commanding Officer Keith Lawrence kindly lent him one of his old hats to wear.

After the coastal air base at Kalafrana had been bombed, David used some of the wood from the destroyed buildings and some canvas from the pre-war sailing club to make a canoe, using dope from the flying boat base to waterproof and shrink the canvas. When off duty he enjoyed many hours with his friend Robert Sim in the canoe or swimming.

Towards the end of June David had a close call with what today would be known as 'Friendly fire'. Four aircraft, led by Flt Lt Halford, had been scrambled by 185 Squadron to intercept six Me109s. One of the other pilots, Flt Sgt Shorty Reid, shot down a Me109 and David was in pursuit of another one when he was forced to pull out of the chase.

'I was diving very steeply down after a 109; didn't look at the speed, but the controls became very hard and it took all my strength to pull out without breaking something! I'd seen tracer going past me and that's what caused me to pull out. Probably just as well or I might have dived in. It was another Spit firing at me. Found out it was Halford firing at me.'

Malta: The Spitfire year 1942. C. Shores, B. Cull, N. Malizia
(Grub Street. 1991)

July continued with more interceptions. On the first day of the month David flew twice, firstly to attack a force of over twenty Italian fighters and bombers, but, although contact was made and he fired at the enemy, he made no claim. During the second sortie later the same day, he flew a patrol for just over an hour around the island of Gozo. On July 3rd he was scrambled three times and once on the fifth, but again no claim was made.

The only crashed aircraft David went to view whilst on Malta was of an Italian bomber, the wreckage burning with the dead pilot still at the controls. He said that he and the other pilots did not have the interest or the transport of any kind to move easily around the island looking at crashed enemy aircraft.

**David sitting on the wing of a 222 Squadron Spitfire in 1942,
a pose he recreated in 1986 (P Ferraby)**

On the morning of July 7th 'B' Flight were at readiness and were soon in action when a force of around 12 Ju88 bombers, with a large escort of 24

Me109s and 30 Italian MC202 fighters approached targeting the airfield at Luqa. A total of eighteen Spitfires took off, six from 185, the rest from 249 Squadron. The massed dogfight that followed the meeting of the two opposing air groups led to losses on both sides.

David's aircraft was one of those shot down by a Me109 fighter setting his Spitfire (AB500) on fire. He described what had happened:

'The first two Spits to take off left a dust cloud right down the track. I took off by myself as close to the dust cloud as I could. My No.2 failed to take off due to dust and I hoped I would be able to join up with some other Spits but, as was often the case, I didn't see a plane in the sky and climbed to 10,000 feet by myself. I can't have kept a good enough look out, because soon there was a loud bang and flames belted into the right side of the cockpit. The hood was open (we mostly flew with them open for better visibility) and I pulled the harness release handle and shot half out of the cockpit. I have very long thighs and my knees jammed on the rim of the windscreen. Still got the scars. So I had to pull myself back in and straighten my legs. The parachute had caught on the head pad, which stuck out a few inches behind one's head. The plane was going down at about 450mph with engine still on -forgot to shut throttle – and there was no control from stick. Anyway, got out in the end and pulled ripcord. I much enjoyed floating down and saw a Spit circling me. Turned out it was Dodd, a good pal. Just missed a ten-feet high wall in a village; 'chute went in over the wall and I landed in a lane. I suppose all the women who gathered round didn't know if I was English or Jerry, but they kept touching my bleeding knees for some reason; burns were just down my right leg from knee down. I'd been flying in shorts and gym shoes!'

Malta: The Spitfire year 1942. C. Shores, B. Cull, N. Malizia
(Grub Street 1991)

The burns and other injuries David sustained meant that this was his last combat flight over Malta and he spent the following six weeks in Mtarfa Hospital.

David had landed in the village of Zebbug and believed his Spitfire had crashed into the sea.

'As far as I can tell, my Spitfire after I'd baled out, showed a plume of smoke for a while and flew itself, gradually losing height, till it more or less landed in the sea somewhere: I should think on the south east side of

the island.'
Battle Over Malta: Anthony Rogers (Sutton Publishing 2000)

Research by the author Anthony Rogers found that another pilot, Flt Sgt Tommy Parks from 249 Squadron, had been shot down by anti aircraft fire around the same time as David. He also baled out and landed in the village of Zebbug. John Galea, a resident of Zebbug, believed David's aircraft crashed within the village not the sea.

'I am positive that both David Ferraby and his Spitfire fell in the same area, David against a wall in a narrow street…and his plane in a field not far from his fall…a woman who was a girl then…told me that she remembers seeing the plane going round in circles at speed until it crashed in a low lying field beside a chapel… I saw David sitting in a RAF jeep with those who came to pick him up just off the church.'
Battle Over Malta: Anthony Rogers (Sutton Publishing 2000)

On the outskirts of Zebbug, in 1998, wreckage was found in a field directly below the Chapel of Our Lady of the Abandoned. An aircraft had indeed crashed here but it could not be determined whether it was David's, Tommy Park's or another pilot's.

On July 13th David was one of six pilots stood down from flying duties, the others included his good friends Flt Sgt Robert Sim and Sgt William Dodd, who had ensured that David's recent decent by parachute did not come under enemy attack.

David left Malta having flown over 45 Operational hours over the island. He was fortunate in being unable to take the first of the two available Lockheed Hudsons off the island, as this crashed on take off. David recalled the cold of his six-hour flight to Gibraltar dressed just in shorts and a shirt. When he did reach Gibraltar he remained there for six days, before embarking during September, on a former passenger liner back to England. A further period of recuperation and leave followed before his next posting.

In October 1942 David began as an instructor at 61 Operational Training Unit based at Rednal in Shropshire. The unit had various aircraft including Miles Masters, Spitfires, Lysanders, twin engined Oxfords and Miles Martinets, which were used for target towing duties. Night flying training in Spitfires was also carried out at the satellite airfield of Montford Bridge.

Fatalities at training units were a constant reminder of the danger involved in teaching novice pilots. On December 14th a Spitfire of 61 OTU crashed in

Wales whilst on a training flight from Rednal. The pilot, Sgt Degail, survived the crash but had broken both legs and was unable to move and died of exposure. The following day a Westland Lysander from the unit, which had been sent out to search for the Spitfire, was also lost when it was caught in a sudden downdraught. The pilot Acting Flt Lt D. H. Walder was killed.

In December David received confirmation of another promotion from Pilot Officer to Flying Officer. He continued at 61 OTU into 1943 with a period of six weeks spent at the Fighter Instructors School at Hullavington, Wiltshire, before leaving in February 1944, to transfer to another training unit.

No.57 OTU was based at Eshott, Northumberland, and also used an airfield at Boulmer approximately 15 miles away. Miles Masters and Spitfires were the main aircraft used by the unit.

Pupil pilot Edward Sparkes wrote home his first impressions on arrival.

'Have just arrived in Eshott, north of Morpeth Northumberland. Am even further off the map than when I was at Watton. There is a lot of Bull here, everyone is on their toes to salute and we get periodical parades. I do not think much of that side of it. Being new I am without friends as yet but am in no hurry until I can see the lie of the land. We are four to a nissen hut with a stove in the centre which is lighted about 4 pm.

'They are certainly going to keep us busy. We work literally from dawn to dusk and for the first three weeks there is not one hour free. Beyond that I have no idea as the orders have not been posted. The food here is truly excellent. A very unusual mess in that respect. These Spits are wizard kites and I enjoy being here and being among the chaps who have done the work in the famous tussles.'
Contents Of The Mumblings of Edward Sparkes (Web site 1998)

In the Imperial War Museum, Lambeth, London, is Spitfire MkI R6915, a surviving aircraft from the Battle of Britain, 1940, during which it achieved three confirmed kills. It is displayed suspended by cables from the ceiling. This aircraft was almost certainly flown at some later stage by David as it spent six months between October 1942 and March 1943 at 61 OTU whilst David was there. Then, coincidently after being damaged in an accident and having been repaired, it then went to 57 OTU and was there for 2 months at the same time as David.

In July 1943 David was once again posted to an operational squadron when he joined 64 Squadron based at RAF Ayr at Prestwick on the west coast of

Scotland. The squadron flying MkV Spitfires were mainly involved in convoy patrolling but also under took air sea rescue searches and reconnaissance flights. During the first week of August the squadron moved to RAF Friston, approximately five miles from Eastbourne in Sussex, where they were engaged in coastal patrol work before the squadron moved once again, this time to RAF Gravesend on August 19th 1943.

No.64 Squadron began to be involved in escort missions to protect bombers attacking targets in France. On August 27th David was part of an escort for American Flying Fortress' flying through France to strike within Germany. The MkV Spitfires did not have sufficient duration to go all the way to the target and were forced to turn back, refuelling at RAF Hawkinge before returning to their base.

On August 16th Operation Starkey was launched continuing until September 9th. This was a feint attack by British, Canadian and American forces on Boulogne in the Pas de Calais region of the French coast, intended to divert German troops from Italy and draw the Luftwaffe into large-scale combat with RAF fighters over the channel. Bombing was carried out against airfields, fuel dumps, transport links, industrial targets and gun positions. The final day of the operation saw the most Naval activity with over 350 ships sailing towards the French coast, although no large Capital ships were involved. After approximately 90 minutes sailing the large armada received the codeword 'Backchat', which was the signal to perform a 180-degree turn and return back to their English ports.

David was involved in providing air cover for 18 Lockheed Ventura bombers attacking targets around Boulogne on September 4th. On the 8th he flew as protection to bombers attacking the airfield at Cambrai, then, on the 9th he flew above the armada of ships. The Operation, on the whole, was not deemed a great success, as the Germans did not take the bait and failed to respond in large numbers to the ruse.

During the first week of September 64 Squadron moved to RAF West Malling, Kent, where it continued with escort work and sweeps over northern France attacking ground targets, these were known as Ramrod missions. Around this time David met up again with one of the original Operation Spotter pilots when Flt Lt John Plagis, DFC and Bar, joined the squadron.

They were not to serve together for long as David was once again posted in October to Flying Training Command to be an instructor, this time with 41OTU at RAF Hawarden, Flintshire, North Wales, and later at RAF Poulton, Cheshire. The unit operated Miles Masters and Harvards, leading the pupils on to being able to fly the Hawker Hurricane MkII and North American Mustang MkI.

In November David spent a week at the School of Artillery at Larkhill, Salisbury Wiltshire, then he returned to 64 Squadron, which had moved to RAF Coltishall, Norfolk. He only spent a further two months with the squadron before joining No.2 Flying Instructors School at Montrose, Scotland, where he commanded 'C' Flight as an instructor using the twin engined Airspeed Oxford. On the 12th April 1944 he was posted to No.11 Advanced Flying Unit at Calvely, Cheshire, again instructing on Oxfords with the emphasis on night flying and cross-country navigation exercises. Whilst with the unit in June, he was promoted to the rank of Flight Lieutenant.

On August 16th David spent a week on a course at No.1 Beam Approach School, RAF Watchfield, Oxfordshire. The school used Oxfords and Ansons carrying painted bright yellow triangle identification. They were fitted with equipment that received two radio transmissions as a way of finding and lining up an aircraft onto the runway, designed to be used in poor visibility, due to weather or at night. The two transmissions were one of the Morse letter A, the other of the letter N. When on the correct course for the runway a continuous tone would be heard instead of two tones. The aircraft would either have had a blind screen to block visibility out of the cockpit during the training, or it had green windows with the pilot wearing red tinted goggles that allowed the aircrafts instruments to be seen but did not allow vision out of the cockpit. Further training continued for David at the Beam Approach Training Flight at Newton, Nottinghamshire.

In January 1945 David was posted overseas to India where he instructed recruits to the Indian Air Force, initially at No.1 Service Flying Training School, Ambala and then at Poona. A variety of aircraft were available including Oxfords, Harvards, Vengeances, Hurricanes and Spitfires.

On February 28th David was awarded the Air Efficiency Award, which was granted for efficient service in the Auxiliary and Volunteer Air Forces of the United Kingdom and the Commonwealth.

In May 1946 David, by now with the rank of Squadron Leader, left the air force to become a civilian. During his time with the RAF he had been known by many of his colleagues as Nick, he claimed, though, that he never did know why.

David rejoined the family firm of Ferraby and Hare Ltd and travelled to Hull every day by train from his home in Hornsea, Yorkshire. In 1948 he met Pamela Naughton, who also made the same train journey from Hornsea to her job in Hull with the toiletry and pharmaceutical company Rekitt & Coleman. The couple started seeing each other and David introduced her to his great interest of motorcycling. At the time he owned four motorbikes, one of which he later had fitted with a sidecar for Pamela, although she was not content to sit just in the sidecar, and later she passed the test to gain her own motorcycle license.

In April 1950 David and Pamela were married, and in May the following year their first child, Nicholas, was born, with another son, John, in 1954. Two years later they welcomed a daughter Barbara.

David stayed with the family firm until 1972 when he became disillusioned with the company and decided to leave. He then became a postman happily walking the streets of Hornsea, the town he was born in. Around this time he also went back to his love of motorcycles. He particularly enjoyed repairing and riding old machines and both he and Pamela became active members of the Vintage Motorcycle Club. The couple also enjoyed caravan holidays together and David was able to combine their two hobbies by adapting their own caravan to carry a motorcycle.

In 1985 David was able to spend more time on his interests when he retired from the Post Office. In May 1992 he made his only visit back to Malta to coincide with the fiftieth Anniversary of the award of the George Cross to the island. The celebrations welcomed Queen Elizabeth and, with the President of Malta Dr. Censu Tabone, they

David on a return visit to Malta in 1992 (F Galea)

inaugurated the Siege Bell in Valletta, a ten tonne bronze bell now rung daily to honour the 7,000 people who lost their lives in the 1940 –1943 Siege of Malta.

David Lake Ferraby died on 17th November 2007 at the age of 87 after a short period in hospital. He was cremated on the morning of 22nd November with a memorial service held in the afternoon at the United Reform Church, Hornsea. His ashes were interred at the Edenfield Cemetery, Marlborough Avenue, Hornsea.

Stanley Bernard Grant

The Grant family had been indigo planters in Bhagalpur, India from around 1800. They were involved in growing Indigofera, the plant from which indigo dye is obtained. In February 1911 Harry Alexander Gwakin Grant married Marjorie Gladys Hoyle at Christ Church, Lucknow, India. The couple had five children, two daughters and three boys, all born in India with the exception of their last child Stanley, who was born at Sendhurst Grange in the village of Send near Guildford, Surrey.

Stanley was born on May 31st 1919, and, along with his two older brothers Cecil and Robert, was educated at Charterhouse Public school in Godalming, Surrey. Cecil joined the army and served with the Royal Tank Regiment during the Second World War. Robert went to university at Cambridge and then studied medicine at St Bartholomew's Hospital. He later joined the RAF, rising to the rank of Squadron Leader and after the war he became an Orthopaedic Surgeon.

In January 1937 Stanley passed the stringent selection process required for RAF Cranwell, Lincolnshire, and started a two-year course as a Flight Cadet, enabling him to become a permanent Officer in the RAF. During his time there he became a Flight Cadet Corporal, and represented the college at soccer. He graduated from the course on December 17th 1938 and was awarded the rank of Pilot Officer, service number 33417.

Stanley was able to build up the number of hours he flew gaining plenty of flying experience during the 'Phoney War,' the period of little military activity between the declaration of war in September 1939 and the invasion of the Low Countries and France in May 1940. Early in 1940, Stanley joined 65 Squadron, a part of 11 Group Fighter Command then based at Northolt, Middlesex. The squadron was equipped with the Spitfire MkI fighter, which was armed with eight Browning.303 machine guns in the wings.

In March the squadron moved further forward to Hornchurch in Essex, where two other Spitfire squadrons, 54, and 74, were also based. Three chimneys from the nearby Ford factory made a convenient reference point for the pilots when seeking the airfield prior to landing.

On the morning of May 17th the squadron, led by Squadron Leader Desmond Cooke, flew a patrol of twelve aircraft to Ostend and along the coast. The Battle of France, which had begun only a week earlier, was not going well for the allies. The troops of the British Expeditionary Force had begun to be pushed back, along with French and Belgium forces, towards the coast at Dunkirk. Here, surrounded by the Germans, a defensive perimeter was set up, protecting around 500,000 allied troops now trapped and awaiting rescue.

Within the grounds of Dover Castle are tunnels dug into the white cliffs of Dover, originally constructed as barracks for troops in 1797, during the threat of a previous invasion by Napoleon, a naval headquarters was set up under Vice Admiral Bertram Ramsay. Here plans were laid down for the rescue of the trapped forces, using the limited number of naval vessels available, along with a flotilla of commandeered boats and ships of all sizes. Operation Dynamo, as the plan was called, began on May 26th 1940 with the intention of retrieving around 45,000 troops. With the benign weather and the failure of the German forces to push forward their advantage, at the end of the nine-day operation over 338,000 men had been rescued. What was a retreat became looked upon as almost a victory due to the large number of men saved.

On the early morning of that first day of the withdrawal of troops, Stanley was also in action. Sqn Ldr Cooke led twelve aircraft of 65 Squadron over France in the region of Calais where they met 20 Me110 aircraft flying in four groups of five. An air battle followed in which Cooke damaged the engine of one aircraft, Pilot Officer Nicholas struck the engine of another, and Flying Officer George Proudman set another aircraft on fire, witnessing it crashing below. Stanley fired 1126 rounds during the engagement, which resulted in a victory for him, described later in his combat report:

'The Squadron had engaged several Me110 and individual dogfights were in progress when I attacked an enemy aircraft from the rear. I fired a two second burst at 450 yards but saw no effect. Then I fired a further 4 seconds burst closing in to 200 yards and smoke appeared from one engine. I broke away as another of our fighters engaged. I then attacked another Me110 as another of our fighters broke away. I fired several bursts and the enemy aircraft lost height rapidly, finally crashing to the ground.'

The following morning Stanley was once again in action in the Calais area as part of a squadron of twelve aircraft. At around 7:50 a group of Dornier 17 aircraft were seen and engaged. Stanley reported:

'I was No.2 in Green Section when we sighted twelve Do.17s in Vics of 3. I attacked No. 2 of one section from astern firing bursts totalling about 8 seconds with no apparent effect. I broke away and attacked No.2 of another section from below with a burst of 4 seconds which silenced

173

the lower rear gun. I broke away to the right and keeping the same level as enemy aircraft, came in again and fired the remaining ammunition in an astern attack by which time the enemy aircraft had dropped back from his formation considerably, with smoke coming from one engine.'

Stanley claimed a shared probable, possibly in conjunction with Flying Officer George Proudman who also fired at one of the Dorniers, but was then struck by return fire from one of it's gunners, wounding him in the leg, the bullet passing clean through and ending up in his parachute pack. Stanley wrote of his colleague:

'George Proudman was one of the stalwarts of the squadron; he used to smoke his pipe in the cockpit while climbing to gain height, a foolhardy thing to do but amusing at the time. Always the joker he kept our spirits up when things were looking black but we finally lost him early in July. I think, when the convoy attacks started in the first phase of the Battle of Britain. I was on a few days leave at the time when the whole of Green section failed to return. Had I been there I would probably not be writing this letter because I always flew in that section.'
Air Battle For Dunkirk. Norman Franks. (Grub Street 2000)

At one in the afternoon the remaining eleven Spitfires of 65 Squadron, without Fg Off Proudman, made their second sortie of the day. Fifty minutes later, north of Dunkirk, they encountered a mixed force of bombers flying in groups of three and five at around 7,000 feet. Sqn Ldr Cooke led them into the fight. Two of the German aircraft were seen to crash after the attacks with several others damaged. Stanley made a claim for another probably damaged:

'I was leading Green Section when we encountered a great many Me110s just north of Dunkirk. I attacked from above and slightly behind one Me110 which was doing a steep turn. I kept inside his turn firing all the time, and used about three quarters of my ammunition. I then broke away because another Me110 was approaching my tail, by which time my targets rear gunner had ceased fire and smoke was pouring from one engine.'

On May 28th the pilots of 65 Squadron were woken early to prepare for the first of their two patrols that day, but only eight aircraft were still serviceable after the recent air battles. Due to the much greater numbers of German forces 65 Squadron had begun to operate as a wing with the Spitfires of 19 and 54 squadron.
Stanley noted:

'All our aircraft were damaged in one way or another and when, after one last sortie over the area on 28th May, we were withdrawn to Kirton-In-Lindsey to refurbish. Practically every aircraft had a bullet through the main spar which technically made them unfit to fly even in transit! Three days later we returned to Hornchurch but by this time it was all over bar the shouting.'
Air Battle For Dunkirk. Norman Franks. (Grub Street 2000)

It was June 5th when 65 Squadron returned to Hornchurch. During the month their role included reconnaissance and offensive patrols over Northern France, plus the protection of shipping in the channel, wth practise combat exercises also carried out whenever possible.

On June 17th Stanley was promoted to the rank of Flying Officer, and was no doubt proud to wear his new rank on his uniform ten days later when King George VI visited Hornchurch along with Hugh Dowding, to present medals to some of the pilots based there.

The Battle of Britain officially started on July 10th 1940 with attacks on shipping in the English Channel, although there had been many encounters with German aircraft prior to that date. Two days earlier Sqn Ldr Desmond Cooke had been shot down into the sea, and on the 9th Stanley was in one of three sections from 65 Squadron detailed during the afternoon to intercept raiding aircraft off the Kent coast near North Foreland:

'I was No.2 of Blue section patrolling over Margate when I sighted 6 Me109s which we attacked. I attacked an enemy aircraft from above and behind. I fired a 3 second burst and white smoke poured from the aircraft. He dived but I did not follow because I knew there were at least 2 other enemy aircraft behind me. I fired very short bursts at two other Me109 with no apparent effect.'

Following the death of Sqn Ldr Desmond Cooke, Sqn Ldr Henry 'Sam' Sawyer took over command of 65 Squadron, frequently leading them from the forward airfield at Manston. Soon after taking command he was also killed, on August 2nd when his Spitfire stalled during a night-time take off. Sqn Ldr A L Holland subsequently took over command of 65 Squadron.

On August 5th the Chief Test Pilot for Supermarine, Jeffrey Quill, joined 65 Squadron in order to gain operational experience of flying and fighting in the Spitfire. During his time with the squadron he was involved in several air combats, resulting in the destruction of an Me109 and the shared destruction of a Heinkel

175

bomber. He was recalled 19 days later back to Supermarine. The experience he had gained led him to improve the vision through the side panels of the Spitfires cockpit, with the rear view enhanced by changes made to the canopy and the rear fuselage. He also recommended that the fabric-covered ailerons be changed for metal ones, which required less force on the control column at high speeds.

At the end of August the squadron were posted to Turnhouse in Scotland, becoming a part of 13 Group, this allowed a period of rest, and enabled replacement pilots to be trained. The squadron also carried out some patrolling but no contact with the enemy was made. At the end of November the squadron once again moved forward this time to Tangmere in Sussex for more patrol work and convoy escorts.

In February 1941 Stanley became an instructor at 55 Operational Training Unit based at Usworth, 7 miles south east of Newcastle. The unit had at this stage mainly Hurricane MkI aircraft; here Stanley endeavoured to pass on his flying experiences from the Battles of France and Britain to new pilots before their first posting to an operational squadron.

By August, Stanley, now promoted to Flight Lieutenant, had returned to 65 squadron as a Flight Commander, 65 were then stationed at Kirton-in-Lindsey, Lincolnshire, flying the Spitfire MkII on Circus operations- the escorting of a small number of bombers over northern France, protected by a large number of fighters.

The squadron often flew from the forward airfield of West Malling, Kent.

Stanley wearing a 'Mae West' life jacket in 1941 (F Galea)

On one occasion, on the afternoon of August 21st they were flying as part of a wing with 121 and 401 squadrons on a patrol around Gravelines in France. Stanley was leading three aircraft from Red Section of 65 Squadron when around 15 Me109s began diving out of the sun through the Spitfire formation, and then back up again. One of these 109s was claimed as shot down. The Spitfires, now running low on fuel, turned for home, but when crossing the French coast they came under fire from anti aircraft guns. Stanley believed he saw a Spitfire plunge down out of control trailing white smoke behind it.

Two aircraft were missing from Stanley's Red Section, but it was not known how or when they had disappeared, or whether it was the result of the flak or the German fighters. Sergeant Baxter became a prisoner of war, but 21-year-old Sergeant William Kay was killed, his recovered body was later buried at Dunkirk.

In December 1941 Stanley was posted to 601 Squadron as a Flight Commander and continued forays into northern France. No.601 had recently been the first squadron to trial a new aircraft, the American Bell Airacobra. The aircraft turned out to be a poor performer above 20,000 feet and not as fast as anticipated, engine problems meant the trial finished early, and by the time Stanley joined, the squadron had re-equipped with Spitfires.

In the Operation Spotter file held at the National Archives at Kew, Surrey, there is a list of the pilots who would take part in the first flight to Malta. Flight Lieutenant Stanley Grant's name is at the top of the list, below him is Flight Lieutenant Norman Macqueen's name, the title Squadron Leader prefixes Macqueen's rank. This may have been an administrative error, or perhaps later the decision may have been changed, because it was 22-year-old Stanley who was promoted to acting Squadron Leader and it was he who led the Spitfires to Malta.

On the day of the flight to Malta the pilots were waiting for the wind to increase to a level, which, added to the speed of the wind over the aircraft carrier, would enable them to take off safely. Stanley was apparently asked to meet the ships Captain, where he was politely offered, and accepted, a glass of sherry before his onward journey.

Stanley was the first to fly off the carrier leading seven other aircraft behind him. Followed by Flt Lt Norman Macqueen leading a section of six behind him, both flights landed safely at Takali airfield on Malta.

Although now a Squadron Leader, Stanley and 249 Squadron were both under the firm leadership of the Canadian Squadron Leader, Stan Turner. He, along with several other pilots, had flown to the island aboard a Sunderland aircraft the previous month.

Stanley's first flight on the island was the second day the Spitfires went into action on March 11th. Stanley in Spitfire AB262/GN-B led four Spitfires, joining 16 Hurricanes intercepting a raid made by two Ju88s, with an escort of six Me109s. The bombers turned for home before dropping their bombs when they were engaged, with a number of dogfights between the opposing fighters taking place over the Grand Harbour. Stanley fired at two 109s, one of which was seen to be heading down to the sea upside down and it was awarded to him as probably destroyed.

On March 14th Sqn Ldr Turner was promoted to Wing Commander in charge of the Takali Wing, allowing Stanley to take over command of 249 Squadron, which he had been told he would lead before he was posted to Malta. He still flew whenever he could and, on the afternoon of the 17th he damaged a Me109 that was part of an escort to Ju88s bombers attacking the airfields. A week later on the 25th he was able to claim another two victories. A large formation of Ju88s and Ju87s had approached the island targeting the Grand Harbour and the shipping within. Stanley attacked one of the Stukas destroying it, Plt Off Plagis also claiming one shot down. Plagis was then attacked by one of the escorting Me109s and received damage to his aircraft. The 109 was chased by Stanley who caught it, shooting it down into the sea just off Gozo. The pilot Fw Max Fischer was able to bale out, and was later rescued by a Dornier 24 air sea recue aircraft based in Sicily.

April 1st saw Stanley involved in several combats during the day. In his first encounter in the morning he damaged a Ju88 over the Grand Harbour. At approximately 16:30 a Do24 rescue aircraft, with Me109s for protection, was seen five miles off Valletta, Stanley led a flight of Spitfires into attack, claiming a 109 as damaged. Later the same afternoon a force of over fifty Stukas, with escort, approached the harbour and were intercepted, Stanley claiming one Ju87 as probably destroyed and one as damaged.

Early on the morning of April 21st a force of over 35 Ju88s and around 30 supporting Me109s commenced a series of raids on the airfields and the Grand Harbour. Six of the bombers, that had just bombed Luqa were intercepted and Stanley and Plt Off Plagis singled one out. Stanley attacked first, setting the starboard engine on fire, followed by Plagis who did the same to the port engine, with no reply now coming back from the rear gunner. The aircraft was seen diving steeply toward the sea pouring smoke from both engines and was credited as destroyed, the victory was shared between the two pilots.

On April 29th Stanley was informed that Group Captain Woodhall would be coming later that day to the officers mess at Xara Palace, Mdina, to see him along with Flt Lt Laddie Lucas, Flt Lt Ron West, Flt Lt Buck McNair and Fg Off Daddo-Langlois. When Woodhall arrived they gathered for drinks together, then went to the privacy of the Intelligence Room at the end of the terrace overlooking Takali. The group were then informed that they were to bring in the next delivery of Spitfires that were to be flown in off the American aircraft carrier USS Wasp, in conjunction with HMS Eagle. They, the most experienced pilots, would leave by Hudson aircraft the following night to go to Gibraltar to meet with Wing commander John McLean who had been involved in previous aircraft transfers to Malta, including Operation Spotter.

A preceding delivery from USS Wasp, Operation Calendar, on April 20th had successfully delivered 46 Spitfires, but, within 48 hours, constant bombing and strafing had reduced the number serviceable to only 7. This time, for the next delivery, code named Operation Bowery, preparations had been made for each aircraft once landed. The Spitfires would be met and then led to a protective enclosure, where they would be quickly refuelled, rearmed and then flown back into the air at the hands of an experienced Malta pilot, all within 15 minutes of the Spitfires touching down.

Stanley had the chance to take some rest away from the constant bombing whilst at Gibraltar and enjoyed the benefits of proper meals unlike the severe rationing imposed on Malta. A week later Wasp left with fifty Spitfires aboard, along with HMS Eagle carrying a further 17 fighters, both under the protection of an escorting Naval force which included 9 Destroyers.

At 06:43 on May 9th Stanley led off the first flight of 16 Spitfires to Takali, followed by Flt Lt Ron West leading another flight to land at Luqa. However, not all went as planned with the rest of the delivery, one aircraft failed to gain height and plunged in to the sea, disappearing beneath the carrier which was unable to avoid crushing it beneath the keel, the body of Flt Sgt Bob Sherrington the Canadian pilot was not recovered. Another pilot, Plt Off Jerry Smith, found his extra fuel tank was not delivering fuel, and therefore he did not have sufficient fuel to be able to reach Malta, he subsequently made an unauthorised landing safely back on the carrier. Two other Spitfires failed to reach the island having attacked an Italian Floatplane, they either collided with each other, or more probably the floatplanes fighter escort shot them down.

The other three 249 pilots who went to Gibraltar with Stanley, remained there until the aircraft carrier Eagle had returned, they then led nine days later another delivery of 17 Spitfires (Operation LB) to Malta.

Stanley was not prepared to just rest after his arrival back on Malta, and by 11:00 he was leading a flight of the new Spitfires into the air, to protect against a large incoming force of bombers and fighters that were attempting to destroy the reinforcements whilst still on the ground. Both sides lost aircraft in the ensuing air battles. The next day the German forces again attacked the

A DFC Medal ribbon now adorns
Stanley's uniform, June 1942
(F Galea)

airfields. Stanley, leading a flight in response, claimed a Ju88 shot down, which was seen to fall in flames. The anti aircraft gunners, however, also claimed one destroyed, and possibly they both fired at the same aircraft.

In June Stanley was awarded the Distinguished Flying Cross the London Gazette published confirmation of the award on June 5th the citation read:

'This officer is an excellent fighter pilot. On one occasion he led a force of fighter aircraft over many miles of sea to Malta. On the same day, after his aircraft and been refuelled, he took off and destroyed a Junkers 88. For the rest of the day he remained at the head of his squadron in a series of fierce battles over the island. He has destroyed at least 4 enemy aircraft and damaged many more.'

The citation stated that he shot down the Ju88 on the same day as the delivery flight, the 9th. Although Stanley did fly immediately on return to the island, his claim for the 88 was actually made on the following day the 10th. Whichever day it was, Stanley was certainly a very deserving recipient of the award. He was highly regarded by those who served with him; one of those was Laddie Lucas who wrote of him:

'Finely trained by the Royal Air Force in peacetime, Stan Grant knew how to run and lead a squadron. He retained firm overall control but delegated detail to his two flight commanders. He was an excellent officer to serve under. Not only was he thoroughly proficient in the air, but on the ground he took the view that a flight commander was there for one purpose-to manage his flight. He left things to him. If all went well, the maximum encouragement and the minimum interference were dispensed. If things went badly, the reaction was sharp and immediate.'
Five Up. Laddie Lucas. (Sidgwick and Jackson 1978.)

'Stanley Bernard Grant, an English officer of stature, looks and impressive credentials. Charterhouse and Cranwell educated, Stan Grant fastened an easy, yet assertive grip on 249 the moment he took over. He knew what he wanted from the unit and what he expected from his subordinates flight commanders.
'After my first half hours talk with him, I was certain we would hit it off in the exceptional circumstances, which we both knew, weren't easy. He was efficient, liked things to be buttoned up and expected his flight commanders to get on with the job without being told. He didn't interfere provided we delivered the goods. He stood back until it was necessary to intervene...

'I could see at once he was a good general in the air, never selfish or individualistic, but always with a comprehensive grip of what was going on. He seemed to be thinking of his clutch, but that didn't stop him going hard for an opening if he saw one. When he could, he got in close to the enemy and wouldn't let go. He flew precisely and accurately and this made his aircraft a good gun platform. From what I saw of him he didn't waste ammunition on unpromising targets, he shot when he reckoned he was in with a worthwhile chance to score. This wasn't always a common habit. I judged him to be a high class all rounder.

'Stable and friendly... he was undoubtedly at his best when under the whip, and the enemy was certainly getting it out now."
Malta: The Thorn In Rommel's Side. Laddie Lucas. (Stanley Paul 1992)

Stanley's humour can be seen in a discussion he had with Plt Off Jeff West regarding what was known as Malta Dog, a form of dysentery, which induced diarrhoea from which most of the pilots suffered at some stage.

Stanley: 'How are you today, Jeff?'
Jeff: 'Better sir, thank you. I could do a trip of forty minutes, no more'.
Stanley: 'But Jeff, can you fart yet without danger? That's always the test'.
Jeff: 'Not yet sir, but I don't want to'.
Stanley: 'Right, then you're stood down'.

Brian Noble, the author of Hero, wrote a biography of the maverick, yet gifted Canadian pilot George 'Buzz' Beurling, who would be the highest scoring ace on Malta and go on to be credited with 31 victories during the war. Nolan describes a meeting between Stanley and Beurling, where Stanley asked Beurling if he was interested in being promoted to the rank of an officer. His stark reply was only one word **"No."** Stanley, realising he would make no headway with Beurling, equally curtly responded, **"You may leave."**

On June 10th a flight of nine Beaufort torpedo bombers were on their way to Malta from Gibraltar, a radio message had been received asking for help from the aircraft as they were under attack. Stanley led off eight Spitfires to meet the aircraft, but before they could reach the aircraft they were redirected to intercept a large formation of Italian bombers and fighters coming towards the island, additional Spitfires were also scrambled to join the defence. Stanley, flying Spitfire BR170/C-25, was able to shoot down a RE2001 fighter into the sea, the pilot, believed to have been Serg Giovanni Dringoli was killed. This was to be his last action for a while as Group Captain Woodhall had deemed him to be due a rest, and so on June 24th Laddie Lucas was promoted to take over as the new Squadron Leader of 249.

Stanley was also promoted to become acting Wing Commander. He spent a week at the RAF command centre in Lascaris, Valletta, and then on the 30th he was posted to a staff job at RAF Headquarters in Egypt.

Stanley would not be away from the island for long. During August 1942 he returned and took over the command of the Takali Wing comprising 229, 249 and 185 Squadrons, after Wing Commander Arthur Donaldson had been wounded. One of his first actions was to reduce the number of operations from Takali, to remove the danger of attack, accidental or otherwise, on the nearby Mtarfa Hospital, and instead used Krendi airfield, relocating 249 and 229 Squadrons to be based there from November onwards.

Although designated as Wing Commander (Flying) his chances to fly, were

Sqn Ldr Stanley Grant and Group Captain "Woody" Woodhall (Centre) with two colleagues in Malta, July 1942 (M Woodhall)

much less than previously because of his administrative commitments. He was despite this able to claim his last two victories on December 11th 1942. Stanley, flying Spitfire EP622/T-P, was leading eight Spitfires as escort to six Beaufighters, the group were on an offensive patrol close to the islands of Pantelleria sixty miles off Sicily, and Kirkennah off the Tunisian coast. Midway between the two, is the small uninhabited island of Lampione, and it was at this point the fighters met a formation of Ju52 troop carrying transport aircraft flying at sea level. Flying with them were three BF110s and two Ju88s, plus an unidentified four-engined aircraft all flying around 1500 feet above, and acting as escort to the Ju52s.

In the fierce air battle that took place the Beaufighters claimed the destruction of five of the Ju52s with others damaged, although with the loss of one Beaufighter. The Spitfires initially tackled the escort, Stanley sharing in the destruction of one of the Bf110s with Plt Off Bill Locke. In the confusion, several pilots made claims for the destruction of the Bf110s, one crashed into the sea and the other two force landed on Pantelleria. The Spitfires then focused on the transporters and Stanley was one of the two pilots who each made a claim for destroying one of the Ju52s. This was to be his last victory of the war.

By November 1942 Malta had five operational Spitfire squadrons and now, with very few bombing sorties being made against the island, it had moved more to the offensive. Bombing attacks on Sicily, with Spitfires carrying up to 500lb of bombs beneath their wings, now became a regular task of the squadrons, particularly against trains and transport targets. Stanley led the escort on one such attack in early January. This time the target was Comiso airfield, with explosions seen on the buildings and runways, all part of the softening up of Sicily prior to the invasion that would take place seven months later.

At the end of January 1943 Stanley was awarded a bar to his DFC for his part in the attack on the Ju52 troop carrying aircraft, the citation stated:

'In December 1942 this officer flew the leading aircraft of a formation acting as escort to a force of fighter-bombers. During the flight, 63 enemy air transports escorted by five twin-engine fighters were intercepted. Leaving the fighter-bombers to attack the transports, Wing Commander Grant led his formation in an attack on the enemy fighters, all of which were shot down. This officer, who displayed great dash, destroyed two of them. He has participated in many sorties and, as a result of his outstanding work, much success has been achieved. He has at all times proved himself to be an inspiring and courageous leader.'

The quoted figure of 63 enemy transports in the citation is curious, Stanley had written of the incident:

'...We suddenly saw twenty four Junkers 52s, escorted by one Junkers 88 and four Me110s. We took a heavy toll.'

In May 1943 Stanley was moved away from front line action and took up the first of a series of staff jobs. The first of these being with 203 (Training) Group at RAF Heliopolis in Egypt, who were responsible for the operational training of all units in the Middle East. The Battle of Britain pilot Billy Drake, who had also been with Stanley on Malta, was also with 203 Group at this time, and mentions in his biography his happiest memory of that period was drinking with and getting to know Stanley.

Stanley as Commander of H Q British Forces Gulf in 1968
(www. acesofww2.com)

This posting may have been followed by a period at an RAF Staff College, possibly leading on to his next move in May 1944, when he became Command Training Officer at the Advanced Head Quarters Mediterranean Allied Air Force in Italy.

In January 1945 Stanley was Mentioned In Despatches, a military award for bravery or commendable service issued by the King. He was to receive the same award again the following January.

After the war Stanley continued in the RAF working at the Air Ministry as Director of Policy from 1946. In 1948 he was posted to Flying Training Command based at Shinfield Park, Reading, Berkshire. In 1948 Stanley also found time to get married in Westminster to Miss Barbara Jean Watts, the couple would later have a son and a daughter.

In June 1955 Stanley became Senior Air Staff Officer for 13 (Fighter) Group, which had been disbanded in 1946, but was then reformed once again.

His stay would not be long, for the following year, he became a Staff Officer in Bangkok, Thailand, for the Southeast Asia Treaty Organization. SEATO was planned to be a Southeast Asian version of the North Atlantic Treaty Organization (NATO) in which the military forces of each country would be coordinated to provide for the collective defence of all the other member countries.

Stanley's stay in Asia was for three years until July 1959 when he returned to England with the rank of Group Captain to take over command of RAF Stradishall in Suffolk. The airfield had front line jets based there including the Gloster Javelins of 85 Squadron and Hawker Hunters from 1 and 208 Squadrons.

**Air Vice Marshal Stanley Grant CB DFC and Bar in 1969
(www.acesofww2.com)**

In January 1962 Stanley, recently promoted to Air Commodore, attended the Imperial Defence College at Seaford House, Belgrave Square, London, in preparation for his next posting, which was on December 21st when he became Assistant Chief of Staff (Intelligence) at the Allied Forces Head Quarters at Fontainebleau in France, one of two NATO strategic command centres. This was followed by a return to England three years later, when in July 1965 he became Senior Directing Staff (Air) at the Imperial Defence College, London.

In 1963 Stanley's wife Barbara had died. Later, when he returned to Fontainebleau, he met Christiane Marie Py (nee Bech) and they were married on May 31st 1965, which added a stepson and two stepdaughters to his family.

A final promotion was awarded to Stanley on January 1st 1966 when he was made Air Vice Marshall. Two years later on April 4th he was made Commander of British Forces in the then Persian Gulf. In 1969 he was awarded a C.B. The Most Honourable Order of The Bath, Companion.

The Times newspaper announced in November 1969 that Stanley was to be Air Officer in charge of Administration at Strike Command. This role, if he took it up, may have been his last with the RAF. Strike Command based at RAF High Wycombe in Buckinghamshire was the successor to all the wartime commands such as Fighter Command and Bomber Command.

Stanley retired the following year in June 1970 possibly on health grounds, at the age of 51. He moved to Brignoles in Provence, Southern France remaining there until his death aged 68 on July 4th 1987.

James Joseph Guerin

James Guerin was born on January 12th 1914 to parents Daniel Joseph and Mary Guerin, in Wollongong, a port city approximately 50 miles south of Sydney in New South Wales, (NSW) Australia. At the end of his school education he worked for three years at the Mount Isa Mines in Queensland, NSW, involved with the smelting of copper, lead, silver and zinc. He left there to work for four years as a Furnace man, in the production of steel, at the Broken Hill Proprietary Company, known locally as B.H.P. in Newcastle, NSW.

On June 26th 1940 James enlisted to join the Royal Australian Air Force at the No.2B mobile unit in Hunter Road West, Newcastle. Later that year, on the 9th December, at the No.2 Recruitment Centre in Sydney, he signed his enlistment papers for **"the duration of the war and twelve months thereafter."** His personal details noted that he was, aged 26, 5 foot 7 tall and weighed 168lbs. He had to have a medical examination and, although he had lost the top from his index finger on his left hand, he was passed fit for flying duties.

James became an AC2 (Aircraftman second class) service number 403136 and was sent to the No.2 Initial Training school at Lindfield, NSW to be taught the basics of military life. On February 6th 1941 he joined Course 9 at No.5 Elementary Flying Training School at Narrowmine, NSW, to begin the basics of learning to fly in the Tiger Moth Biplane. At this stage he received his first promotion to LAC (Leading Aircraftman). Whilst at the training School one of the things he was required to do was to complete his Last Will And Testament, which he did on March 1st, officially witnessed by two of the flying instructors.

James (centre) whilst at 57 OTU Haward, Cheshire in September 1941 (C Shores)

On April 3rd 1941 he was posted to No.2 Embarkation Depot, RAAF Bradfield Park, NSW, where he was supplied with his full kit and underwent a final medical examination. His flying training continued abroad under the Empire

187

Air Training Scheme. On April 22nd 1941 he embarked at Sydney Harbour to set sail to Canada, where he arrived on May 14th 1941 at Vancouver, he then travelled by train on to his next base.

From May 16th James was attached to the Royal Canadian Air Force, based at No.11 Service Flying Training School at Yorkton, Saskatchewan, in western Canada. James's flying training continued on the Tiger Moth and the Harvard MkII, a fast two-seat monoplane training aircraft. The course culminated two months later on July 27th when he successfully gained his 'Wings,' the coveted badge of a pilot, and a promotion to Pilot Officer.

In early August James travelled to No.1 'Y' Depot in Halifax, Nova Scotia, to await embarkation by ship to the United Kingdom where he would become attached to the RAF. On August 9th he passed through No.3 Personnel Reception Centre in Bournemouth where the Commonwealth pilots were first sent prior to their next posting. James then went on to No.57 Operational Training Unit based at Hawarden, Flintshire, in North Wales, his initial flight with the unit is listed as September 7th and his last on October 11th. During this time he flew a Spitfire for the first time. Between the 14th and 27th October 1941 James was able to enjoy two weeks leave before joining his first operational squadron.

James was posted to 501 Squadron, which was at the time based at RAF Ibsley in Hampshire, although the pilots would also fly from RAF Warmwell in the neighbouring county of Dorset. The National Archive Of Australia holds only limited details from James's Flying Logbook. It is known that on November 8th he took part in a patrol over a shipping convoy, and on December 12th a scramble from base to intercept an unidentified aircraft.

On December 18th he flew an escort patrol to Brest to protect bombers flying to the French port, where they attacked the two German Battle Cruisers Scharnhorst and Gneisenau, a similar mission was flown on December 30th in Spitfire W3840. These two ships, along with the Heavy Cruiser Prince Eugen, had been trapped in the docks whilst undergoing repairs and maintenance and were repeatedly attacked by the RAF until their daring escape through the English Channel in February 1942.

During the end of November and into December, James had two further weeks of leave. His logbook shows him to have also taken part in another scramble on January 6th 1942. Having at some stage volunteered for service outside of the UK, James was advised later in the month of his posting to Malta.

The diary of Plt Off Peter Nash mentions that he and James went into Blackpool for a drink and dinner at the Clifton Hotel on February 9th, the evening before they were due to leave by ship. They returned to their base at

Kirkham, near Preston, around 11:00pm where they stayed up untill 1:30am drinking and talking with the padre.

On arrival on Malta, James joined 249 Squadron along with the other pilots who had flown from HMS Eagle. With the surplus of pilots in comparison to the 15 Spitfires available, it is probable that James may not have flown many times between his arrival on the 7th and his death two weeks later.

The Maltese village of Rabat is set just beyond the dry moat and substantial bastions of Mdina, the old capital of Malta. It has commanding views across the island, making it an ideal location for the guesthouse, named the Point de Vue, which was built there in 1889. During the Second World War it was requisitioned by the RAF to be used as an Officer's Mess and billet for the airmen based at the nearby Ta-Kali airfield.

On the afternoon of March 21st the island suffered several raids by Ju88 bombers against the airfields. Bombing from a greater height than previous raids, bombs were scattered over a large area with many residential districts being struck. A large bomb fell in Rabat, just outside the main entrance of the Point de Vue hotel, killing five pilots, one of whom was James Guerin. Another 249 Squadron pilot, Fg Off John Booth, was also killed, plus two from 126 Squadron, Flt Lt Cecil Baker and Plt Off William Hallett. An RAF intelligence officer, Flt Lt Arthur Waterfield, also died. Another pilot from 126 Squadron, twenty year old American Plt Off Edward Streets, who had lost a leg and been blinded during the raid, died later in hospital from his injuries.

Several other pilots who were in the area were lucky not to be killed, including Flt Lt Bud Connell and Fg Off Ron West who, along with Flt Lt Robert McNair known as 'Buck,' had just left the cinema in Rabat and were returning to the Point de Vue. McNair, who was caught in the blast, later vividly described the carnage that he witnessed as he reached the building:

'When I came round, I didn't know where I was. I didn't feel I was dead, I didn't feel whole. My eyes were open, but my jaw and chest didn't seem to be there. There was no pain, I just didn't seem to have jaws or chest. I felt for my tin hat, then I started to be able to see just as if the sun was coming up after a great darkness. I explored myself with my fingers and found that I had a face and a chest, so I felt better. 'It started to get light — the darkness had been due to the showers of dust from the stone building. I felt for my revolver, the one Stan Turner had given me at Hornchurch, back in England. I mucked around and found it, knocking the dust off it and checking it to make sure it was loaded. 'As I became more conscious, I found I was upstairs; but I knew I shouldn't be upstairs — I should be

downstairs. Then I realised I had been blown upstairs, either through a door or through an opening at the turn of the staircase. I'd been thrown up 20 or 30 feet.

'I went out onto the roof and back down the main staircase which was barely hanging in place. I saw the bodies lying at the foot of it. They were in a heap. There was no blood. The raid was still on — the All Clear hadn't sounded — but everything seemed very quiet. Heavy dust covered the bodies. I looked down at them, studied them. One was headless, the head had been cut cleanly away from the top of the shoulders. I didn't see the head, but I could recognise the man by his very broad shoulders.

'I heard a moan, so I put my hand gently on the bodies to feel which of them was alive. One of them I noticed had a hole, more than a foot wide, right through the abdomen. Another's head was split wide open into two halves, from back to front, by a piece of shrapnel. The face had expanded to twice its size. How the man managed to still be alive I didn't know. I thought of shooting him with my revolver. As I felt for it, I heard Bud Connell's voice behind me: "Look at this mess!"

'I put my hand against the wall, but it slithered down it. It had seemed dry with all the dust, but when I took my hand away I found it was covered with blood and bits of flesh stuck to it — like a butcher's shop when they're chopping up meat and cleaning up a joint. I turned to Bud. "For God's sake, don't come in here." Then I noticed that my battledress and trousers were torn and ripped.

The bombed Point de Vue guest house used as an Officers Mess in 1942 (Grub Street)

'Ronnie West appeared. It seemed natural to see him. He had been in the building with us, but he didn't say anything about me being there. He didn't seem to want to talk.

'Now an ambulance and a doctor arrived. The doc asked me to help him with the bodies. I said, "Get someone else, I've seen enough." But I did get one chap onto a stretcher. He was still alive, but I couldn't recognise him. I put a cloth over his face and then a stupid orderly took it off. It was the

190

most horrible sight I've ever seen and I've seen chappies with heads off and gaping wounds and horrible burns.

'The realisation of what had happened began to dawn very slowly. My left arm had gone out of joint when I was blown upstairs by the bomb, but I had shoved it back in place. Ronnie and I sat on the kerbside and talked about it. As we discussed it we began to understand the awfulness of it all. Then we started cursing the bloody Huns; it was maddening that all we could do to them was curse. We were inwardly sick, sick at heart.

'We decided to get drunk. When we got over to the mess, the orderly refused us anything to drink and wouldn't open the bar. We broke our way in and each took a bottle.....it helped relieve the tension.'

Buck McNair: Canadian Spitfire Ace. Norman Franks. (Grub Street 2001)

James' gravestone at the Capuccini Naval Cemetery, Kalkara

Flying Officer James Joseph Guerin, aged 28, was buried on March 23rd 1942 at the Capuccini Naval Cemetery, Kalkara. Plot E Grave 19. He lies in a shared grave with four others who were killed by the Point de Vue bomb. His name is also listed on the Australian War Memorial, Campbell, Canberra, on Panel 123 in the Commemorative Area. In 1944 his records stated that he was retrospectively promoted to the rank of Flying Officer with effect from January 28th 1942. This rank is on his grave, a promotion he did not live to see.

Philip Whaley Ellis Heppell

Philip was always destined to fly, being born into an illustrious flying family; his father Philip Forsyth Heppell had been a fighter pilot with the Royal Flying Corps during the First World War. He had survived being shot down in an aerial battle over the Somme in 1916, receiving gunshot wounds to his hands and legs. He was captured, and treated for his wounds, by the Germans, and remained a prisoner of war until the end of the conflict in 1918.

Philip senior's interest in aviation had not been diminished by his experiences during the war, and in 1925 he was one of the founder members of the Newcastle Aero Club based at Cramlington, Northumberland. The club moved a decade later to Woolsington, which later became Newcastle Airport, where the club had an aircraft fleet of 3 Gipsy Moths, one Puss Moth, one Tiger Moth and a B.A. Swallow.

In 1940 Philip senior rejoined the RAF in the Balloon Branch. He was transferred in 1941, holding the rank of Squadron Leader to the Administration and Special Duties Branch for the duration of the war. There he became a senior Administrative Officer at an U.S. Army Air Corps Training Centre, involved with the training of British pilots based in Alabama, USA. He finally retired from the RAF on health grounds in June 1945.

Philip, and his wife Dorothy, had three children, daughters Sheila, and Rhoda Elinor Fairbairn were born in 1920, and a son, Philip Whaley Ellis, who was usually known just as Whaley within the family. The children where taught to fly by their father as soon as they were old enough to do so. Rhoda gained her flying license in May 1939 at the age of 19 and went on, during the war, to join the Air Transport Auxiliary, ferrying new and repaired aircraft to airfields all over the country. She became the first woman to be commissioned as a Pilot Officer.

Whaley was born in Newcastle on June 24th 1921 and attended the Newcastle Preparatory School and then Uppingham School in Rutland. With war inevitable, Whaley joined the Royal Air Force Volunteer Reserve on June 26th 1939 at Newcastle as a pilot under training, (Service number 745110). He made his first RAF flight on July 3rd 1939 in de Havilland Tiger Moth N6599 with No.42 Elementary and Reserve Flying School at Woolsington, an airfield he was very familiar with. Two weeks later, although already a qualified pilot, he made his first solo flight whilst under training with the RAF.

On December 3rd 1939 Whaley began his basic training with No.3 Initial Training Wing at Hastings, East Sussex, being billeted in a local guesthouse. On May 13th 1940 he joined No.4 Elementary Flying Training School at Brough, Yorkshire, where further training continued in Blackburn B.2 bi-planes, followed by a period flying from RAF Cranwell, Lincolnshire. At the end of the course he was rated as **"Above average"** and commissioned as a Pilot Officer (Service number 86370) and was then able to enjoy a period of leave before starting, on September 28th, at No.7 Operational Training Unit at Hawarden, Flintshire, Wales. After one week of flying alongside an instructor in a Miles Master, he was able to make his first flight in a Supermarine Spitfire on October 5th 1940.

Ten days later he joined his first squadron, 616 based at Kirton-In-Lindsey, Lincolnshire, where he made his first flight from the base of 55 minutes in Spitfire MkI X4186 on October 24th. This officially made him a Battle Of Britain pilot as he had flown operationally between the official dates of the battle, 10th July to October 31st. Further familiarisation flying training continued over the next few days. On October 28th Whaley made a 30-minute local flight but, on returning to land at Kirton, instead of landing into wind,

'A' Flight of 616 Squadron taken early 1941at Tangmere . Back row Sgt James McCairns, Plt Off Heppell, Flt Lt Ken Holden, Plt Off 'Johnnie' Johnson and Sgt Sydney Mabbett. Front row Sgt Jeff West and Sgt Ronald Brewer (P Heppell)

the direction of which could clearly be seen from looking at the airfields windsock, he approached downwind; resulting in the aircraft landing too fast and over shooting the end of the runway, the Spitfire was subsequently damaged during the heavy landing.

The embarrassment for a new member of the squadron committing such a basic error was compounded by the entry written in his Logbook in red ink by Wing Commander Howard Burton:

'P/O Heppell crashed Spitfire X4330 at Kirton Lindsey... Due to GROSS CARELESSNESS in landing DOWN WIND'

Whaley made his next operational flight, an uneventful convoy patrol, during November, no doubt keen to make up for his error.

Rejoining 616 Squadron in December, after a period of recuperation from an operation on his shoulder, was a pilot who later became the RAF's highest scoring ace. James Edgar Johnson known as 'Johnnie' Johnson, wrote in his biography of the new officer who had joined 616 in his absence:

'A new member to the squadron was Pilot Officer Heppell from Newcastle. "Nip" as he was generally known, belonged to a well-known flying family, for his father had fought in the Royal Flying Corps and his sister ferried various aeroplanes across the country. Nip, not yet twenty was apt to be absent-minded and something of a dreamer, but once in the air he seemed to assume an entirely different personality, for he pressed home his attacks in no uncertain fashion. Since he was the youngest and most junior member of the squadron he was subjected to somewhat more than his fair share of leg pulling, which he accepted with a considerable amount of patience and good humour.'
Wing Leader. Johnnie Johnson. (Chatto & Windus1956)

Hugh Dundas, another pilot with the squadron, wrote along similar lines:

'Heppell- commonly known to one and all as 'Nipple' or 'Nip'- was very young, slightly built though tall and- misleadingly- rather soft looking... You would not have thought, when he joined us, that he could say boo to a goose. But he was an above average pilot, an intelligent man and an exceptionally brave one.'
Flying Start. Hugh Dundas (Stanley Paul and Co. Ltd 1988)

On February 26th 616 Squadron moved south to Tangmere, Sussex, and became a part of Douglas Bader's Tangmere Wing. The wing was now not a large mass of fighters but was made up of smaller units able to control a greater area of sky. The convoy patrols they flew later gave way to offensive patrols, with fighter sweeps flown into occupied Europe.

On May 9th 616 moved to Tangmere's satellite airfield at Westhampnett, a grass airfield close to the Goodwood racecourse, where there was more space available and the grass field was considered less likely to come under enemy attack than a more prominent airfield.

July 2nd whilst flying a MkII Spitfire with 'A' Section, brought Whaley his first victory, as he described, no doubt excitedly, in his Combat Report, which contained many crossed out and added words:

'I was Yellow Three when the squadron took off from Westhampnett at 11:50 hours. When over France we were patrolling slightly north of Lille when W/C Bader's section attacked about 14 109s. Three of these turned northwards straight for our section, I don't think that they had seen us. When they were (unreadable) with us and about 500 feet below on our port side I broke underneath my section leader in a steep turn, diving slightly and came up behind one of these aircraft which I recognised as 109Fs. I gave him a burst at about 250 yards but saw no result. The enemy aircraft then turned steeply to the left and I turned inside him, giving him a good 3 seconds burst closing from 150 yards to about 50. I saw a sheet of flame burst from the engine and a bit of the enemy aircraft flew off and hit my hood which it smashed the latter hitting me on the head. I pushed the hood over the side and looked to see where the e.a. had got to, I saw a parachute just opening and the machine going down in flames.

'This has been confirmed by other pilots of the squadron and is claimed as destroyed.'

He did not have to wait long for his next contact with the enemy. Eight days later on the 10th he was flying as a part of Wg Cdr Douglas Bader's Section with the call sign Dogsbody on another fighter sweep over France.

'I was Dogsbody 4 flying in W/C Bader's section and being number two to F/L Dundas. We took off from Westhampnett at 11:38 hours on patrol over France as high cover to the bomber escort. The Wing was patrolling in Calais area just prior to returning to Tangmere, when we sighted a section of 3 ME109s several thousand feet below travelling in the opposite direction in a wide vic. We did a half roll and dived after them and below attaining a speed of about 400mph. We were diving almost line abreast Wing Commander Bader on the left, Flight Lieutenant Dundas the centre and myself on the right, I was slightly father back than the other two. The e.a. on the right which I was attacking saw the other two delivering their attack and turned to the left just as I was about to fire. I fired at him on the turn for a few seconds and then broke under him, by this time he was going down in a gentle dive with glycol streaming from him, I also saw the aircraft which had been attacked by W/C Bader in a perpendicular dive on fire.

'I then rejoined my section and returned across the straits making landfall at Dover.'

It was only a couple of days before Whaley was again amongst the enemy whilst on another fighter sweep over France:

'I was Dogsbody 4 when the Tangmere wing took off from Westhampnett at 09:25 hours. F/L Dundas, Dogsbody 3, broke away just after the squadron was airborne because his R/T packed up. I then changed over to number 3 position.

'The wing crossed the French coast just south of Boulogne and did a sweeping turn over France and up towards Gravelines at about 25,000 feet. Just south of Calais we saw 6 Me109s flying in a westerly direction at roughly the same height. The e. a. were flying in line astern and so Dogsbody Section turned to the left to engage. The 109s had apparently not noticed our arrival. We picked the back 3, Sgt Smith taking the fourth one Wing Cmdr Bader the fifth and I took the last at the end of the line.

'I opened up at about 250 yards firing until I saw the Wing Cmdr breaking in front of me. I then turned in behind the e.a. who took evasive action giving him a burst while he did a gentle diving turn to the right. Suddenly he went into a steep dive and I followed him down firing at him. Just before I broke there was a big stream of glycol come from him and something appeared to fly off from underneath his belly.

'I then broke away violently as I thought one of the other 109s might be following me. The last I saw of the e.a. it was still in a vertical dive with glycol coming from it. I then managed to find Sgt Smith and a few minutes later found the Wg Cdr, and continued our patrol. Sgt Smith had said that he had seen this e.a. diving down with glycol coming from it. This 109F is claimed as damaged.'

Although primarily a daytime fighter pilot, Whaley was also expected to fly at night, making constant reference to his instruments to ensure the aircraft was flying in the correct attitude. It was easy to become disorientated with the ground below being invisible, as it would have been during the blackout with no lights showing. Many pilots were quite happy to admit they did not like flying under these conditions.

One evening Whaley was retuning to Tangmere low on fuel and requested a homing signal to help him find the airfield. At the time German bombers were dropping their loads nearby at Southampton. Smoke from both the bombing, and the reply from the anti aircraft guns made visibility even worse. Whaley became worried by how close the gunfire from the ground was to him, and above him was further danger. At 5,000 feet above him was a Beaufighter night fighter flown by Johnnie Topham who was closing in on a Heinkel bomber, he fired hitting one of the bomber's engines causing the aircraft to dive down. Topham followed in pursuit determined to ensure its destruction. Flying through the murk, Topham saw a white light in front of him, which he took to be the Heinkel and fired at it, but it was in fact the rear light of Whaley's Spitfire. Luckily the Spitfire was not hit but Topham, recognising the aircraft for what it was, and now in front of it, felt sure that the pilot would assume that he was an enemy aircraft and come after him.

Both pilots however landed safely. Topham found out from the controller who had been flying the Spitfire and came over to apologise, and thanked Whaley for not firing at him. Whaley told Topham that with everything going on around him he had just wanted to land, adding **'That's the last bloody time they get me up at night.'**

It was, of course, not the last time, and Whaley was involved in another nighttime incident whilst flying from Westhampnett. He was waiting his turn to land and had been asked to switch on his navigation lights by Ken Holden, the officer in charge on the ground, and to circle the airfield at 2,000 feet while the other Spitfires took their turn to land. Finally Whaley was the last

Whaley with a war weary looking Spitfire (P Heppell)

Spitfire remaining waiting to land. The controller, looking up, was astonished to see the red and green lights on the edge of Whaley's wings changing places- he was passing the time doing slow rolls, forgetting his lights would give him away. The controller called to him to 'cut it out' and land straight away. Whaley became alarmed at realising he had been caught out and, now somewhat distracted, he came in immediately to land, making a perfect approach, but he had not realised that his undercarriage was not down, and landed the aircraft on its belly and ploughed it into the grass runway. He was uninjured, except for his pride at the foolish mistake he had just made.

On July 21st Whaley flew twice, both times making contact with German fighters:

'I was Red 1 when 616 Squadron took off from Westhampnett led by W/C Bader at 07:40 hours. We crossed the French coast at approximately Le Touquet at about 24,000 ft, my section being stepped up to the right of the W/C. When we reached Lille we went into a left-hand orbit and I led my number 2 into line astern of the leading section. A 109 dived underneath the section in front and I gave chase with my number two. The e/a turned diving towards the East and so I broke away after giving him a burst at about 400 yards.

I then found that I lost my number two and so turned around and joined the bomber escort. Just before we reached Gravelines two e/a dived to the right-hand side of the escort, with a Hurricane I gave chase and they dived inland. I again broke off as getting low and the Hurricane had left. I climbed up and was some distance behind the bombers when I saw two e/a coming up astern. I did a climbing turn to the right and stall turned meeting them head on. They both fired at me and I could see from the tracer coming from the wings that they were 109Es. Another two arrived which were 109Fs. I did a violent evasive action of every type I knew, firing occasionally. I then fired at one who came straight through my sights and was a 109F. I very nearly collided with him. I did a steep turn to the left to avoid another who was firing at me and saw that the one I had just fired at was going down in a gentle dive with black smoke coming from him, one of the other 109s went after him. I then went into a steep dive doing turns over the coast and the last I saw of the one who had followed the smoking e/a, he was weaving about him. The other couple dived away to the South West. I then returned at sea level. About four miles from Dover I saw an e/a flying at sea level. I found it was a 109E and squirted it all around one turn without result. My ammunition ran out and I saw another 109 preparing to attack me from above. I did some very steep half turns and went hell for leather for Dover. I saw the 109s climb up to about 4,000ft five miles off Ramsgate. I landed at Hawkinge to refuel. I claim the 109F with smoke as probable.'

The second contact this day was made in the Merville area of France during the late evening, the events were written later in his combat report:

'I was Dogsbody 4 when 616 Squadron lead by W/C Bader took off from Westhampnett at 19:50 hours. While on patrol over the target area our section was flying in an Easterly direction when about 6 Me109s were sighted travelling to the south and about a thousand feet blow us. Our section did a steep turn diving slightly. I took the e/a on the extreme right, diving slightly below him until I was within range. I then pulled up getting my sights on to him and giving him a burst with cannons and machine guns from dead astern. Then someone called over the R/T telling us to break as there were more e/a behind us. Just before I broke I saw glycol start to stream from the 109 and his nose dropped slowly and went into a steep dive. I then lost sight of the e/a in my turn and Red 1 (P/O Johnson) gave him a squirt. When I had turned around and seen there was nothing close behind me, I looked down and saw e/a was about five to ten thousand feet below still in the same attitude, pouring out glycol and black smoke. I then joined up with some other Spitfires, who were shooting at other 109s, who were diving for the ground.

'Shortly afterwards we made our way back to the coast coming out over Boulogne, where we received very heavy and accurate flak. We made landfall at Dungeness, without any further excitement, and returned to Tangmere.'

Whaley claimed one as probably destroyed shared with Plt Off Johnnie Johnson. During this sortie Johnson's wingman, 21-year-old Sergeant Sydney Mabbett, was shot down, his body was recovered by the Germans and buried at St Omer.

Whaley and Johnson were good friends who often went hunting wild fowl together, something that they continued to do once a year after the war. In his biography, Johnson tells of a time when the two friends drove to Brighton one afternoon, the local Padre kindly lending them his car. After having dinner and a few drinks the pair picked up two other pilots in the early hours of the morning and set course back to Tangmere, Whaley at the wheel while the others slept. Going through Hove, Whaley heard shouting and confusion and glimpsed some sort of barrier in the road but continued on. Later the little car began to over heat and the engine to run roughly. The next day when they examined the car they spotted a bullet hole below the rear window. Following the trajectory of the bullet it had passed, luckily, between the two pilots in the backseat and between Johnson and Whaley in the front, finally exiting via the cars radiator. The confusion the night before had been a military checkpoint, which they had blundered through without stopping.

August 9th was to be a memorable day for Whaley. The Tangmere Wing was to be part of Circus 68 providing cover for a bombing raid on Bethune. Three sections from 616 Squadron met with a further twelve Spitfires from 610 squadron. In addition 41 Squadron were due to join the wing but were not at the rendezvous point at Beachy Head so the wing continued on without them.

The Form F Combat Report again gives Whaley's account of his days action, whilst flying Spitfire MkVb W3456, a presentation aircraft from the Watford Spitfire Fund, in Hertfordshire. It had Watford and the town's coat of arms painted on its side, plus the word Audentior, meaning bolder.

'I was Yellow 3 when 616 Squadron took off from Westhampnett at 10:40 hours. Shortly after crossing the French coast south of Boulogne, the squadron went into a left hand orbit. After a few minutes about 20 109Fs were seen to the east and several thousand feet below, climbing up over white cloud. W/C Bader led the squadron in to attack in a steep dive, when I got down to their level the e/a had split up.

'I climbed up to the right and saw a 109F come up in front of me. He appeared to be on the top of a stall turn and so I gave him a long burst closing to point blank range. I saw on the side of his aircraft as he turned to the left a large '6' just behind the cross on the fuselage. He then went in to a very slow gliding turn to the left and I had vivid view of his hood flying off and the pilot jumping out of his machine. I watched him falling and turning over and over until he had dropped down to some low white cloud, his parachute had still not opened so I assume he was killed. This a/c is claimed as destroyed.

The camouflage was a dirty grey and black in addition to the usual cross there was a 6 behind it, the tail was painted orange and the spinner black and white.'

As well as being the day Whaley achieved his second confirmed victory, he would recall this as the day that the legendary Wing Commander Douglas Bader was shot down. Research carried out by the author and aviation historian Andy Saunders, whilst researching who had been responsible for the shooting down of Sqd Ldr Douglas Bader, identified the German pilot who had been shot down by Whaley, as twenty one year old Unteroffizier Albert Schlager of 3/JG 26 he was flying only his second combat mission. The young pilot's parachute had failed to deploy when he bailed out, and he plunged to his death near the village of Widdebrouck, France.

Bader, who had to bale out of his aircraft, on this mission, believed his aircraft had been brought down in a collision with an Me109, that resulted in his aircraft losing its tail. Feldwebel Max Meyer of II. Jagdgeschwader 26 claimed that he had shot down Bader. Historian Andy Saunders, however, believes that Bader may have been shot down in error by one of his own side.

Flt Lt 'Buck' Casson, claimed an Me109 shot down around the same time noting that the **"..tail came off and the pilot bailed out."** Flt Lt Casson's aircraft was also damaged on the same sortie and he was forced to crash land near St Omer where he was captured and became a prisoner of war.

Bader survived bailing out; during which one of his false legs became trapped in the cockpit pinning him to the aircraft, until its bindings to his body broke away. He became a prisoner of war, which later included a period at the notorious Colditz Castle.

The pilots of 616 Squadron had not seen Bader once the combat started and so no one was sure as to when or where he had been brought down. On landing, the aircraft were quickly refuelled and rearmed and a search for the two missing men was set in motion led by Hugh Dundas, with Whaley and Johnnie Johnson volunteering to go along. It was believed that the two missing men might be in the sea close to the French coast so a low level search was started, at one point a dinghy was seen but it proved to be empty. Whaley spotted something unusual in the sea and went for a closer look, deciding it was a small enemy submarine he opened fire at it without result. They searched until their fuel became low, then flew to Hawkinge to refuel and afterwards started back again to France to continue the search, but within a short period Group Captain 'Woody' Woodhall recalled them all back to their base at Westhampnett.

Whaley Heppell, his uniform bearing the DFC ribbon won in September 1941 (P Heppell)

It was five days before news of the two pilots being prisoners was received. 'Woody' himself gave the news over the Tannoy at the airfield, before rushing off to see Bader's wife Thelma.

Ten days after Bader had been shot down, Circus 81 (a bomber escort) was flown late in the morning. Six Blenheim bombers with a large fighter escort were detailed to bomb the power station at Gosnay, near Bethune. There was also another objective for this mission, the Luftwaffe had agreed to the RAF dropping a replacement leg for Douglas Bader on to St Omer airfield. Whaley was part of the escort in Spitfire Vb W3456. The leg was parachuted safely down from Blenheim R3843 in a crate marked with the Red Cross symbol. With the leg dropped the truce was considered over and the airfield was then attacked. The main mission, the bombing of the power station, was however cancelled due to poor weather.

In September recognition was given to Whaley with a promotion to the rank of Flying Officer and the award of the DFC. The citation read:

'This officer has participated in thirty-three operational sweeps over enemy territory. He has destroyed two and damaged a number of other enemy aircraft. Throughout, Pilot Officer Heppell has supported his leader with great courage and skill.'

On October 7th 1941, 616 Squadron were transferred to RAF Kirton-In-Lindsey for a period of rest, where they were predominately involved in flying monotonous patrols over convoys in the North Sea.

January was a month in which Whaley, now with a further promotion to the rank of Flight Lieutenant, was able to fly without coming into contact with enemy formations. Flying became for him, practising manoeuvres such as line astern and formation flying, plus aerobatics with air firing and cine gun camera work also included. By the end of the month his logbook showed he had flown 170 operational hours including 410 hours on Spitfires. Squadron Leader Colin Gray, Officer Commanding 616 Squadron, endorsed his logbook with an assessment of his flying as being **'Above Average'**.

Having previously volunteered for overseas service, he was now ready for his next posting which turned out to be Malta. Whaley described how he found out the news:

'Drinks were coming in fast at the Haycock Inn, Wansford, on Friday, 29th January 1942, at about 9:00pm. When in came our C.O. Colin Gray, to say that I had been posted as a Flight Commander to Malta. The party ensued with my old friend Johnnie Johnson pushing the boat out in a big way.

'Having only moved to Kingscliffe that day, and being only half unpacked, to be faced with another immediate move was confusing- with a large size in hangovers I succeeded in catching the 10:15 to Kings Cross.

'I recollect thinking that I had not done too badly to get my kit aboard leaving my Churchill shotgun and golf clubs in Johnnie's possession.

'I was unable to think why I should be heading for Portreath in Cornwall. I was sure that the posting to Malta, which Wing Commander Ken Holden at 12 Group H.Q. had asked me about a few days earlier, could not sail from there. I had given my acceptance provided it was not on "Hurricanes"- By now totally outclassed by the Me109F.

'Suddenly I remembered I was short of cash and I was arriving in

London after 12pm on Saturday. This presented a problem. On arrival I took my baggage by taxi with my last pound or two to Paddington for the evening train. Returning to the Berkley Hotel I phoned the four people I knew in town – no answer – all away at the war, and the banks were closed. The Berkley did not cash cheques for Flight Lieutenants without a reference. Having only about 30 shillings left, I drifted into Green Park to think. Sitting watching a robin and the snowflakes falling, I thought Oh for a friend with some cash; I had a rather deserted feeling.

'As dark came I took a tube to Paddington and sat reading the Evening News but the blackout lighting was very bad.

'I had calculated that I had enough for 2 drinks and the train was leaving about 11pm so I went into the Paddington Hotel Cocktail Bar. I recall thinking time goes very slow in such circumstances.

'Suddenly I spotted a one-armed ATA pilot (formerly a film stunt man) coming over, and there was Captain Corrie, a friend of Douglas Bader, who had come to see us on many occasions on deliveries at Tangmere.

'On telling him my predicament he said, "I know the Manager and he will cash you a cheque" – which was promptly done.'

On February 1st Whaley reported to RAF Portreath in Cornwall to be kitted out for his new posting and to meet some of the other pilots. Plt Off Peter Nash noted in his diary: **"Flight Lieutenant Philip 'Nip' Heppell arrived. Good lad".** On the 3rd he began a weeks leave at home in Newcastle and in London prior to his embarkation to Malta and his new squadron 249 based at Takali.

The Spitfires first went into action on March 10th but the day before Whaley flew a 25-minute flight to test a Spitfire's cannons, firing at the small island of Filfla situated 3 miles south of the cliffs of Dingli.

At around 10:30 on Tuesday 10th seven Spitfires, along with eight Hurricanes from 185 Squadron, took off from Takali to intercept a bombing raid by Ju88s and their escort of Me109s. Whaley flying Spitfire AB262/B described the events:

'First Spitfires operating from Takali with Wing Commander Stan Turner leading, and I led the 2nd section of four, we climbed to over 20,000 feet to intercept 3 Ju 88s and 4 Me109Fs. There was some layered cloud and the sections lost contact. I spotted 8 German aircraft about 3 or 4,000 below and immediately attacked getting a long burst into the first Me109 which slowly turned over onto its back and dived into the sea just off the Grand Harbour. I must have hit his slipstream at close range and the shock partly inverted the Spit and made me think I had been shot from behind – I pulled into a steep turn and jettisoned the canopy and called my No2, who said all was well and he was still with me. My No3 P/O John Plagis also destroyed a Me109 and P/O Nash damaged another.

'Landing at Takali I saw a Hurricane on the approach with wheels and flaps down being attacked by an Me109 warned him on the R/T and he successfully took violent evasive action narrowly saving his life.

I held a post mortem with Stan Turner and admitted to surprise that we had lost contact, clearly my fault.'

During this sortie, Whaley fired all his ammunition claiming the first victory for a Spitfire over Malta and also the first for a Spitfire not based in Great Britain. Both Plt Off Plagis and Plt Off Leggo confirmed his claim. The victim was Fw. Heinz Rahlmeier from 8/JG 53 who was killed his aircraft Black 11 crashing into the sea. The elation of the first success was quickly tempered by the first loss, the Australian Plt Off Murray, killed on the same sortie.

The following day Whaley flew against an incoming raid but no contact with the enemy was made this time. On the 13th he flew Spitfire AB264/H and operated alongside several Hurricanes in trying to protect the airfields from a bombing raid by Ju88s and their escort. He wrote in his logbook:

'Me109F Damaged. Attacked by 109s, followed one to sea level and got cannon strikes on fuselage lost sight of enemy aircraft in haze. Squirted at Ju88 guns ran out no effect.'

On March 15th he was directed up and beneath six Ju88s and their escort and attacked, but saw no result from his fire. Early on the morning of the 17th Whaley flew a forty-minute patrol in search of a Liberator aircraft, which had left Gibraltar the previous day but had not arrived in Malta, no trace of the aircraft was found.

Later on Whaley led four Spitfires along with eleven Hurricanes against a force of Ju88s and Me109s that were attacking Luqa airfield. Just before 10:00am another group of seven Ju88s, with four protecting Me109s, approached the island and once again Whaley, flying AB334/J, led four Spitfires into attack. Climbing up under the fighters, the Spitfires were attacked by four Me109s who were quickly reinforced by another twelve. Now in a dangerously disadvantaged position, Whaley decided it was better to withdraw rather than fight the much greater number of enemy aircraft and called for the Spitfires to dive down to low level over the sea, where they could not be attacked from below, and return to the airfield. During this manoeuvre Flt Sgt Ian Cormack's aircraft plunged into the sea near Filfla island, possibly the pilot blacked out in the dive, or more likely he was shot down by one of the opposing fighters.

With the loss of another Spitfire, pilot Whaley must have no doubt spent time considering whether he had made the right decision in heading back for the airfield. Flt Sgt Ferraby later said, **'Why they didn't just turn towards the 109s, I don't know.'**

Whaley flew seven times during the rest of March, including a patrol over an incoming supply convoy, and to cover the arrival of a squadron of Hurricanes that had flown in from Libya, but no further contact was made with any enemy aircraft despite several attempts to catch high flying Ju88 reconnaissance planes. During the month, he had flown over 15 hours in Spitfires, which now gave him a total of 425 hours on the fighter. He signed his logbook as Philip W E Heppell Flt Lt Officer Commanding 'A' Flight, which was counter signed by Sqd Ldr Laddie Lucas, the Officer Commanding 249 Squadron.

A group of pilots includingWhaley far left, enjoy a cold beer in the Malta sunshine. 1942 (M Woodhall)

Laddie Lucas described a day some of the pilots spent relaxing away from the airfield at a rest house at St Paul's Bay. They took a small rowing boat from the rest house and headed the mile or so out into the bay towards St Paul's Island:

'One day we were half way across to the island when the air raid sirens started wailing out their misery. Soon the unmistakeable 'blue note' of the Daimler Benz engines was to be heard up above as a

couple of staffeln of Me 109s, at around 8,000 feet, swept in ahead of the incoming raid. Suddenly, and apparently for no good reason, two of their number peeled away from the rest and started down on a fast, curving dive towards the Bay. Could they really be going to draw a bead on our boat?

'Mostly naked, except for our hats to keep the sun off, we prepared to leap bravely into the water while Philip Heppell, 249's Northumbrian jester, sitting right up in the bows, kept up a jocular commentary on the 109's progress and intentions. Quickly, he changed his tune. "Take your hats off, fellers," he shouted "they'll see we're officers"!

'The 109s passed right overhead, straightening out at about 50 feet at the bottom of their hell-bent dive. Why they did that if they weren't going to fire we weren't quite sure.'
Malta: The Thorn In Rommel's Side. Laddie Lucas. (Stanley Paul 1992)

Laddie Lucas wrote of Whaley:

'Philip Heppell came from Newcastle of a well-established Northumbrian family. His background gave him an independence of spirit which allowed him the luxury of pretending that few things on this earth, and particularly in Malta, should ever be taken seriously, least of all the opinions of senior officers. Nip Heppell was the necessary jester in 249's pack, the English antidote to the inevitable intensity which sprang from our critical circumstances.'
Five Up. Laddie Lucas. (Sidgwick & Jackson 1978)

April 8th proved to be a day of mixed fortunes for Whaley. At around 1:30pm three Spitfires and seven Hurricanes took off to intercept six Ju88s and their escort approaching over the Kalafrana seaplane base. Whaley, flying Spitfire AB346/K, climbed up through the light cloud to 20,000 feet before diving down on the bombers. He fired at one noting strikes on the cockpit, fuselage and an engine, then fired on another seeing hits on the wings and fuselage. One Ju88 crashed into the sea off the Grand Harbour, which, Whaley believed, was his victory, although Sgt Boyd, a Hurricane pilot, also claimed a Ju 88 shot down and it is possible that they both may have fired at the same aircraft. An Axis air sea rescue aircraft based in Sicily later successfully picked up the German crew of the shot down aircraft.

The Spitfires, having been refuelled and rearmed, were ready again when, at 3:00pm, a large raid of over fifty Ju88 and 26 Ju87 bombers, with fighter escort, approached to bomb Luqa airfield and the Grand Harbour. Whaley led three Spitfires along with nine Hurricanes, which joined the battle. Intercepting the bombers coming in over St Paul's Bay, he climbed up under them firing at one seeing hits on the port engine which started to give off smoke. He then turned his attentions to other enemy aircraft as he described:

'I intercepted the next wave coming in from Kalafrana and dived in behind the leading Junkers 88 as we entered the very heavy anti aircraft barrage over the Grand Harbour, Valletta. I knew that the 109's did not venture into the barrage, and I saw it as the only safe place to attack the bombers. I recall my fire striking the bomber in the wings and tail…rear gunner dead.

'My next recollection was falling head first towards the harbour sans aircraft. At about 120mph you get a vivid impression of the earth below and dream like believe this is not happening to you. I grabbed the parachute rip-chord (which I still have), the 'chute opened and there I was suspended at about 10,00 feet. Bombs drifting passed and blowing up below. Flak exploding all around and continuous rattle of machine gun fire, very frightening since one feels every one is shooting at you alone. With my good arm I pulled on the 'chute harness and avoided landing in the harbour.

It seemed that I was on a sky-hook and not apparently losing height, until suddenly the earth shot up and I crashed into a bomb hole full of stone, still conscious but unable to move. I shouted "I'm British" in case the Maltese attacked me, they seemed to think anyone shot down was a Hun. God knows why! However they were deep in the bomb shelters and I think I was bemused by the fact that I was still alive.

'Some Army types got me on a stretcher and into a shelter. A Medical Officer gave me a shot of morphia. I was taken to Imtarfa Hospital and shortly afterwards found myself on the operating table to have the gashes in my head and legs sewn up. Three times the lights went out (effects of the bombing) as I was about to be anaesthetised. And the third time I fell off to sleep on the table before the pentathol was injected.

'I woke up about noon the next day. I was black, green, blue etc and it was almost a week before I could sit up in bed without assistance. My stomach muscles were so damaged by the blast, which had disintegrated my Spitfire. My aircraft (AB346/K) had received a direct hit from the anti aircraft guns, wings and tail falling off and blowing me out. The only part that was found was in Sliema cemetery, the tail, which had fallen like a leaf, the rest no doubt fell in the harbour.'

Whaley remained in Imtarfa hospital until April 20th when he was discharged and given two weeks sick leave. He was then classed as fit for flying but only of non-operational aircraft. On May 1st he flew as a passenger in a Wellington making three stops in the ten-hour journey to Cairo, Egypt. There he spent two weeks further sick leave at A.H.Q, and two weeks later he joined an Air Delivery Unit in Cairo. In June he was attached to Port Sudan, Sudan, as a test pilot on Curtiss Kittyhawk fighters and Martin Baltimore light bombers both of which he had never flown before. However, he flew solo on both types on June 22nd.

In December 1942 Whaley became operational again joining 1435 Squadron as a Flight Commander again on Malta, based at Luqa. The squadron had reformed earlier in August having previously been a night fighter unit, to become a day fighter unit flying the Spitfire MkV.

By now Malta aircraft had control of their own air space and had gone on the offensive with sweeps over Sicily attacking trains and other transport, not only by gun fire, but also now the Spitfires could carry one 500 pound bomb under the fuselage, or two 250 pound bombs under the wings.

During the first two weeks of January 1943. Whaley acted as Fighter Controller on HMS Orion, a Leander Class Cruiser which, having been previously badly damaged during the evacuation of Crete in 1941, had now recently taken up position in the Mediterranean as part of the 15th Cruiser Squadron. It was tasked with interception of enemy convoys and the defence of Allied convoys. The Fighter Controller ensured all gun crews were up to date on aircraft recognition to ensure that there were no incidents of 'friendly fire'.

On January 28th Whaley was the section leader of a group of four Spitfires, which, after a search, successfully found a downed pilot, Sgt Don Goodwin of 229 Squadron who had been forced to bail out of his Spitfire after an engine problem. He was located, having lost his dingy, floating in his Mae West life jacket around forty miles off the coast of Malta. The high-speed launch HSL107 based at St Paul's Bay, was already on its way to join the search, and, with the guidance of the Spitfires, was able to successfully recover the pilot. Two days later Whaley himself would be grateful for the services of the rescue launches.

Whaley was flying Spitfire AR561 on the afternoon of the 30th along with his number two, Plt Off Ron Wood. Their bombing target was a group of SM79 bombers on the airfield of the small island of Lampedusa, situated approximately 125 miles from Sicily. Possibly due to an electrical fault, one of Whaley's two bombs failed to detach correctly from his aircraft and was suspended under the wing close to the wheel, making a landing impossible. Having advised Operations on Malta, he was left with no alternative but to bail out, which he did off the Maltese coast at Kalafrana, protected by his number two until he was picked up by the alerted rescue launch HSL166. He described the incident later:

'My Spitfire was carrying two 250-lb instantaneous bombs with rod

attachments, one of which hung up when over the target – Lampedusa. I heard a bang when making a stall turn over the target and this may have caused it. On the way back to base Red 2 told me that my starboard bomb was hung up. I returned to base intending to drop it on Filfla. The bomb did not come off so I asked Red 3 to look at it and was informed that the tail of the bomb was off and the rear end of the bomb was hard against the mainplane, causing the rod and nose to point downwards. As landing was impossible I decided to bale out. I climbed to 6,000 feet about one mile off Kalafrana to the South, the rescue launch being out off Delimara Point. I attempted to jettison the hood but although the starboard side cleared the port side stuck. I pulled it off from the outside and had to hammer very hard at the hood to release it. I then released straps and R/T. Ran west to east towards the launch and when above it, trimming nose down, rolled over onto my back, and was halfway out when the aircraft dived and held me in. I grabbed the stick and righted the aircraft, returning to the cockpit. I then took off oxygen mask, which had blown up, obscuring my vision, regained height and tried the same procedure. My parachute caught in the faring behind the pilot's head position and my shoulders were against the aerial mast. The aircraft was again diving and I think that I kicked the stick forward because I suddenly dropped out. I was turning head over heels in the air and pulled the rip-cord after dropping about 500 feet. I looked around and saw the launch a little way behind me and as I was facing downwind, remained that way. I blew up my Mae West and turned parachute release to 'red' position. As I hit the water and submerged, I pressed release and kicked. When I surfaced, I was entirely free of parachute, which was drifting away. The launch picked me up within two minutes. The aircraft, after I left, continued in its dive and plunged into the sea 200 feet from the launch, the bomb exploding immediately. I heard the explosion and felt the concussion from it 3,000 feet up. The people in the launch did not have effects from it. Beyond feeling bruised about the legs and ribs, I did not receive any injury.'

Whaley also described the incident in a letter to his sister, Rhoda, whilst wishing her a belated 23rd birthday. He mentioned that he had lost a boot during the parachute descent, and that he was now trying to dry out the belongings he had carried with him at the time.

February continued with more bombing attacks. On the 5th Whaley in partnership with Sgt F Thomson, attacked a steam train at Cassibile railway station, then, not finding any further suitable targets, once again returned to Cassibile to ensure the train was destroyed.

Three days later Whaley and the Canadian, Sgt Mush Sharun, whilst flying low, spotted another train on the move and approaching Noto in the south east of Sicily. Both pilots attacked the train seeing their cannon shells hit the engine and its tender. The train entered a tunnel but, on appearing out the other side, the two pilots continued their attack along the length of the train, although it did successfully reach Noto station. The two fighters were driven off by accurate anti aircraft fire, which damaged Whaley's Spitfire but he was able to land safely.

The month of March continued in the same manner; on the 6th Whaley and Plt Off Wood found a stationary train near Sampieri, which they fired both their cannons and machine guns at until the engine blew up. On their return to Malta they were tasked with finding a lost RAF Hudson aircraft, which they subsequently were able to do, and guided it to the island.

The 22nd saw Whaley's section again on the hunt for trains and one was destroyed or badly damaged near Sampieri. Moving on, within a quarter of an hour the group had found another train, which they attacked, the engine left pouring steam and smoke. The following day Whaley, along with Sgt T. Atkinson followed a Sicilian railway line until they came upon a train, which was subsequently left surrounded by billowing clouds of steam and smoke.

On April 13th Whaley was promoted to Squadron Leader taking command of 229 Squadron based at the airstrip at Krendi, Malta. 229 Squadron were involved with a similar role to 1435 Squadron, providing convoy protection and low level attacks on targets in Sicily, although they did not have bomb armed Spitfires until the following month.

April 16th brought an increase in Luftwaffe attention to Malta as two Royal Navy destroyers approached the island following an attack on an Italian shipping convoy. Just after 6:00am Whaley led a section from 229 Squadron on patrol along with his former squadron 1435. They spotted a Ju88 bomber and all eight Spitfires in the group, led by Whaley, attacked from the aircraft's rear. The aircraft, after multiple strikes, turned onto its back with one engine on fire and crashed into the sea.

In the area at the time were several Italian aircraft on their way from Sicily to the island of Pantelleria. Comprising of five MC202 and nine MC200 fighter aircraft, they saw the German aircraft shot down and turned in to intercept the Spitfires. An air battle between the two forces broke out, during which Whaley's aircraft was struck in the wingtip and the instrument panel. He and his number two, Plt Off Robinson, turned to face their attackers to make themselves a smaller target and to allow them to return fire. Both pilots hit their adversaries' aircraft and both claimed a damaged, although one aircraft was actually shot down into the sea unseen.

Whaley started back to base in his damaged Spitfire but was followed and attacked by two of the Macchis fighters, one of which fired at him. He was wounded in the thigh, chest and arm but, despite these injuries, he was able to land back at Luqa safely. Whaley was taken to the 45th General Hospital, which had been converted from a former school not far from the Grand Harbour. Here he stayed for nearly three weeks. The serious nature of his injuries meant that he was returned to the UK for further treatment. On May 5th he left Malta and was flown to the Army General Hospital on Gibraltar. Five days later he was flown back to England and admitted to the Princess Mary's RAF Hospital at RAF Halton, Buckinghamshire. Here he remained until the May 17th when he was sent on 21 days sick leave, to return for readmission on June 7th. Having been granted an extension to his sick leave, Whaley was not required to report for duty until 16th June 1943.

On July 2nd Whaley was posted to a staff appointment with 13 Group at RAF Inverness, Scotland, where he remained until mid November. Whaley returned to flying duties in two temporary positions, the first as a Supernumerary Squadron Leader with 222 Squadron at Hornchurch, Essex.

222 were a part of the 2nd Tactical Air Force, carrying out offensive sweeps in Mk XII Spitfires over France in preparation for the forthcoming invasion. His stay with 222 was brief as he left at the end of the following month to take up his second Supernumerary position as Squadron Leader with 129 Squadron who were also based at Hornchurch performing the same role. After a short period, on the 19th January 1944, Whaley left the squadron, as a position was now available for him as Commanding Officer of 118 Squadron, who were based at Castletown, Scotland.

Within two days of Whaley taking over the squadron, they were posted to Detling, Kent, where they took up, once again, offensive operations over Europe. The squadron had recently changed to the Mk IX Spitfire from the Mk V, and their first mission on the 14th was to provide escort to American Liberator bombers attacking V1 flying bomb sites in France.

The war had not prevented Whaley from finding romance, and the Times newspaper of March 9th carried the following announcement in the personal columns:

'The engagement is announced between Squadron Leader Philip Whaley Ellis Heppell. D.F.C., R.A.F.V.R., only son of Squadron leader P.F. Heppell and Mrs. Heppell, of Gosforth, Northumberland, and Section Officer Jean Muir Wilson, W.A.A.F., only daughter of Major A. Wilson and Mrs. Wilson, of Lulworth Cove, Dorset.'

They were married the following year.

On March 10th the squadron once again returned to Scotland to Skeabrae, Orkney, providing the defence of Scapa Flow, with long patrols against enemy reconnaissance aircraft, and occasionally air sea rescue searches. On July 12th the squadron returned to Detling, once more forming a part of a wing with 504 and 124 squadrons, carrying out bomber escorts in support of the Allied forces as they fought their way through France.

August 9th saw 118 Squadron in Scotland this time, for a brief posting to Peterhead, followed on the 28th by a move south to Westhampnett, Sussex. They carried out some fighter sweeps but the majority of their work was as escort to bombers. In September, Whaley flew his first mission over Germany as the leader of the escort of a daylight raid by over 200 Lancaster and Halifax bombers. A week later 118 provided escort to 600 gliders and 400 aircraft containing parachutists on their way to Eindhoven, Nijmegen and Arnhem, as part of Operation Market Garden, the planned capture in Holland of several bridges across the Maas and two arms of the Rhine, the Waal and the Lower Rhine.

Two days after his first flight to the Arnhem area, he returned to the area to escort a supply drop despite the poor weather conditions noting:

'Dicing with death! Weather bloody awful.'

The following day there was another supply drop, the conditions had not improved but the mission had to be flown to ensure further supplies were received in Holland. Whaley wrote in his logbook:

'Informed by planning that the supplies had to get through even if all the Stirlings and the Westhampnett Wing were lost in the attempt.'

118 Squadron, on the 25th September 1944, moved to Manston, Kent, along side 124 and 229 Squadrons to continue their escort work with the bombers to German industrial targets. As the bombing raids penetrated further and further into Germany more squadrons began to convert away from the Spitfire to the Mustang because of its greater endurance. 118 were one such squadron and, in mid December, they moved to Bentwaters, Sussex, to join five other Mustang squadrons 64, 126, 129, 165 and 234 to form a wing led by Wg Cdr Kai Birksted.

In early February 118 had received its full complement of the Mustang III and had carried out their conversion training. Their first operational flight was on the 14th when Whaley, flying Mustang NK-A, led 12 aircraft as escort to 18 Lancasters sent to bomb the viaduct at Paderborn in Germany. Although the flight took over four hours, Whaley wrote: **'An enjoyable first trip on Mustangs, but not quite long enough!'**

In March 1945 Whaley's Operational flying career ended when he began a staff appointment with the General Staff Headquarters, 11 Group at RAF Uxbridge. One of his duties was flying senior officers around the Group in aircraft such as Oxfords and the Percival Procter, a world away from the front line fighters he had been used to.

The Supplement to the London Gazette announced in June 1945 a Bar to Whaley's DFC. He had also been awarded the Croix de Guerre with three Palms from France, the French War Cross awarded to Allied Forces for an individual feat of arms mentioned in a despatch. In addition, he had gained the Air Efficiency Award for efficient service in the Reserve Air Force.

In April 1946 Whaley left the RAF. During his time in the RAF he had flown with some of its greatest pilots and characters, men like Douglas Bader, Johnnie Johnson, Hugh Dundas and Laddie Lucas. His logbook showed he had flown over forty different types of aircraft and had landed at 170 different airfields. Whaley, though, held no great affection for Malta and never returned to the island.

After the war, Whaley qualified as an Auctioneer, Chartered Surveyor and Estate Agent becoming a fellow of the Royal Institute of Chartered Surveyors and Auctioneers Institute. He joined a Newcastle company called Lamb and Edge. He worked for 37 years at the company and later succeeded his father as the senior partner, before his own retirement.

Whaley was also on the board of the Newcastle Building Society and, in 1966, became its Chairman, the Society was one of his great loves. He would be proud to know both companies are still running successfully today.

Flying was still another of Whaley's passions and he continued after the war by flying in air races, as did his sister Rhoda. In August 1949 he flew an Auster Autocrat aircraft in a weekend of flying events held at Elmdon Airport, Birmingham. He came in joint fifth tied with a Miss Curtis out of twelve competitors in the Siddeley Challenge Trophy, a three-lap event for light aircraft. Whaley would no doubt have been pleased to meet up with former colleague Sqn Ldr Hugh Dundas, who was also there taking part in an inter squadron race.

The following year he won a prize of £25 for the best time for an aircraft under 500 Kg in Heat Two of the Grosvenor Cup. In 1951 Whaley took part in an air display at Woolsington, Newcastle, although weather conditions curtailed most of the events. Whaley and another pilot chased balloons downwind trying to burst them with their aircraft. An impromptu air race between 7 aircraft, over five laps within the airfields perimeter was also organised. Whaley duly won on his home ground in an Auster.

In 1952 he again took part in the Grosvenor Challenge Cup in Tiger Moth G-AMLH the front cockpit was completely faired in to make it more aerodynamic and the struts and wires were also described as 'tidied up' he was, therefore, given further handicapping, resulting in him coming in 7th place.

Whaley's exuberant flying led to him to be brought before the Law Courts at Newcastle charged with flying: ' In such a manner as, by reason of low altitude, to cause unnecessary danger to any person.' The charge was that he had flown a Tiger Moth from Woolsington Airport over Gosforth (where his parents lived) at between 300 and 500 feet, and executed a number of shallow dives and rolls. The case was, however, subsequently dismissed.

Whaley had three sons and a daughter and all were taken flying as the family tradition dictated. He, himself, had become a fighter Ace and had flown with some of the war's greatest pilots; he was shot down and wounded twice, and rose to the rank of squadron leader.

In October 1987, whilst on holiday in Bournemouth, his full life came to an end when he died after a short illness, aged 66. Philip Whaley Ellis Heppell DFC and Bar, AE, CdeG, is buried in Ward 15 section 4K of All Saints Cemetery, Jesmond Road, Newcastle.

Whaley with his wife, Jean, at the premiere of the film Battle of Britain in 1969 (P Heppell)

Raymond Brown Hesselyn

Raymond's father was born George Albert Hesselin being of Swedish descent, but during the First World War he decided to change the spelling of his surname to the less Germanic sounding Hesselyn. In June 1916 George married Marjorie Moore Stewart Wilkie in Dunedin, New Zealand. Their first son, Bill, was born the following year, two more boys followed, Norman in 1919 and Ray on March 13th 1921.

When Ray was two, the family moved to Oamaru on the east coast of the South Island of New Zealand. At the age of five, Ray started primary school then moved on to the Waitaki High School for boys in 1934. In 1935 tragedy struck the family when Ray's older brother, Norman, died aged just 15 from Peritonitis.

In 1937 the family moved to Invercargill and Ray attended the Southlands Boys School for a short period, before starting an apprenticeship as a machinist with the joinery company George Poole and Sons. Ray also joined the Territorial Army and, by 1939, he had become a Corporal in the Southland Regiment. However it was the Air Force, which appealed to him, and so on June 23rd 1940 aged 19, he signed up with the Royal New Zealand Air Force, (RNZAF)

Ray started his basic training at RNZAF Levin. In December 1940 he transferred to No.1 Elementary Flying Training School at Taieri, Dunedin, where he was instructed on the de Havilland Tiger Moth. On February 9th 1941 he was sent to No.2 Flying Training School at Woodbourne, here he would make his first solo flight and gain his pilots 'Wings'. Confident and headstrong during his training, Ray performed an unauthorised low level 'beat up' of a passenger train whilst at Taieri, and also another one of the airfield whilst at Woodbourne. These incidents led to him being disciplined, and quite possibly he only remained in the Air Force because of the urgent wartime requirement for pilots.

On April 26th 1941, having enjoyed a period of leave, Ray began the start of his journey to England. Now nicknamed 'Hess' by his fellow pilots, he embarked on the liner Aorangi at Auckland for the first stage to Canada. Ray and the other trainees arrived at Victoria, British Columbia, on May 13th and travelled on to Vancouver where they boarded a train. After a tedious 5-day train journey, they arrived at Fairfax near Halifax, where they boarded a troop ship, which sailed as part of a convoy, en route to the United Kingdom. After 9 days at sea, the pilots arrived at Gourock on the river Clyde, Scotland, where they were held on the ship for two and a half days before going ashore to board a train. The train took them to the RAF Reception Centre at Bournemouth in England, where they received additional items of kit, and after a few days, they were released for a period of leave.

On July 23rd Ray joined No.9 Flying Training School at Hullavington, Wiltshire. Here he received further tuition flying the Miles Master trainer and the Hawker Hurricane fighter. After 2 months Ray joined 61 Operational Training Unit based at Heston, Middlesex, where he flew the Supermarine Spitfire for the first time. The period was marred by the loss of two of his fellow course members in separate fatal accidents.

Ray, now a Sergeant Pilot No.404362, joined his first operational squadron 501, based at Ibsley in Hampshire, although he only remained with them for a few weeks before being transferred to 234 Squadron on the same airfield. 234 were involved in convoy protection duties, bomber escort and fighter

**Ray, far right, at Taieri, New Zealand; with fellow trainee pilots by a
Tiger Moth biplane (N Nicholl)**

sweeps over the channel into occupied France.

In February 1942 Ray was one of the sixteen pilots chosen to take part in the reinforcement of Malta. He flew a Spitfire from the carrier, HMS Eagle, over 600 miles to the island. On approach to Takali, their destination airfield, Ray, flying AB338, found he was unable to get the undercarriage down, and subsequently he was the last to land by the time it had finally locked into place. He, along with the other pilots, joined 249 Squadron led by Squadron Leader Stanley Turner.

The day after the debut of the Spitfires, March 11th, Ray flew his first mission but it was not until April 1st that he made his first victory claim, destroying a Me109. Over the next 5 months he became one of Malta's most successful pilots with 12 victories and several probables and damaged claims. His own accounts of his flying are given within the original text of Spitfires Over Malta.

In May 1942 the Supplement To The London Gazette noted the award of the Distinguished Flying Medal to Ray, the citation read:

'Sergeant Hesselyn is a skilful and gallant pilot. Undeterred by odds, he presses home his attacks with outstanding determination. He has destroyed 5 enemy aircraft, 2 of which he shot down in one engagement.'

Above him on the list of those awarded the medal, was the name of his good friend, Paul Brennan.

Not long after, on May 18th, Ray was awarded a Bar to the Distinguished Flying Medal, and soon after promoted to the rank of Pilot Officer. The citation stated:

'During a period of four day's operations in May 1942, this airman destroyed five enemy aircraft, bringing his victories to ten. Although fighting at great odds in the heavy raids on Malta, Flt Sgt Hesselyn never hesitates in his efforts to destroy the enemy. His courage and devotion to duty are outstanding.'

Ray flew his last operational flight over Malta on July 15th 1942 without encountering any enemy aircraft. He and Paul Brennan enjoyed a period of rest at Sliema before their departure back to England. They left towards the end of July, flying first to Gibraltar and then onward, a few days later, to the UK where they enjoyed a well earned three weeks leave.

Ray's next appointment was as an instructor for six months with 61 OTU based at Rednal, Shropshire, this was the same unit where he had been a novice pilot under training only the previous year. During this time he wrote a letter to his parents outlining some of his time on Malta:

'When we arrived at Malta, the Maltese cheered us everywhere we went. In their eyes we were heroes who had come to save them, and we did, too.
'You've all read what it was like and how hectic it was. All I can say is that it was worse than any description the newspapers ever gave it. There

was quite a lot of damage when we arrived there, but when we left there was hardly a decent building left standing.

'The Hun certainly used a lot of his poison there, and he got a lot back. The Hurricanes were trying to hold him back. The first time the Spitfires went up (four of them) they shot down six enemy machines. It was a good start and boded ill for the Hun.

'During March I spent most of the time dodging bombs and canon shells, and generally summing up the situation and the Hun tactics as a whole.

'Then on April 1st, in company with the Commanding Officer, Stan Grant, his No.2 Johnny Plaggis, and Buck Buchanan, all of whom flew together as a team and later received decorations, I started a fairly good page for the month…

'…The month of April was hectic in every sense of the word. "Jerry" increased his bombing one hundred fold both by day and by night. It was almost impossible to get a decent sleep and we were beginning to think it was safer in the air than on the ground. Food was getting shorter and very poor. Tinned beef was the staple diet morning, noon, and night.

Reinforcements of Spitfires were coming in and being bombed before we could get them off the ground, and we old hands (as we called ourselves now) had to keep going until the new boys got used to things. Mosquitoes were getting more numerous, flies were beginning to bite, and we were all getting touches of dysentery. Chaps were cracking under the strain, and we were all getting jittery and bad tempered.

'We were still shooting them down, but the odds were terrific, and as we were coming into land, nearly out of petrol, out of ammunition, and dog tired, the "Jerry" fighter would try to shoot us up. How we stood up to it all I still wonder. The stamina and guts of everyone were marvellous, especially the ground crews, who worked night and day keeping our machines in the air, and the gunnery boys. During April, the anti aircraft shot down 102 enemy aircraft, and probably destroyed and damaged a score of others. Our own squadron's score was mounting up, and was about 40 to 1.

'In May, Wing Commander Gracie took over when we had no aircraft left, and had to sit and take all the bombing and gunning without doing anything about it. Gracie made a big difference. We were expecting a new batch of reinforcements. 60 brand new Spitfires, the latest England had, were coming, and Gracie had everything ready for them. Ammunition, petrol, oil, glycol, and crews and pilots were in every dispersal pen.

'We reckoned to get every aircraft in the air within 20 minutes of landing. Next day they arrived, sixty-four of them, and within ten minutes half of them were in the air, and did the Hun get a shock! Experts say it was even better than the Battle of Britain. From May 9 to May 14 we were battling all day and we won.

'During 24 hours we destroyed 112 aircraft, and we kept at it until the Hun gave in. We had won the Battle of Malta.

'By May 11 I had brought my score to eleven. Our own losses were not heavy in comparison, but I had lost a lot of Cobbers, and missed them, too.

'Things slackened off after that. We had certainly given the Hun something to think about. He sent over a few fighter sweeps and the Italians started to come over. They didn't worry us. They were yellow. They still kept up their night bombing though.'

Ray's next posting was again to one of his previous squadrons, 501, who were then based at Aldergrove, Northern Ireland, before their later move to Westhampnett near Tangmere, West Sussex. In April 1943, 501 Squadron formed part of a wing with two other Squadrons, 601 and 485, and carried out offensive sweeps and escort missions of bombers into Northern France.

During June, Ray appears to have spent some time attached to 277 Squadron who were an Air Sea Rescue unit. On the 22nd whilst flying an elderly Spitfire MkII as escort cover for a Walrus seaplane, he encountered an FW190, which he fired at seeing strikes around the engine and cockpit area. He was credited with a damaged only, although the Walrus pilot believed he saw the FW190 crash into the sea.

In July, Ray was posted to 222 Squadron based at Hornchurch, Essex. The squadron were equipped with MK IX Spitfires and

Ray outside Buckingham Palace, London in May 1943 (N Nicholl)

flew as part of a wing with 129 Squadron in offensive sweeps over Northern France, sometimes flying two or three sorties a day. The Wing Commander was a fellow New Zealander, William Crawford-Compton, who said he regarded Ray **'as the fastest and quickest thinking New Zealander he had ever seen**

in the air'.

In the early afternoon of August 17th the squadron took off from Manston airfield in Kent on an escort mission of American Flying Fortress bombers. Over Holland, 12 enemy fighters were spotted. Ray attacked one of the Me109s seeing hits to the wings and fuselage, with smoke pouring from it, the aircraft turned onto its back and crashed. Ray then turned his attentions to another 109 ahead of him at 3,500 feet, and closed in to around 300 metres before firing from immediately behind it. At 250 metres Ray fired again, and saw the cockpit canopy come off and the pilot bale out, the plane's tail tearing off as it plunged down. Two days later, Ray shared in another victory with Flt Lt Tripe of a Me109 above the Dutch town of Sluis.

In the early evening of August 22nd the wing were flying their third sortie of the day, crossing the coast into France. Close to Abbeville they spotted seven FW190s, which they attacked. Ray fired both his cannons and machine guns in pursuit of one of the aircraft, seeing many strikes on the fuselage and wings. As both aircraft had been in a high-speed dive at low level, Ray believed the German would not have been able to pull out in time before crashing, but as a crash was not witnessed he was only credited with a possible.

On August 27th the wing was acting again as escort to Flying Fortresses, this time bombing the marshalling yards at St Omer, France. The bombers were intercepted by nine FW190s, which the wing engaged. Ray fired at one from 350 metres, and then again at 300 metres. Closing up further he used up all his remaining ammunition on the aircraft, which finally crashed near the town of Guines.

Ray had flown 27 operational sorties during the month of August, and September was to bring him further successes. On the 4th the wing were once again providing escort, on their third mission of that day. This time B-26 Marauders were targeted with bombing the marshalling yards at Hazebrouk. Me109 fighters attempted to attack the bombers. Ray saw an aircraft below him climbing up, he dived down behind the 109, closing upon it and firing a 10 second burst. The German aircraft was hit in the radiator, and leaking Glycol coolant, crashed east of Audruicq.

During September Ray was able to have two weeks leave and was also pleased to be promoted to Flight Lieutenant, flying his first mission with his new rank on the 24th.

On the 27th 222 and 129 Squadrons took off on an escort of B-26 Marauder bombers tasked with attacking Beauvias airfield. Over the target, the bombers were attacked by 20 FW190s, which the Spitfires intercepted, 12 Me109 fighters also joined the air battle. Ray fired brief bursts at two enemy aircraft one of which was about to attack another Spitfire. He, along with Fg Off Bass, saw four FW190s climbing to his left and went into attack. Ray used all his remaining ammunition on one of the aircraft which went into a dive losing part of its wing and the canopy, although the pilot was not seen to bale out, the aircraft crashed at Beauvais, south east of Forges.

October 3rd 1942 saw Ray flying one mission in the morning with 222 as escort to bombers attacking Schiphol airfield in Holland. Later a second mission took off from Hornchurch at 4:30pm, as escort to Marauder bombers targeted to strike Beauvais Airfield again. The target was reached around 5:30pm and bombed, but, as the aircraft were leaving, a large group in excess of forty FW190 and Me109 aircraft dived down to attack the bombers. 222 Squadron followed the fighters down and Ray caught up with the last enemy aircraft, setting it on fire and crashing down to its destruction. After the war Ray claimed that he had in fact shot down three aircraft during this day's action.

The section then climbed back up but were immediately intercepted by two 190s with one firing at Ray. His aircraft was struck below the cockpit, which set the aircraft on fire, with several shells also striking the protective armour behind his seat. Ray became trapped in the plane, now spinning wildly, and he struggled to get out. Eventually he managed to stabilise the aircraft enough to allow him to release the canopy and bale out of the now fiercely burning Spitfire. His parachute, fortunately, had not been damaged by the fire and opened normally, although part of his uniform was still burning as he floated down. On reaching the ground near Beauvais, he was quickly surrounded by German troops. He was taken to a dressing station for his wounds to be treated. He was then taken away by the Luftwaffe for interrogation, here the German officer speaking in perfect English said to him,

'Ah –Hesselyn it is nice to see a big shot like you' and then went on to describe how he knew Ray had been in London with Paul Brennan and the journalist Eric Baume, and even which restaurants they had frequented. Ray had to admit he was impressed with their intelligence.

Ray spent several weeks in Beauvais hospital receiving treatment to the shrapnel wounds in his legs and the burns on his hands, he left on September 29th and was taken to Dulag Luft the interrogation centre near Frankfurt, Germany, where he was held until November 6th.

Ray's parents received a telegram on October 5th stating that their son was 'missing' confirmed by a letter later from the New Zealand Defence Department acting on information received from the Air Ministry in London.

Although held in captivity and unknown to him, Ray was awarded on October 23rd the Distinguished Flying Cross, his parents were also informed by telegram. The citation stated:

'This officer has destroyed at least 17 enemy aircraft. His successes are a fine tribute to his great skill, courage and keenness.'

On November 11th 1943 Ray was transferred to Stalag Luft 1 close to the town of Barth on the Baltic coast. The camp had first opened in late 1941 for British and Commonwealth prisoners, but had then closed in April 1942, only to reopen six months later in October. Not long after, it started to receive the many shot down American aircrew that parachuted from stricken bombers into captivity.

In the late afternoon of January 22nd 1944 Ray, along with Warrant Officer R.B. Olliver, escaped from the camp by hiding in the roof of the theatre until 7:00pm. They made their way across the roof and down to the ground near a gate leading to an adjacent compound. They avoided two patrolling sentries to climb over the gate, and out into the surrounding countryside. Ray had made a jacket and a cap to wear from a camp blanket but was still wearing his RAF trousers. He had some money, maps, food and a compass, but carried no identity papers. On the morning of the following day, the two men had reached the area of Velgast where they hid in a wood until midday.

A German photograph of Ray taken during his period of captivity (N Nicholl)

They tried to enter a railway marshalling yard but were caught by four policemen and were returned, the same day, to Stalag Luft 1. Both men were sentenced to 14 days in the cells on only bread and water. Ray spent another five months as a prisoner of war, before the advancing Russian forces liberated the prison camp on May 1st 1945, and within two weeks, Ray had returned back to England.

In 1947, when he was back home in New Zealand, Ray confided in his father and brother, that whilst held by the Germans, he had been castrated. This possibly had been carried out as a reprisal, because the Germans knew he had been a successful pilot, as shown by the publication of the book Spitfires Over Malta with Paul Brennan, and that they had been honoured by many important people after the book's publication.

In December 1945 Ray was awarded the M.B.E. (Member Of The Order Of The British Empire) for work he had carried out whilst held prisoner. The citation stated:

'Whilst a prisoner of war at Stalag Luft 1, Barth, Germany, this officer was appointed personnel officer in the camp. He completed this task in a most efficient and cheerful manner and was able to hand permanent records, including confidential reports on 1400 aircrew, to the Air Ministry on release. These reports were largely the result of Flight Lieutenant Hesselyn's own efforts. During periods of starvation and depression, this office contributed very considerably to the well-being of British and American prisoners of war by his unstinting efforts on their behalf.'

After a period of recuperation, Ray continued his career within the RAF after the war, in April 1946 he joined No.1 Squadron as a Flight Commander. They were, at the time, based at Tangmere on the south coast, equipped with the Griffon engined Spitfire MkF.21, which was capable of flying at over 450mph. During early October the Spitfires were replaced by the first jet fighter aircraft in RAF service, the Gloster Meteor, powered by a Rolls Royce Derwent engine that allowed the aircraft to exceed over 500mph.

In 1947 Ray returned to New Zealand where his proud parents were keen to parade their hero son, although Ray was not that interested in the social functions. He found it a difficult time and started to drink heavily and then not be able to sleep afterwards.

In June 1947 Ray took up a permanent commission in the RAF and joined 56

Ray with his parents, his brother Bill, wife Esme, and their children Rae and Lynne. Circa 1947 (N Nicholl)

Squadron based at Duxford, Cambridgeshire. He also attended several training placements, including nearly three months on a Junior Commanders Course at Hornchurch, Essex. He moved to No.226 Operational Conversion unit at

Molesworth, Cambridgeshire, for instruction on the Mk4 Meteor. In 1948 he was appointed supernumerary at 12 Group Headquarters and moved on to Fighter Command headquarters at Bentley Priory in an administrative role.

On August 17th 1948 Ray married Elfreda Bellairs at Marylebone registry office. Known as 'Babs,' she was a divorcee nine years older than he was and for these two reasons the family did not approve of her, although they never actually met her. Ray, however, described himself to be **'wonderfully, gloriously happy.'**

In 1950 Ray was sent on a year long course at the RAF Staff College Bracknell, and afterwards to the Staff College at Andover. After a further short period at Bentley Priory, Ray joined No.41 Squadron at Biggin Hill, Kent. The following year, in January 1951, he was promoted to Squadron Leader, and subsequently Officer Commanding Flying until November 1952. He was then posted to No.233 Operational Conversion Course Unit based at Pembrey in South Wales, where two squadrons of Vampire jets were based along with a flight of target towing Tempests. Whilst here he gained a reputation for being rather cantankerous, in particular to non-flying personnel.

He had also become a heavy drinker, not just in company, but often alone in the mess. On two occasions he performed unauthorised aerobatics over the airfields, for which he was lucky not to have faced a Court Martial, a lack of discipline reminiscent of his early training days when he had buzzed an airfield and a train.

In 1954 Ray did have to face a Court Martial after an incident at a rifle range. He and two others, instead of firing at the range, were firing across an estuary at some ducks, a woman on a nearby boat was accidently hit by a spent bullet. Ray pleaded guilty to two charges of Conduct Prejudicial to Good Order and Air Force Discipline. The subsequent sentence received is not known, but Ray was quickly posted away the following month to Headquarters 83 Group Second Tactical Air Force based at R.A.F. Wahn in Germany.

Ray photographed in 1962 the year before his death (N Nicholl)

In the late 1950s Ray returned to England based at RAF Horsham St Faith, and then at 217 Signals Unit at Meatishead. This was followed, in January 1960, by a return to Bentley Priory as an Administration Officer in the plans department initially, and then later as Weapons Officer.

In late 1962 Ray returned home to New Zealand although not accompanied by his wife. On his return to England, his interest in the Air Force was on the decline, and he considered the possibility of working in New Zealand although aware that Babs, his wife, may not have been willing to move out there with him. Ill health was to prevent any possibility of this ever happening.

In April 1963 Ray wrote to his brother, Bill, from the Princess Mary RAF Hospital at Halton in Buckinghamshire, telling him that he had been ill for sometime with a very painful stomach ulcer. The doctors believed Ray had been bleeding internally through the bowel for a long period and had lost a great deal of blood; he was subsequently diagnosed as suffering from cancer of the stomach, an illness that proved to be terminal.

A gun salute is fired at Ray's funeral by the Guard of Honour (N Nicholl)

On the 14th November 1963 Ray died whilst at the RAF Hospital Uxbridge, he was aged just 42.

Raymond Brown Hesselyn MBE DFM and Bar, DFC received a guard of honour and burial party provided by the Queen's Colour Squadron (a unit of the RAF Regiment). His name is listed on the Roll of Honour at the National Memorial Arboretum, Staffordshire. He is buried within the RAF section of the Hillingdon and Uxbridge Cemetery, Hillingdon Hill, Middlesex. Grave location: QD18.

Norman William Lee

In the summer of 1914 in Willesden, a suburb of north west London, the marriage took place between William Alexander Lee and Edith Grimwood. William, a successful local solicitor, went on to become Secretary of the Mining Association Of Great Britain rising to the position of Chairman and was later awarded the CBE for his valuable work.

The couple had four children, two girls and two boys, one of whom was Norman born on April 10th 1919. Norman's education began at Bowden House Preparatory School and then, in 1930 continued at Uppingham, which at the time was a boys only fee paying boarding school in Rutland, Leicestershire. In 1937 Norman attended Clare College, the second oldest of Cambridge's 31 colleges. Leaving in 1938 he joined the RAF Volunteer Reserve although it was not until 1940 that he was called up to commence his training. Enlisting at RAF Cardington in Bedfordshire he was issued with his first uniform and his official service number of 954159.

Norman started his RAF career in June 1940 at No.3 Initial Training Wing based in the coastal town of Hastings, Sussex. Moving later to Torquay, Devon, the pupil pilots stayed in guesthouses requisitioned by the RAF, whilst under going kitting out, medicals, basic drill and receiving instruction on RAF life and its requirements.

Norman began his flying instruction in July at No.1 Elementary Flying Training School located at the de Havilland School Of Flying at Hatfield in Hertfordshire. The school taught both civilian and RAF pilots in de Havilland 82A Tiger Moth Bi-planes, which were painted a striking maroon and silver. On July 31st Norman completed his first solo flight in Tiger Moth G-ACDB and by the end of the course in September he had received over 20 hours of dual instruction, and flown solo for nearly 32 hours, plus ten hours instrument training in a Link trainer. The Chief Flying Instructor wrote in his logbook his assessed rating of **'Above Average.'**

The next stage of Norman's training was with No.12 Service Flying Training School at RAF Grantham in Lincolnshire. This included flying the under powered Fairey Battle, a single engined monoplane that could carry a crew of three. These had been relegated to training use after suffering heavy losses during front line service, particularly during the Battle Of France in May 1940. Having successfully competed this course with an assessment of **'Average,'** Norman was awarded his 'Wings' Flying Badge on November 27th 1940 and was promoted to a Pilot Officer, his service number changing to 88724.

In December Norman was posted to No.56 Operational Training Unit to prepare for frontline service. 56 OTU were based at Sutton Bridge in Lincolnshire and were equipped with the Hawker Hurricane Mk1. Having successfully completed the course in January 1941, Norman joined his first Squadron, 504 who were also using the Hurricane and at the time were based at RAF Exeter in Devon. 504 were mainly involved in convoy protection patrols along the south coast from Plymouth to Portsmouth. They aimed to keep at least two aircraft circling in an anti-clockwise direction at all times over a convoy whilst it was passing through their sector. During this period some night time patrols were also flown. Further training also continued and on February 4th they used the firing range at Crichel Down, Dorset, for air to ground firing practice.

504 Squadron at Exeter in 1941. back row left to right; Sgt Boreham. Plt Off Norman Lee, Sgt Douglas Haywood, Flg Off Michael Rook, Plt Off Henry Hunt, Flg Off Salter, Sgt Waud, Sgt Nurse, Sgt Lewis. Seated Sgt Ray Holmes, Medical officer, Flg Off Blair White, Sqn Ldr John Sample, Flt lt Tony Rook, Flt lt Trevor Parsons, Flg Off Wilkinson Barnes, Flg Off Clennell. Two at front not known (P Lee)

In early 1941 merchant shipping losses in the Atlantic ocean were increasing, with ships being bombed and destroyed by the long range German Focke-Wulf 200 Condor aircraft. These aircraft were able to roam freely as they flew beyond the reach of the land based single engined Spitfire and Hurricane fighters. One answer to the problem was to place Hurricane fighters on-board a ship to be fired off when the danger arose of attack by enemy aircraft. This led to the setting up on May 5th 1941 of the Merchant Ship Fighter Unit (M.S.F.U) located close by the River Mersey at RAF Speke in Liverpool. The unit used, old war weary Hawker Hurricanes, which were mounted on to Catapult Aircraft Merchant Ships (C.A.M. ships). These were ships under construction, that had been adapted to take the catapult ramp from which the Hurricane was fired, existing merchant vessels had the ramp fitted to the front of the ship and were known as Fighter Catapult Ships.

The ships were fitted with either a rocket powered or a hydraulic catapult sledge, which propelled the aircraft into the air; the aircraft were nicknamed Hurricats or Catafighters. These ships became part of a convoy and continued to carry their own cargo. The majority were owned by the Ministry of War Transport and were known as Empire Ships as all of their names began with the word Empire.

Once launched against a hostile aircraft there was no way to recover the aircraft back to the ship, so unless the ship was close enough to shore to allow a landing, the pilot would be required to bail out of the aircraft and take to his parachute, and then to clamber into his dingy to await recovery from the sea.

Due to the great danger to the pilots from the initial launch of the aircraft, possible combat with an enemy aircraft and then a parachute jump and recovery, the pilots were all volunteers. Norman courageously put himself forward for this unit and was posted to RAF Speke on May 28th to begin training, followed by detachment to RAF Abbotsinch in Scotland. For the first week in June Norman spent time practise flying in Sea Hurricane V7647, this included an actual catapult launch from the S.S Empire Spray followed by a landing back at RAF Abbotsinch. Later in the month Norman sailed as part of a convoy in one of its sister ships, the S.S.Empire Foam, from Greenock, Scotland, to Halifax in Nova Scotia, Canada, returning in July to Liverpool, England in the same ship. August continued with more practice flying followed by another sailing, this time in the M.V Empire Spray to New York in America, and again returning to Liverpool. He was lucky enough not to be required to take to his aircraft on either of these trips.

Between 1941 and 1943 when the M.S.F.U was finally disbanded, there had been only nine combat launches, one of these aircraft was able to make it to land, and the others were all ditched at sea. One allied pilot was killed with eight German aircraft destroyed and one other damaged.

After eight trips pilots were rotated off the unit to allow them to keep their flying skills current, as they would probably not have flown very many hours during their time with the M.S.F.U.

At the end of a round trip to Canada or the United States, rather than the slow and laborious job of hoisting the aircraft from the ship the aircraft were flown off at the end of the voyage, to be inspected, serviced and de-salted. Most pilots returning to an austere wartime Britain took the opportunity of bringing back with them various items of contraband such as cigarettes, silk stockings, and liquor; these were concealed within the aircraft. Flights directly backs to Speke airfield were avoided, as they needed to steer clear of the Customs men based there. So pilots having flown off found a reason to stop off at another airfield to unload their items before continuing on to Speke. The practise appeared to be widespread and condoned by many at the time.

In October Norman returned from the United States on the Empire Spray as part of a large convoy, which included four Camships. All four aircraft were stashed with contraband items. The four pilots were all fired off back to the mainland at around the same time, but soon found they were running into rain and low cloud conditions. One of the pilots headed for Rhyl, another for Sealand, both of whom landed without incident. The third tried to find Valley

The 7,300 ton Empire Spray built by William Doxford and Sons Ltd in May 1941. She survived the war and was finally scrapped in 1969 (P Lee)

airfield also in Wales, but eventually had to crash-land in a field near Bangor. Norman became lost in the poor visibility and was eventually forced to make a landing with wheels down on the beach at Leasowe Castle, near Wallasey, in the Mersey estuary where there was a good stretch of firm sand available; he landed safely close to an anti-aircraft gun position. The men from the gun battery were soon persuaded to drag the aircraft up the beach and away from the incoming tide. Meanwhile, Norman went off to telephone Speke to advise them of his position, and that he would fly the aircraft off again once the weather had improved and the sand had dried out.

On his return from his telephone call, Norman was horrified to see that only the tail of his aircraft now appeared uncovered by seawater. He had inadvertently left the breaks of the Hurricane on, and, although there had been twelve men struggling with the machine, they had been unable to save it from being swamped by the waves.

A salvage party was later sent out to recover the Hurricane, and the contraband items were discovered within the aircraft, that, plus the damage to the aircraft meant an official enquiry was ordered. Wing Commander George Pinkerton a former Battle of Britain pilot who was head of flying at Speke led the enquiry. Pinkerton apparently understood and appreciated that minor smuggling did go on, but also that some action was needed to be seen be to be taken, so Norman was posted away from the unit.

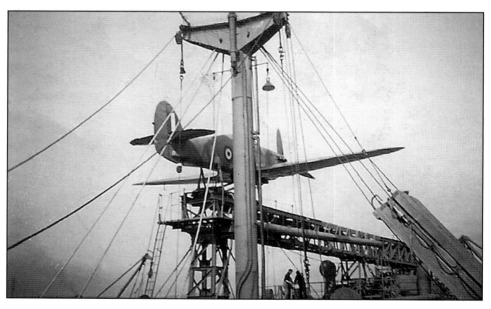

A Hawker Hurricane awaiting launch from the Empire Spray 1941 (P Lee)

On November 14th Norman began a brief period with 276 Squadron, an Air Sea Rescue squadron based at RAF Harrowbeer in Devon. This was quickly followed on the 29th by a posting to RAF Perranporth, Cornwall, to join 66 Squadron flying long range Spitfire IIs, which were fitted with an extra 30-gallon fuel tank in the starboard wing. This was the start of another period of coastal patrolling, but also included offensive forays, and flying escort protection to Blenheim bomber aircraft into occupied France. Whilst with 66 Squadron Norman met three other pilots Raoul Daddo-Langlois, nicknamed Daddy Longlegs, 'Junior' Tayleur and Percy 'Laddie' Lucas who would all later meet up again on Malta, where they would all serve with distinction.

In December Norman was promoted from Pilot Officer to the rank of Flying Officer. At the end of January 1942 Norman was advised of his imminent posting to Malta, and, having flown Spitfire Vb AB377 off HMS Eagle to the island, he was subsequently transferred to 249 Squadron at Takali.

The Spitfires first went into action over Malta on March 10th, although Norman did not fly until the following day and then did not make any contact. He flew 4 times during the following days and on the 18th made his first claim. In the early evening a raid of 24 Ju88s with a large fighter escort began bombing the airfields, six Hurricanes and four Spitfires were scrambled to intercept. Norman fired at the Me109s with out success, but also shot at and claimed a Ju88 as damaged using up all his ammunition in the process.

A week later Norman made his second claim this time for a Ju87 Stuka bomber as probably destroyed, noting excitedly in his logbook that there were **'Hundreds of bloody Stukas.'**

On the 28th Norman, along with three other 249 Squadron pilots, attacked a loan reconnaissance Ju88. Although they were unable to shoot it down, it was sufficiently damaged that they all claimed a quarter share of it as probably destroyed. Norman's aircraft was struck by return fire from the Ju88's gunners, and although his Merlin engine was damaged, he was able to land safely.

April 1st brought another raid by Ju88s along with their fighter escort. Norman was one of those scrambled but during the interception, in which he claimed a Ju88 as damaged, he became separated from the others and was attacked by six Me109s and was, as he later wrote, 'shot to hell.' He received a shell splinter in the ankle of his right foot, which required a visit to the hospital. He was well enough, however, to be able to spend some time with fellow pilot Peter Nash socialising in Valletta over the next two days.

Norman flew again on the afternoon of April 10th when six Spitfires and ten Hurricanes intercepted a large force of around 80 Ju88 and Ju87 bombers attacking Malta's airfields and the Grand Harbour. Norman claimed one Ju88 damaged and another shot down whilst it was attacking Takali airfield, the aircraft breaking up in the air with the German gunner's turret falling away from the aircraft, and landing with the dead gunner still inside it onto the airfield. Although also claimed by the airfield gun battery, Norman believed that this was his victory and apparently kept the dead gunner's cap as a souvenir.

The following day Norman, along with Peter Nash, went to the Mtarfa Military Hospital to visit some of their injured colleagues, and whilst there also saw several of the German aircrew who had been shot down and who were also receiving medical attention.

In the darkness of the evening of April 21st, Norman along with several others pilots, left Malta in a Wellington aircraft to fly to El Ballah airfield in Egypt in order to collect and return with some replacement Hurricanes for 229 Squadron. They spent over two weeks testing the Hurricanes and their cannon armament. On one test flight Norman became lost in a sand storm and mistakenly landed at Gazala in Libya only four miles from the German lines. On May 7th Norman flew Hurricane IIc BN537 on the dangerous four and half hour flight over the sea from Gambut in Libya to Hal Far airfield on Malta. On his return he noted in his logbook the death of two of his fellow pilots, Norman Macqueen and the Canadian Gordon Murray, who had both been killed during his time away.

May 9th saw Norman taking off three times on interceptions, on the first two no contact was made, but on the third occasion he closed in on a group of Ju87s only to find his cannons would not fire and his own aircraft was struck in the coolant radiator by one of the 87s.

On May 10th a bombing force, made up of 20 Ju87s and ten Ju88s, approached the Grand Harbour protected by a large Me109 escort. Recent Spitfire reinforcements from the carriers HMS Eagle and the American USS Wasp meant a substantial defending force was now available and 37 Spitfires and 13 Hurricanes took off to intercept. In the frenzied mêlée that followed Norman was able to line up against a Ju87, which he attacked, initially claiming it as probably destroyed which was later given as confirmed.

Two sorties were made by Norman on the 12th, although no contact was made on the first, on the second he was able to swoop down from 23,000 feet upon four Me109s damaging one before his cannons jammed, his own aircraft was then struck in the aileron of the wing by a cannon shell. He had a similar experience two days later when, having bounced 3 Ju88s from out of the sun, again his cannons stopped firing and his own aircraft was hit by return fire.

On the morning of May 15th the Italians attacked the island with three SM84 bombers escorted by around 30 MC202 fighters. Norman was able to damage one of the bombers before once again he found his own cannons would no longer fire.

On May 17th Peter Nash was killed and Norman noted in his logbook:

'That leaves only 5 left of the original "Cape Hawke" fifteen'

In fact the number of survivors at that time either with 249 or 185 Squadron was nine with six having been lost. He also noted that since 249 Squadron had arrived they had destroyed 100 enemy aircraft, 72 of them since the Spitfires first went into action on March 10th.

Apart from a ten-minute flight as a passenger in a Beaufighter that was undergoing a cannon test, Norman did not fly again for ten days until May 25th when he flew against an attacking Italian force. He damaged one bomber but was then himself again struck by return fire causing a coolant leak and an immediate return to base.

During June Norman, in addition to intercepting raiding Axis aircraft, was involved twice in escort duties, first to Swordfish and then to Albacore torpedo bombers as they attacked Italian naval shipping off the coast of Sicily. When 'Laddie' Lucas took over the command of 249 Squadron during this month he chose two pilots who he knew well for his flight commanders:

'It was to two Englishmen of solid worth and ability that I turned for my flight commanders. Norman Lee and Raoul Daddo-Langlois, two well-educated products of the British public school system, became the linchpins in the team on whom I could always depend. They quickly gained the respect of their overseas comrades. Authority came easily to them.'
Five Up. 'Laddie' Lucas. (Sidgewick and Jackson Ltd. 1978)

'(Norman's) rather diffident approach cloaked more than his fair share of purpose and resolve.'
Malta: The Thorn In Rommel's Side. (Stanley Paul and Co.1992)

Norman took over 'B' flight from Buck McNair and was also promoted to the rank of Fight Lieutenant. On July 6th another Italian raid comprising of Cant Z1007 bombers and a large escort of Reggiane 2000 and Macchi 202 fighters approached the island. Norman led a flight of eleven Spitfires head on at the Cant bombers unnerving them enough that they dropped their bombs into the sea and retreated. Norman only flew on a few more occasions before he left Malta including an escort for the high-speed launch used for sea rescues. His final flight was on the 15th to test the cannons of a Spitfire.

In the late evening of July 20th a Lockheed Hudson was waiting to take some of the tour expired aircrew from Malta to Gibraltar. Norman was amongst the group, which also included Paul Brennan, Ray Hesselyn and Laddie Lucas, who described his feelings as the aircraft took off just after midnight on its six and a half hour flight:

'The moon was on the wane as we became airborne, but still the whiteness of the island down below, framed by the darkness of the sea around it, stood out, boldly as ever. Drenched in nostalgia, none of us could credit that we were actually leaving Malta and going home. It was as if we had never known any other life and that our sojourn on the island had lasted for an eternity.'

Malta: The Thorn In Rommel's Side. (Stanley Paul and Co. 1992)

The group stayed a few days on Gibraltar before continuing their flight on July 24th in the Hudson, taking over seven hours to reach RAF Hendon in London.

Norman and his bride Pamela after marrying in London in October 1942 (P Lee)

After a period of leave, Norman was posted in August 1942 to 53 Operational Training Unit based at Llandow and its satellite airfield Rhoose in Glamorgan, Wales. Here he became an instructor passing on his knowledge and experience to pilots preparing to join their first squadrons. 53 OTU were, at the time, using the Miles Master two-seat trainer and Spitfire MkII fighters.

On September 18th the Supplement to the London Gazette announced confirmation of the award of the Distinguished Flying Cross to Norman, an award won for his time flying on Malta with 249 Squadron. The citatation was as follows:

'This Officer has been engaged in active operations over Malta for three and a half months, most of which were during the period of heavy air attacks, when the number of our own aircraft were few, and every operation involved fighting against great odds. He has destroyed three

enemy aircraft and damaged several more. Flt Lt Lee has on all occasions led his flight with great gallantry.'

The following month on October 17th Norman married his fiancée, Eileen Mary Pamela Barlow, at Marylebone Registry Office in London. Preferring to be called Pamela, she worked in the capital as a civilian for the Admiralty. Norman and his new bride enjoyed a honeymoon together before he returned to instructing on October 31st and throughout the rest of the year.

The early months of 1943, however, saw Norman flying a rather different aircraft during his ongoing duties with 53 OTU. The Westland Lysander was a large single engined aircraft with a high monoplane wing and a fixed undercarriage; this limited its speed to a maximum of 220mph. The Lysanders had been converted for target towing duties and carried a crew of two, Norman being the pilot and to the rear of him a winch operator who streamed out a Drogue behind the aircraft. This was the target for the Spitfire pilots to practise firing at. The exercises normally took place at a designated firing range in the Bristol Channel, three Spitfires taking it in turns to come in and attack the Drogue with different coloured painted ammunition. The target would then be dropped over the airfield and checked for successful red, green or blue coloured strikes on it.

On April 4th the constant dangers of flying were illustrated when one of Norman's friends and colleagues at 53 OTU, and a pilot from his days on Malta, was killed. Anthony Barton, three weeks after Operation Spotter, had led the second Spitfire delivery to Malta off H.M.S.Eagle on March 29th 1942. Having reached the rank of Squadron leader with the DFC and Bar, he was killed at the training unit when he was forced to make an emergency landing when the engine on his Spitfire cut out as he tried to land at Llandow. His aircraft was involved in a collision on the runway with another Spitfire waiting to take off. The pilot of the other Spitfire, 21-year-old Sergeant Charles Hamilton, also lost his life. To remember Anthony, Norman secured a photograph of his former friend into his logbook.

At the end of April, Norman was attached for a period to 122 Squadron, then based at Hornchurch in Essex, in order to gain experience on the MkIX Spitfire prior to his next posting which would again be overseas, this time to North Africa.

In May Norman embarked on the S.S. Duchess of York, a 20,000-ton former transatlantic liner built in 1928, she had been requisitioned in 1940 by the Admiralty for use as a troop ship. Norman arrived safely at the port of Algiers in Algeria on May 27th 1943. Two months later the S.S. Duchess Of

York was attacked by German bombers and was subsequently sunk off the coast of Portugal with the loss of 27 lives.

On June 10th Norman was flown in a Dakota from Maison Blanche in Algeria to Mateur in Tunisia to join 324 Wing. The next few weeks were spent on becoming familiar with the local area and practice flying sessions.

July 1943 saw the start of Operation Husky, the Allied invasion of Sicily; this had only been seriously planned six months earlier, in January. The invasion began on July 10th and continued for 39 days until August 16th when all Axis resistance ceased. Air superiority had been gained using 25 squadrons of Spitfires based on Malta and the smaller adjacent island of Gozo.

Norman was to play his part in the invasion and on July 8th he was flown by Dakota to join 93 Squadron who were also a part of 324 Wing. The former Battle of Britain pilot Wing Commander Hugh Dundas led the wing, which now comprised of 93, 43, 72 and 243 Squadrons. The MkV and MkIX Spitfires of 93 Squadron were based at Hal Far airfield on Malta. A year after leaving, Norman was once again back on the Mediterranean island.

On the day of the invasion, Norman flew two sorties to cover the troops landing near Syracuse. On the second sortie the aircraft of 93 Squadron were attacked by six Italian MC202 fighters, Norman fired at one but without result. The next two days were spent on patrolling the beaches and the south east of Sicily. On the 12th around 7:00pm 93 Squadron spotted below them six Me109s. Norman, flying a MkIX Spitfire (LZ837 HN-W) along with Sqn Ldr Wilf Sizer, dived down to attack, chasing one at low level and damaging it, before his cannons jammed. The following day, this time in a MkV Spitfire (JK306 HN-U) whilst flying near Augusta on the east of Sicily, 93 Squadron came across eight MC202 fighters, which they attacked. Norman flying with Flt Sgt Raymond Baxter (who would after the war become a well known BBC television broadcaster) believed that between them they had destroyed one of the Italian aircraft. Norman also claimed two others as damaged, with no losses from their own Squadron.

On July 14th 93 Squadron relocated from their base on Malta to the captured airfield at Comiso near the south coast of Sicily. It had the benefit of a long concrete runway and the pilots were curious to examine the several-damaged enemy Me109 aircraft that littered the airfield. One of these fighters was subsequently repaired and painted bright yellow and having been given prominent British markings, was to be flown to evaluate its performance in front of a crowd of interested pilots. The flight did not turn out well as, after becoming airborne, the engine of the aircraft caught fire, although the pilot was able to bale out and made a safe parachute landing.

The remainder of July was spent patrolling and providing escort to the bombers, twin engined B-25 Mitchell bombers and the single engined Curtiss P-40 Kittybombers. These carried two 250lb bombs side by side under their fuselage, which were dropped whilst the aircraft executed a shallow dive. The B-25 Mitchells required the long concrete runway at Comiso resulting in the Spitfires moving out to Pachino on Cape Passaro on the south east of Sicily. Here the airstrip was within a cleared vineyard and only around 800 meters long. The aircraft of 324 Wing were disbursed amongst the vines on cleared track ways, and everything became covered in the thick red dust thrown up by the aircraft. The pilots and crew also had to suffer from the constant presence of flies, which fed off any cut or scratch to bare skin.

August was to continue as July had ended with more rendezvous with bombers to escort them to their Italian targets. On the 15th Norman was posted to join 43 Squadron as the Flight Commander of 'A' Flight, still within 324 Wing. The first day in his new role was an uneventful escort of B-25 Mitchells, but the next day was much more dramatic.

On the afternoon of August 17th Norman led a flight of Spitfires on the thirty-minute flight to the nearby airfield of Lentini where a Supermarine Walrus MkI air sea rescue plane from 284 Squadron was based. They were to act as escort for the aircraft as it searched for a shot down airman off the coast of Bianco at the toe of Italy.

Also in that area at the same time were two A-36A Invaders, the dive-bomber version of the North American Mustang fighter. These were flown by two RAF pilots Fg Off John Griffith DFC (HK947-A) and Fg Off William Gilliland (HK956-E). They were both from 1437 Strategical Reconnaissance Flight and were flying over the east coast of Italy returning from an inland sortie. The two pilots, seeing aircraft below them, mistook them for Me109s and swept down to attack. Fg Off Griffith fired at the leading aircraft, which was Norman's, and shot it down, luckily not injuring him, allowing him to bale out and parachute into the sea. The escorted Walrus (X9506), flown by Warrant Officer Ken Hall with Wireless Operator Flt Sgt J. R. Berry, promptly landed and picked him up.

The two A-36A Invaders continued along the coast and carried out a low level strafing run against a column of vehicles, Griffith's aircraft was struck by return fire from a 20mm flak gun setting his engine on fire, although he was able to gain sufficient height before baling out into the sea 100 meters off the coast of Cape Bruzzano. Fg Off Gilliland circled overhead and saw his colleague climb safely into his dingy, he then radioed his position and called for assistance. Within a short time a Walrus rescue plane appeared to pick him up. This was the same aircraft that had retrieved Norman from the water, and so Norman, and the pilot who had just shot him down, were forced to share an awkward journey together back to Cassibile airfield on Sicily.

A Supermarine Walrus amphibious biplane based on Malta similar to the one that rescued Norman and Fg Off John Griffith (Bill Lazell)

The rest of the month continued with bomber escorts and practise flights. On the 31st Norman and Fg Off Anthony Snell, pursued at 33,000 feet, a German Ju88 reconnaissance plane, but Snell's aircraft suddenly left the formation and crashed down into the sea killing the 22 year old. It was believed his oxygen supply had failed causing him to black out.

In early September Norman was flown out of Sicily by Dakota to No.2 Base Personnel Depot in Tunis, Tunisia, where he was based for several weeks until being posted to 144 Maintenance Unit at Maison Blanche, Algiers, in November. At 144 MU he acted as test pilot on aircraft that had recently undergone service or repair including Spitfires, Kittihawks and the Fairchild 24, known to the RAF as the Fairchild Argus.

On January 3rd 1944 Norman was test flying a Spitfire MkVIII (JF787) when, whilst in the circuit to land, the engine suddenly cut out and an emergency landing had to be made. In the ensuing crash Norman was seriously injured and was taken to the No.2 RAF General Hospital where he remained for 14 days. It was decided to return Norman to the UK to recover and so, on January 30th at Algiers, he boarded the 23,000 ton S.S. Strathmore, another former passenger liner converted to a troop ship, for the voyage home to England.

After a period of recuperation, Norman was posted in March 1944 to 691 Squadron at Roborough, Devon. Formed four months earlier, the squadron was used primarily for anti-aircraft cooperation duties with the army and navy in the south west of England. Norman made a couple of Flights in a Hurricane during his time there before his next posting to 22 Operational Training Unit based at Wellesbourne Mountford, Warwickshire.

22 OTU was a bomber training unit training crews mainly on the Wellington bomber. Norman's role would have been fighter affiliation either by flying a Miles Martinet aircraft which would have towed a drogue target behind it allowing the Wellingtons' gunners to aim and fire at it, or by making dummy attacks in a Hurricane fighter, to allow them to become familiar with the types of approach a fast moving fighter would make. The gunners would not have fired live ammunition at the Hurricane but would have had cine cameras attached to their guns, with the film being evaluated later on. It is believed that there were six Hurricanes used by the unit, one of these Hurricane MkIIc (LF738) almost certainly flown by Norman is now preserved at the RAF Museum in Cosford, England.

The middle of December saw Norman posted once more, this time to 154 Squadron as a Flight Commander based at Biggin Hill,

Norman and his wife Pamela with their first child Patrick (P Lee)

Kent. The squadron had been disbanded at Naples in early November but had been reformed on the 16th and issued with Spitfire MkVII fighters capable of over 400mph. On February 1st the squadron began long-range bomber escort duties, requiring a landing to refuel at Ursel in Belgium. The need for refuelling was over come on February 14th when North American P-51 Mustang IV fighters replaced the squadron's Spitfires. These aircraft, with external tanks, had a range of over 1,650 miles, and a maximum speed of

430mph. During March Norman flew sorties deep into the heart of Germany including escorts to Essen, Hanover and over the Ruhr.

On the afternoon of 27th March Norman made his final claim of the war whilst flying over Lubeck, Germany:

'While flying as Yellow 1 in 154 squadron sweeping Lubeck area, Token leader was engaged in a mêlée of Fw190's at 4,000ft approx. I was above him at 8,000 ft when I sighted 4 Fw. 190's several thousand feet below. I bounced them attacking the starboard Fw.190 (short nosed yellow engine cowling with yellow band round fuselage), as my speed built up to about 400mph and they turned out to be doing only a climbing speed of 150 mph, my closing speed was so great that I only had time for one short burst observing strikes on starboard wing plane, then I overshot him, so I climbed away almost vertically to avoid being fired at by the enemy. E/A not seen again. This I claim as damaged with P/O Todd Yellow 2.'

Norman left 154 Squadron at the end of March and was posted to his last wartime squadron 122 based at Andrewsfield in Essex, a former American airbase taken over by the RAF in October as part of 11 Group. The Polish 150 Wing comprising 129, 306 and 315 squadrons were soon joined by 122 Wing 19, 65 and 122 Squadron, all flying Mustang fighters in escort duties to RAF bombers now also flying daytime missions, and the interception of V1 flying bombs.

With bombers now escorted by fighters all the way to their German targets by both day and night, and with the advancing allied troops in the capital Berlin, Germany surrendered on May 8th 1945. Norman drew a cartoon Chad/Kilroy figure in his logbook declaring **'Wot no more ops ?'**

Norman had flown over 900 hours in 25 different types of aircraft from over 80 airfields and from at least 2 ships. In January 1946 he left the RAF for civilian life once more.

Norman and his wife Pamela set up home in an apartment in Clifton Court in the St John's area of London, their first child Patrick, was born the following year. Norman attended the Regent Street Polytechnic in London, now known as the University of Westminster, where he studied Architecture. A second son, Michael, was born in 1951. Successfully passing his examinations, Norman became a member of the Royal Institute Of British Architects.

In 1957 Norman and his family moved to Canada where job prospects were better, settling in Don Mills, a residential area close to Toronto. He became a civil service architect with the Ontario Provincial Government for five years and for a time lived in Ottawa. In 1961 he worked for the Canadian Government and for a while livid in Toronto. Ten years later, on his retirement, he returned once more to the Don Mills area.

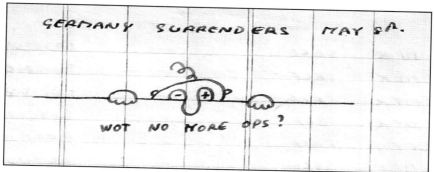

Norman's comical addition to his Log Book
after the end of the war is announced (P Lee)

Norman never returned to Malta, although he did return to England, the country of his birth several times. On 30th December 1979 Norman William Lee DFC passed away at the Sunnybrook Veterans Hospital, Toronto. He was aged only sixty.

Douglas Cecil Leggo

During the late 1950s a small boy growing up in Bulawayo in Southern Rhodesia (Now Zimbabwe) everyday gazed above his bed at a black and white photograph of a man in uniform. The portrait was of a man in his early twenties with a neat, clipped moustache, he looks directly into the camera in a formal portrait; he wears an Air Force uniform, and on his chest is a badge in the shape of a pair of silver wings denoting that he is a pilot, visible on his sleeve are 3 stripes - his rank is that of a Sergeant pilot, above these are a shoulder flash with the single word RHODESIA.

The boy was Gavin Cooper, the pilot was Douglas Leggo, the brother of Gavin's mother. The photograph left a deep impression on Gavin, who wanted to learn more about this man. At an early age, Gavin read the original Spitfires Over Malta book and became determined to find out more about the circumstances of the death of his uncle, believing that the description given at the time, and subsequently in other books, to be incorrect. Gavin was later able to correspond with the German pilot attributed to shooting down Douglas, and to 'Laddie' Lucas who flew on the same sortie as Douglas when he was killed.

Douglas Cecil Leggo was born on July 13th 1919 in Cape Town, South Africa, although he and his family initially lived in Portuguese East Africa (Now Mozambique), and then later they moved to Southern Rhodesia. He was born to parents Albert and Lillian, a brother for their first child, a daughter, Joan, (Gavin's mother), another brother, Lionel, was born later.

Albert Leggo was himself a former pilot having been in the Royal Flying Corps during the First World War, before returning to Southern Rhodesia and Portuguese East Africa. He later became a farmer, railway worker, telegrapher and professional big-game hunter. He was a strict disciplinarian who held traditional values dear, such as good manners and etiquette, and also a sense of fair play, all of these qualities he passed on to his children.

Douglas first went to school in Umtali (Now known as Mutare) in Southern Rhodesia, and then on to Milton School, an all-boys secondary school in Bulawayo, Rhodesia. He was a high-spirited child who was good at sports, particularly boxing, later representing his country successfully between the ages of 16 and 18 at flyweight and later at welterweight, as did his brother, Lionel. He was brought up in the Gorongoza, a wilderness paradise of exotic animals and bird life, where he became an expert shot, under the guidance of his father.

As a child, Douglas read of the first Siege of Malta in 1565, when the

Knights of St John defended the fortress of Malta against the Ottoman Empire's onslaught, and was greatly impressed by this battle of good versus evil, a story no doubt recalled later when he himself was sent to defend Malta.

A month after the outbreak of war in September 1939, over 2/3rds of the manpower of Southern Rhodesia had volunteered to serve in the armed forces. Douglas joined the Royal Air Force Volunteer Reserve. With the assistance of the British Government, the first Rhodesian Air Training Group was started in May 1940 with around 360 technical staff, helping to create the first Empire Air Training Scheme. Only one year later, 9 similar training schools were up and running.

Douglas began his training at No.25 Elementary Flying Training School at Belvedere airfield near Salisbury, flying the de Havilland Tiger Moth. He then moved to the nearby No.20 Service Flying Training School at Cranborne, where the faster Harvard aircraft were used for training. Take-offs and landings were made interesting at Cranborne as the runway had a hump in the middle not allowing a full view of the runaway until the pilot was over the rise.

At the end of the course, and having successfully completed examinations and a final flight with the Chief Flying Instructor, Douglas was awarded his 'Wings', the badge of a pilot, at a passing out parade. It is believed that during his training, Douglas first met with John Plagis who went on to become a high scoring fighter ace. The two became inseparable friends and flew

John Plagis and Douglas as recently qualified Sergeant Pilots in 1941 (G Cooper)

together later in their first squadron posting, and from HMS Eagle to Malta. Having completed his training in Rhodesia, Douglas was entitled to a period of leave, and during this time, before his embarkation to the UK, he married his fiancée, Eva Mells.

From February 1941 the first Rhodesian trained pilots began arriving in England. Douglas joined No.57 Operational Training Unit at Harwarden in Flintshire, Wales. At this unit his flying ability was assessed on Miles Master aircraft, before his introduction to the Spitfire.

Douglas was posted, after completion of his training to No.266 Squadron, known as the Rhodesian Squadron due to the large number of pilots from that country. Its Squadron badge featured a Bataleur, a medium sized, but agile eagle native to Rhodesia. The squadron, led by another Rhodesian Flight Lieutenant Charles Green, was based at Wittering in Northamptonshire and flew MkII Spitfires. The squadron, in addition to intercepting intruding Luftwaffe aircraft, took part in sweeps over northern France and in anti-shipping strikes off the coast of Holland.

At 266 squadron Douglas was reunited with his friend, John Plagis, and

The two good friends together John Plagis astride a Spitfire with Douglas standing below (G Cooper)

when they flew together they spoke to each other in 'Shona,' an African dialect that they were both fluent in, so any enemy listening was not able to understand them. In September the Squadron moved to Martlesham Heath in Suffolk, and then in October to Collyweston, and King's Cliffe, both in Northamptonshire. From October they also began to use the improved MkV Spitfire, Douglas's aircraft carried the name of his wife Eva painted beneath the cockpit.

On November 25th Douglas was promoted to the rank of Pilot Officer, his service number changing from 777652 to 80356.

A secret telegram was sent to Malta RAF Headquarters on February 1st 1942 confirming that the head of Fighter Command, Air Vice Marshall Sholto Douglas, had hand picked a list of pilots to fly the first Spitfires to Malta. The names of Plt Off Douglas Leggo and Plt Off John Plagis both appeared on that list.

The night before he left England, Douglas went with James Guerin and Plt Off Peter Nash into Blackpool for a quiet drink at an hotel, returning around 11:00pm, after which all 3 stayed up until 1:30am drinking and chatting to the Padre.

Having docked at Gibraltar on February 21st Douglas, along with Plt Off John Plagis and Plt Off Peter Nash, went for lunch at an hotel, returning later to the ship. In the evening they all went out again for drinks at a club and, after the pubs had closed at 9.30pm, they met up with some army officers and went back to their mess until 1.30am. Peter Nash described the two Rhodesian friends as both being a bit **'Squiffy.'**

Along with the other pilots, Douglas successfully flew to Malta on March 7th to become part of 249 Squadron at Takali. On the following day, along with Plt Off Peter Nash and Plt Off James Guerin, Douglas visited the Rabat museum and the remains of a Roman Villa, and probably spent the evening in the cinema along with other pilots.

The Spitfires first went into action on the morning of March 10th to intercept an incoming raid of Ju88 bombers; seven Spitfires were scrambled in two groups. Douglas flew in a group of four led by Flt Lt Heppell along with Plt Off Nash and his friend Plt Off John Plagis. All, apart from Douglas, made claims.

It is not known if Douglas flew again between this day and March 20th when he was killed, there were certainly more pilots available than there were Spitfires or Hurricanes to be flown.

Douglas on-board HMS Eagle on the journey to Malta (G Cooper)

Just after 8.00am on Friday March 20th 12 Hurricanes and four Spitfires were sent to intercept an incoming raid by Ju88s protected by Me109 fighters. The Spitfires were led by Flt Lt Laddie Lucas, with Flt Lt Buck McNair, Fg Off Raoul Daddo-Langlois and Douglas in Spitfire AB337 (GN-A). The Spitfire pilots, at 11,000 ft, spotted 6 Me109s close to the island of Filfla below them, they dived down to attack. Buck McNair was credited with the destruction of one of the Me109s in this combat.

Douglas's Spitfire was struck by the cannon fire of either Ltn Ernst Klager or more likely Ltn Hermann Neuhoff, both of 7/JG53, forcing him to bale out. The victorious German was pursued by Fg Off Daddo-Langlois who fired all his ammunition but with out success.

Laddie Lucas described the loss of Douglas:

'In my section, we spotted, far away to port, a single Spitfire obviously looking for a mate. As we turned to go to his aid, a lone 109, diving steeply and very fast out of the sun, pulled up, unseen, under the Spitfire. From dead astern, the pilot, who plainly knew his business, delivered a short, determined closing burst of cannon and machine gunfire, sending his victim rolling onto his back and spiralling down to earth or sea. It was a clinical operation. Relieved, we saw a parachute open.

'As we watched the silk canopy floating down in the distance, with the pilot swinging on its end, another single 109, diving down out of broken cloud, made a run at the 'chute, squirting at it as he went and collapsing it with his slipstream as he passed by. The canopy streamed leaving the pilot without a chance. The next thing we knew, the 109 was diving away for Sicily with never a hope of catching it.

'When we landed back at base, we found it was Duggie Leggo who had 'bought it'. When Johnny Plagis, Duggie's countryman and inseparable friend, was told the story he couldn't credit it. Then the reality of it seemed to overwhelm him. For two or three days, he was morose and uncharacteristically silent and brooding.'

Malta: The Thorn In Rommel's Side. Laddie Lucas. (Stanley Paul 1992)

Lance Bombardier Stanley Fraser of the 4th Heavy Anti-Aircraft Regiment Royal Artillery was also a witness and entered the following at the time in his diary:

'Before breakfast we witnessed a dogfight above our site which resulted in a rather sickening start to the day's activities. One of our Spitfires had one of its tail fins practically shot off and the pilot lost control of the plane. It fell like a falling leaf, describing small circles with it's nose downwards. Several times it seemed as though the pilot had managed to straighten out into a glide but no, on it came until, just over a hundred feet from the ground the pilot bailed out. He was too low. His parachute just billowed until the cords were taut. He reached the ground about the same time as the plane which just pancaked in the next field only a couple of hundred yards from our camp. When we picked the pilot up he was

246

grasping the harness of his parachute with both hands but he was dead. We placed him on a stretcher covering him up with the parachute and carried him into the Medical Inspection room. I thought at the time of his family in Rhodesia somewhere, just having breakfast maybe, oblivious of the horrible shock which awaited them; a telegram depriving them of the pride which they felt in having a son, so young, in his early twenties, and a Pilot Officer in the RAF.'

The Guns Of Hagar Qim: The Diaries Of Stan Fraser. 1939-1946
(Bieb Bieb Enterprises Ltd 2005)

Two other gunners also remembered the same incident later to the author Tony Rogers:

'The pilot of a Spitfire which had sustained bad damage ejected from his plane but was too low for his 'chute to properly open. He dropped between the gun-position and a line of hills, known as Gebel Cantar. Several of us ran to see if we could be of assistance…on arriving at the scene it was obvious the young man was quite dead. On his shoulders was the word RHODESIA.'

SNCO George Lord.

'His body was brought in on a stretcher by our medical orderly, Lance Bombardier Jimmy Corr…and placed on the floor of the MI hut. I saw him there and noticed he was dressed in blue battledress with one shoe missing and a large hole in his sock, which somehow seemed to make the whole incident more tragic. Later, the RAF came and took him away.'

Acting Bombardier Howard Bell.
The Battle Over Malta. Anthony Rogers. (Sutton Publishing Ltd. 2000)

These eyewitness accounts give us two versions of how Douglas was killed, it is accepted that Ltn Hermann Neuhoff is the more likely of the two German pilots to have shot him down, he was a very experienced fighter pilot having flown in the Battle of France, Battle of Britain and against Russian forces on the Eastern Front. Douglas was his 38th claimed victory.

The anti-aircraft gunners on the ground clearly witness Douglas' aircraft being struck in the tail fins making it uncontrollable, but it did not plunge to the ground in a violent dive. It appears, that with aircraft, particularly Spitfires, being so valuable at this stage of the war on Malta, Douglas may initially have tried to crash land the aircraft to try and make it salvageable, but jumped from it too late, not allowing his parachute enough time to billow and inflate with air, the subsequent impact with the ground killing him. The diary account was written on the same day rather than having been recalled from memory years later.

Laddie Lucas' account has Douglas shot down by one Me109, and then over flown by another so closely that the slipstream collapsed the parachute. Maybe he was mistaken, possible if his account was not written at the time, maybe even confusing Douglas' death with that of Plt Off Murray who was killed 10 days earlier, again amidst talk of being attacked whilst under his parachute by a close flying Me109.

Gavin Cooper corresponded after the war with Neuhoff who informed him

that whilst he could no longer recall individual combats he was adamant that neither he nor any of his men would attack a man in his parachute, as they would not have attacked any man once he had surrendered.

In the same battle, as well as Douglas being shot down, the German Uffz Fankhauser was also shot down by Buck McNair and was seen in the sea, he had almost certainly taken to his parachute, did this create the confusion, maybe his was the parachute that was over flown. Uffz Fankhauser did not survive, his body was washed up on Sicily seven weeks later.

The allied pilots at the time believed that a pilot had been killed unfairly and a Canadian pilot was later said to have sought revenge by deliberately shooting at and killing three-downed German aircrew

A photograph of Douglas that appeared in a local newspaper announcing his loss in 1942 (G Cooper)

in their dingy. John Plagis was particularly upset by the loss of his friend, he vowed to shoot down 10 German aircraft in revenge.

Ltn Neuhoff was himself shot down on April 10th and although injured, parachuted safely to become a prisoner of war.

Today the picture of Douglas, that was above Gavin Cooper's bed as a child is now mounted proudly above the bed of his own son Justin Cooper.

Pilot Officer Douglas Cecil Leggo aged 23 is buried in a shared grave in the Capuccini Naval Cemetery, Kalkara. Malta. Plot E. Grave 18. His name is also remembered on a war memorial plaque at Milton School in Bulawayo, Zimbabwe.

The temporary grave maker for the shared grave of Plt Off Kenric Murray, Plt Off Douglas Leggo,and three others. Strangely all five dates shown are incorrect, but were corrected when the permanent stone was installed
(D Thornton)

Norman Carter Macqueen

Laddie Lucas, the Commanding Officer of 249 Squadron on Malta in 1942, enjoyed many walks around the island with Norman during their periods off duty, and described him as being a modest and transparently honest man, with fair curly hair, good looks and with the personality to match.

Twenty-two year old Norman would never leave the island. His Spitfire fighter, having come under fire from an opposing Luftwaffe aircraft, plunged to the ground, his death tragically witnessed by many of his colleagues and friends. He was the fifth of the Operation Spotter pilots to be killed.

Norman was born on April 17th 1920 in Bloxwich Road, Leamore, Walsall in the West Midlands, a second son to parents Doctor Joseph Gordon Macqueen and his wife Helen Fairley. Their first son Kenneth Gordon was born three years earlier. Norman had the middle name Carter passed down to him from his mother, as it had been her maiden name prior to their marriage in December 1914. His parents had both originated from Scotland, Helen from Castle Douglas and Joseph from Balmaclellan approximately three miles away, areas that are now a part of Dumfries and Galloway.

Joseph qualified as a Doctor in 1911 and during the First World War he served with the Royal Army Medical Corps seeing service on the Western Front; by the end of the war he had risen to the rank of Captain. In 1921 the Macqueen family moved to Hyde in Cheshire where Joseph joined a medical practice in Church Street with Dr Paterson. Here, in June the following year, another son Ian Gordon was born. In 1930 the family moved once again, this time to Rhyl, a seaside town on the north east coast of Wales. There they took over Clarence House a large detached property in Russell Road to form a Doctors surgery on the ground floor, with living accommodation above.

At around eight years of age Norman was sent to become a boarder at the Cargilfield Preparatory School in Edinburgh, Scotland. In 1933 Norman joined his brother Kenneth at Fettes College, Edinburgh. Norman proved to be a good pupil becoming a prefect, and an accomplished sportsman. He also joined, within the college, the Officer's Training Corps, an association designed to encourage those with an interest in joining the regular or reserve armed forces. Norman became a Sergeant, marching, no doubt, proudly in a kilt to the sound of the drum and bagpipe band. He left the college aged 18 in July 1938.

Within a week of the outbreak of the Second World War Norman had signed up with the RAF Volunteer Reserve as an Aircraftman 2nd Class at No.3 Depot Padgate, Warrington, and was issued with the Service Number 968025. On

November 3rd 1939 he was called up to RAF Wick in Scotland staying until December 28th when he was posted to No.4 Initial Training Wing at Bexhill, near Hastings, East Sussex, holding the rank of Leading Aircraftman. On May 20th Norman was posted to No.7 Anti Aircraft Cooperation Unit, which had formed the month before at RAF Castle Bromwich, Birmingham, although his role with the unit during the three-weeks he stayed is unclear, as he was not as yet a trained pilot.

On June 10th Norman joined 50 Group Pool. Pools were formed to hold trained or part trained pilots before they could be sent on to a specific unit. On July 27th he was able to join No.5 Service Flying Training School based at RAF Sealand in Flintshire, North Wales. Tuition was on the Miles Master, a two seat advanced trainer monoplane.

In the second week of October 1940 Norman passed his flying and written examinations to gain his coveted 'Wings' badge as a qualified pilot. This also brought a promotion to the rank of Sergeant. Norman, on October 19th, transferred to No.57 Operational Training Unit at RAF Hawarden, Flintshire for additional training on Masters, also whilst here he flew a Spitfire for the first time. At the end of the course he was classed as ready to join an operational squadron.

The London Gazette confirmed in November that Norman had been granted a commission as a Pilot Officer, his Service Number changed to 86689 with the promotion backdated to the previous month when he had joined 57 OTU.

Norman's first squadron was 610 based at Westhampnett, a satellite airfield to Tangmere, both in Sussex. His stay here was only brief as fourteen days later he was posted to 602 Squadron who were also at the time based at Westhampnett. 602 had been in the front line since August, which included the Battle of Britain period, but, having suffered several casualties, they were on the December 17th posted to Prestwick, Scotland, to rest and train replacement pilots, one of whom was Norman. This was a good opportunity for Norman to learn from the experienced pilots who had fought during the Battle of Britain, before they were promoted and moved onto other squadrons. 602 were flying from Prestwick and Ayr taking part in convoy patrols and training exercises around the west coast of Scotland.

In January 1941 602 Squadron were chosen to provide aerial footage for Twentieth Century Fox who were making a film called A Yank In The RAF! The film, released the following year, starred Tyrone Power and Betty Grable and featured scenes of the aircraft on the ground and in the air, and a shot of the pilots running from the Old Mill at Prestwick to their Spitfires.

July 1941 saw the squadron, under the command of Sqn Ldr P E Meagher, move south again, as part of 11 Group based at Kenley, Surrey, to take part in offensive operations over occupied Europe. Their Spitfire MkII aircraft in August were replaced with the cannon armed Spitfire Vb. During this month the command also changed to Sqn Ldr Al Deere. 602 flew sometimes two or three times a day mainly operating as a part of the Kenley Wing which included 452 (Australian) Squadron and 485 (New Zealand) Squadron, flying large numbers of fighters as escort to a small numbers of bombers in the hope of drawing the Germans into battle. They did not have things their own way though; the Me 109F had recently come into service with the Luftwaffe and this could match the Spitfire V in performance.

In the first two-months since their move, 602 had flown over forty sorties back and forth across the English Channel the pilots were additionally equipped with personal survival dinghies in case of the need to bale out over the sea. Norman is attributed as saying:

"They couldn't have chosen a worse position in the dinghy pack to place the CO2 bottle it's almost indecent"
Nine Lives: Al Deere. (Hodder and Stoughton Ltd 1959)

On Sunday September 21st whilst on an incursion into France, Norman made a claim for damaging a Me109, after firing five two second bursts. He was now flying as the Flight Commander of Blue Flight. His Combat Report read:

'I was Blue 1. On crossing French coast at Le Touquet at 20,000 ft. many e/a seen ahead and above. Squadron did a wide sweep to the right and the leader ordered Blue Section to attack three e/a well below. I dived down and caught e/a up at about 6,000 ft. Over Hardelot One Me.109E immediately dived in to France and I fired several bursts at another Me.109F. Black smoke was pouring from it and it was gliding down to coast when a further Me. 109 attacked me from behind. I fired one short burst at it and having finished my ammunition returned to base at 0 feet.'

Two pilots were shot down on this sortie; 21 year old Sgt. Andre Hedger missing believed lost in the sea, and Sgt. Patrick Bell who crashed in France and, with the help of the Resistance fighters, was able to eventually make his way back to England four months later.

Losses were not only the result of enemy action; two 602 pilots were killed the following month flying low in poor visibility due to the weather. The weather and shorter daylight hours of winter did however, lead to the squadron flying fewer missions. Two new types of sortie were introduced at this stage; the first was the close escort of Beaufighters attacking hostile shipping, and the second the escorting of Hurricane bombers attacking targets in northern France.

In October Norman was promoted to the rank of Flying Officer, the announcement of confirmation appearing in the London Gazette on November 25th. Within the same month he had received another promotion to that of Acting Flight Lieutenant. Having previously volunteered for service abroad, the rank was confirmed as standing for his posting to Malta.

On Sunday February 1st 1942 Norman made his way by train to RAF Portreath, Cornwall, where he met the other pilots destined to go to Malta. Here they began their journey to the Mediterranean, with Norman leading the second of the two flights of Spitfires off HMS Eagle to Malta, where they became part of 249 Squadron.

The Spitfires first went in to action on Tuesday February 10th 1942; there had already been three raids that day by the time Norman was scrambled at around 4:30pm against another incoming raid. Forty enemy aircraft were approaching the airfields of Luqa and Hal Far. Eleven Hurricanes from 242 and 185 Squadrons along with four Spitfires were sent to intercept. Seven of the pilots including Norman claimed damage to German fighters or bombers in the dogfights that followed.

On March 14th Norman flew again as the leader of four Spitfire pilots, but when he found his radio had failed Plt Off Peter Nash took over. They intercepted three Ju88 bombers with a large escort of Me109 fighters, three of whom were seen to be circling around the island of Gozo apparently searching for their colleagues shot down earlier in the day. Norman dived down on one firing all his ammunition which he could see hitting the fuselage of the aircraft. The 109 appeared not to take any form of avoiding action and the pilot Uffz Adolf Jennerich baled out, to be retrieved from the sea by an Axis rescue plane later in the day.

Four days after his first confirmed victory Norman was successful again. In the early evening of March 18th 24 Ju88s with a large fighter escort penetrated inland to bomb the airfields. Six hurricanes and four Spitfires were scrambled but were attacked whilst still climbing by four Me109s. One of the Spitfires, flown by 20-year-old Plt Off Harold Fox, was shot down and he was killed. Norman attacked the aircraft that he believed was responsible closing to 100 metres firing until it crashed in to the sea off Wied iz-Zurrieq. The pilot Ltn

Kurt Lauinger from 7 Stab III/JG53 was rescued by High Speed Launch 107 (HSL107) with wounds that included a broken leg. He later told his own account of events.

Norman has time to enjoy the Mediteranean sunshine of Malta (F Galea)

'(We) were flying over Malta at 12,000 feet in two pairs stepped up in an echelon when (we) sighted three Spitfires below and dived to attack. I fired a burst at one of the Spitfires and then did a climbing turn in order to keep at the same height as the section leader. By this time one of the other Spitfires had turned inside me and attacked, shooting away (my) rudder. (I) Baled out, landed in the sea and was picked up after dark by a rescue launch".

Spitfires Over Malta: Brian Cull with Frederick Galea. (Grub Street. 2005)

Norman and some of the other pilots went to see Lauinger when they visited their own injured colleagues at the Imtafa Hospital. It was apparently his first mission and because he was intent on sticking close to his No.1 he did not see Norman's aircraft until it was too late. He was not an ardent Nazi but did believe that he would be rescued when the Germans invaded Malta. Laddie Lucas described one visit:

'He was an intelligent and agreeable man of twenty one, full of good humour and, considering his predicament, also of spirit. Macqueen was naturally interested to exchange notes with his victim.

'Lauinger gave no secrets away, and most correctly and politely, put up the shutters when we turned the conversation to the strength and disposition of Kesselring's forces in Sicily.

'But he was obviously fascinated by flying and, when we told him about the 'names' among the pilots we had with us on the island, he was quite prepared to talk about the qualities of the German squadron and wing leaders he served with, their victories and their foibles.

'He was ready to give his opinion on the few Italian fighter squadrons which were now beginning to appear in small numbers in Sicily. He and his comrades obviously thought little of them. I remember when we asked him what, in particular, he thought of the standard of the fighter pilots in the Regia Aeronautica, he picked up a torch from the table beside him and started shining it under the bed as if he were looking for something. Grinning away he said "We do not see them. They are not anywhere. They are not. Please. How do you say, battle happy!"

Five Up: Laddie Lucas. (Sidgwick and Jackson. 1978)

Around 6pm on March 22nd Norman flew with two other Spitfires as escort to five torpedo carrying Albacore biplanes intent on attacking Italian shipping. Two 109s attacked them from out of the sun, Norman turned towards one that was on the tail of one of the other Spitfires, then turned away to the other 109 which was firing at one of the more vulnerable Albacores. The 109 started going down in a shallow dive, and was seen to be close to the surface of the sea, when Norman saw a splash he claimed the aircraft as destroyed.

In the early afternoon of the 23rd Norman, in conjunction with another Spitfire flown by Plt Off Sergeant, along with two Hurricanes from 185 Squadron, intercepted three Ju88s. All three were damaged; one had its engines set on fire after an attack from both of the Spitfires. The next day at around 2:00pm Norman, along with Fg Off Daddo-Langlois, was scrambled to intercept a reconnaissance Ju88. They pursued it to close to the Sicilian coastline both firing at it with Daddo-Langlois expending all his ammunition, and noting in his logbook that his air speed indicator had shown 380mph during the chase. It was not seen to crash, so both pilots claimed another damaged only. However, a Ju88 and its crew were lost in the sea off Catania although records recorded this as being due to an accident.

The light cruiser HMS Penelope had been severely damaged by bombing raids whilst in Malta and was under repair in the dry docks and became a target during further bombing raids. Her hull was holed so many times in the bombing she acquired the nickname HMS Pepperpot. Her crew had helped fight fires around the docks and her anti aircraft defences added to the dockyards own defences. On the evening of the 4th April she again came under attack by sixty Ju87 and Ju88 bombers. Norman, leading four Spitfires, attacked one of the Ju88s, its starboard engine caught fire. He then turned his attention to the port engine and the aircraft turned on its back and dived vertically away. It is believed to have crashed on return to its base at Comiso. Four days later, after temporary repairs had been completed, HMS Penelope was able to leave the docks and Malta.

In the late afternoon of April 10th a combined force of over 85 Ju88 and Ju87 bombers attacked the Grand Harbour and the airfields of Takali and Hal Far. They were intercepted by ten Hurricanes and six Spitfires, one flown by Norman, who, along with Fg Off Norman Lee fired at a Ju88 which had its gun turret blown away with the gunner Uffz Paul Boger still inside, it crashed onto the airfield at Takali. The airfield anti aircraft defences also claimed this aircraft as shot down.

Four days later Norman made another shared claim this time with Plt Off Sergeant. They had been sent to cover the return of a reconnaissance Maryland aircraft and found it being pursued by Me109 fighters. Between them they shot one Me109 down its pilot being picked up by the Malta air sea rescue launch. Plt Off Sergeant wrote later:

'Cover for Maryland. Attacked by two Messerschmitts with three below. A good squirt at one 109 and a quick squirt at another. A 109 went in so Mac and I split the bag-half destroyed, half damaged.'
Spitfires Over Malta. Brian Cull with Frederick Galea. (Grub Street. 2005.)

In mid April Norman was notified of his award of the Distinguished Flying Cross. The citation read:

'This officer carried out a large number of sorties over enemy occupied territory and destroyed one enemy aircraft whilst based in this country. In the Middle East he has destroyed a further four hostile aircraft. Throughout his operational career. Flt Lt Macqueen has rendered most valuable service. He has displayed great skill and leadership.'

Flt Ltn Tim Johnston wrote in his diary on April 18th:

'A party to celebrate gongs for Macqueen and Johnny Plagis. Whisky, gin and liqueurs still seem plentiful, but there isn't very much serious drinking, just an occasional celebration. Personally I daren't to fly here with a hangover would be the shortest cut to glory I know.'

Tattered Battlements. Tim Johnston. (William Kimber and Co Ltd 1985)

Pilots watch an air battle above the balcony of the officers mess in Mdina, now the Xara Palace Hotel. (M. Woodhall)

The award was confirmed in the London Gazette on May 1st, three days before Norman was killed.

Around 5:15pm on April 20th Norman was the leader of a flight of six Spitfires from 249 Squadron, and, along with six from 126 squadron, they had been scrambled to intercept a large incoming raid of over sixty Ju88 and twenty-five Ju87 bombers, with an escort of in excess of 30 Me109s. The ground controller held them off to the south of the island to save fuel and await the mass of aircraft approaching. Then, on his command, they swept in to attack. With the advantage of height Norman was able to dive down onto a Ju88 from above firing his guns and saw the strikes on the aircraft, which he believed crashed down to disappear into the sea below.

The following afternoon he was again successful. Having bombed the airfield at Takali a number of Ju88s and Me109s were withdrawing to head out over the small islet of Filfla towards their bases in Sicily. Norman was again able to destroy one of the fighters and claimed damage to a Ju88. The danger for him was not over though, as coming into land he was pursued by two Me109s. When around 50 feet up and only a few seconds from being an easy target on the ground, Norman spotted one of the fighters firing at him from behind and quickly whipped up the Spitfire's undercarriage and turned sharply away. Short on fuel he quickly came in to land again and with the ground defences chasing off the German fighters he landed safely. Only one of the Me109s had fired but he had been a poor shot and missed the Spitfire. Norman's flying skill and luck had held, so far, in all the air battles he had been in, his aircraft had not received a single strike from the enemy.

**Spitfire MkVc BR226 being hoisted aboard the USS Wasp,
Norman would lose his life flying this aircraft on May 4th 1942.(F. Galea)**

On the morning of Friday May 1st Norman and Plt Off Les Watts were conducting an air test of their aircraft around Filfla islet, when the ground controller advised them of a small formation of fighters in the area. They soon spotted four Me109s each fitted with a long-range fuel tank and gave chase as they attempted to reach Sicily. Having caught them up one of the 109s was shot down into the sea and was shared as destroyed between the two pilots. The 109 pilot survived the attack and the ditching of his aircraft into the sea and his own forces later recovered him.

The death of Norman on Monday May 4th was unfortunately witnessed by many of his friends and colleagues watching from the veranda of the mess at Xara Palace, they knew him now just by his nickname of Mac. At the time Norman had taken over temporary command of the squadron from Stan Grant, an indication of how his career might have progressed had he survived.

In the late afternoon a force of five three-engined Cant Z1007 Italian bombers, along with a mixed force of Italian and German fighters, flew over the island to bomb the Grand Harbour. Norman led off three other Spitfires from 249 Squadron as part of their response; Flt Sgt Paul Brennan and Plt Off Ossie Linton, with the less experienced American Plt Off Fred Almos flying as No.2 to Norman. Once airborne the group of four inadvertently became separated and were now in two pairs. Norman and Almos, and Brennan and Linton, and were soon caught up in a twisting dogfight with the 109 fighters. Brennan successfully shot down one of the 109s. Almos then called on the radio that Norman was in trouble and wanted to land, Linton having been in his own dogfight had by then landed at Takali.

It is believed that Norman's radio was not working and he was not aware of messages from Almos warning of an imminent attack. A 109 swept down onto his Spitfire but overshot. Then the German's wingman followed behind and pulled up underneath, firing at Norman's aircraft. Those who witnessed the action saw the strikes beneath the cockpit area. No doubt now wounded, Norman appeared after a few moments to have control of the Spitfire (BR226), which was trailing smoke and was approaching to make a landing when suddenly the nose dropped and the aircraft plummeted down to the ground at San Pawl Tat-Targa on the outskirts of Naxxar. It is believed that Norman had lost consciousness due to his wounds. He had been shot down by Uffz. Walter Manz of III/JG53, the first of the eight victories he went on to claim during the war.

One of those to witness Norman's loss was Flight Lieutenant Denis Barnham of 601 Squadron whose account was later published:

'Cyril's (Flying Officer Cyril Hone) seen something: two dots curving downwards, two fighters swinging round over the bomb dust heading towards us, Spitfires, but they're too late, the bombers have gone.

'Approaching our hillside the Spitfires start to turn: I'm not particularly impressed by the way they are crossing over. Look out! A black shape is hurtling upon them; swerving, but it's going too fast: it can't bring its guns to bear. Its engine howls as the 109 passes low in front of us; it wavers as the pilot twists in his seat to see if he is being followed, then, with sudden power, it bounds forward, behind Naxxar's square buildings, reappearing above the skyline in the distance, a tiny dot streaking away

northwards.

'A 109 by itself? Never. Where's its number two? We all searched the sky. The two Spits are climbing in vic formation much too close together, tactically vulnerable, why doesn't the second Spit take up its wide line-abreast formation for mutual protection? If there is a second 109, watching, the Spits are asking for trouble; there's nothing we can do to help them. They circle left, still in tight vic formation, and with their engines murmuring lazily they pass above us. The second German! With horror we watch a black dot dive vertically down the blue just this side of Valletta; it eases out of its dive about two miles away, and now, low behind the grain store it's rushing towards us. The Spitfires haven't seen its angled shape growing larger and larger; they can't hear its roaring engine. Turn, you fools, turn…turn…the 109, making for the second Spitfire, lifts gently over our heads, then, swerving towards the leader, opens fire. Although the second Spit breaks violently right, the leader continues straight and level for that critical instant longer: a flash of a shell striking below its cockpit before a 109 streaks upwards and away.

'The Spitfire circles to the left, wobbling a little, trailing a wisp of smoke, but now, as both machines level out and pass slowly over our heads, the smoke has stopped, the leader's engine is running smoothly, it flies steadily while its companion, after making an inquisitive turn towards it, moves out into wide line abreast where it should have been all the time. The section heads towards Naxxar, lucky to have escaped; but no, the leading machine trembles as if an uncertain hand is holding the controls. It steadies itself again. It's turning. Its nose is dropping. It is plunging straight down. Pull out…pull out…with engine roaring it seems to hang for an instant between the twin towers of Naxxar church, then drops out of sight. Scotty (Pilot Officer T. W. Scott) puts his fingers in his ears: wuump, a sprout of black smoke is mounting higher and higher above the buildings.

'I turn to my pilots "have you learned the lesson from that?" I demand angrily. "Number two's fault, he was too damned close. If you fly like that in our squadron, I'll shoot you down myself."

'The second Spitfire is circling the smoke pillar. We run – but what is the use of running? As we pass the church we are joined by a crowd of small boys. I find myself leading a strange party through the narrow streets and out along the road beyond the town, for the plane has crashed near the army camp. Although a platoon of soldiers is called to attention as I pass, I know they salute the officer who has just died. Nearing the place I send back the children; I also tell my pilots there is no need for them to see the wreck, but they follow me; over the stone walls towards a gully where dark red flame fringed with black smoke gushes up. It is a place of humped rock, disturbed red earth and burnt grass; there are a few pieces of telescoped metal; everyone looks very tall; a Sergeant Major and a Corporal are shovelling earth onto flames near a flat disc which may have been a wheel; two other soldiers are searching among scattered fragments, while a Private next to me with a rifle slung round his shoulders stares down at a twisted piece of propeller mechanism. My pilots are climbing back towards the road, but I am sketching the scene in my diary. It is silent but for the fire which crackles and spurts. As I stare down at the wreckage, drawing unrecognisable pieces, I seem to feel someone I know, I seem to be in the presence of Mac, Peter's (Pilot Officer Peter Nash) friend. Quietly in inner silence I bid him farewell.

'A car has drawn up on the road above us: the short plump figure of Gracie, now a Wing Commander at Takali, is climbing over the rocks towards me. Two army officers have joined him and now all four of us stare down at the pieces. As Gracie prods a large lump of earth, the soldiers hand him their finds: a wallet, a photograph of a girl, two postcards from England, and a ring which have miraculously been thrown clear. Again Gracie prods the lump with his foot; with horror I realise I could have been standing on what is unrecognisably Mac's body.

"What do you want us to do with it?" asks the army officer.

"Dig it in," says Gracie.

"No. Don't dig it in", I interrupt hotly; an air battle is waging but invasion has not yet started, the soldiers must have plenty of time to bury him. "His girl in England" I continue, "or his family may want to visit his grave one day".

"Any monument in a cemetery will do", replies Gracie.

"Don't dig it in – give him a proper burial", is my only retort. I am much junior to Gracie, I don't know if I will be obeyed or not. Gracie's only concern is with the efforts of the living to save Malta, and he's magnificent at that; Mac's dead body is now irrelevant. I know it is a discarded thing, empty of essence, but for the sake of those who come after us please God let a stone or a cross mark the actual spot where this moist earth is finally laid to rest.'

One Man's Window. Denis Barnham. (William Kimber and Co. Ltd. 1956.)

Flight Lieutenant Tim Johnston wrote in his diary of the event and another incident before when Norman came close to losing his life:

'**Poor Mac, he was the most likeable and modest person; also one of the most successful, with seven confirmed plus probables in the two months he'd been here. He'd had one narrow escape, after following an 88 too far, when six 109's jumped him out at sea; in his evasive action his motor had cut out and at 1,000 feet he'd tried to bale out, but had been unable to open or jettison his hood; he'd given himself up as lost, and then at 200 feet his engine, for no reason, had cut in again and brought him safely home. Even then, and I think on all his other flights, neither he nor his machine had been hit, and now a casual burst from a 109, which was much more interested in getting home than in fighting, proved fatal. It's difficult to follow. When someone is shot down you shut your mind to it and carry on as if he was away on leave. It was only when I saw that Macqueen's bed, which stood opposite the door, and all his personal kit, including a photograph of a girl, had been taken away, that it came home to me what had happened.'**

Tattered Battlements. Tim Johnston. (William Kimber and Co Ltd. 1985.)

Laddie Lucas said the loss of Norman was '**felt deeply for he was universally liked with his sunny and modest personality which bore ill to no man. Life was a game to be played to the full until the final whistle.' They both shared an interest in photography and each had their own camera on Malta. Laddie's camera was, however, stolen from his room one day and Norman, hearing of this, said that if he should ever be killed then he wanted Laddie**

The inscription on Norman's shared grave stone
at the Capuccini Naval Cemetery, Kalkara.

to have his German made Kodak-Retina camera. The adjutant was told so that he could confirm the wish later if required. Norman's camera was recovered undamaged in the shattered wreckage of the Spitfire and Laddie used and treasured his friend's camera from then on. He said 'I

never felt that Norman ever had a premonition that he might not see out the battle. He was too happy and jolly to harbour any such maudlin thoughts.'

P/O Peter Nash Wrote in his diary at the time:

'Macqueen and his boys had a lot of trouble with 109s from the start and later one 109 bounced Macqueen and his No.2. He attacked No.2 who turned but Macqueen turned too late and 109 hit him. He stayed in control for about a minute and then dived straight in just east of Mosta and was killed instantly. So dies the lion hearted fighter who has shot down 6 and a half enemy aircraft also some probables and damaged and got a DFC in just two months. Cheerio Mac and happy landings in your hunting grounds.'

Even Kurt Lauinger the German pilot who had been shot down by Norman and who had been visited by him in hospital had been touched by his personality, and had somehow acquired a charred photograph of Norman, which he kept.

For many of the allied pilots Norman's loss was a warning of their own mortality. Paul Brennan later admitted to becoming over confident having shot down his sixth enemy fighter the same day Norman was killed, but realised that if a pilot as good as Norman could be shot down then he too was vulnerable. This awakening may have saved his life in the air battles to follow.

Norman's name is remembered on the Rolls of Honour where he was educated within the Memorial Chapel in Cargilfield Preparatory School, and also on the Fettes College War Memorial, Edinburgh. In his hometown Rhyl in Wales his name is in inscribed on the memorial within the Garden of Remembrance on East Parade. Norman's father Joseph, outlived all of his sons and his wife. He died in 1979 and, as he wished, his ashes were scattered near to the Rhyl memorial, the closest he could get to be reunited with his son.

In April 2010, after research by Rhyl local historians Charles Leach and George Hornby, a presentation ceremony was held to commemorate Norman's life within his hometown. A copy of his DFC and a written profile of him was presented to the Mayor of Rhyl at a ceremony held at the Public Library, this was attended by around 25 invited guests including the Air Commodore For Wales, Adrian Williams, and representatives of Fettes College, Edinburgh.

Flight Lieutenant Norman Carter Macqueen DFC aged 22 was buried in the Capuccini Naval Cemetery, Kalkara, Malta. Within a shared grave, Plot E. Grave 2.

Kenric Newton Lathrop Murray

Kenric Murray was born on Sunday 23rd October 1921 in Melbourne, Australia, to parents Elia and Hugh Murray. He grew up with his older sister, Mon, in the town of Toorak, Victoria, and went on to attend the Anglican Melbourne Grammar Boys School in South Yarra.

He was described by Stewart Brooks, a contemporary of his school days as:

'... A very strong fellow, rowed 4 seat, very heavy build, and very quiet. Colossal crew member, never argued or got upset when Wally Ricket (The Rowing Coach) blew his top. Others got taken aback, Ken didn't.

... Not over friendly but if he liked you he'd talk to you, very quiet bloke...very serious fellow, took rowing very seriously, one of the stronger members of the crew... very fit, we used to row 5 evenings a week after school and on Saturday mornings.'

Although well built and being around 5'11" tall he was not an aggressive man and was described as a **'Gentle man in every respect'**.

19 year old Ken during his training in 1940 (Thornton)

On June 23rd 1940 aged 19 Ken enlisted with the Royal Australian Air Force and was allocated the service number 400152. Basic training took place at a Flying Training School in Australia, before he departed to Canada as part of the Empire Training Scheme. Over 50,000 Commonwealth pilots were eventually trained under this scheme during the Second World War, safe in the Canadian skies away from the attentions of any enemy aircraft.

The first Australian contingent left for Canada on November 14th 1940. Ken could possibly have been amongst these as, in a letter he sent home in February 1941, he wrote that it had been 3 months since he had left Australia, at that time he was with No.1 Flying Training School, in Borden, Canada.

Writing and receiving letters was an important part of Ken's service life, and during his time abroad he sent a letter home every two weeks, to his mother and sister or girlfriend Daphne. In one of his early letters during training, he mentions early problems with instrument flying, and his worry that this may lead to him failing his 'wings' exam.

Weather conditions could be very harsh in Canada and in another letter he describes a period of two weeks when no flying was possible and how, on the January 31st 1941, he was forced to land his aircraft due to bad weather and was only able to fly back to base three days later when conditions had improved.

On February 4th 1941 two student pilots from Ken's course were killed when their aircraft (possibly a Harvard) crashed whilst flying through a blizzard, the aircraft plunged down, breaking up on the ice covering a frozen lake. Ken was particularly upset by the loss of one of the students, his good friend 19 year old Claude Murray Ross, and admitted in a letter home how he **'All but broke down'** after being told that wreckage had been seen on the ice. The body of his friend was never recovered. Many of his future letters would refer back to the death of this close friend, in one that he wrote to his mother he said:

'I have been set an example and am going to try my hardest to reach and maintain the high standard that Claude has left with me.'

Ken passed his instrument flying test with an **'above average'** mark and on February 6th he received his RCAF wings at a passing out parade.

Ken on leave at home in late 1940 (Thornton)

The following day announcements of those Commissioned to the rank of Pilot Officer were given out. Ken did not receive a Commission and at the time said he was glad he had not received one. However, he did later refer many times to his desire to become a Pilot Officer, but for now he remained a Sergeant pilot. On the 9th February he attended a parade to receive his Royal Australian Air Force wings, these he claimed were **'100% better than the RCAF ones.'** He then went on to a pre-embarkation camp at Ottawa before departing by ship for service in the UK.

During April Ken was given four days leave which he spent partly in London, staying at the Cumberland Hotel, and past the evenings with other pilots in the bars and nightclubs of the city. Here he also witnessed the results of an evenings heavy bombing of London by the Luftwaffe.

In early May Ken was posted to 602 Squadron based at Ayr in Scotland, flying MkII Spitfires. He was not very pleased to find that he was the only one from all of the Australian pilots to be sent to this squadron. During this time he mentions his feeling of becoming home sick, and how he had started to suffer from occasional styes in his eyes, no doubt missing the Australian climate, he mentions the possibility of seeking a transfer to the East or Egypt, this possibly may have been the start of his journey to Malta.

In late June Ken wrote home to say he had intended to send some photographs back but the Police had seized three quarters of them on security grounds, even though some were of towns in Canada taken from the air. He also wrote of his hope that he may soon become a Pilot Officer. During July Ken received a new Spitfire, which was a Presentation Spitfire, an aircraft paid for by a group or country. This was one of three Spitfires bought by the Government and people of Tasmania with a donation of £18,000. The aircraft, a MkIIa P8183, had Tasmania III written on its side, Ken declared he would also like to have painted on the side, a picture of a Kangaroo with Hitler in its pouch.

Ken standing in front of a 602 Squadron Spitfire in 1941 (Thornton)

On July 10th the squadron flew south to be part of the Kenley Wing based at Kenley and its satellite airfield Redhill in Surrey, now re-equipped with the Mark V Spitfire the squadron undertook operations over the channel into Northern France, escorting bombers and trying to draw the enemy fighters into combat.

In the early evening of Sunday August 3rd Ken was flying his Tasmania III over Northern France. His combat report described the events leading up to his claim for the destruction of a Me109.

'I was Yellow 4, 602 Squadron on offensive sweep over St Omer area. 4

Me109F's seen 1,000ft above and to starboard of squadron over Marquise. One enemy aircraft stayed up and three dived down onto yellow section, who flew in echelon to the left. One enemy aircraft dived onto me quarter head on. I turned up to get him in my sights, fired a short 1-second burst at 150 yards. Enemy aircraft turned to the right in front of me. I saw sparks coming from the engine and little pieces falling which seemed to come from the engine cowling. I made a second attack from quarter astern, firing a short 1-second burst from 100 yards, black smoke was pouring out of enemy aircraft's engine. Enemy aircraft turned slowly to the left, dived and started to spin. F/Lt Hopkin saw enemy aircraft spiralling down and Sgt Gardon saw it burst into flames before entering cloud. I dived down across channel, rejoined section and returned to base'.

Back row, Ken Murray, 7th from the left; with 602 Sqaudron at RAF Prestwick in 1941 (Thornton)

On October 10th 1941, two weeks before his 20th birthday, confirmation was finally received of his commission to the rank of Pilot Officer.

At the National Archives in Kew, Surrey, a document is held listing the names of eighteen pilots who had been interviewed by Wing Commander H. Pearson Rogers, for the proposed reinforcing of Malta with Spitfires. Ken Murray's name did not appear on this initial list, but two of the pilots who are mentioned are noted as having insufficient experience, and were subsequently withdrawn from the final selection. Ken indeed received his earlier wish of a transfer to a warmer climate, and he was posted to join 249 Squadron based at Takali, Malta.

The last letter received from Ken was sent from the port of Gibraltar and dated 1st March 1942. The aircraft carrier HMS Eagle had returned early from the mission to fly off the Spitfires, having been aborted due to the problems with the underbelly fuel tanks not functioning correctly.

The days that HMS Eagle had been at sea, Ken refers to nonchalantly as a **'cruise around the Mediterranean'** not wishing to write of the worry and fear he must have held prior to his first ever take off from an aircraft carrier. He did though mention he was suffering from several ailments, including a stye on both eyes, boils, a rash and 'Flu. Perhaps these had been brought on by the stress of the impending event.

In this last letter he is again thinking reflectively of home, it is now a year and a half that he has been away from his family, and leaving familiar parts of England seems to have made him feel even further away from his loved ones. He thinks of his sister's birthday later that same month, and of a time after the war when they can be together, and the family will all be reunited once again.

Fellow members of Ken's Squadron, headed by Ft Lt Whaley Heppell, carry his coffin into the Capuccini Naval Cemetery, March 1942 (Thornton)

Three days after their arrival on the island, the Spitfires went into action for the first time on March 10th against an incoming raid of Ju88 bombers and their fighter escort. In the late afternoon another raid came in to attack the airfields, and Ken was one of four Spitfire pilots, along with several Hurricanes, who were scrambled to intercept. In the mêlée of battle between the two opposing forces, Ken was either shot down by Hptm Karl-Heinz Krahl, an experienced pilot already with 18 claimed victories, or Fw Hans Schade. Ken's aircraft plunged down to crash at Ta' Zuta. Ken was able to bale out of his damaged Spitfire but his parachute failed to open fully, and he sustained severe injuries when he plummeted to the ground. He died in hospital later that evening. It was believed by some that Ken might even have been deliberately over flown by a Me109 fighter, flying so closely that this had caused his parachute canopy to collapse and fail.

Pilot Officer Kenric Murray, aged twenty, was the first of the HMS Eagle Spitfire pilots to be killed. He was buried on the morning of March 12th within a joint grave at the Capuccini Naval Cemetery, Kalkara, Malta. Plot E, Grave 18. His name is also remembered on a Roll of Honour in Toorak, Australia, and on the Australian War Memorial, Campbell, Canberra. Panel 127 in the Commemorative area.

Peter Alfred Nash

In early 1921 the marriage was held within the St Pancras area of London between Mr Edward Nash and Miss Hilda Noakes. On December 22nd of that same year their first child Peter Alfred was born at their home, at 112 Station Road, Barnes, London.

In 1931 from the age of ten Peter attended the Alleyn's School, a fee-paying boy's public school in Dulwich, South East London. He left in 1937 and began work with the Times Newspaper as a reporter, his father a News Compositor almost certainly also worked for the same well-known national daily newspaper.

Peter's RAF career (service number 113759) began on July 1st 1940 when

Peter Nash relaxing, the insignia on his sleeve denoting his rank as a Pilot officer (F. Galea)

he joined No.1 Receiving Wing in Babbacombe, Devon, where he was kitted out with his uniform and underwent medical examinations and inoculations. After two weeks he moved to No.5 Initial Training Wing where he remained until September 8th for drill and basic training, this led on to No.13 Elementary Flying Training School (E.F.T.S) at White Waltham where Peter began to learn to fly.

The former De Havilland School of Flying at White Waltham Berkshire had been established to train reservists, but after the outbreak of war it became No.13 E.F.T.S. Here it was, on September 9th 1940, that Peter had his first flight as a passenger in a de Havilland Tiger Moth bi-plane, followed by an explanation of the layout of the cockpit. For the next two weeks Fg Off Wesson his instructor taught him the art of flying, starting with straight and level flight, then turning, taxing, taking off into the wind, landings, stalling, and how to control spins. On September 24th in Tiger Moth DH82a (G-ADHS) he flew his first solo flight of twenty minutes. Further practices continued including instrument flying, low flying, forced landings, and aerobatics.

At the end of the course on October 12th Peter's training had consisted of over 20 hours of dual instruction, plus 21 hours 20 minutes solo flying, and 3 hours in a Link trainer. His logbook was endorsed with his assessment rating as **'Average.'**

The next stage of training with No.5 Service Flying Training School was divided between RAF Sealand in Flintshire, Wales, and RAF Ternhill in Shropshire. Flying instruction was in the two seat Miles Master, an advanced single wing aircraft having a maximum speed of 260mph, with an enclosed cockpit and retractable undercarriage. Peter flew his first solo on the type on October 27th 1940. In December Peter gained his coveted 'Wings' and was promoted to the rank of Sergeant.

Further practice and training continued to include formation flying and navigation, plus long cross-country flights, until, early in April 1941 with over 122 hours in his logbook, he was transferred to No.53 Operational Training Unit. 53 OTU were formed in February 1941 at RAF Heston in Middlesex its grass runways were used to train fighter pilots for Fighter Command using Spitfire MKI and II aircraft.

After a few days of reconnaissance of the area surrounding his new airfield and with additional practice flights in a Miles Master, on April 20th Peter had an air examination with the Chief Flying Instructor Wing Commander John A. Kent. For 19-year-old Peter this must have been a daunting prospect, 27-year-old Wing Commander Kent, a Canadian former test pilot, had already shot down 7 aircraft with several others as probables, and had been awarded the DFC and AFC.

Peter was successful and a white piece of typed paper was affixed to his logbook stating.

'Sergeant Nash is permitted to fly Spitfire aircraft, having passed written examination and cockpit drill tests to my satisfaction.'

As there were not any dual control Spitfires available at the time, Peter's first flight on April 20th in Spitfire MkIA X4616 was also his first solo.

Training continued with more new procedures constantly being added, these included cloud flying, dog fighting, climbing to altitudes of 30,000ft, formation attacks, and the firing of the guns into the sea off Littlehampton. On May 26th Wing Commander Kent signed his logbook with another assessment of his ability, again his evaluation was noted as **'Average.'** He had now flown over 190 hours in total, 151 of them solo, and was now ready to join No.65 Squadron, his first operational squadron.

65 Squadron were based at RAF Kirton located 15 miles north of the city of Lincoln in Lincolnshire, they were equipped with the heavier but slightly

more powerful Spitfire MKII. Part of 12 Group, their main roles were the defence of northern England and convoy patrols.

On May 30th with the offensive being taken more and more against the Luftwaffe, Peter, with 65 Squadron, flew down to West Malling in Kent to refuel, then, as part of a wing, they took part in an offensive sweep over the English Channel to the French towns of Le Touquet, St Omer and Gravelines. A similar sweep was carried out again a week later. Peter left 65 Squadron on July 5th and probably enjoyed some leave before joining his next squadron 609 who were based at Biggin Hill in Kent. A famous Battle of Britain Squadron, 609 had been the first Spitfire squadron in October 1940 to reach 100 victories against the enemy.

The forward location of Biggin Hill close to the channel and occupied France meant that the squadron, commanded by Squadron leader Michael Robinson, were heavily involved with fighter sweeps over the channel, and above the French coastal ports and towns. Within two weeks of joining 609 on July 14th Peter had flown 12 offensive missions and was now flying the improved MkVb Spitfire, these carried 4 machine guns and two 20mm Hispano cannons, in place of the eight machine guns of the earlier Spitfires. In mid August Peter had his first successes when twice he was able to damage a Me109 whilst flying over France.

During August and September the Squadron was based at Gravesend continuing their fighter sweeps, or acting as escort for bombers striking shipping and the French coastal ports, on one of these escorts Peter was again able to see his fire hit but not destroy an Me109. His first victory was scored on October 13th achieved over a Me109 fighter whilst on a bomber escort, flying Spitfire Vb AD202 (PR-U) he wrote in his logbook:

'He made 4 attacks on the squadron. Flew right across me. Got in good quarter (shot). Flamer.'

609 Squadron contained many commonwealth and other nationals including several from Belgium, one of whom was Flight Lieutenant Jean Offenberg who commanded 'B' flight in which Peter flew. Offenburg wrote a diary that was later edited and published under the title Lonely Warrior, in which Peter is mentioned:

'But Sergeant Nash was the star turn of the day. A Messerschmitt passing within firing range, he gave him a long burst in the engine. The German had time to bale out and his machine exploded in the sea.'

Further success was achieved on November 7th during an offensive sweep around Dunkirk and Le Touquet. Whilst flying the same Spitfire Peter claimed a Me109 destroyed and a Focke-Wulf 190 probably destroyed. He described the events later in his Combat Report:

'I was flying Red 4 during this operation, but became separated from the formation owing to a previous attack. I was about 3 miles off Le Touquet when I was attacked by six bandits, three of which were Me109F's and three were FW190's. A very close-quarter dogfight ensued during which I was able to get a starboard quarter shot at a Me109F. It immediately emitted a quantity of white smoke and went straight down into the sea. I then managed to get a short port quarter attack on a Fw190 which threw out volumes of black smoke and rolled on it's back. This was at 4000 ft. and about 5 miles off the French coast. The height of the combat ranged between 18,000 ft and 1,000 ft, and lasted 10 minutes.'

On November 27th the squadron was moved to RAF Digby in Lincolnshire, part of 12 Group and away from the excitement and danger of the Channel sweeps for a period of rest. There followed days of patrols and practice formation flying, Peter noted in his logbook after his arrival:

'My first flip at Digby. Not impressed by the place.'

On December 1st Peter was promoted to the rank of Pilot Officer. At the end of the month his total hours flown were totalled and added to his logbook he had now flown over 353 hours, the page was signed off by Flight Lieutenant Jean Offenberg DFC. The following month Flt Lt Offenberg was tragically killed over Digby airfield on a training exercise, when a Spitfire from another squadron collided with his aircraft. Peter came back from a weeks leave to be told the news; he later acted as a Pallbearer at the funeral held in the village of Scopwick. He wrote in his diary:

'I saluted him for the last time about 3:30pm, that writes finis to the best man I have known. I guess quite a few of us will end up the same way before this is all over.'

On Friday January 30th 1942 Peter was called in to see 609's Commanding Officer Squadron Leader George Gilroy who informed him that he was to be posted, and that he was to report to RAF Portreath in Cornwall prior to onward passage to Malta. Peter contacted his parents and arranged to meet them in London the following day. After seeing them he caught an overnight train to Redruth in Cornwall, then on to Portreath where he would meet some of the others for the first time also on their way to Malta, including Flt Lt Stan Grant, Plt Off John Plagis and Plt Off Doug Leggo.

Having been advised he needed to be at RAF Kirkham near Preston on February 8th he went home on leave to see his parents who were now living in Beckenham, Kent, and his girlfriend Renée whom he had hoped to marry sometime in the future, but his parents at this stage had forced a postponement.

Having arrived at Kirkham the afternoon before, Monday February 9th involved more inoculations, and then some free time in the afternoon. In the evening Peter went into Blackpool with the Australian Plt Off James Guerin for a meal and a drink, returning to the base to continue drinking and talking with the Padre until 1:30am. They did not get much sleep as the next day at 4:00am they were taken by lorry to Liverpool docks where they boarded the freighter MV Cape Hawke on the start of the journey to Malta.

Peter was fourth to take off in Spitfire AB336 from HMS Eagle on March 7th and flew for over 4 hours at low level to Malta, arriving at Takali at 3:15pm local time.

The next day, with the Spitfires requiring work before being used in action, Peter explored his new surroundings including visiting a Roman Villa and museum in Rabat with Douglas Leggo and James Guerin, and then later going on to the Adelphi cinema to see Racket Busters (1938), an American gangster movie with Humphrey Bogart. He also hitchhiked into Valletta to send telegrams home and was able to witness a German Ju88 bomber being shot down over the Grand Harbour, before taking a horse drawn gharry to return back to base.

Tuesday March 10th was the first day the Spitfires operated over Malta being scrambled to intercept an incoming raid by Ju88 bombers. Peter was flying number two to Flt Lt Heppell with Plt Off Plagis and Plt Off Leggo three and four. Climbing to 21,000ft and seeing three Ju88's approx 4,000ft below, they attacked. Flt Lt Heppell shot one down and Peter and Plt Off Plagis claimed a probable, Plt Off Plagis also chased one off Peter's tail. Peter described it in his logbook as:

'Very good party, had a lovely bounce'

Plt Off Ken Murray was killed later on the same day, the first of the HMS Eagle pilots to die, and two days later Peter attended his funeral. He wrote in his diary:

'I think it is a bad thing for pilots to go to funerals. It kind of rubs it in!'

Peter flew again on March 14th taking over the lead after Flt Lt Norman Macqueen's radio failed. They tried to attack three Me109s but lost them in the mist, although Flt Lt Macqueen was credited with a victory.

The next few days saw the loss of another of the HMS Eagle pilots. Peter himself was lucky not to be closer when the Point de Vue Hotel, which was being used as accommodation for the pilots, was bombed, killing Plt Off Guerin along with several others. He wrote in his diary that he got there two minutes after it happened to witness a terrible sight.

On March 25th Peter achieved another victory. At around 3:30pm a large raid of over 50 bombers with fighter escort approached the Grand Harbour. Having initially attacked the fighters flying Spitfire AB335 (GN-F), he then followed the first Ju87 Stuka Bomber as it started its dive and was able to hit it seeing white smoke emit from it. Originally listed as a probable, this was later upgraded and confirmed as destroyed. Two days later he shared a probable with three other pilots after attacking a Ju88.

Peter was now sharing a room with Plt Off John Plagis, and four other pilots from 126 squadron within Mdina's protective Bastions allowing commanding views across a large area of Malta including Takali

Peter wearing a Malta style camouflaged steel helmet (F. Galea)

Airfield which they could look down upon. They also had the benefit of 3 young Maltese boys to act as batmen.

The last two days of March were spent filling sandbags and old petrol tins full of earth to be used to build aircraft pens, to try and protect the aircraft from being damaged by blast and shrapnel during the constant bombing of the airfields.

April started well for Peter with two more victories on the first day. In the afternoon 15 Ju88s with fighter escort approached the Grand Harbour, Peter fired at one of the bombers hitting it in the fuel tank, it turned over on to its back in flames and crashed into the sea. Later a large raid by Ju87s, again heading for the docks, was intercepted, Peter attacked one that subsequently blew up in mid air, **'Another fine party'** he wrote later.

During the next few days he had some time off and paid a visit to Valletta to celebrate his victories and noted how the bombing was sadly destroying the historic city:

'If this goes on much longer Valletta will be nothing but a shambles. Raids seem to consist of 109's sweeping first, then wave number one of about 20-30 88s then another wave about the same. Sometimes varied by 87s. I watched them from the Bastions today. 109s embarrassed the boys landing this afternoon. Plt Off John Bisley RAAF got one 88 and one 87 probable. He was shot up and broke undercarriage landing, wounded in one leg. Johnson one 109, Plt Off Hiram'Tex' Putnam RCAF got one 88. A lot of trouble with 109s. The weather is getting pretty hot lately too! Four Hurricanes and three Spits against 83 bombers and 50+ 109s!! <u>This is Malta.'</u>

On April 6th he flew an uneventful sortie although landing at the second attempt as his air speed indicator was not working, it was later found that a bee had got into and blocked the Pitot Tube, the device that measured the airflow moving through it to give a reading of speed.

On the 7th Peter went with Plt Off Don Mcleod, a Canadian, to the pilots rest house at St Paul's Bay, and while they were there they were outraged to see 109s flying low and shooting randomly at the boats and houses of the Maltese. Having returned to the rest house again the next afternoon, the 9th was spent filling sandbags again in the hot sunshine.

The 10th was also a busy day this time in the air, Peter wrote in his diary:

'On this afternoon just managed to get four Spits on the line with 12 Hurricanes. Terrific balbo. Scramble at twenty to six and had 120 plus on my hands. More 109s than I have ever seen in one mass. They bombed Grand Harbour, Takali and Hal Far. The Hurricanes had a terrible time there, being shot up the whole time on the circuit. Buchanan led the Spits. He got a 109 when we were first bounced. I came down to the deck and

Lee joined up. We went to Grand Harbour and I got an 87 with smoke pouring out of it. Was well and truly bounced by six 109s. Managed to get a damaged when they thinned out a little. Landed while 109s were shooting the joint up. Got strikes on (my) wing and rear of cockpit from one. Not sorry to get down again today!

'Frantic time shoving the kites into bays with the help of two very game airmen who were above ground.'

Malta Aviation Museum

Peter did not fly again for ten days and spent sometime visiting the injured pilots at Mtarfa hospital and visiting Valletta where he sent telegrams back home. He was also pleased to receive a letter from Renée, which, although she had posted eight letters previously, this was the first one he had received. There were also many more sandbags to be filled and aircraft pens to be built ready for the next anticipated delivery of Spitfires.

Pilots, ground crew and soldiers all helped in the building of protective pens for the Spitfires (F. Galea)

The reinforcements arrived on April 20th when Operation Calendar brought 47 Spitfires from 601 and 603 Squadron, which were flown off the American carrier USS Wasp. Peter along with Sqn Ldr Stan Grant and Plt Off John Plagis flew protective cover as the new pilots arrived over the island. Peter on seeing all these new fighters wrote in his logbook:

'Now let battle commence General Kesselring !'

The following day Peter was scrambled to an incoming raid only to find his aircraft had a flat battery and would not start. When he subsequently did get off, he found that the radio and other electrical items were not working, and then when a wing panel over the guns blew off he decided it would be better to land again.

With the raiders bombing Takali airfield he took cover near the dispersal, but seeing a Spitfire burning in one of the protective pens he rushed out to see what he could do, but he was caught out in the open when the next wave of Ju88s started dropping their bombs. He later recalled hearing a short intense whistling sound and then all the breath was sucked out of his body, the force of an explosion threw his body around 15 metres across the airfield. He believed he lay unconscious for 15 minutes whilst the raid continued around him. Having been left very badly shaken he was taken off flying for the next 48 hours.

No doubt still affected by his experience the previous day, Peter wrote in his diary:

'They have bombed us at such a terrific pace that by this afternoon we had six Spits serviceable out of Mondays 50! P/O Frank Jemmett was killed this afternoon. This cannot continue. The boys are feeling the strain very heavily now. I don't think it is possible to keep a fighter force on this island.'

It would, in fact, be four days before he flew again and then he was forced to land early after the failure of his radio. Peter spent some time writing letters home and was cheered to receive some letters including one from Renée, which had been posted only seven days earlier. Later, four letters were received together from her that had all been posted two months earlier.

On April 30th Peter flew one of seven Spitfires sent to intercept four Italian bombers north of Gozo, but they had been sent too late and although they chased them to within 20 miles of the Sicilian coast, they were unable to catch them.

Sunday May 3rd Peter was on duty at 5:30am and was sat in the cockpit on 'standby' three times before he was actually scrambled to intercept an incoming raid, this time with over 40 aircraft approaching he took off. Peter along with Plt Off Milburn were designated airfield defence and waited approximately 20 miles out at sea at 12,000 feet below the cloud that covered the island. They swooped down on four 109s at 4,000ft over Hal Far airfield, in the dogfight that followed Plt Off Milburn became separated and Peter chased two 109s at low level shooting one of them into the sea, using the port cannon only, as the starboard side had misfired and jammed.

On May 6th Peter and Plt Off Milburn carried out some test landings on Hal Far airfield, which was used by Hurricanes and Swordfish aircraft to see if it would be suitable for use with the Spitfire. On one of the take offs Plt Off Milburn punctured a tyre and had to do a wheels up belly landing at Takali.

With more reinforcements expected on the 9th the 8th was spent with a rehearsal of the plan to get all the new aircraft down and then prepared to be put straight back into the air again with an experienced Malta pilot at the controls. Peter was on duty at dispersal from 5:30am. During the day over 40 Ju87s bombed Takali forcing him in to seek shelter in a slit trench.

Having received some photographs and written to Renée he wrote in his diary that he now had **'Bags of moral for tomorrow.'**

The new Spitfires arrived around 9:30am and were refuelled and rearmed immediately as planned. Peter was allocated BR108, a Spitfire MkVc, and took off soon after to intercept an incoming raid of over 60 Me109s:

'I was leading D'arcy (P/O Milburn) Almos and Linton. Sent to Hal Far to deal with 109 trouble. We bounced them at 3,000ft from 15,000ft, mine went into the sea off Hal Far. Formed up again, and attacked by three 109s. One stuck around above us. Got to him and gave a short burst. Spun down. Lots of black smoke, five miles east of Malta.'

Whilst returning to the airfield to land, Peter's No.2 19 years old Plt Off Harold Milburn, known as D'arcy, was shot down and killed near Safi. Later, around 1:15pm, another raid of Ju88s and their 109 escort headed towards Takali and Hal Far. 24 Spitfires and 6 Hurricanes took off to intercept including Peter, scrambled too late to catch the bombers he attacked and damaged a 109, again whilst having only one cannon working.

The same day Peter was one of four Spitfires from 249 Sqn who chased some Ju87s, which had just bombed the Grand Harbour, one of which he claimed as a probable:

'Chased recco 88 but unable to find him even over Sicilian coast. Stuck

around at 27,000ft for big raid. Bounced 87s over Grand Harbour. Only one cannon working again. He went on his back belching black smoke.'

On May 10th Peter claimed two more victories. He was on duty from 4:00am, and scrambled at 6:00am to chase away a reconnaissance Ju88, and later two 109s. In the Grand Harbour were two Naval cruisers partly obscured by a smoke screen, these were the targets for a large raid by the Stukas:

'Terrific party over Grand Harbour. I got, one destroyed and one probable. Everybody got something. The Stukas stuck! Starboard wing came off one, the other disappeared into smoke screen at 200 feet.'

Over 55 Luftwaffe aircraft approached the island on May 11th the majority of them Me 109s, 23 Spitfires were sent to intercept them. Sgt Paul Brennan became involved in a fierce dogfight and called for assistance on the radio, Peter was one of two pilots who drove away the attackers and then he himself attacked a 109:

'Got one of them two miles off Grand Harbour (he) went Straight in from 5,000ft. Only fired 20 rounds of canon all from one gun from 50 yards.'

Peter was later praised by Wing Commander 'Jumbo' Gracie on his recent good showing and apologised to him for the fact that he had not yet been awarded a medal. The following day, however, Wg Cdr Gracie was not so pleased with him. When taxing in, Peter collided with a steamroller that was used to flatten the repaired bomb craters, damaging the wing of his Spitfire (BR108). He was partway through being reprimanded by Gracie for this misdemeanour when a lone Me109 dropped a bomb close by forcing them both to take cover. Gracie, getting up to inspect the damage, said he would finish speaking to Peter later, but the incident was never mentioned again.

Spitfire BR108 was flown several times by Peter (also Stanley Grant) during which he claimed one Me109 shot down, plus another damaged and a probable, along with two Ju87s destroyed, plus another probably destroyed. This aircraft, which had been flown off the U.S.S. Wasp on May 7th was later shot down on July 8th when piloted by Flt Lt Lester Sanders. After an encounter with two 109s Sanders was forced to ditch into the sea off the coast of Gozo. He survived the ditching only to lose his life later the same year whilst flying as a test pilot, when a new Spitfire Vb he was flying broke up in the air over

Cannock Chase near Birmingham and he was killed in the resulting crash.

The Merlin engine from BR108 was later successfully raised in 1973 from the seabed of Marsalforn Bay, Gozo, and can now be seen on display in the National War Museum in Valletta.

Peter now had a few days off including two days with Plt Off John Plagis at the rest house in St Paul's Bay. There they watched some of the air battles overhead before going for a meal at the Harbour Bar, returning in the evening to listen to the radio.

Early in the afternoon of May 16th a single Ju88 approached Malta supported by around 26 Me109s. Eleven Spitfires were despatched including Peter and Plt Off John Plagis, they both shared in the destruction of one of the fighters by shooting its wing tip off:

The recovered engine of Spitfire MkVc BR108 in which Peter destroyed 3 enemy aircraft.

'Damn good party with Me109s off Kalafrana Bay. They attacked in pairs but Plagis and I fixed one from 300 yards. This is the 100th enemy aircraft destroyed on Malta by 249 Squadron.'

He wrote in his diary:

'Party tonight, but on at dawn so will wait till tomorrow night!'

If there were indeed a party the next day Peter would not have been there to

281

attend it. On Sunday May 17th six spitfires from 603 Squadron plus Peter and Plt Off Lawrie Verrall from 249 Squadron, were scrambled around midday to meet an incoming raid. During a dogfight with several Me109s both pilots claimed a victory each over an Me109. Plt Off Verrall returned safely to base but Peter did not return, he was shot down and killed when his Spitfire BP951 crashed near Dingli. He was the victim of a pilot from 6/JG53 believed to have been either Uffz Erich Paczia or Ltn Hans Marksetter.

An unknown member of 249 squadron completed the last entry in Peter's logbook:

'P/O Nash with F/Sgt Verrall attacked 5 109s. Both destroyed one. P/O Nash was shot down and killed by one of the 109s.'

Laddie Lucas, later Commanding Officer of 249 Squadron, said of him:

'Punctilious, precise and coolly efficient, Peter Nash was the most undemonstratively successful pilot in the squadron. If the truth be told he was probably, all round, taking one day with another, the most accomplished. The squadron recognized this.
'…The quality and balance of Pete Nash's flying placed him in a category which few, if any others on the island could quite attain.'
Five Up. 'Laddie' Lucas. (Sedgewick and Jackson Ltd 1978)

'Pete was, day in and day out, probably the best of some exceptional performers and, maybe, the most accomplished fighter pilot on the island during the worst of the battle…
'The early loss of both Norman Macqueen and Pete Nash had deprived the Squadron of two outstanding performers- and potential leaders.'
Malta: The Thorn In Rommel's Side. Laddie Lucas. (Stanley Paul 1992)

A month after his death in early June came confirmation of his DFC, which was published in the London Gazette. The citation stating he had displayed **'High courage and devotion to duty.'**

The Times Newspaper published a tribute to its former employee in July 1942. An unknown RAF Officer from Malta also added in a letter:

'Pilot Officer Nash was top scorer in Malta's finest Squadron, and had shot down 2 enemy aircraft during the day I was shot down. His total

score of 14 destroyed was brilliant, and led the whole island. I was a good many years senior in age to Pete Nash, but we were extremely good friends, and I could best express my own feelings by saying that I hoped my own son would turn out as good a fellow.'

In 1943, a year after his death, his parents published a memorial to him in the Times:

'NASH- In proud and happy memory of Pilot Officer Peter Alfred Nash. 22 Forest Ridge. Beckenham. Kent. Who was shot down over Malta. May 17 1942.'

Pilot Officer Peter Alfred Nash DFC aged twenty is buried in a shared grave in the Capuccini Naval Cemetery, Kalkara, Malta. Plot E, Grave 2. His name is also written in gold letters on the Roll Of Honour boards at the Alleyn's School, Dulwich, London.

'John' Ioannis Agorastos Plagisos

Ioannis took the Christian name of John, and Plagis, a shortened version of his surname, as he considered it easier for his colleagues and friends to pronounce. His parents, Agorastos along with his Egyptian wife Helene (nee Rosselli) had originated from the Greek island of Limnos, and had emigrated to Southern Rhodesia seeking land and a new location to raise a family and start a business, safe from a Europe being torn apart during World War 1. They settled in Hartley where Agorastos became a farmer. The couple went on to have five children Thomas, Helen, Constantino, Katerina, and Ioannis (John) who was born on March 10th 1919. Blackwater Fever, a complication of the disease Malaria, claimed two members of the family, firstly Constantino at an early age, and then some years later the children's father, Agorastos.

John attended Hartley Junior School before going on to Prince Edward School, a public school in what was then Salisbury, now known as Harare, Zimbabwe. During this time his parents divorced, with his mother later remarrying a Cypriot, Theophanis Passaportis. They moved to Gadzema with the children where they ran a small hotel, trading store and fuel station that served the nearby gold mine. Helene went on to have four daughters with her new husband. John was always closest to his natural sister Katerina who he adored, she called him Jay and he called her Kay, a name that he later had painted on many of his aircraft. He often sent her presents of small personalised pieces of jewellery from the many countries he visited.

At the outbreak of war in 1939, John applied to join the Rhodesian Air Force but his application was rejected, as he was still officially a Greek citizen. The RAF was not so pedantic, and John began training as a Greek subject with the Royal Air Force Volunteer Reserve in Rhodesia during October 1940 (service number 778350). It is believed that he trained with another future Operation Spotter pilot, Douglas Leggo, with the two of them becoming good friends.

Initial training was on the de Havilland Tiger Moth at 25 Elementary Flying Training School at Belvedere near Salisbury, he then moved to the nearby 20 Service Flying Training School at Cranborne flying the North American Harvard. During his training John was classed as **'Above average'** in all of his flying assessments. In May 1941 he was posted to the UK to continue his training at No.58 Operational Training Unit based at Grangemouth, Scotland. It was here he gained his 'Wings' as a pilot, flew his first Spitfire and gained promotion to the rank of Sergeant.

John's first operational posting was to 65 Squadron flying Spitfires from Kirton-In-Lindsey, Lincolnshire, at the end of June 1941. His stay with them was only for a matter of weeks as on July 19th he joined 266 (Rhodesian) Squadron, another Spitfire equipped unit based at Wittering, Northamptonshire. The squadron were involved in intercepting intruding German aircraft, carrying out fighter sweeps over northern France and attacking shipping off the coast of Holland. At 266 John met up once again with his friend, Douglas Leggo. Both pilots were fluent in 'Shona,' an African dialect that they spoke to each other on sorties, in order that any listening enemy would not understand them.

In September the squadron moved to Martlesham Heath in Suffolk. In October they moved to Collyweston, and then on to King's Cliffe, both in Northamptonshire, where they started to fly the improved MkV Spitfire. In December 1941 John was promoted to Flight Sergeant, and then early in 1942 to Pilot Officer (Service No.80227). He moved with the squadron, in January, to Duxford where, having at some stage volunteered for service overseas, he was advised at the end of the month, that he was to be posted to Malta. On March 7th he flew Spitfire MkVb AB343 off HMS Eagle to Takali to join 249 Squadron. He described Takali as the:

'Land of burnt-out Wimpys (Wellington Aircraft) and bowsers!'

On July 17th 1942, four months after John had landed on Malta, he spoke about his arrival on the island to a BBC reporter,

John aged around 22 as a Sergeant Pilot feeding the pigeons in Trafalgar Square, London 1941

he had at that stage returned back to England a week earlier:

'I can well remember the day when we first arrived on Malta. It was a clear sunny day and the sight of those battered buildings came rather as a shock to me. But as we came in lower I got a foretaste of the unbelievable spirit of the people of Malta, and our own men there who are helping to defend it so stubbornly.

'For, in addition to the ruins I could plainly see the people waving excitedly their welcome was simply over whelming. I was amongst the

first few Spitfires to land on the aerodrome, and immediately after I landed a ground staff sergeant rushed up, and kissed the wing of my aeroplane out of sheer joy.

'My God Sir' he said "We'll knock the so and so's down now" and knock them down we did. How right he was.

'Almost immediately after landing we were ready to take to the skies and meet the Hun in combat. I shall never forget our first scrap over the island when 4 Spitfires brought down 3 enemy fighters without loss. Before the Spitfires arrived in force it happened quite often that we were outnumbered by as much as ten to one. I remember one day when only 5 of us were airborne, and we encountered and engaged well over 200 enemy aircraft.

'We were still gaining height when 40 109s came in, and their job apparently was to ground us so the strong force of bombers which were following close on them could do their damage without interference from us. The 5 of us didn't have much of a chance and they actually beat us

John sitting on the wing of his Spitfire which clearly shows the name of his sister Kay, and his eleven victories, June 1942 (D Ritson)

from about 15,000 to 6,000 feet, but then we managed to hold our height till the bombers came in and as they dived down on Grand Harbour we tore in to them and managed to get 4 before we broke away and tried to land. This was not so easy with all the fighter escort they had. Time after time as my wheels touched the ground, I had to go up again to avoid being shot to pieces on the ground. **By that time we had run out of ammunition, and all we could do was to make dummy attacks, but it was the same old story we couldn't get down and land. One chap eventually landed, taxied 50 yards and ran out of petrol.'**

(Imperial War Museum Sound Archive: Catalogue Number 1163)

Although John's report implies the aircraft went straight into action the same day, it was actually three days later on the morning of March 10th that the Spitfires first flew against enemy aircraft. Seven Spitfires and twelve Hurricanes from 185 and 126 Squadrons were sent to intercept a group of nine Ju88 bombers with escorting fighters, some of the bombers had just attacked the airfield at Luqa. John flew as part of a flight of four aircraft led by Flt Lt Heppell. Having reached an altitude of around 19,000 feet, they spotted the enemy formation and dived down onto them, the German pilots had not seen the defenders and were caught off guard. In the air battle that followed John was able to fire at an Me109 that was on the tail of Plt Off Peter Nash, and claimed it as probably destroyed. John was involved in attacking another escorting Me109 fighter on the 17th but only claimed this as damaged.

John in his personal Spitfire in a photograph sent to his friend and former Air Controller 'Woody' Woodhall (M Woodhall)

On March 20th John's good friend, Plt Off Douglas Leggo was shot down in combat with German fighters, he was able to bale out successfully but, either too low or possibly another Me109 flew very close to his parachute

287

causing it to collapse and stream, and Douglas plunged to his death. John was extremely upset and angry over the manner and death of Douglas. Laddie Lucas noted that for the next two or three days, he was morose and uncharacteristically silent and brooding. John made a promise to avenge the loss of his friend:

'Swear to shoot down ten for Doug-I will too, if it takes me a lifetime.'

On March 23rd John began to avenge the loss of his friend, although on this day he was only able to damage a Ju88 4 miles off the Grand Harbour. Two days later John was able to claim his first victory shooting down a Ju87 bomber and damaging another before he was forced to withdraw when cannon fire from an Me109 struck his aircraft.

John was one of four pilots that attacked a Ju88 on the 28th but, although all four pilots used up all their ammunition, the bomber flew on and could only be claimed as a probable, shared between them, a claim of a quarter each. Such were the odds against the Spitfires John said:

'In fact if four of us were airborne and we encountered twenty enemy fighters and bombers, we considered it a reasonable flight.'

April began well for John with several claims made on the first day. In the afternoon John was one of six pilots scrambled to intercept four Me109s. When the Spitfires intercepted, one of the 109s broke away which John (AB335/F) immediately went after, shooting it down into the sea south east of the Grand Harbour. The pilot was believed to be Fw. Hans Schade from III/JG53, an experienced fighter pilot with 13 victories of his own, including possibly Plt Off Kenric Murray, the first Operation Spotter pilot to be killed. Within the same hour John had landed and then scrambled straight away again to intercept 15 Ju88 bombers, protected by their fighter escort that were bombing the harbour and docks. John followed the bombers through the anti aircraft barrage and out to sea where he shot down one of the Ju88s a quarter of a mile off the Grand Harbour. In the same battle he also claimed another bomber as probably destroyed, shared with a Hurricane pilot from 185 Squadron.

At around 4:30 in the afternoon John was sent up on his third sortie of the day. A Dornier flying boat, accompanied by a covering force of Me109s, had been seen five miles off the coast searching the sea for Hans Schade and other downed aircrew. John was one of four Spitfires along with a Hurricane that intercepted, he was able to position his aircraft against one of the fighters, which he shot down into the sea. The aircraft was Black 5 from JG53 flown by Uffz. Gerhard Kitzenmaier. Sgt Ray Hesselyn had also claimed an Me109 in this encounter and, as only one Me109 had been shot down, it is believed that they both probably attacked the same aircraft.

The Spitfires landed to rearm and refuel and were soon off once again as a large force, including over 50 Ju87 Stukas with fighter escort, approached the Grand Harbour and Hal Far airfield. John began his fourth sortie of the day, four Spitfires against over 180 bombers with around 80 escorting fighters, again he was rewarded, shooting down a Stuka, noting that its engine was on fire and that the aircraft had spun down in flames. John stated later:

'My score for the day 4 aircraft destroyed, one damaged and one probably destroyed. On landing back at base my aircraft was badly damaged and I received superficial wounds.'

During this attack four Stukas were claimed as destroyed by Spitfire pilots, with two more by the anti aircraft guns. In addition, five others were claimed as probably destroyed and three more as damaged. In the confusion, with so many fast aircraft twisting in the sky, several of the Stukas must have been hit by more than one pilot and probably also by the anti aircraft gunners.

John's fighting on April 1st had not gone unnoticed and he was recommended for the DFC, which was confirmed the following month, the citation stating:

'It is difficult to single out one fighter pilot and make comparisons but Pilot Officer Plagis shot down four enemy aircraft. He is worthy of special mention. He flies a Spitfire and with it he is devastating. Since the beginning of March 1942 this officer has destroyed 4 and probably destroyed a further 3 hostile aircraft. With complete indifference to odds against him, he presses home his attacks with skill and courage. In one day alone, he destroyed 2 enemy fighters and 1 bomber. He has set an outstanding example.'

On April 18th the diary of Flt Lt Tim Johnston noted that a party was held for John, his roommate, along with Flt Lt Norman Macqueen to celebrate their forthcoming awards. Johnston also mentions that John had a Maltese girlfriend, Anne Pullicino, who apparently had an endearing and amusing habit of mispronouncing English phrases.

John was able to make multiple claims once again on April 21st. The day before, Operation Calendar had delivered a further 47 Spitfires to the island, and a big response was expected from the Luftwaffe. The first raid came in at 7:30am with 35 plus Ju88 bombers and an escort of over 30 fighters. John (AB263), in conjunction with Sqd Ldr Stanley Grant, attacked one of the bombers that had just bombed Luqa airfield. Grant set one engine on fire, John followed setting the other engine ablaze, the aircraft was last seen in flames leaving a trail of black smoke as it plunged into the sea. John then turned to fire at one of the Me109s, but was only able to damage it. Just after noon a second raid of 20 Ju88s plus 15 Ju87 bombers with around 35 fighters approached the coast, the airfield at Takali and the harbour were targeted. John was again in the air and spotted that Sgt Ray Hesselyn's aircraft had a Me109 on its tail, Hesselyn knew it was there and was taking evasive action. John caught the pair up, but initially could not fire for fear of hitting his colleague. Eventually the 109 broke away and John seized his chance to fire, seeing strikes on the aircraft, which he claimed as probably destroyed.

John's next claims were made early on the morning of May 10th when he damaged an Me109 that had been escorting a reconnaissance aircraft. Later the same morning a combined bombing force of Ju88 and Ju87 attempted to bomb two cruisers in the Grand Harbour. The recent arrival of more Spitfires allowed a large defending force of 37 Spitfires and 13 Hurricanes to counter the attack. John shot a Stuka down into the sea north east of the harbour, and noted, with so many allied aircraft in the sky his difficulty in finding a suitable target:

'Flew seven miles out to sea to find a Ju87 which didn't have Spit on its tail.'

John mentioned this battle later, with a little poetic license making good propaganda for the listeners, when talking later in England to a BBC reporter:

'You'll be able to understand how we fighter pilots felt when at last we could meet the Hun on an equal footing, which we did the afternoon of May 10th over Grand Harbour it was just one big mass dog fight. There were probably well over 100 fighters in the air at the same time. The ack ack gunners put up a terrific barrage, but the boys in the Spitfires were so keen to get at the Hun that they couldn't resist the temptation of rushing through our own barrage. I was in this dogfight and so was my friend Ronnie. (Flt Lt Ronald West). 87s were everywhere, dropping everywhere

in planes, with their tails and wings blown off. And the Maltese cheered themselves hoarse. The actual fight was in easy sight of the island and that afternoon the shelters of Malta were empty. It was undoubtedly the biggest fight since the arrival of the Spitfires, and more than 20 enemy planes went down into the sea.

'We gave the Hun such a hiding that he didn't dare show his face again for a whole week. That's what happens when we met the enemy on equal terms. But through all this fighting I think the people who really deserve the praise were the ground staff personnel. They never failed to see us in safely whether bombs were dropping or not.

'And I think we all owe our success in the air to the boys who took care to keep our aircraft in tiptop fighting condition. Working on my aeroplane I had a crew of Scotsmen, they were the most cheerful the most hard working the most wizard lot of chaps I have ever known in all my life.

'We also take our hats off to the Maltese ack ack gunners for their terrific good marksmanship and powers of endurance during the bad blitz's.'

(Imperial War Museum Sound Archive: Catalogue Number 1163)

A reconnaissance Ju88 with fighter escort flew over the island early on the morning of May 11th. Three Spitfires, including John, pursued these back towards Sicily. As they approached Sicily eight Reggiane 2001 Italian fighters came out to intercept them, although the Spitfire pilots miss-identified them as the more proficient Macchi 202 fighter. John pursued one from around 10,000 feet down to almost sea level, whilst he himself had an Italian behind him, and another of the Italian fighters made to attack him from his left-hand side. John, now outnumbered, instinctively turned in head-on making himself a smaller target and ploughed straight at the Italian. The Re.2001 pilot realised that maybe the aircraft coming towards him intended to ram him and he hauled his aircraft upwards, but so steeply that the aircraft stalled and it fell back into the sea. John had destroyed an aircraft by intimidation only without firing a shot. He wrote later:

'I thought my last minute had come and decided to sell my life dearly. I flew straight at the nearest machine with the intention of ramming it. I did not fire a shot, but the Macchi pilot, suddenly realising his number might also be up too, took violent evasive action, stalled and crashed into the sea.'

291

John was now very low on fuel and asked control for a course back to the island, 'Woody' Woodhall, the controller, responded and also despatched two Spitfires to meet him, so that his position would be known should he have to ditch in the sea. With only around three gallons of fuel remaining, John safely reached Takali. John and Woody became good friends with John becoming Godfather in 1943 to Woody's son, Martin.

On the afternoon of May 16th a lone Ju88, with an escort of around forty German and Italian fighters, attacked the Naval base at Kalafrana. John was one of eleven Spitfires that intercepted, flying with Plt Off Peter Nash, they both fired from around 300 metres at a 109, which set fire to the engine. The pilot believed to be Uffz. Felix Sauer bailed out successfully into the sea. Peter Nash noted this as being the 100th enemy aircraft shot down by 249 Squadron.

Two days later John was not so successful, an Italian air-sea rescue plane, protected by Reggiane 2001 fighters was searching for downed aircrew. John was one of over a dozen Spitfires that attacked and chased what he believed to be Italian Macchi 202 aircraft away from the island:

'Chased a Macchi which strafed Hal Far. Caught him up, fired every round at him from 200 yards-and he got away-never forgive myself. Only damaged him.'

John was no doubt particularly angry with himself at not being able to destroy this aircraft, as Peter Nash, who he had shared his last victory with, had the previous day been shot down and killed.

At the end of May John was flown out to Gibraltar, along with Sqn Ldr Anthony Barton and an American pilot Flt Lt James Peck, to lead back to Malta the seventh delivery of Spitfires. This was Operation Style, 32 MkVc Spitfires that had been shipped in crates, their pilots and assembly crews also on-board. At Gibraltar the aircraft were assembled and transferred to the aircraft carrier HMS Eagle. Then on June 2nd they departed under naval escort to Malta. The aircraft were safely launched from the carrier, but this time there were Luftwaffe aircraft in the area.

As the flights of aircraft neared the island of Pantelleria they met a group of Me109s from II/JG 53 escorting a twin engined FW58b light transport plane. Other Me109s may also have taken off from the airfield on Pantelleria, alerted that Spitfires had been spotted. Two pilots, Fg Off Jim Menary and Plt Off David Rouleau, attacked and shot down the FW58 before the escort could intervene, but they in turn were then shot down into the sea.

Sgt Len Reid, an Australian flying as one of nine aircraft in the flight led by John, noticed that the other pilots were ditching their extra under fuselage fuel tanks, so he did the same. He described his encounter with the German fighters:

'Near Pantelleria we saw some Messerschmitts sitting out there watching us for five minutes. I could see them getting in position, saw them closing. I recall 'T' (Believed to be Flt Sgt T F Beaumont) shouting the 109s were attacking. I saw them coming. Plagis suddenly rolled over and dived for the sea. He left the rest of us up there like sitting ducks. Those 109s just flew in behind us and shot 'T' out of the sky. 'T' was alongside me; he was shot, obviously, as the stick came back in to his stomach, and I saw him go up, smoke coming out. He was probably dead, and it was a matter of rolling over and diving for the sea. Everybody had to look after himself. I had one or two on my tail- tracer bullets flying past but fortunately they didn't hit me- and followed right down to the sea. I remember zig-zagging madly across the water, and in the finish I was on my own. I didn't know where I was, but knew I had to steer a certain course which might bring me to Malta. It did. I was supposed to land at Takali, but landed at Hal Far, as I came in from that direction.'

Spitfires Over Malta. Brian Cull, Frederick Galea. (Grub Street 2005)

Laddie Lucas, in his book The Thorn in Rommel's Side, described John as greatly shaken after the event and attributed the following quote to John:

'With about 150 miles of the 700 mile flight still to go- and petrol reserves "dodgy"-this was no time to stay around and mix it with the 109s. We were lucky, I suppose, not to have lost more. If the Huns or the Eyetyes are really going to start making an effort to disrupt these flights from the carrier, we've got another think coming...'

Flt Sgt Thomas Beaumont and Canadian Flt Sgt Hugh Macpherson were the two other pilots lost. All four are remembered on the Malta Memorial in Floriana, erected to honour those with no known grave. This was the only time that a delivery flight of Spitfires was ever intercepted.

On returning back to Malta, John found that he had been promoted to Acting Flight Lieutenant and posted to 185 Squadron as the Flight Commander of 'B' Flight based at Hal Far airfield. It was not long before he was able to make his first claim with his new squadron. On the afternoon of June 6th a

Cant Z506B, a three-engined floatplane, was searching for missing aircrew under the protection of around 20 Italian fighters. Four Spitfires, led by John (BR321 GL-J), went out to intercept, followed soon after by 4 others from Blue section. John's flight pursued a group of fighters out to sea:

'Intercepted about 10-12 enemy aircraft 30-40 miles east of Malta-joined by another 36 e/a. Reid got one RE2001. Blue Section got blood wagon. I got two RE2001 destroyed. Both pilots baled out!! RIP.'

The white floatplane painted with the red cross symbol was considered fair game as the RAF rescue launches were constantly being attacked by the enemy. Although initially Plt Off Ogilvie flew alongside and tried to signal the aircraft to turn to land at Malta, others were not so patient and it was unceremoniously attacked from the rear by 3 Spitfires, with their fire causing the fuel tanks and the aircraft to explode.

The following day John was one of 11 Spitfires that took off to meet a flight of around 15 Me109s, one of which he attacked, 5-7 miles east of Delimara Point this he claimed as destroyed. It was to be his eleventh and last victory on Malta. At the end of the month he was notified of the award of a Bar to his DFC. The citation stated:

'This officer has displayed exceptional skill and gallantry in combat. He has destroyed at least 10 enemy aircraft. 2 of which he destroyed in one engagement. Undeterred by superior numbers of attacking aircraft, he presses home his attacks with great determination.

'On June 6th in one combat he destroyed two enemy aircraft 40miles east of Malta. During this enemy engagement he lead his section of four Spitfires into superior numbers without hesitation. His example and courage have been unsurpassed at all times.'

On July 7th John was flown by Whitley to Gibraltar and then later by Sunderland back to England. The harsh conditions of Malta had taken there toll physically on John, and on his return he was sent to an RAF Convalescent Home to recover, suffering from scabies, exhaustion and malnutrition, his body weight had dropped from 200lbs to just 135lbs.

In August 1942 John became an instructor at 53 Operational Training Unit based at Llandow, Glamorgan, along with its satellite airfield at Rhoose also in Wales. He became Flight Commander of 'B' Flight instructing on Miles Master and Spitfire Mk1 aircraft, and during his time at the OTU he was graded as '**Exceptional.**'

Tragically, training was a dangerous time with many novice pilots losing their lives. One accident took place on February 6th 1943 when John was leading a formation flying exercise, with two pilots under instruction. After an hour and a quarter he left the formation to land, instructing his two pupils to continue local flying and to land within 15 minutes. The first pilot landed but the second pilot became over due and could not be contacted on the radio. A report soon came into the base that a Spitfire had crashed around seven miles away. Flying Officer Neville Fleming, a 20-year-old Australian, had been killed.

In July 1943 the former Commanding Officer of 249 Squadron on Malta, Laddie Lucas, was promoted to take over the Coltishall Wing in Norfolk. The two previous Wing Leaders had been lost in quick succession and Lucas was brought in to bring some order back to the wing. He quickly dispensed with the out-dated method of flying in line astern, for the proven line abreast formation, two aircraft flown fast 200 metres apart, and wide-open sections of four aircraft. Lucas also needed two flight commanders and personally chose John to be one of them. John led 64 Squadron in around 200 incursions over enemy territory. Lucas noted that John's **'exceptional experience, record and authority on the other pilots in the wing was immediate.'**

John as a Flight Lieutenant with 64 Squadron in 1943 (Harder)

The wing comprised Typhoon and Spitfire squadrons, the Spitfires were the MkVb with clipped wings, giving them a comparable performance to the German fighters up to 13,000 feet, but above that they were known to be inferior. The wing was tasked with low level shipping strikes supporting Beaufighters off the coast of Holland, and escorting American B17 and B24 bombers across 140 miles of the North Sea into occupied Europe.They also flew regularly from more southerly airfields such as Manston, and Tangmere. Also with John at 64 Squadron at that time was Flying Officer David Ferraby, another former Operation Spotter pilot.

On September 24th John took off in

Spitfire MkVb BL734 (SH-B) with thirteen other Spitfires from West Malling airfield led by Squadron Leader Michael Donnet DFC. They escorted a flight of Marauder bombers, which successfully attacked Evreux airfield in France. On the return, near Rouen, an Me109 approached the fighters. John described what happened in his Combat Report:

'I was flying as Charlie leading a section of aircraft (Spitfires 'A' Flight 64 Sqn) I was flying on the port side of the O.C. and nearest the bombers to which we were acting as close escort. The bombers had turned port 90 degrees after bombing airfield near Evreux, when I observed a lone aircraft which had manoeuvred from dead astern of our squadron and then to 800 yards astern of the last box of bombers. I turned towards this aircraft to investigate and as I closed in I observed and reported it as a Me109. When about 400 yards away it saw me and went in to a steep dive and I immediately followed it with full throttle, from 12,000 down to 1,000 feet. In the initial dive, the 109 pulled away to about 700 yards but I rapidly gained on him and closed into about 200 yards before giving him my first burst with cannon and machine guns. I continued shooting away at him closing in the whole time to about 120 yards. I saw strikes along the fuselage and engine and also in the roots of the wings. Glycol started pouring out also brown black smoke increasing in volume all the time. I broke off the engagement at 1000 feet and immediately climbed full throttle.

'I watched this 109 continue gliding for about half a mile and then observed it crash and go up in flames in a big wooded area, on the edge of the woods about 10 miles ESE of Rouen.

'This Me109 had a brownish grey camouflage and also had a cannon undserslung beneath each wing.'

This was John's first victory since his time on Malta. On the afternoon of November 23rd he gained another off the coast of Holland whilst flying the same MkV Spitfire. His combat report stated:

'I was flying as CHARLIE 1 leading a section of 4 Spitfires which was acting as escort to Beaus on an anti shipping prang.

'On reaching the enemy convoy I observed 2 enemy aircraft flying in line astern very close to enemy convoy from seaward towards Holland at 500 ft. These enemy aircraft started to climb to attack Beaus. Which were making their approach on target from E. to W.

'I immediately climbed at +12 with my section to intercept but was too late in stopping them from attacking a Beau. After making their attack they dived down to sea level. I led my section down and intercepted them before they reached the enemy coast.

'I opened fire from about 400 yards closing in all the time and giving short burst at line astern and about 10 degrees off eventually closing to 300 when I broke off attack. I observed strikes but no smoke or bits falling off.

'About 10 seconds after breaking off my attack, FW190 went into sea N.N.E. of Den Helder. CHARLIE 3 also observed this enemy aircraft in the sea.

'Enemy aircraft had a bright blue camouflage on the under side of aircraft.'

During January 1944 64 Squadron spent some time recuperating in the quieter area of Scotland based at Ayr, before returning again to Coltishall, Norfolk, to continue their escort and ground attack work. At the end of April they were posted to Deanland, Sussex, then at the end of June they moved to Harrowbeer, Devon. This was within the sector controlled from Exeter by John's friend from Malta, 'Woody' Woodhall.

Whilst at Harrowbeer John was promoted to the rank of Acting Squadron Leader and became Commanding Officer of 126 Squadron, a squadron that specialised in attacking ground targets, trains and military vehicles, along with coastal gun and searchlight positions, plus strikes against enemy shipping. He was not away from his colleagues at 64 for very long, as on July 3rd the pilots of 126 Squadron were also posted to Harrowbeer.

John's personal new year message to his friend 'Woody" Woodhall 1943 (M Woodhall)

On July 24th John claimed another victory whilst flying Spitfire IX ML214 (5J-K). This was one of six presentation aircraft that had been donated by the Persian Gulf Fighter Fund and had been named Muscat, which was written on the side in front of the cockpit in Arabic and English. Below the cockpit was also painted John's sister's name, Kay, possibly John had chosen to use this particular aircraft as its identification code letter was 'K'.

The details of the sortie were written in his Combat Report:

'I was leading Shell Mex Squadron of 8 aircraft consisting of 2 Sections of 4 aircraft each. My section was Johnny section, and F/Lt Collis was leading Mild section. We were detailed to sweep to TRIGUIER, RENNES, S. of Angers, LAVAL, and home to HARROWBEER.

'At 19:30 hours as I was turning North from ESE of ANGERS at 4,000ft. I observed four E/A about 300 yards below and behind my Section, and also observed Mild Section just to starboard of these E/A. I immediately broke my section to Port in a steep climbing turn at +16lbs of boost. The Huns (Keen types) followed us in this turn and with the 90 gallon tanks still slung underneath the Spits we managed to hold our own and if anything turning slightly better. At this moment 2 other E/A joined in the fray from down sun. I dropped my 90-gallon jettison tank in this climbing turn as the engine was beginning to cut with the G and the fact that I was at high boost. I fully expected the tank to damage my aircraft, however, it came off quite uneventfully.

'The 2 Huns that endeavoured to bounce us from down sun pulled up from 3,500 feet in a climbing turn from Port and into sun, and levelled out at approximately 5/6000 feet, I managed to get in two bursts of 1-2 seconds at 50-70 deg. Deflection, range 200-250 yards, on the No.1 of the 2 E/A from port Quarter below and behind. I observed strikes on his port fuselage and he did a violent break to Starboard and upwards, and two flick rolls and then went down in a series of slow rolls and hit the ground inverted just ENE of Angers, and West of the wood that is NE of the junction that runs E. From Angers.

'E/A Pilot baled out and his parachute opened at about 1000ft. I also observed F/Lt Collis engage one of the Me109's that bounced my Section, and saw him shoot down one of them, which crashed into the ground ESE of railway junction. This pilot also baled out. One of the E/A managed to evade Johnny 3 by climbing into a fair sized solitary cloud E of Angers.

'After the destruction of these E/A the light flak (Bofors) was quite considerable from the vicinity of junction E. of ANGERS. The other E/A rapidly dispersed themselves. I reformed the Squadron over the river LOIRE and took them on a course for LAVAL at zero feet in hopes of re-engaging, but with no success.

'Those E/A were of a dark camouflage normally adopted by us, and they

also had black and white stripes on the wings and fuselage, though their stripes on the wing seemed nearer to fuselage than ours and if anything, narrower than ours. I did not observe any black and white stripes of the spinners of E/A.'

Interestingly, at the end of the report, John describes an attempt by these German aircraft to disguise themselves as Allied aircraft by attempting to mimic, unsuccessfully, the black and white stripes that were painted on all Allied aircraft prior to the D-Day landings in June 1944. The Allied stripes (three white and two black) were 18 inches (457 mm) wide and were painted across the width of the upper and lower surfaces of both wings and around the fuselage. The outer edge of the wing bands was 6 inches (152 mm) inboard of the RAF roundel and the rear edge of the fuselage bands was 18 inches (457 mm) forward of the tailplane.

John in Spitfire MkIX ML214 a presentation aircraft from the Persian Gulf Fighter Fund named Muscat. 1944 (Aces Of WW2)

John led 126 Squadron Spitfires, armed with bombs, on July 29th 1944 to attack Scrignac in Brittany, France. The Germans, with a Gestapo Headquarters set up in two former school buildings, had occupied the village. The Spitfires attacked early in the morning at very low level devastating the village, destroying the school buildings, several houses and damaging the church. Regrettably, although the French resistance, who had apparently objected to the planned attack, were aware of the raid and had warned the villagers,

299

around 20 civilians were killed.

On August 3rd both 64 and 126 both moved again to Bradwell Bay, Essex, to become part of a Spitfire Wing along with 611 Squadron. Their role continued to be to provide escort, now mainly of Lancasters, on daylight bombing raids, and also fighter sweeps into France to support the advancing Allied forces.

John claimed two more victories and a damaged before the end of the war, with all three being on the same day, and on the same sortie, whilst again flying Spitfire Mk IX ML214 in the late afternoon of August 14th:

'I was leading "Johnnie" Squadron on a sweep around Paris. 2nd sweep in 10 Group Rodeo 202, and was approaching Melun when I decided to sweep further south. I had just turned S. from a point W. of Melun when my No.2 saw some E/A flying on the deck, at the time we were flying 8,000 and it was easy to see these E/A on the deck from that height - they cast a very conspicuous shadow on the ground.

'Johnnie 2 went down first and attacked what seemed to me the front port FW.190. I attacked the starboard FW.190 in the second section of FW.'s I opened fire from above and behind about 380 yards, closing in very rapidly. I closed in firing in dead line astern to 50 yards, and just before stopping fire I observed strikes on port side of fuselage and port wing root. The FW.190 did a slow dive and turn to port and hit the ground.

'I still had my 90-gallon tank on and firing accurately was most difficult owing to yaw of aircraft and the flak-Bofors and light MG was in abundance and accurate. This F/W was camouflaged very dark indeed – almost black.

'I observed Johnnie 2's F/W do a curve to starboard go into the ground and burst into flames just south of the airfield in a wood.

'As I was attacking my F/W I noticed 2 fighters parked on the ground on the airfield.

'I pulled up to port and did a steep climbing turn at +18 boost into a gaggle of ME109's and at the same time endeavoured to jet my tank – pulled too hard and broke cable, so had to continue fighting with jet tank on.

'I managed to manoeuvre into a 40-degree angle of attack on an ME109 and continued firing short bursts of MG closing into 75-100 yards. At 20° - 30°, I observed no strikes by canon or MG. – but this 109 about ½ second after I stopped firing (only MG by then) did a violent break and flipped to starboard at 5-6,000ft, and did two long downward vertical turns and went straight into the ground 3-4 miles N. of BAULNE near a river. I took a short film of this aircraft burning on the ground.

'I attacked another 109 stern with MG from 100 yards and observed MG strikes but had to break off engagement as I was attacked by another two 109's. I observed another Spit being attacked by a 109 and gave a general break, which undoubtedly saved him as the 109 had him in a good position for a kill.

'My ammunition was by now expended and I had a climbing fight with 4 109's from 5,000 to 15,000 using the throttle through the gate the whole time.

'With the jet tank on and full throttle I held my own with the 109's from 5 to 10,000 ft and still had more manoeuvrability. From 10,000 to 13,500 I had difficulty until my second blower came into action, then it was a piece of cake to climb away.

'I had used +18 for about 12 minutes during the whole of the combat and at 15,000 ft my radiator temp was 138, and my engine was very rough and not responding properly.

'I throttled back to 0-2 and 18,000 revs and glided to 8,000 ft till engine cooled off and everything seemed OK – so came home.

'I find combat extremely difficult with 90-gallon tank – and at high and slow speeds aircraft very slovenly and difficult.

'I observed 4 aircraft in the vicinity of Hun airfield.

'ME 109's were of light camouflage with a black band or spiral around spinner. 1 claimed 2 destroyed and 1 damaged.'

During this busy summer period John, now aged 25, made time to marry his 23-year-old fiancée, Joan Ann Bolton, in Peterborough, Northamptonshire. She was apparently a very attractive woman who preferred to use the more elegant name of Penelope. For a while John replaced his sister's nickname Kay from beneath his Spitfire's cockpit with a painted copper penny for Penelope. The couple had a daughter together, Romayne, who sadly died of a brain abscess with other complications in 1960, aged just 13. John had sought out the best medical treatment for her and when she died he took her death very badly.

One sortie in September John, whilst taking off, lost the back wheel from his Spitfire, but continued on to complete the sortie before safely crash landing back at the airfield. Later on during this month John had another more serious crash landing. While flying in the Arnhem area of Holland his aircraft was struck by anti aircraft fire and he had to make a forced landing at over 200mph, during which John received minor injuries. The Squadron Operation Record book does not mention this incident, and the records of known Spitfires that John flew during this period do not document an aircraft being lost or damaged in that area. It may have been during Operation Market Garden (September 17th - 25th 1944), when an unsuccessful airborne invasion of Holland was attempted involving over 3,500 allied aircraft, including 500 gliders towed by bombers. John did write after the war that the anti-aircraft fire was so heavy over Arnhem that he lost 7 out of his flight of 12 Spitfires because of it on just one day.

On September 19th John was providing escort to Dakota aircraft, flying at very low levels to ensure the accuracy of their despatch of medical and other supplies to the allied troops on the ground at Arnhem. One Dakota, although severely damaged with a wing on fire from its first run, attempted a second drop as it still had two crates remaining. The pilot, Flt Lt David Lord, carried out the drop successfully but, while trying to allow his crew to bale out, the aircraft exploded, with only one survivor. David Lord was later posthumously awarded the Victoria Cross.

After the war in 1946, John, because of his actions over Holland, was awarded the Dutch Distinguished Flying Cross, a silver cross with an orange striped ribbon, with the inscription "Initiatief - Moed - Volharding" (Initiative, Courage, Perseverance) engraved on the medallion. The Maharaja of Mysore, India, also awarded him the Mysore Medal for his wartime actions.

In early October John flew several times on Ramrod Missions, the escorting of short-range bombers to and from their targets. Leading a squadron of 12 aircraft on the 3rd to the Dutch island of Walcheren, on the 5th to Nijmegen, the 6th to Gelsenkirchen in Germany, then the following day to Emmerich, Germany. On this last mission John flew Spitfire ML214 Muscat for the final time, when it was damaged requiring repairs, after which it was returned back to the squadron in November. The aircraft survived the war and was believed written off in 1949. From mid October onwards John regularly used Spitfire MkIX NH295 (5J-E).

In early October John was awarded the Distinguished Service Order confirmed in the London Gazette the following month. The citation read:

'Since being awarded the Distinguished Flying Cross this officer has participated in many varied sorties. During which much damage has been inflicted on the enemy. Shipping, radio stations, oil storage tanks, power plants and other installations have been amongst the targets attacked. On one occasion he led a small formation of aircraft against a much superior

force of enemy fighters. In the engagement 5 enemy were shot down, 2 of them by Squadron Leader Plagis. This officer is a brave and resourceful leader whose example has proved a rare source of inspiration. He has destroyed 16 hostile aircraft.'

Into November and through December John continued with further Ramrod missions. On December 18th 126 Squadron began to convert to the Mustang III, the British name for the Merlin powered P-51B and P-51C aircraft almost identical to the American version but having a bubble style canopy similar to that of the Spitfire to improve visibility. It had the renowned endurance that all Mustangs had that allowed them to roam far into Germany in support of the long-range bombers.

The 126 Squadron Operations Record book noted on December 12th:

'Squadron leader Plagis promoted to Wing Commander and posted to RAF Station North Weald for Deputy Station Commander.'

This was only a brief appointment as, in early January 1945, John was posted to Bentwaters in Suffolk which had recently become part of 11 Group Fighter Command. That same month two of John's previous squadrons, 64 and 126, relocated there also, along with 234 and 309 Squadrons to form a wing. John led another wing comprising of 165 and 118 Squadrons both newly converted to the Mustang. The six Mustang squadrons then became interchangeable flying in two wings, one led by Wing Commander Harold Bird-Wilson and one by John.

John continued in this role until the end of the war. One notable raid, in which he led his wing, was to provide cover during Operation Carthage, this was a low level attack by 20 Mosquito bombers against the Gestapo Headquarters in Copenhagen, Denmark. After several requests by the Danish Resistance to attack the building, several weeks of planning were required before the raid was carried out on March 21st 1945. The building, formerly owned by the oil company Shell, was known as Shell House, and housed many prisoners in the sixth floor attics, many of whom had been tortured with executions believed imminent for some. The building also contained records and details on many other resistance suspects.

The Mosquitos broke up into 3 groups with their Mustang escorts and approached from 3 separate directions. One of the low flying Mosquitos struck a lighting tower at the nearby railway yards and crashed at a school starting a fire. Other aircraft following behind took this to be the target and dropped their bombs into the flames resulting in the tragic death of 86 children and 17 adults. Realising the error, the remaining aircraft continued on to hit Shell House with eight 500lb bombs starting a fire, which swept through the building by the wind, destroying most parts of the structure. 18 of the 26 prisoners survived the raid with around 100 Germans and Danish collaborators killed. Four Mosquitos and two Mustangs were lost killing nine pilots and crew, with one of the Mustang pilots captured.

In mid April John began a period of rest and then returned to his homeland of Rhodesia where he was given both a Civic and a Government Reception. He took over command of RAF Kumalo, Bulawayo, the home of No.21 Service Flying Training School, the airfield reportedly had a single concrete runway with a sewage farm at one end and a cemetery at the other. John's stay was only until late October when he returned to England, at the personal request of Lord Tedder, Chief of the Air staff, joining 234 Squadron in June 1946. The squadron had replaced their Spitfires with the Meteor F3 jets six months earlier and were based at Boxted, Essex.

On June 8th 1946 the London Victory Parade was held celebrating the victory of the British, Commonwealth, Empire and Allied forces over the German, Italian and Japanese forces. The military parade included representatives from most of the countries involved and was followed in the evening by a fireworks display. The parade began with the British Chiefs of Staff along with the Supreme Allied Commanders, passing the Mall where the saluting base was, where members of the Royal family, Prime Minister Winston Churchill and other dignitaries were seated. A column of 500 military vehicles nearly 4 miles long followed them, with a marching column 2 miles long of men and women from the military and civil services. A flypast of 304 aircraft from 39 squadrons led by a single Hurricane fighter flew over Admiralty Arch, the Mall and on to Buckingham Palace. Amongst the aircraft were six Gloster Meteor III aircraft, one of which was proudly flown by John.

On September 1st 1946 234 Squadron were disbanded and renumbered 266 (Rhodesian) Squadron, John became the commanding officer of the squadron he had flown with back in 1941 leading up to his time in Malta. In January 1947 the squadron moved to Wattisham, Suffolk, then in April to Tangmere, Sussex.

In June 1947 it was the turn of 266 Squadron and John to spend two months training at Lubeck, Germany, along with 222 Squadron. The squadrons arrived with their ground crews for armament and close support training. The first month was spent in the study and implementation of close air support using no live ammunition, but gun cameras to judge their success against various targets. The second month live ammunition was used in air-to-air and air to ground firing and bombing. At the time a journalist from Flight magazine was covering the exercises for an article, having watched four Meteors attacking targets he wrote:

'To round off a good morning's work, S/L Plagis DSO DFC, Officer Commanding 266 squadron, acquainted the visitors with the recognition characteristics of the meteor travelling at 500 mph and at 50 feet. We all hoped that his aerobatics were enjoyed by our Russian neighbours.'

The journalist later watched John lead four meteors down to attack some ten-foot square targets, which John had earlier put all of his 160 20mm shells into. The journalist waited eagerly for the score, this time John had managed to get 156 of the 160 shells on target. John's prowess in the Meteor led to him being selected to provide aerobatic displays to many foreign delegations in Europe during his last year in the RAF.

John stayed with 266 Squadron until December 1947 and finally left the RAF in May 1948 when he returned home once again to Rhodesia. He became a Rhodesian citizen, and settled in Salisbury (Harare), when, around 1952, he opened a business, The John Plagis Bottle Store, selling alcohol. He was well known in the community, and, being a keen golfer, he sponsored the scorecards at the Old Royal Harare Golf Club. He was always pleased to welcome old friends and colleagues including, one day Douglas Bader, who was then working for the Shell Oil Company, who made a much publicised visit to his store.

John was honoured in the late 50s by having a road, John Plagis Avenue, in Alexandra Park named after him where he subsequently lived. A neighbour was the author and founder of the Church of Scientology, L. Ron Hubbard, a controversial and later discredited figure. In 1966 Hubbard and John, along with a local garage owner, Aubrey Davies, purchased the Bumi Hills Hotel set on a hill overlooking Lake Kariba. Two months later, in July, the Ministry of Immigration advised Hubbard that his residence permit would not be renewed and he was forced to leave Rhodesia. John was also involved in developing residential properties in Harare and other areas, which were subsequently sold on.

In the early 1950s John and Penelope separated and were later divorced. John went on later to marry Angela Gann, with the couple having together one daughter, Jill, and three sons, John, Jason and Michael. John referred to his children as his **'Diamonds,'** although he and Angela would eventually part, John then moved with the children to a house in Earl's Road.

During the early 1960s John had a short political career when, in 1962, he represented the Rhodesian Front for the Salisbury City area in the Southern Rhodesian General Election. This widened even further his extensive list of important contacts. He polled 44% of the vote but was unsuccessful, although his party were overall winners and started the steps towards the country's eventual declared independence from the United Kingdom in 1965.

In 1964 John had become a member of the board of Central African Airways, the airline had moved to a new headquarters facility at Salisbury Airport in 1956 and were flying Vickers Viscounts to and from Europe. The airline established three subsidiary airlines, Air Malawi, Zambia Airways and Air Rhodesia. The declaration of the country's independence in 1965 brought sanctions by the United Nations Security Council, this affected the ability of the airlines to fly to Europe and other countries. John subsequently joined a steering committee in 1966 set up by the new government's Department of Transport to look in to fuel supplies and other matters, which were affecting the country as a result of the economic sanctions that had been imposed.

John with his beloved sister Kay after the award of John's Greek medal in 1974 (Ritson)

In 1974 John was awarded the Order of Medal of St Mark, a Greek award either from the government or more likely the church, as it is presented in the presence of a Greek Orthodox Archbishop.

A personal view of John by his niece Daphne Ritson

'My first memory of my precious uncle Jay, was when I was five years old and my parents were moving farms. My Mum "Kay" his favourite sister and I lived with him in his Northampton Crescent Home (Harare) for a few weeks. He used to come down the stairs singing and dressed to perfection-wearing wonderful aftershave-he was off to work! He was the kindest human being I would ever know. He opened his home to anyone who needed a place to stay and his generosity was enormous.

'During my teenage years, I went to boarding school, and in those days we were only allowed out on limited weekends. Naturally, my parents and I went to Jay's home where again the hospitality was superb and best of all, we could drive the Bottle Store scooters around the neighbourhood, or swim, or listen to new music.

'When I needed to take my driver's license, I needed funding so I worked in the Bottle Store during school holidays. As soon as I could drive, he lent me his Bottle Store pick-up truck to go home to visit my parents. He was a fun loving uncle who loved to share.

'In his final years, he was decorated by the Greek Government who bestowed a decoration on him, at a ceremony held in Harare. My mum and dad were privileged to attend.

'The greatest tribute I can pay to him is that he was the uncle that made the whole family very proud. He was kind, generous with himself and gifts, considerate, consistent in his devotions for the cousins, a man who attracted people, loved to gamble, loved to party, loved to tell a good joke, loved to share and most of all was a personality of note. He adored his children. He was exceptional and his loss left a huge hole in our family.'

On August 27th 1975 John took his own life, a great shock to his young family. A family, that is still fiercely proud of John for what he did during the war, and for what he achieved during his life. John Agorastos Plagis DFC and Bar, DSO, DFC (Dutch). Died aged 56. He is buried at the Warren Hills Cemetery, Harare, Zimbabwe.

Robert James Sim

Robert Sim was born on June 28th 1919 to parents Peter and Lilas Sim, in Gisborne, a town on the north eastern side of New Zealand's North Island. He attended Gisborne High School, and, as a keen sportsman, he represented the school at both cricket and rugby. On leaving school he went to work as a Cost Clerk at the Cook Hospital And Charitable Aid Board also in Gisborne. He applied to join the Royal New Zealand Air Force in September 1939, the same month that war was declared.

On October 26th 1940 at the age of 21, he enlisted in the Royal New Zealand Air Force, (Serial No. NZ403995) and started at the Ground Training Station at Levin as an Airman Pilot Under Training. Here, after medical examinations and being kitted out with his uniform, he learnt the basics of service life which included lectures on navigation, morse code, airmanship, plus marching, drill and discipline. The course of around six weeks duration, led to the next stage at No.3 Elementary Flying Training School based at Harewood near Christchurch, where Robert began learning the skills required to fly an aircraft.

The course at Harewood was of around eight weeks during which Robert was given flying instruction in their brightly painted yellow de Havilland Tiger Moth biplanes. On December 4th Robert flew solo for the first time, all pilots needed to complete at least 25 hours of flying time solo, out of the 50 hours, which were flown during this course.

In mid January 1941, after a weeks leave, Robert's training continued at the No.2 Flying Training School at Woodbourne, situated on the South Island, 5 miles from the town of Blenheim. At the school, pilots flew the Harvard II, a faster monoplane aircraft with a retractable undercarriage, variable pitch propeller, and an enclosed cockpit, very beneficial with increased flying speeds now of around 170mph. The training also introduced for the first time the added danger to the pilots of night flying exercises. After around eight weeks the Chief Flying Officer tested each pilot's flying ability, this was followed by a written examination, and the successful pilots were later presented with their 'Wings' badge, which Robert received in early March 1940. An additional advanced part of the course included formation flying, cross-country navigation and firing the Harvard's wing mounted machine guns at a ground and an air towed drogue target.

On the completion of the course on April 12th Robert was promoted to the rank of Sergeant Pilot, and at the end of the month on the 29th he began his embarkation to the UK via Canada arriving on attachment to the RAF in England on June 29th 1941. Before he left for service abroad Robert married his fiancée Patricia Tooman from Mairoa, Auckland.

In June the Personnel Reception Centre at Uxbridge allocated Robert to continue his training with No.58 Operational Training Unit based in Grangemouth, Stirlingshire, Scotland, where he flew the Supermarine Spitfire for the first time. At the end of the course he was retained as a Staff Pilot where he remained until his posting to an operational squadron.

In September 1941 Robert joined 130 Squadron based at Portreath, Cornwall, flying the MK IIA and later the MK V Spitfire in defence of the counties of Cornwall and Devon. On November 1st he was promoted to Flight Sergeant. Robert flew 29 operations, including 18 convoy patrols, seven scrambles to intercept enemy aircraft and four fighter sweeps into occupied France. Having volunteered for service outside of the UK, he was chosen as one of the Spitfire pilots to be sent to Malta.

Robert joined 249 Squadron based at Takali, and flew his first operation over the island on March 14th when he carried out a search at sea for a shot down allied pilot. Whilst in the company of three other Spitfires, they intercepted and attacked several Me109 fighters. By April 13th there were very few Spitfires still serviceable and consequently several pilots, including Robert, were transferred to 185 Squadron (B Flight). Here he flew the Hawker Hurricanes that were available, based at Hal Far airfield until further Spitfire reinforcements could be flown to the island.

On May 11th Robert attacked and damaged an Me109 causing it to emit black smoke, 3 Spitfires that attacked it immediately afterwards finally shot it down. He was also involved in interceptions of enemy aircraft that were carried out on the 15th, when, flying with Sgt Jack Yarra, the pair attacked seven Me109s and 4 Macchis Italian fighters, returning only when they had run out of ammunition, Yarra claiming two destroyed. On the 19th in conjunction with Flt Lt Keith Lawrence, Robert, fired at a group of Italian bombers and their escorting fighters, although no claim was made by either. The following day, and now flying as part of 'A' Flight, Robert's aircraft ran out of fuel after an interception and he was forced to make an emergency landing at Takali airfield.

The 185 squadron diary mentions that on the 23rd Robert was ill with 'Malta Dog,' the vomiting and diarrhoea sickness which affected so many on Malta:

'Quite a lot of chaps are down with that insidious malady "Malta Dog" Flt Sgt Sim, is the latest victim-he even looks like a dog'.

The diary entry on Monday June 15th for a now recovered Robert also describes his first success:

'**F/Sgt Sim was beetling along after an 88 who was making rapidly for home. He was having some difficulty in catching the 88 when he noticed another one flying in formation with him. The pilot in the 88, noticing the evil look on F/Sgt Sim's face immediately buzzed off, hotly pursued by "Simmie", who proceeded to shoot great pieces off the enemy bomber. However, the aforementioned pieces kept bouncing off Sim's Spitfire and tore some holes in various places, but did not prevent the destruction of the Ju88, or the safe return of F/Sgt Sim.'**

Left to right: Sgt Robert Sim, Sgt John Yarra, Plt Off Ian 'Skip' McKay and Plt Off Ron Noble of 185 Squadron, Malta 1942. In the original book the two pilots on the far right had been erroneously identified (T Rogers)

Robert landed the Spitfire (BR126/GL-O) wheels up at Luqa airfield with an overheating engine caused by a glycol coolant leak.

The squadron diary on the June 16th shows that a posting back to the UK had come through for him, although it was several weeks before he was actually able to leave the island. June had also seen another promotion for Robert to the rank of Warrant Officer.

Fellow Operation Spotter pilot, David Ferraby, recalled one of Robert's favourite expressions he would repeat was **"our old mate the wily Hun"** referring to the German pilots. June 21st saw another victory for Robert over 'the wiley Hun,' whilst flying Spitfire BR321/GL-D, he shot down an Me109 that was attacking another Spitfire, having fired at it a 12 second burst of both cannon and machine gun fire. Robert's third and final victory on Malta occurred on July 12th when, en route to escort in a Sunderland Flying Boat, flying the same Spitfire as during his previous success, he shot down into the sea another Me109 fighter. The following day, after a total of 70 sorties, he was stood down from operations to await his return to the UK.

Before his return the Squadron Leader endorsed his Log Book recommending a medal, which sadly was never awarded:

'Recommend that this pilot be recommended for DFC when he has destroyed one more enemy aircraft. A very reliable section leader'

On July 23rd he started the journey back to England, flying the first stage as the second pilot in a Hudson aircraft to Gibraltar, continuing after a stop over, he arrived back in the UK on July 29th where he enjoyed a period of leave.

In August 1942 Robert was appointed as an instructor on Spitfires with 52 Operational Training Unit based at Aston Down in Gloucestershire. During his time as an instructor he was promoted again in October 1942, to a Pilot Officer. The following year in early May 1943, and

Robert Sim Malta 1942

now with the rank of Flying Officer, he was posted to 616 Squadron flying the high altitude Spitfire VI from Ibsley, near Ringwood, Hampshire. Also at 616 was Squadron Leader 'Laddie' Lucas who Robert had flown with in Malta. Their role consisted of fighter patrols, the escorting of bombers, fighter sweeps over northern France and strikes on enemy shipping. It was during one of these last types of missions that Robert lost his life.

In the early hours of June 15th 1943 four German minesweepers followed by an armed trawler, were heading at around 8 knots through the English Channel close to the Channel Islands, destined for Cherbourg, where they would be protected during the day by the port's anti aircraft defences. At the time two sections of MK VI Spitfires were in the air, eight from 616 Squadron in an armed reconnaissance role seeking out enemy shipping, and eight from 504 Squadron as their escort. The fighters had rendezvoused with four bomb-ladened Westland Whirlwinds from 263 Squadron that had taken off at 05:40am from the south coast airfield of Warmwell, Dorset. The group, led by Squadron Leader 'Laddie' Lucas of 616 Squadron, then flew out towards France, the four Whirlwinds in line abreast behind 616 Squadron, with two sections of Spitfires from 504 on either side of them, all flying at sea level to avoid being detected by radar.

At around 6:20am the German ships were spotted 3 miles north east of Sark, they were sailing line astern, in two pairs, with the armed trawler approximately 700 metres behind them. One of the front pair was the minesweeper M483. Over 62 metres in length, her two coal-fired boilers powered two 900hp engines, which gave her a speed of over 17 knots, she carried a crew number of around 80 men. She was heavily armed with a 10.5cm gun at the stern, a 3.7cm gun at her bow, and seven 2cm anti-aircraft guns along her deck.

New Zealands Weekly News announces Robert Sim missing in 1943 (AucklandWar Memorial Museum Cenotaph Database)

The Spitfires of 616 Squadron attacked first diving down at very low level, their cannon fire seen to be tearing into the ships. Then the four Whirlwinds, each with two 250lb bombs beneath their wings, came in low from the left hand side, the bombs had an eleven second delay to allow the aircraft to clear the area before the explosions. One of the Whirlwinds, flown by Australian, Pilot Officer Max Cotton DFC, dropped his two bombs from around mast height ensuring that they would hit or be very close to the minesweeper M483, one of the other pilots saw them splash amidships of the vessel.

The anti-aircraft fire from the defending gunners was fierce and, at the low level flown by the aircraft, very accurate. Plt Off Cotton's Whirlwind was struck near the cockpit area, possibly by a 40mm shell, setting the aircraft on fire, the aircraft with its pilot plunged down to break up on the surface of the sea. The M483 had been severely damaged, having been struck by more than

312

one bomb, and sank quickly approximately 10 miles north east of the island of Sark. The four other ships in the convoy were all damaged during the air strike but were able to escape to safety.

The accurate return anti-aircraft fire also hit Flying Officer Robert Sim, who was flying Spitfire MkVI (BR319/YQ-C) on his 97th wartime operation. The 616 Squadron Operations Record Book stated that:

'The attacks were pressed home to a point blank range and strikes were obtained on the ships by all pilots. During the attack F/O Sim flying as Yellow 3 was heavily hit by a Bofor shell and his aircraft was seen to catch fire. He pulled away from the formation and was last seen at 300 feet with his aircraft on fire and a dead propeller, going down towards the water in a shallow dive. No one saw him ditch nor yet to bale out.'

The name of Flying Officer Robert James Sim, aged 23, is listed on the Air Forces Memorial, for those with no known grave at Runnymede in Surrey, England. On panel 198. His name is also written within the Rolls of Honour, held in the Hall of Memories at the New Zealand National War Memorial in Wellington, New Zealand.

John Lovett Tayleur

By October 1940, the aerial duels of the Battle Of Britain between the pilots of the RAF and the German Luftwaffe, had been taking place in the skies above Britain for three months. John, who had recently left school, was living with his aunt Florence at Chilworth near Southampton. He was keen to join up and play his part in defending his country having met with some of the traumatised small children who had been moved from the Southampton docks area, after it had been heavily bombed. However, at the age of seventeen he was not yet eligible to enrol with his chosen service, the RAF. So he did what many others had done before him, in both the First and the Second World Wars, he lied about his age. With a little assistance from his Aunt Flo, who agreed to sign his RAF application, which showed the year of his birth as being 1922, instead of the correct year of 1923. This date of birth went uncorrected right through John's RAF career.

John came from a military family background and, as a consequence, his father, Guy Lovett Tayleur, was not pleased when John chose the air force instead of the army. Guy had been in the 2nd Dragoon Guards (Queens Bays), before the First World War. In October 1914 he joined the 4th Battalion, Devonshire Regiment, and was later promoted to 2nd Lieutenant. In 1918 Guy was seconded to the Indian Army, progressing the following year to the rank of Captain.

In 1914 Guy married Evelyn Maud Gwynne at Christchurch, Devon. Their first child Pamela was born in 1918, their second daughter Joan was born in Hampshire in 1920. Evelyn later followed her husband who had been posted to India, where their next two children were born. John was born on February 25th 1923 at Rawalpindi, with another sister, Constance, born in 1927.

In 1928 the family returned to Britain, where a third daughter, Pamela, was born. They settled in Cardiff, Wales, where Guy was seconded to the Territorial Army, serving in the 53rd Welsh Division Royal Corps Of Signals. He was later posted to Catterick, North Yorkshire, and, around 1935, once again returned to India. He rose through the ranks and was promoted to Lieutenant Colonel in 1937. His active military service ended in 1940, although he did not finally retire until July 1945 when he left the army with the honoury rank of Brigadier.

John began his formal education, age nine, in September 1932 as a boarder at Aysgarth Preparatory School in North Yorkshire. With his parents being in India part of the time, the Doctor of the school became his official guardian. John was keen on sports and excelled at both swimming and rugby. He left in July 1936 aged thirteen and became a boarder at Wellington College in Berkshire. The Prime Minister in the early 1850s had proposed the college in memory of the Duke Of Wellington. It was to be a charitable educational institution open to the orphans of army officers, although the sons of living officers were also accepted.

John was in Combermere Dormitory, one of several Houses that the boys were divided amongst. With its military background, the college ran a Cadet Force with each House being represented and with all the Houses making up a Combined Cadet Force. The boys performed drills and weapons exercises, with regular competitions held amongst the Houses. The Combermere House Platoon comprised three sections, with Section Two under the command of Lance Corporal John Tayleur. During the summer of 1940 there was a very real threat of a German invasion of Britain and so the Combined Cadet Force also became part of a Local Defence Force, which carried out exercises, patrols and watches around the College grounds.

On October 4th 1940 John, Service No. 1380093, began his RAF training at No.1 Receiving Wing based at Babbacombe, Torquay, on the Devon coast. Having passed his medicals, he was kitted out with uniform and equipment and then commenced his basic drill training, before he moved further along the Devon coast to No.4 Initial Training Wing at Paignton, where he was billeted in a requisitioned local hotel. At the end of November he received his first promotion from Aircraftsman 2nd class to Leading Aircraftsman. On January 8th John joined No.6 Elementary Flying Training School at Sywell, Northamptonshire. His first flight of 25 minutes, as the pilot of a Tiger Moth (R5016), was with Flt Lt Love as the instructor. On February 21st John flew his first solo flight, of ten minutes duration. Further dual and solo training continued until the end of the course on March 6th when he was assessed and rated as an '**Average**' pilot.

John received further training abroad under the British Commonwealth Air Training Scheme. On April 1st he boarded a ship, which travelled in convoy on a weeklong voyage to Canada. After the ship had docked he spent a couple of days travelling by rail to his final destination of Moose Jaw, Saskatchewan. This was the location of No.32 Service Flying Training School. Here he was billeted in one of the long wooden huts, which were fitted with three large stoves to keep out the freezing temperatures, each housing up to 86 men.

At the end of April the commanding officer of 32 SFTS felt it necessary to admonish John for having an untidy Log Book, with too many blotches. Having written this in red ink he unfortunately then smudged his own entry.

John received instruction on flying the North American Harvard, culminating in him successfully completing the course on June 18th 1941, he then gained his pilots 'Wings' and received a promotion to the rank of Sergeant. At the end of July, having safely made the voyage back to England, John attended No.3 Personal Reception Centre in Bournemouth to await a posting to an Operational Training Unit. The wait was only a matter of days, as he joined 53 Operational Training Unit on August 3rd, which was then based at Llandow, Glamorgan.

John's training continued with 53 OTU, initially with 3 flights on August 7th on the dual controlled Miles Master aircraft. He was then, on the same day, considered proficient enough to make his first flight in a Spitfire (X4897). The unit also had, at the airfield, target towing Fairey Battle aircraft; these aircraft towed behind them a drogue target that the pilots were able to practise firing at with the Spitfire's machine guns.

On August 31st John flew Spitfire X4901 during a training exercise. On returning to the airfield to land he stalled the aircraft resulting in a very heavy landing that ripped off the aircraft's undercarriage. This was deemed as due to carelessness and his log book was endorsed in red ink stating so.

Having successfully completed the course, and with 43 hours experience on flying the Spitfire, John was then posted to his first frontline squadron. On September 22nd 1941 John joined 'A' flight of 66 Squadron based at Perranporth on the north coast of Cornwall, being billeted at a nearby hotel. The squadron was under the command of the former Battle Of Britain pilot, Sqn Ldr Hubert 'Dizzy' Allen DFC, and was equipped with the Spitfire MkII, which carried the squadron's identification code letters LZ on the fuselage. The Spitfires included an ungainly 30-gallon fuel tank permanently fixed to the port wing. This led to great care being required on take off as the aircraft had a tendency to pull to the left. A visiting Commanding Officer was alarmed one day to see three damaged Spitfires covered with tarpaulins, which had been the result of careless take offs. The squadrons main task was protecting the shipping travelling around the coast. This mundane work was interspersed with providing escort to bombers, including those, which attacked the German battle ships Scharnhorst, Prinz Eugen and Gneisenau that were trapped in the French port of Brest.

In addition, offensive sweeps were carried out over the North French coast. One such attack took place on December 9th. Six Spitfires led by Sqn Ldr Allen, took off in the early afternoon to attack the German radar station at Ploumanche on the French coast. Having crossed the channel at 200 feet, they ventured inland and noted several French people giving friendly waves to them as they passed overhead. Not being able to find the radar site, they looked for another suitable target and spotted some railway goods wagons with workers alongside at Kermaria. The formation swept down, all firing their machine guns with the De Wilde incendiary and armour piercing ammunition hitting the railway trucks. These were considered unusable as a result of their attack, although it was noted that, had the aircraft been fitted with cannons, the wagons might have been completely destroyed. John's aircraft was the only one fitted with a cine gun camera, which he used during his attack. The aircraft left the coast and headed back to base at very low level. On their way they spotted a Ju88 flying at around 2,000 feet, which they attacked and damaged, but Sqn Ldr Allen ordered the pilots not to pursue the aircraft. All aircraft and pilots returned safely to their base.

On December 15th the squadron moved further down the coast to Portreath, commandeering several houses to the rear of the harbour to provide accommodation, with meals taken at the station mess on the airfield. Sqn Ldr Byron Duckenfield, another former Battle of Britain pilot, had now taken command of the squadron. Also with the squadron were three pilots with whom John would meet up with later again on Malta, Percy 'Laddie' Lucas, Raoul Daddo-Langlois, nicknamed Daddy Longlegs, and Norman Lee.

John remained with 66 Squadron until February 8th when, having at some stage elected for a posting overseas, he found out his destination was Malta. At this stage he had flown over 70 hours in Spitfires and nearly 270 hours in total. During his time with 66, John had been given the nickname 'Junior' as he was the youngest in the squadron, this name stayed with him when he joined 249 Squadron on Malta, having flown off HMS Eagle in Spitfire AB334 on March 7th 1942 with the other Operation Spotter pilots.

The first flight by John over Malta took place on March 11th when he tested the cannons of Spitfire AB337, and later flew two defensive sorties over the airfield. On the 15th just before midday, three Ju88 bombers with fighter escort bombed Valletta and the airfield at Luqa. Two soldiers and eight civilians were killed in the raid. Four Spitfires, piloted by Flt Lt Heppell, Flt Lt Connell, Plt Off Jeff West and John in Spitfire AB334 (GN-J), were scrambled to intercept, along with seven Hurricanes. Plt Off West and John both attacked one Ju88 causing some damage before they were forced to withdraw by the escorting fighters. The Germans claimed two Spitfires as shot down in the fight when in fact none of the aircraft were lost.

John flew again on the morning of March 17th when four Spitfires and several Hurricanes engaged over twenty Ju88s that had attacked Luqa airfield and damaged several aircraft. Residential areas had also been targeted with many civilians killed and injured. John was flying along with Flt Sgt Paul Brennan and both were on a course to intercept the fighter escort when, suddenly, John's pilot seat came away from its supports, throwing him forward hard against the control column. His Spitfire, AB337/(GN-A), plunged down out of control from 20,000 feet to around 8,000 feet before John was able to recover sufficiently to pull the aircraft out of its dive. John flew three times that day and in his Log Book he noted the death of Flight Sergeant Cormack, the second Operation Spotter pilot to be killed.

At around 10:00am on the morning of April 20th a further reinforcing consignment of 46 Spitfires arrived on the island. They had been flown as part of Operation Calendar from the American aircraft carrier U.S.S. Wasp. The pilots were from two complete squadrons, 601 and 603, as opposed to a selection of men from various squadrons, as was the case with Operation Spotter. The Luftwaffe were fully aware of the new arrivals and, just after midday, the first of their bombing raids began, with a force of over 50 Ju88 and Ju87 bombers with fighter escort attacking the three main airfields.

Around 1:00pm John, flying Spitfire AB465 as No.2 to Flt Lt Buck McNair, was one of six Spitfires all led by Laddie Lucas that were scrambled to intercept along with three Hurricanes from 185 Squadron. Climbing to 10,000 feet south of the island, they continued to the north side turning back over the island when they encountered the German aircraft. The sky became full of twisting and turning aircraft, the fighters seeking to gain an advantage to attack the opposing aircraft, the bombers trying to avoid being attacked, but also, still seeking a target on which to drop their bombs before they could withdraw.

John dived down on one fighter and saw strikes from his guns damage the other aircraft, this he believed to have been so badly damaged that it would not be able to return to its base in Sicily, he therefore later claimed it as probably destroyed. Another Me109 pilot came to the aid of his colleague and charged head on at John's aircraft with its cannons firing. A 20mm shell struck the canopy of John's Spitfire causing the Perspex to shatter, his face being lacerated by the pieces, with many tiny fragments going into his eyes. Although now bleeding heavily from his facial wounds, John could make out one of the Stuka bombers in front of him and closed in on it, he saw his fire hit the Stuka and he claimed it as damaged.

John, with his visibility now very limited from the Perspex fragments and blood that had run down his forehead into his eyes, made a safe landing at Takali where he was promptly taken to M'tarfa hospital.

On April 27th Plt Off Peter Nash and some of the other pilots visited their colleagues in the hospital:

'Went up to M'tarfa to see James (P/O Jimmy James). He is quite OK also saw Sgt Tayleur. He is very rough. His eyes are bad and his nerves very shaky. Shocked at the difference between the officers and NCOs wards. It's a terrible scandal, Tayleur's ward resembles an extremely shabby barrack room and his food is very bad while the officers is very good indeed.'

Many years later John's wife admitted that she had cried when she had read about the discrimination between the wounded officers and the Sergeant Pilots, and the poor conditions John had to endure while in hospital recovering from his injuries.

In May John was promoted on an Emergency Commission to Pilot Officer. He, however, remained at the hospital until June 13th when, because of his injuries, it had been decided that he should return to England.

He wrote in his Log Book:

'Spent between April 20th & June 13th in 90 General Hospital, Imtafa, Malta. Where they tried unsuccessfully to remove 150 perspex splinters from my eyes.'

On July 8th he began the journey home, flying as a passenger in an Armstrong Whitworth Whitley to Gibraltar, with an Air Transport Auxiliary pilot. Two days later another Whitley began the journey back to England, but had to turn back and return to Gibraltar with a failed port engine. Three days later John landed safely at RAF Whitchurch, Shropshire, the base of No.2 Ferry Pool, A.T.A.

Having been virtually blinded for a short period, John regained full vision in both eyes. He later reflected that the wounds he received may have saved his life, before he left Malta six of the pilots that had flown out with him had been killed, men he considered to be better and more experienced pilots than he was. After a period of recuperation John travelled out to India to visit his father, who was now retired from the army and in charge of the British Red Cross in Southern India.

In August 1942 John returned to the UK, his rank had changed from the emergency commission of Pilot Officer whilst on Malta to Flight Sergeant in July. John became an instructor at 52 Operational Training Unit based at Aston Down, then at Chedworth, Gloucestershire. The unit was equipped with Miles Masters, Harvards and Spitfires. Also based, as instructors at 52

OTU were some familiar faces from Malta, including Plt Off Paul Brennan and Flt Sgt Robert Sim, both former Operation Spotter pilots. In addition he met, once again, Flt Lt Raoul Daddo-Langlois and Fg Off Robert 'Barney' Barnfather who had been in the hospital at the same time as John on Malta.

In November John was promoted to the rank of Flying Officer, he stayed as an instructor until early April 1943. The Operational Record Book for the unit noted:

'F/O R.R. Barnfather and P/O 'Junior' Tayleur, who have been with the unit for more than six months, are leaving us for further spells overseas. Tayleur was commissioned with us and has been a popular member of both the sergeants and officers messes.'

In May 1943 John was posted to join the Practice Flight of 325 Wing at Setif, Algeria. Here he flew a Hawker Hurricane for the first time in addition to Spitfires in training exercises. At the end of the month he moved to 322 Training Flight in Tunisia. Then on June 7th John was transferred to 232 Squadron, one of 5 squadrons, which made up 322 Wing based at Takali, Malta.

John was once more back at Takali and no doubt pleased to be back in proper accommodation rather than the tents that had been in use during his time in North Africa. The Canadian Sqn Ldr Charles Arthur, nicknamed 'Duke' led 232. The squadron became involved in offensive sweeps over Sicily and provided escort to Mitchell and Marauder bombers attacking airfields, railways and power stations, all as part of the preparation for Operation Husky, the Allied invasion of Sicily.

A little before 10:00am on the morning of July 1st John flew, along with Fg Off J. G. Woodill, out to sea to investigate the report of unknown shipping off the north east of Malta. They noted a large oil slick around seven miles off shore. Shortly after, they spotted three narrow vessels heading east. On realising they had been seen, the ships altered their course to the south. The two pilots flew lower to get a better look at the craft but were unable to find them again in the haze, despite searching for several minutes. They then flew close to the coast of Sicily on patrol before returning back to Takali.

By July 9th, when the invasion of Sicily began, 232 was one of 23 Spitfire fighter squadrons based on Malta and its sister island of Gozo. These provided air defence and carried out patrols around the Sicilian coast. After the ground forces successfully landed, they advanced across Sicily, allowing 232 to relocate onto the island on July 22nd to be based at Lentini, around six miles from the north east coast and, at that time, only ten miles from the front line. The escort operations continued although they rarely saw any opposing aircraft at this stage, the greatest risk was from ground fire. On August 11th an Me109 was seen to fly over their airfield on a reconnaissance mission, which resulted, the following night, with the airfield being bombed. Several men were caught out in the open whilst trying to make for the protection of a ditch. Seven men were killed, including three pilots. They were buried the following day at a site close to the camp. Six days later Sicily surrendered to the allies.

With the momentum with the Allies, on September 3rd the invasion of the Italian mainland began, 322 Wing continued its support for the ground forces. John flew over the invasion beaches of Italy on September 9th, noting that it was necessary to use a 90 Gallon overload fuel tank to allow greater range flying from their airfield.

As the battle progressed the squadron, now flying the Mk IX Spitfires, were moved to bases on Italy, initially to Asa, then Serretelle, and then Gioia Del Colle. In December 232 Squadron was posted to Bab el Haoua in Syria for a period of rest and also to provide local air defence cover.

John stayed with the squadron for a brief period in Palestine, then in April 1944, the squadron moved to Corsica, a Mediterranean island similar to Malta in that it was now home to hundreds of allied aircraft, all continuing the support

John Tayleur who was shot down and wounded on his fifteenth sortie over Malta in April 1942 (P Green)

to ground troops fighting their way through Italy. Initially, John was based at Alto airfield then, between April and July at Poretta, both airfields positioned on the east coast of Corsica. The squadron was involved in escorting bombers and also strafing targets of opportunity over Italy. In late April John attacked two freight trains and also a convoy of trucks. Anti-aircraft fire was still the greatest danger to the fighters, John recorded in his Log Book the death of the South African Lt Rosendorff due to the flak on one mission.

In May John received another promotion to Flight Lieutenant. June continued as before with patrols and attacks made on road transport, during one attack his aircraft was struck by return fire but was only slightly damaged. On the last day of the month, flying in the region of Florence, he encountered 6 Me109s. John fired all of his ammunition at one but without result. On July 11th the squadron transferred to Calenzana, Corsica, and began patrolling areas of the south of France. The battle for Italy continued for another six months until their surrender in April 1945.

In late August the squadron relocated to Frejus on the south coast of France, approximately 20 miles from St Tropez, the Allied forces having landed on the northern beaches of France on June 6th two months earlier. From here the squadron patrolled the coastal area between Cannes and Marseilles, until 232 Squadron were disbanded at the end of September.

John returned to England and in November attended at No.1 Personal Despatch Centre, West Kirby, Merseyside. A series of short postings then followed as a Flying Instructor on Spitfires, starting in January 1945 at No.61 Operational Training Unit at Rednal and Montford Bridge, Shropshire. In February 1945 he transferred to No.41 OTU at Hawarden, Flintshire, followed by a period of instruction at No.58 OTU at Poulton, Cheshire.

In March 1945 John attended a Junior Commanders Course at the RAF training school at Cranwell in Lincolnshire, returning to 58 OTU afterwards. His records show he spent three months from June with the Air Transport Auxiliary's No.12 Ferry Unit, based at Cosford, near Wolverhampton but in a non-flying role. John's Log Book for June shows just two flights, including a two-hour flight in an Anson carrying out a map reading exercise.

On April 18th John was flying a MkV Spitfire (BM476) when it caught fire whilst in the air shortly after take off, he turned the aircraft around and returned to crash back onto the airfield. He managed to escape from the aircraft but not before he had received minor burns to his face, hands and leg. The aircraft was so badly damaged that it was scrapped.

In August 1945, with the war in Europe now over, John was posted to the Far East, undertaking a three-day journey by Dakota to India. On September 6th he attended No.3 Refresher Flying Unit at Poona, where he gained experience on the MkXIV Spitfire. This included training for taking off from an aircraft carrier, an experience that certainly was not new to John.

On October 5th John was posted to join No.11 Squadron, India, as a Flight Commander. Later that month the squadrons MkXIV Spitfires were loaded by crane on to HMS Trumpeter, an American built Escort Carrier, and shipped to Port Swettenhamm where the aircraft were flown off the carrier to Seletar on Singapore island. The Japanese forces had surrendered the previous month in September 1945, after the devastation that followed the dropping of two Atomic bombs on the 6th and 9th of August.

On the last day of October John was performing an air test of Spitfire NH790 when the engine suddenly cut out and he was forced to make a crash landing, the aircraft was severely damaged and later written off, John was lucky to escape uninjured.

In January 1946 the squadron transferred to Kuala Lumpa in Malaya and then in April, 11 Squadron were sent to Japan to be based there as part of the British Commonwealth Occupation Force. The squadron, along with 4 and 17 Squadron, were transported on HMS Vengeance, at Cochin their Spitfires were loaded aboard by crane. The voyage took two weeks, from Cochin to Iwakuni, on the Japanese island of Kyushu. The weather became noticeably rougher as they approached Japan. They arrived at Iwakuni on 23rd April 1946, where the aircraft were unloaded and taken ashore by barge. During May the squadron moved to Miho, 90 miles to the northeast and situated on the West Coast of the main Japanese island of Honshu, which was their base for the rest of their stay in Japan.

John as a Flying Instructor preparing to board a Gloster Meteor Circa 1953 (P Green)

The majority of John's flying, normally in Spitfire NM822 was air patrols and the testing of serviced aircraft. However, on July 15th he flew Spitfire NM866 as part of a flypast over the burial of one of the squadron pilots, 21 year old Flt Lt Desmond Quick from Rhodesia who had been killed in an accident the previous day, he was buried at the temporary cemetery of Kure. A flypast over the grave by the whole wing was also carried out two weeks later.

On September 17th John began his journey back to England, with his Log Book showing he had now amassed a flying time of 898 hours. He left the RAF on October 27th and was finally released on February 4th 1947.

The RAF had set up Reserve Command in 1946 and, in March 1947, an appeal was made to former pilots to join the newly constituted RAF Volunteer Reserve. Pilots were granted a £35.00 annual retaining fee, later increased to £55.00, plus some travelling expenses. They received a minimum of 40 hours flying training each year over a fifteen-day period. Training initially was carried out on Tiger Moth Biplanes, the same type of aircraft that they had trained on several years before as fledgling pilots.

John was one of over 1300 pilots who applied to one of the RAF Reserve Centres. He went to No.24 Reserve Centre, signing up for five years service. He had to relinquish his wartime rank of Flight Lieutenant and reverted back to being a Flying Officer. His training began in June 1947 at No.8 Refresher Flying School at Woodley, Berkshire, where once again he began flying the Tiger Moth performing the exercises he had carried out six years earlier. For the next three years John flew 3 or 4 days a month at Woodley.

John flying Spitfire FRXIV NH866 with 11 Squadron over Japan in May 1946
(P Green)

With John now only infrequently attending the RAF, he spent time with his family who were now living at Weycroft Hall, Axminster, Devon. He also set up a Market Garden business with some former RAF colleagues. On Easter Sunday 1949 John was having a drink in the Crown Inn, East Burnham, Buckinghamshire. Whilst there, he noticed a young lady, Phyllis Harris, out with her friends. Having been introduced, they chatted for a while, and then John returned to his group telling them boldly, **"I am going to marry that girl one day."**

John was correct in his prediction; he and Phyllis were married in 1951, and set up home in West Lodge, Stomp Road, Burnham. On one of the days when John was flying he brought his Tiger Moth aeroplane low over their house circling it several times. Unfortunately, nearby at the time, was Air Vice Marshall Donald Bennett who made a note of the aircraft's number and reported it, John was later reprimanded by his Commanding Officer.

During 1951 John was once again promoted to Flight Lieutenant. From July he continued his flying at No.1 Flying Training School at Oakington, Cambridgeshire, flying the Harvard. In September he attended No.102 Flying Refresher School at North Luffenham, Rutland, where he flew Spitfire Mk LFXVIe aircraft in the build up to converting to the de Havilland Vampire jet aircraft. The de Havilland Vampire was the air force's second jet. It had made its first test flight in April 1945, six months after the Gloster Meteor, the RAF's first jet, and incorporated many features from the highly successful de Havilland Mosquito, including the part wood and part metal construction. It had a single Goblin jet engine, a tricycle undercarriage, and a distinctive twin boom tail, with a top speed of around 540mph, and a maximum ceiling of 40,000 feet. Its role was as a fighter-bomber with four cannons and either two 1,000lb bombs under each wing, or eight 60lb rockets.

John far right with other RAF officers visting the Brabazon aircraft Circa 1950 (P Green)

John made his first flight of fifty minutes in a single seat Vampire MkV on September 24th 1951, flying several times during that month and in October. Over the next ten months John once more flew propeller aircraft back again at Woodley, including a new type, the de Havilland Chipmunk.

In September John also attended a 14-day course at RAF Full Sutton in Yorkshire, at No.207 Advanced Flying School, which was equipped with the single seat Mk4 Gloster Meteor and the 2-seat Mk7 Meteor. John had two hours flying alongside his instructor then flew his first solo on the type on September 16th.

The Meteor had first flown in 1943 entering service with the RAF in 1944 and had seen some wartime action, mainly in countering the V-1 rockets being fired towards England. The aircraft had two Derwent jet engines, an all-metal construction and could climb to 40,000ft in 8 minutes and reach around 600 mph. In its role as a fighter it was armed with four 20mm cannons, it could also carry rockets beneath both wings.

In May 1952 John extended his commitment to the RAF Volunteer Reserve for another 5 years. However, in January 1953 he relinquished this commission and rejoined the RAF full time on a Short Service Commission as a Flight Lieutenant. He commenced training, which led him to become a full time Flying Instructor. In February and March 1953 he undertook two courses with the Central Flying School. These were the 'Basic' course flying Harvards, Prentices and Provosts at South Cerney, Gloucestershire, and then in June he was posted to Little Rissington, Gloucestershire, for the 'Advanced' training programme using the Meteor jet. This programme also included a Flying Instructors course that John passed to qualify as an instructor on the Meteor.

Spitfire F22 PK399 used by 102 Flying Refresher School, RAF North Luffenham in September 1951(P Green)

In 1949 the RAF had opened its first training school purely for jet pilots, based at Driffield, Yorkshire, this was 203 Advanced Flying Training School. Previously pilots, having mastered the Harvard, would have gone on to Spitfires, but now with no piston engined aircraft in use on the frontline, they went straight on to jets cutting three months off the previous training period. In August 1953 John started at the school as a Qualified Flying Instructor, with his wife Phyllis, moving into married quarters.

The students, prior to their jet flying, had four weeks ground training, learning about the jet engines, airframes and the new skills required to fly these fast aircraft. The course took around two months to complete. There were two squadrons within the school, No.1 used the Gloster Meteor T.7 and No.2 Squadron flew the de Havilland T.11 Vampire, both equipped with two seat dual controlled training aircraft.

The pupil pilots would have been greatly impressed with the change from their 200mph Harvards, to the jets able to fly at almost three times that speed. They were taught basic and aerobatic manoeuvres, formation flying, instrument flying and navigation. In June 1954 the school was renamed No.8 Flying Training School and, in July 1955, John moved with it when it relocated to Swinderby, Lincolnshire. This was to be his last posting.

In 1954 John was diagnosed as having a malignant tumour, which required him to have an operation for it to be removed. Having undergone the procedure, John spent some time in a nursing home in Hull to recover. Sadly, Phyllis and John were able only to share two more happy years together. In 1956 John attended the RAF Hospital at Uxbridge where it was discovered that the cancer had returned. Phyllis was taken to one side by one of the doctors, who gave her the devastating news that her husband had only between three and nine months to live.

Guy Tayleur arranged that John and Phyllis would stay with Joan, John's sister, so that the family were able to provide support to both of them. As shocking as receiving the news had been of John having only months to live, three days later, on May 6th John died, he was aged just 33.

Tragically, John's mother, Evelyn, who suffered from a weak heart, was taken seriously ill when she was told of the death of her son and three months later she also passed away.

During his RAF career John had flown for over 1,750 hours including nearly 750 hours in Spitfires, he flew ten different types of aircraft, from 55 UK and 36 overseas airfields. He had made his last flight on February 14th 1956 instructing in a de Havilland Vampire.

John's name appears on the Roll Of Honour at the Armed Forces Memorial at the National Memorial Arboretum, Staffordshire. His date of birth still listed incorrectly as 1922.

At 11:00am on Thursday May 10th John Lovett Tayleur was buried at the Biggin Hill Burial Ground, Church Road, Biggin Hill. Grave Section 3, Grave 221.

John William Yarra

Alfred Earnest Yarra joined the Australian Field Artillery during the First World War, and went on to be posted to Europe to serve as a Gunner in France. In September 1918 he was acting as a runner, taking messages back and forth between the front line Batteries at Mont St Quentin and Headquarters in the rear. At the time the area was under constant shellfire including poisonous gas shells. For his bravery under fire he was later awarded the Military Medal due to his 'Gallant conduct and devotion to duty.'

In 1920, back home in Australia, 35-year-old Alfred married Harriet Welch in Toowoomba, Queensland. On August 24th 1921 their first child John William was born in Stanhope, Queensland. Their second child Robert Earnest was born two years later. They were the first of six children the couple were to have. Both of the boys later went on to serve their country as pilots flying with the Royal Australian Air Force during the Second World War.

John, who preferred the name Jack, grew up at 121 Dobie Street, Grafton,

Jack aged around 19 during his pilot training in 1941 (L. McAulay)

in northern New South Wales, a city renowned for its Jacaranda trees with their vibrant purple blooms. Jack enjoyed swimming and sailing in the mighty Clarence River that flowed through the city. Jack also enjoyed boxing, and cycling with his friend Norman Rankin, the two friends later trained together to become pilots. Both boys attended Grafton High School and were joined there in 1936 by Jack's brother Robert.

On leaving school in 1940 Jack became a Printing Apprentice at the Daily Examiner newspaper in Grafton. Whilst in Grafton, on April 29th 1940, at the age of 18 years and 8 months, he enrolled in the Reserve of the Royal Australian Air Force, at the No.2a Mobile Recruiting Office. His medical certificate described him as being five feet seven inches tall, with brown eyes, brown hair, and a scar on his upper lip. His build was noted as slight with his weight as 147 pounds (ten stone seven pounds). He later came to be known as 'Slim' by his Air

Force colleagues.

Jack signed up at the No.2 Recruiting Centre, Sydney, as Air Crew under training with the Royal Australian Air Force Permanent Forces and was given the Service Number 402823. He was posted on October 14th 1940 to No.2 Initial Training School at Lindfield to begin his basic training. The course ended on the last day of January 1941, the month he also received his first promotion to that of Leading Aircraftman.

On February 6th Jack was posted to No.5 Elementary Flying School at Narromine, joining course number 9. Flying tuition was in the de Havilland Tiger Moth biplane. Amongst the other trainees was James Guerin, who also later became one of the Operation Spotter pilots. Having flown his first solo flight and become a confident pilot, Jack became fond of unauthorised low flying, once buzzing a train, and another time flying low over a farmhouse, for which the owner subsequently reported him. The evidence was apparently plain to see, a length of clothes line was wrapped around the rear wheel of his aircraft. On March 18th his Air Force General Conduct Sheet was endorsed:

'Neglecting to obey School Standing Orders. Flying at lower altitude than 2,000 feet.'

He was sentenced to 10 days detention on the airfield. However, his misdemeanour did not mean he failed the course, which he completed successfully during the first week of April. Further training continued overseas under the Empire Air Training Scheme in Canada.

Jack embarked at Sydney docks on April 22nd for the voyage to Vancouver, disembarking on May 14th. He then travelled by train to join No.11 Service Flying Training School at Yorkton, Saskatchewan. Here he received tuition on the North American Harvard MkII. He graduated the course on July 27th and was then awarded his 'Wings' badge as a qualified pilot with a promotion to the rank of Sergeant.

Jack then spent some time under No.1 'M' (Manning) Depot at Halifax, Nova Scotia, until on August 9[th,] he left Canada by ship, to land in England 22 days later on the last day of August. On arrival he came under No.3 Personnel Reception Centre at Bournemouth, Dorset, until he was posted on to 55 Operational Training Unit on September 8th 1941.

55 OTU had been based, since March 1941, at RAF Usworth near Sunderland in the north east of England, and had over 100 aircraft available for pilot training including Tiger Moths, Miles Masters, Miles Martinets, Boulton Paul Defiants and Hawker Hurricanes. Fairey Battles were also used to tow targets

that the pilots would fire at. To accommodate all the aircraft, a satellite airfield at Ouston near Newcastle was established. During all his previous training Jack had been assessed as **'Average'** but at 55 OTU where he had flown nearly 40 hours on the Hawker Hurricane fighter, he was no doubt dismayed to be graded as **'Below Average.'**

Jack's friend Norman Rankin was also at 55 OTU with him and once, whilst chatting, Norman started talking about after the war being back home in Australia. Jack replied in a low voice **'I'm not going back'**. Norman was shaken to hear that his friend believed he would not survive to make it home.

On October 21st 1941 Jack joined his first operational squadron 232, based at RAF Ouston, flying Hawker Hurricanes and involved in defensive patrols of the surrounding area. His stay with the squadron was short, as 16 days later on November 6th he was posted to 64 Squadron at Hornchurch, Essex, equipped with the Spitfire MkII. Their role was convoy patrols and fighter sweeps into northern France. Jack flew just over 22 hours in Spitfires on monotonous convoy patrols with 64 Squadron without making any contact with enemy.

The English autumn and winter climate had left John longing for something similar to his home climate, and he wrote:

'I'll be glad to get back to a decent sun and to some sea water that is not below freezing level, like the English Channel. Seen enough of England to suit me,'

As a consequence, he applied for service overseas not knowing to which part of the world he would be sent to. Later, on finding out he was to be posted to Malta, he described the prospect as **'Sounding pretty Grim.'** Although, once he had met up with Plt Off Peter Nash and some of the others pilots involved prior to their posting, he had changed his mind and had **'Come to the conclusion that we might have a lot of fun in Malta.'** Just before his departure he was promoted to the rank of Flight Sergeant.

Jack did not enjoy the sea trip to Gibraltar in the Cape Hawk complaining of the cramped and poor conditions. He was, however, very glad to be back in a warm climate and in a country not suffering from the wartime austerity of the U.K. The voyage had given the pilots time to consider the feasibility of their first fight from an aircraft carrier, Jack wrote:

'This seemed a pretty tall order to all of us, and although nobody gave away what he thought, I know we all had our doubts. However, we were

in Gibraltar and there was plenty to eat and drink, so why worry.'

On March 7[th,] the day of the launch from HMS Eagle, Jack would not be one of those flying off because his Spitfire had been cannibalised as a donor of spare parts for the other aircraft leaving it unable to fly, so Jack could only watch as his fellow pilots took off.

'When the time came-7am- on the second day out everyone was keyed up and expectant and most of us were wondering if the Spitfires would really get off the deck quite ok… All the aircraft were lined up waiting and everyone was in their cockpits half an hour before the first Blenheim, which was to lead us there, arrived. The Blenheim was sighted and the ship turned into wind. The first motor started and was run up. Suddenly the naval controller gave "Chocks Away" and Sqn Ldr Grant opened his throttle and went roaring down the deck. He lifted off the end, sank slightly below the level of the deck, and sailed away, gaining altitude, proving that a Spitfire can take off an aircraft carrier. All the aeroplanes got off within the hour and we turned back to Gibraltar. I was not going, as my aircraft was u/s. I was to go back to Gib and come out with the next lot of Spitfires.'

Spitfires Over Malta. Brian Cull with Frederick Galea. (Grub Street 2005)

Two weeks after the first Spitfire delivery, Operation Picket delivered 16 more aircraft from HMS Eagle on March 21[st,] and amongst the pilots would be Jack. The first section of nine aircraft were led by Sqd Ldr Edward 'Jumbo' Gracie, an experienced former Battle of Britain pilot. The intention had been to fly off 16 Spitfires but the Blenheim aircraft that were to provide navigation for the second section of Spitfires to Malta failed to arrive. The remaining 7 aircraft did not fly out until a week later on March 29th.

Pilot Officer Donald William 'Mac' McLeod, an American who had previously flown with 121 (Eagle) Squadron, was part of the group of pilots along with Jack who flew off on the 21[st.] He described his experiences:

'Four a.m. The knock, light as it was, sounded like the pounding of a hammer on a brass bell. It brought us out one and all from our sloopy dreaming as to what might happen and put us into a tumult of reality. A quick shave, up to the mess room for a hot cup of tea and a biscuit, then off to the ready room.

'It was dark and dismal. The sun had not yet come over the line of

331

clouds on the horizon. The wind was howling and the carrier tossed to and fro like what to me seemed like a matchbox.

'Then began the process of bringing the Spitfires from below deck to the top. And while we went through the carefully laid plans for the last time, eight 'Spits' were deposited on the upper deck of the carrier. We had been told over and over again, and once more it was repeated: "Don't Panic This can be done. If you get lost, fly a set course and you will strike land and then fly a set course and you will hit Malta," so easily said but...

'Do not fire unless you have to. Obey all signals from the carrier deck on take off. We were given our maps and were just ready to depart when the radio operator rushed into the room and handed a message to 'Jumbo' which was decoded and read to us. "The airfield on Malta (Takali) has been bombed to shambles. Land at the only other one. (Luqa) If that is gone when you arrive, make the best of your situation."

'We couldn't have had anything more to build our moral. This was the crowning glory. Even if we got there, what then?

'Carefully depositing our toothbrushes, a couple spare packs of cigarettes and other small incidentals we knew we would need in the empty gun compartments of our planes (only cannon were loaded, machine guns empty to save weight), we stowed small amounts of candy in the cockpits, and we in Flight 'A' took our parachutes, stowing them in the cockpits and went back to the ready room and awaited further orders.

'By now the sun had risen above the clouds, putting a more cheerful aspect on the scene. The chopping of the waves seemed to have subsided and the wind was blowing as we desired. It was necessary for our operation to be a success that we have a wind of 30 miles per hour. This coupled with the forward speed of the carrier, approximately 27 miles per hour, allowed us to make the remaining 35 to 40 miles per hour on the 400 feet run of the carrier. If we did not obtain flying speed in the short run, obviously the aircraft would tumble into the waves and be run over by the carrier. If a pilot could have gotten out, which was a very remote possibility, a destroyer was assigned to follow the carrier for such happenings.

'At 7am the wind was considered correct and we were told to stand by our aircraft, at 7:15 we were still standing by. At 7:30 we started our engines, getting more nervous by the minute. At 7:31 we were told to cut engines. Valuable gas was being wasted. At 7:45 we started engines again. 'Jumbo', our C.O. was pushed into the starting position. I saw the man with flag. I could see the aircraft shaking as if it wanted to jump. The flag descended and his plane jumped from the start and then seemed to slow down. Actually it was just the lull of the start and the after effect. He rolled down the deck slowly. To me he seemed to have no speed at all. As he reached the end of the deck I saw his plane hover for a second in the air and then disappear downwards from view.

'It was a hollow feeling to know that I was the second from him to go. As I watched him the second plane had been pushed into the starting position. The same roar, the same movements. I still looked once more for 'Jumbo' and no sight of him. The flag went down and the same way, slowly, slowly he got to the end, but instead of doing the same as 'Jumbo', he pulled the stick back hard and his plane shot into the air on one wing and disappeared from my view, as I was being pushed into the starting line. He appeared to be in a very embarrassing position. No sight of 'Jumbo' as yet.

'I remembered, out of the corner of my eye, seeing the deck controller jump on my wing and shout meaningless words. He smiled, patted me on the back. I know he was trying to reassure me, but I was beyond that stage. I again saw that same flag. My engine was wide-open, brakes full set. I was getting every ounce of power, every possible bit of full momentum was being gathered that was within my means of getting. Down came the flag, off came my brakes and down that same deck I went.

'Halfway I passed the main section. It looked to me like I was slowing down. I didn't see how it was possible that I could fly. I could not quit now. Had I tried to stop I would have gone into the drink. I had no alternative left. I must go on. I must get off that deck or I was a gone pigeon. I passed off the deck and seemed to hover. I felt that feeling of emptiness. I knew that I was in the air. One fifth of a second would decide whether I would fly or swim. I hung in the air, seemed to settle momentarily and then received that wonderful feeling of being airborne. I had made it. With a deep sight I said, "It's over."

Jack flew off from HMS Eagle in the now repaired Spitfire AB333, making a total of nine aircraft in the first group. He would later mistakenly put the date of the flight in his logbook as March 25th instead of the 21st. He described his own flight of four hours fifteen minutes:

'The morrow dawned and the weather was lousy. Foggy and raining with a ceiling of 1,000 feet. However we decided to take off and attempt the trip if the Blenheims found us. At 9am the first Blenheim arrived and we started to get off. I was the third man off. When my turn came I taxied into position. I was rather keyed up and my nerves were taut as stay-wires, but as soon as I opened the throttle I lost all my tautness and got that queer kick one always gets when opening up on the world's best fighter aircraft. The old Merlin sounded very sweet that morning as I raced down that little deck and lifted off the end. At that moment the fact that we had 700 miles to travel over water, and hostile water at that, mattered not the slightest. All that mattered was that I was in the air again after nearly three weeks on the ground. We formed up on the leader and began our 700-mile trip. We were right down on the deck all the way, flying through rainstorms and patches of thick mist. We made one attempt to get above the overcast, but as this was unsuccessful we remained on the deck for the remainder of the way. I had trouble with my air pressure all the way. The release valve was not working and I had to keep the pressure down.

'As we were passing Pantelleria we sighted a squadron of CR42s but, as they did not interfere, we were quite happy to let them alone. We could not afford to use up vital petrol dog fighting. After three hours flying I was very much in need of a cigarette but, as I could not find any matches, I had to forgo the pleasure. I could see smoke coming from various other cockpits as the boys were enjoying their smokes. When we were 30 minutes from Malta we tightened up our formation a little and began to keep a good lookout for hostile aircraft. Suddenly Malta showed up on the horizon dead ahead. I, for one, was very pleased, as we had been flying for four hours and we were very tired. Just then I happened to look around and spotted a twin-engined machine approaching from the starboard quarter astern. I immediately thought Me110 and broke away to do a head-on attack. Just as I was about to fire I recognised it as a Beaufort. I very nearly squirted at that guy. He would have been a little brassed if I had! We landed at Takali and put the aircraft away. I then went up to the mess to get a drink and find out how the rest of the boys were. I learned that Mac, Fox, Leggo and Murray were all dead and that out of the 15 Spitfires they had brought, only 2 were left.'

Spitfires Over Malta. Brian Cull with Frederick Galea. (Grub Street 2005)

All of the nine aircraft had landed safely; Jack's account says he landed at Takali airfield, although Plt Off 'Mac' McLeod's version goes on to say that due to the earlier bomb damage of Takali as mentioned in the message that 'Jumbo' read out before they left, they actually landed at Luqa where a dilapidated bus took them to the mess for a meal of stew, followed by tea and biscuits. Then, once more, they boarded the bus to be taken across the island to Takali airfield, which was again under attack by Ju88 bombers.

The bus dropped them off at the mess located at Rabat overlooking Takali where a large crowd had gathered. One of the bombs had struck the Point de Vue Hotel, which was being used as a billet by some of the pilots, and seven men had just been killed in the blast. Plt Off James Guerin from Operation Spotter was one of those killed. Another was the American Eddie Streets who fellow American Plt Off 'Mac' McLeod knew and had hoped to meet up with on Malta.

The newly arrived aircraft were to be shared between 249 Squadron, which Jack joined, and 126 Squadron, which the other newly arrived pilots would reform. Jack wrote in his diary about the bombing of the island he witnessed:

'The Jerries really did some spectacular bombing. The dust covered an area of at least five miles and smoke from burning petrol and oil made black smudges against the yellow dust cloud. I was surprised and shaken to learn that this happens at least three times daily.'

Jack flew his first operational flight on Malta, a scramble on March 26th against forty plus incoming German fighters and bombers. He did not have an auspicious start, noting in his logbook that four Me109s chased him home. Two days later he was again scrambled against incoming bombers and this time he was able to get into a position to fire against a Ju88 but made no claim for any damage. Later the same day he again intercepted a large incoming force during which he engaged an Me109 but, again, without success. On March 29th he was scrambled twice during the day, the first time engaging a mixed force of Ju88s and Ju87s, but on the

Jack leaning on the wing of a MkVb Spitfire on Malta in 1942 (F Galea)

second occasion he was recalled back to base before any encounter with the enemy aircraft.

Jack next flew on April 3rd a 15-minute air test of Spitfire BW824, this proved satisfactory, as he was later scrambled in the same aircraft against a raiding force of German bombers. He used up all his ammunition against a Ju88 bomber but with no result.

There were now more pilots on Malta than Spitfires, so on April 4th Jack, having previous experience of flying the Hawker Hurricane, was one of several pilots transferred to 185 Squadron based at Hal Far. He flew the following day but made no contact with the enemy.

In the late afternoon of April 14th Jack, flying Hurricane MkII HA-D, was one of three Hurricane pilots who patrolled over High Speed Launch 128 as it searched for the crews of two Beaufort bombers shot down close to Filfla island. Other Hurricanes were also in the area at the time. At 17:40 the rescue launch investigated some wreckage including an empty yellow dinghy. A group of Me109s suddenly launched an attack on HSL128, resulting in the Hurricanes fighting to protect the launch and themselves. The boat continued further out to sea to the body of a man floating in a Mae West. The airman was already dead but they were able to recover his body. The Germans were still intent on attacking the launch, which responded by firing its own two machine guns in reply.

Jack's aircraft had been badly shot up by an Me109 in this encounter and he was forced to return to Hal Far where he crash-landed. The launch made its way back to shore, but when close to the cliffs of Dingli a single 109 swooped down, lined up the launch in its sights and fired. A bullet went through the thigh of one of the crew and wood splinters and shrapnel injured four others. The launch pulled close to the cliffs, sheltering in the Blue Grotto for protection and waited for the 109s to leave.

On April 20th 47 MkVc Spitfires, each armed with four cannons, were flown in from the American aircraft carrier USS Wasp, prompting an immediate response from the Germans. Jack was part of the defending force sent up to intercept the large incoming raid of enemy aircraft. The air battle that followed ended similar to his previous one, with his aircraft being badly shot up and he was forced to crash land back on the airfield.

Jack had now taken over writing the records in the 185 Squadron diary. His entries had a humorous and somewhat irreverent tone, along with the sad note of those pilots killed. He described his own feelings, as **"Sgt Yarra is still brassed after having three different kites, in which he was doing readiness, blown up by bombs."** He had now flown over four hours operationally without any success. His luck would change the following month.

At around eight thirty on the evening of May 1st Jack was sent up with three other Hurricanes to intercept a force of Ju88s. The ground controllers guided him towards the enemy. In the receding light he picked up the glow from the exhausts of an aircraft and closed in and fired. The aircraft subsequently disappeared from the radar screens but he was only awarded a probable.

The entry in the squadron diary, written this day by Sgt Gordon Tweedale, mentioned his success:

'The big wigs have taken us off day state to give us a spot of night flying as Jerry seems to have painted most of his aircraft black. Sgt Yarra, the latest Aussie addition to the squadron fired a great burst of sparks into an '88 which induced it to fade off the plot sometime later.'

The next time Jack flew was on May 11th, by then, with the recent delivery of another 64 Spitfires to the island, 185 Squadron were able to replace their aged Hurricanes with the new fighters. Jack's first flight this day, of 35 minutes, along with Sgt Robert Sim did not allow them to get into a position suitable for them to make an attack. Later the same day he was scrambled again, firing at a 109 but without result. The third time he took off he was sent off too late and, although he fired at the many 109s flying across the island, he made no claim.

Jack had somehow brought his gramophone player and several records of the popular music of that period with him, and introduced for the first time, many of the pilots of 185 Squadron, including David Ferraby, to the sounds of jazz and Glen Miller, with the few records available played over and over again. Many years later a former Malta pilot said he often thought of Jack whenever he heard Miller's In the Mood being played.

On May 12th Jack again flew several times, the first time making no contact. The second time he was able to fire at a Ju88 but without being able to observe the results. Four Me109s then attacked him, the leader of which he shot down, he also inflicted damaged to some of the others. Later the same day he was again on patrol over a rescue launch, this time without incident. Finally, he was part of a group that intercepted some Italian bombers and their fighter escort, although he made no claims. He also menaced some Italians who he spotted had been shot down and were floating down in their parachutes. He humorously wrote of his exploits in the squadron diary:

'Sgt Yarra destroyed an Me109. Sgt Yarra also had quite an enjoyable

time playing with some Dagoes who were coming down in parachutes after some destructive person had severely tampered with their Cant 1007. The Italians took a rather poor view of Sgt Yarra's efforts to amuse them. These efforts took the form of placing the parachute canopy in the slipstream of a Spitfire. The canopy promptly collapses and the type has to fall a few hundred feet until the chute opens again. Consequently 4 very sick Dagoes landed in the water off the island.'

In the middle of the afternoon of May 15th a lone Ju88 reconnaissance aircraft came over with a large fighter escort of both German and Italian fighters. Jack found himself battling against 7 Me109s, the leader of which he damaged. He then found himself being attacked by four Macchi 202 aircraft, one of which he shot down, the crashing pilot inadvertently collided with his own wingman, with both the aircraft being destroyed. Jack continued to fight with the remaining two until his ammunition was exhausted.

On the 16th he was scrambled against an incoming radar plot that failed to come in over the island. The following day a force of Italian bombers came over and. although he did fire at and hit an aircraft, he did not make a claim.

Early on the morning of May 18th a large formation of Italian aircraft were in the air covering their countrymen below in motor torpedo boats off the coast of Malta. A group of Hurricanes were sent to attack them. A large group of Axis fighters were now forming and 18 Spitfires were sent to assist the Hurricanes. When the two forces clashed, Plt Off Norman Fowlow was shot down into the sea, but, although slightly wounded, he was able to climb into his dinghy.

HSL128 was sent out just after 11:00am to rescue Plt Off Fowlow. On the way, another aircraft, a Hurricane, flown by Sgt Jim Pendlebury, was seen to crash into the sea. The launch made its way to where some floating wreckage was seen, but there was no sign of the pilot.

Jack was flying as top cover and became engaged in the air battle shooting down an Me109 (White 3), flown by Uffz Johannes Lompa, into the sea off Hal Far. Lompa was seen descending and was picked up by HSL128, which then continued on until it reached Fowlow. The rescued German Lompa helped to get Norman on-board and insisted on shaking hands with him. Both pilots, exhausted by the days events, then slept in the launch as it made its way back to shore.

The aircraft of Jack's wingman, Eric Shaw, had been badly damaged by the attacking 109s and he was forced to return to Luqa to land. Jack stayed alone, fighting off the Me109s over the rescue launch. He claimed another

Me109 during its defence as probably destroyed, this appeared to have been upgraded to destroyed. He later said:

'I arrived over the rescue ship to find at least thirteen Messerschmitt there. I stayed, but it wasn't a case of bravery. I couldn't get away, I had to stay. I sat above the launch, and the Jerries kept coming to have a crack at me. I kept turning into them, firing for all I was worth, and driving them away.'

Eventually he ran out of ammunition but stayed with the launch for around forty-five minutes making dummy attacks on the German fighters until the launch was safe. Jack then headed direct to Takali, short of fuel, but, whilst in the circuit to land, he was set upon by four Me109s forcing him to abort the landing and defend himself by turning into them:

'It nearly cost me dearly, for it caused me to run out of petrol. My motor cut out as I got into the circuit near the aerodrome, and I had to pancake in a hurry.'

The following day, the 19th Jack found time to visit Kalafrana where HSL128 was based and met with crew to see how there were. The crew were pleased to see him and thanked him for keeping the Messerschmitts at bay the previous day. On this day Jack also acted as the leader of a flight for the first time chasing a formation of Italians but they were unable to catch them, and again later that day he led a flight against German Me109s, which he attacked, but without result.

On the 20th Jack led four Spitfires into a formation of Ju88s and their escort, he made no claim, but his own aircraft was struck by return fire. On another sortie later in the day he had a problem closing the hood of his aircraft and, whilst trying to slide it forward, his arm was caught in the aircrafts slipstream wrenching it badly.

On May 24th Jack, leading three others, was providing an escort to some Swordfish torpedo bombers, when Me109s attacked them. One of the Swordfish flew very low to the sea to prevent the fighters getting beneath it, and ripped its own undercarriage off, it managed, however, to fly on safely.

A dawn patrol on the 26th was interrupted when the ammunition in both wings of Jack's Spitfire caught fire, possibly due to the attack of an unseen aircraft, forcing a prompt return to the airfield. Later the same day he flew against a formation of Ju88 bombers, his aircraft being struck by fire from the

Italian escort fighters, but without serious damage. His third flight of the day was no luckier when he was forced to return due to a leak from his oxygen bottle.

The 27th started with a patrol over a rescue launch once again, but this time no enemy were encountered. A second sortie later had to be cut short, as his air speed indicator stopped working. The next day Jack, leading three other Spitfires, chased a number of Ju88s back to Scilly, but then several Me109s appeared promptly and chased him back to Malta.

**Lord Gort the Governor of Malta presents Jack with his DFM in July 1942
(Australian War Memorial UK0200)**

During the month of May Jack had flown just over 25 hours on Spitfires and one hour on Hurricanes with 185 Squadron, before they were exchanged for Spitfires.

On May 31st the following signal was sent to 185 Squadron at Hal Far from Headquarters R.A.F. Mediterranean:

'Secret. On the recommendation of the A.O.C. in Chief, His Majesty the King has been graciously pleased to award the Distinguished Flying Medal to No.042823 F/Sgt. John William Yarra, of No. 185 Squadron, for courage, determination and devotion to duty.'

The award was confirmed in the Supplement to the London Gazette on June 16th 1942, the citation read:

340

'This pilot has shot down 4 enemy aircraft in air battles. On one occasion, when protecting a rescue launch in the face of numerous enemy aircraft, he shot down 1 Messerschmitt and probably destroyed another. When his ammunition was exhausted he made feint attacks and kept the enemy at bay for three quarters of an hour.'

On the afternoon of July 10th in a public ceremony held on the steps of the Auberge de Castille in Valletta, the Governor of Malta, Lord Gort, presented Jack with his DFM, although this would have only been the medal ribbon to be worn on his uniform, and not the medal itself, which he did not live to see. Eighteen months later, on June 16th 1944, the Governor General of Australia, Sir Alexander Hore-Ruthven, First Earl of Gowrie, presented Jack's DFM to his father, Alfred, during a ceremony held at Admiralty House in Sydney.

Monday June 1st 1942, Jack was scrambled leading four other Spitfires against eight incoming, yellow nosed Me109s. Jack, along with Plt Off Broad, attacked four of the fighters approximately 20 miles off Zonqor Point, Jack shot one down and Plt Off Broad damaged another. The next day Jack flew twice but, although having intercepted some Italian aircraft, he made no claim. He flew again two days later attacking, head on, a group of Me109s, but was himself jumped from behind and chased back to the airfield.

On June 6th he was scrambled three times but only once made contact with the approaching Italian aircraft, without any result.

The next day June 7th Jack was returning to the airfield with an engine problem when 3 RE2001 Italian fighters intercepted him. Despite his faltering engine he was able to turn into and damage two of the aircraft and returned safely. Two days later an attacking force of Ju87 Stukas was intercepted, Jack fired all of his ammunition without being able to make a claim, but he did report that some of the aircraft ditched their bombs early to escape the attack.

Jack flew two sorties on the 10th, the first was an attack on a bomber formation in which his aircraft was hit in the front windscreen by return fire, the bullets not penetrating the glass, although he was showered with glass splinters. The second sortie was as an escort to incoming Beaufort bombers and, although Me109s were seen in the distance, he stayed with his charges to see them safely to the island.

On June 12th whilst Jack was leading a group of 8 Spitfires against an attacking force of over 25 aircraft, he led his section on to a group of 12 unsuspecting Me109s. Although he did not personally make a claim, others did, claiming 1 destroyed and 1 damaged. The following two days Jack flew escorts, to incoming friendly aircraft, a patrol over the island, and one over a minesweeper.

On the morning of June 16th a fighter sweep by around twelve Me 109s came in over the island. In the battle that followed, Jack damaged an Me109 but was also, in turn, hit through the exhaust of his aircraft. Two other pilots involved in this fight had to bale out, but both were recovered safely from the sea.

Jack flew a patrol over the island of forty-five minutes on the 20th with out contact and then later in the day he was scrambled in Spitfire BR387 (GL-W) against an incoming formation but had to return early with an engine problem. The following day the fault had been rectified and Jack took to the air again in BR387. On this aircraft, as with others he had flown regularly, he had painted the name NED just below the cockpit, the nickname he had given to his girlfriend, Doreen, back home in Australia.

Just before 7:00pm a reconnaissance Ju88 with an escort of Me109s approached Malta; Jack led off three Spitfires to intercept. He subsequently claimed two of the fighters shot down, including one that lost its tail, and also to damaging the Ju88. Jack described the events in the 185 Squadron Diary:

'A' flight took over at 1 pm and did not scramble until 7 pm, when two sections took off to intercept a 12+ plot which turned into a lone Ju88, protected by fighters, doing a recco. F/Sgt Yarra and his section managed to trick 4 Me109s into coming down. The boys engaged and F/Sgt Yarra sat on one Me109 and shot his tail off with a juicy crunch. F/Sgt Terry had a cannon shell explode over his cockpit and had to crash land on the aerodrome. F/Sgt Yarra then spotted the poor old Recco Ju88 and, madly gnashing his teeth, went down to attack. He managed to damage the Ju88, but was in turn attacked by Me109s. A merry mix up ensued in which one Me109 was shot down. F/Sgt Yarra returned with large pieces bitten out of his dinghy, but otherwise was quite OK.

Jack flew an air patrol of an hour and forty minutes over the island on the 22nd along with Flt Sgt Don Reid, nicknamed 'Shorty' because of his diminutive size. They were engaged by Me109s with Reid claiming one destroyed in the fight. The next time Jack flew was on the 26th in his NED IV (BR387) but again, having led three other Spitfires, he was forced to return with an engine problem. The next day, repaired once more, Jack flew his Spitfire twice against incoming attacks but made no claims. The 28th was a similar day with two scrambles, the first saw no contact with the enemy, the second time he chased, but could not catch a group of Me109s that had **'beaten up a minesweeper.'** At the end of June he had flown operationally for 25 hours, 30minutes.

July's operations began for Jack on the 2nd when he flew three sorties. The first leading four others in a patrol over a minesweeper. Jack and the American pilot Flt Sgt Vineyard, known just as 'Tex,' guarded against some Me109s that were above them, whilst the others attacked an incoming bombing raid, but the Me109s did not come down to fight. His second scramble was against Italian fighters and bombers, but without result. The third time he and Tex again patrolled over a minesweeper and at one stage were **'jumped'** by another section of Spitfires. Jack also spotted a shot down Italian floating in his dinghy and delighted in lining up his Spitfire on him and making dummy attacks, making a mock claim in his logbook for **'1 Wop pilot with ring twitch.'**

On the 3rd Jack flew, once again a patrol over a minesweeper. Eight Me109s were encountered but no claim was made. At one stage during the air battle, Jack's aircraft got into a spin and he was down to 500 feet before he was able to recover from it, no doubt greatly alarming him at the time.

Spitfire MkVc BR387 named NedIV which Jack flew with 185 Squadron
(F Galea)

Although noted as July 4th, it was actually late in the afternoon of the 5th when Jack next flew Ned IV, leading four Spitfires from 185 Squadron against

343

Ju88 bombers and their Me109 escort, Jack noted in his logbook:

'Intercepted four Me109s. Crawled up on them and fired like hell. Broke off and spotted nine Ju88s with Messerschmitt escort. Attacked rear Ju88 and shot it down. Was chased back by 109s; shot up badly-crash-landed.'

Jack claimed 1 Ju88 destroyed, 1 Me109 probably destroyed and 1 damaged. Aviation historian and author, Brian Cull, in his book Spitfires Over Malta, believes Fw Otto Pohl of 2/JG77 was the pilot who most likely forced Jack to crash land.

The next day Jack was scrambled against a radar plot of enemy aircraft, but they did not approach the island so no contact was made.

The last of three raids on the island on July 7th came over around 5:15pm, five Italian Cant Z-1007 bombers flying at high level with an escort of Re2001 fighters. In the air battle that followed Jack, leading a section of three other Spitfires, claimed two of the Re2001s destroyed, but was then attacked by an Me109, which damaged his aircraft, including shooting away some panels from the wing. He had again been successful in NED IV but once again the Spitfire was crash landed back on the airfield. One of Jack's victims was Italian Fabrizio Cherubini from 353 Squadriglia, his aircraft crashing into the sea taking the pilot with it.

Two of the four pilots from the section Jack had been leading, were both shot down in the exchanges and killed, 20-year-old Flt Sgt Peter Terry, and 21 year old Flt Sgt Haydn Haggas. Terry's aircraft crashed onto the island and his body was recovered for burial. Haggas' aircraft had crashed into the sea. High Speed Launch 128 was sent out to around three miles off shore from Dingli, where on finding a pilot's badly mutilated body, the personal effects were removed to confirm the identity and then the body was buried at sea.

Sgt Len Reid, the other Spitfire pilot from the flight wrote:

'We could see the 109s up there, but Slim was trying to get altitude and was a few thousand feet below them. It was the old story, trying to get altitude; I had my speed down to about 120 mph and that's not much to have on the clock. We were sitting ducks. They came down and attacked, and it got all mixed up. It was a general melee that went on, and I think we were attacked by two groups, one from one side, and it's the other group that comes in later that shoots you down, if you are not aware of them. It was a shaky do.'

Against All Odds. Lex McAulay. (Hutchinson 1989)

Jack wrote in the squadron diary that night:

'During this engagement both Sgt Haggas and Sgt Terry were shot down. These two boys had been with the squadron for some time and both had flown very well and done their job. They both died fighting against far superior odds and will be remembered as long as No.185 Squadron remains in operation during the war. The rest of the flight did a very good job. The bombers were forced to ditch their bombs and not one fell on the target area.'

July 8th and Jack's aircraft was available again for the first scramble against a formation of Ju88 bombers. It received, however, two bullets through one of the propeller blades and was unserviceable for the next scramble. The replacement aircraft, (GL-R), fared no better, having to return to base with an oil leak. The next day it was available again but in an attack against Me109s, the Spitfire was hit in the cooling system, which began pouring Glycol. Being too low to bail out, yet another crash landing followed.

On the 10th Jack flew three times, the first on an air sea rescue search but due to low-level fog, nothing was seen, the second time no contact was made with any enemy aircraft and, lastly, a ten-minute air test of a Spitfire. The next day he again flew three times, the first time his radio failed but he continued chasing two Me109s but was unable to catch them, then he was scrambled against a radar plot that did not materialise. The third time Jack made his last victory flying over Malta, he wrote later in his logbook:

'Scrambled after 40+ plot. Joined up with another Spit. Saw two109s and attacked one shot it down. Escorted shot up Spit back to base.'

Flt Sgt Louis de L'ara was flying the badly damaged Spitfire under Jack's escort, de L'ara was able to crash land at Takali but received slight injuries in the process.

The 185 Squadron diary noted on Monday July 13th that six pilots had been stood down from flying operations pending a return to England, included were three Operation Spotter pilots, Flt Sgt Robert Sim, Flt Sgt David Ferraby and Flt Sgt Yarra. Jack also learnt of his promotion to Pilot Officer back dated to June 5th.

It appears Jack may have wanted one more chance to improve his score over Malta in NED IV. His logbook shows he flew on the 14th in a scramble against 70+ aircraft approaching the island. When attacking a Ju88, he found his cannons would not work. His last flight is listed as an air test of his Spitfire on the 16th. NED IV (BR387) survived Malta and was passed on to the Free French Air Force in 1944. It was finally struck off charge in July 1945.

Jack had flown nearly 17 hours operationally during July. On arriving in Malta he had flown 227 hours and when he left five months later he had flown 299 hours. He made 101 flights from Malta, 84 of those operationally, including 54 combat flights. In the pages of his logbook he also recorded the names of each of the many pilots killed, as they were lost over the island.

Jack had returned to England by August 1942 and on the 2nd attended the No.2 Personal Despatch Centre at Wilmslow. On August 20th he was granted leave until his next posting, which was to 453 Squadron on September 10th.

453 Squadron had been reformed on June 18th 1942 at Drem in Scotland and was made up of mainly Australians from the remainder of two Australian squadrons 452 and 457 whose pilots had mostly been withdrawn to operate at home protecting Australia. 453 were equipped with the Spitfire MkV. The squadron became a part of Fighter Command and, on September 26th moved forward to Hornchurch, Essex. On September 15th Jack took over 'B' Flight as Flight Commander and on the 19th he was promoted to Acting Flight Lieutenant.

Jack flew his first sortie on September 29th on a patrol of just under an hour, which passed without incident. 453 were mainly involved in patrols of the coast, the Thames estuary and over convoys, although, during October, they started making fighter sweeps into occupied France.

On one fighter sweep on the afternoon of September 11th Jack flew at 20,000 feet seeing many Fw190, but none came to intercept them, although 6 followed them back to their base without attacking. During their return to Hornchurch two of the Spitfires collided, with the wing of one aircraft ripping off the tail of the other, both pilots crashed to their deaths in the sea below.

Jack flew again the next day as part of an escort to Whirlwinds out to attack German E-boats, but no trace of the reported boats was found.

During November the winter weather started interfering more and more with missions. The squadron diary on the 15th stated that no flying was possible due to the weather and the pilots had taken part in exercises in the Link trainer and watched instructional films. It also confessed that the bar at the station had been open from time to time, and with the diversion of London only three quarters of an hour away this had meant that the training activities had not gone on for the whole of the day.

On the 24th November the pilots and some of the ground crew moved to Martlesham Heath in Suffolk to take part in a two-week air firing exercise. The exercise was apparently very successful with 453 finishing with the highest ever average score. After the exercise the squadron moved from Hornchurch on the 7th to Rochford, Southend. The squadron diary noted how pleased some of the men were that the nearby Cock Inn had not been bombed and still stood, it was a favourite haunt with some of the pilots who had previously travelled down from Hornchurch to visit it. The next few days were spent settling in, with a convoy patrol flown over the Thames Estuary on the 9th despite the poor weather.

At 11.00am on December 10th Jack led off five other Spitfires in his own Spitfire EN824 (FU-U) named as NED V, which carried his twelve victory markings from his time on Malta under the cockpit. They were on a shipping reconnaissance in the area between Blankenberge in Belgium and Flushing, Holland. Around 11:45am, in an area north west of Walcheren, five captured Drifter fishing ships, now being used by the Germans as minesweepers, were spotted. They were the Maria Jacoba (M3401), Toewijding (M3405), Cornelia Classina (M3411), Prins Bernhard (M3416) and the Michel en Piet (M3417), each boat was heavily armed. In addition, coastal anti aircraft positions at Westkapelle were also able to aim their fire at the approaching aircraft.

Jack led the Spitfires, diving down to strafe the ships. In the attack, five of the crew of the ships were killed, with seven others seriously injured and five slightly wounded. One of the ships was set on fire

Jack standing on Ned V the aircraft in which he would lose his life (Aviation Heritage Museum of W. Australia)

and left burning, with a large pall of oily smoke rising to 150 feet above it. The return fire from the vessels had been considerable and both the aircraft of Jack and fellow Australian, 20 year old Pilot Officer Mathew de Cosier, were hit.

Plt Off de Cosier was seen flying slowly, trying to gain height, when his aircraft BL899 (FU-W) stalled and plunged into the sea. Jack also tried to climb in his damaged aircraft and when he reached around 1,000 feet he baled out, but he struck and became caught on the tail plane of his aircraft.

His parachute partly opened streamed behind the aeroplane, just before the burning aircraft hit the seawater Jack became free of the tail, and plunged into the sea, his parachute unable to slow his fall.

The bodies of both pilots were never recovered and, although initially listed as missing, the squadron diary made it clear that they knew both men were lost. This had been Jack's fifteenth flight with 453 and the first real action he had taken part in since leaving Malta five months earlier. Had he been too bold going in to attack? Uneven odds had certainly never bothered him before whilst on Malta and probably would not have done so then.

Jack with his brother Robert, both would be killed whilst flying with 453 Squadron (Australian War Memorial P00943.007)

During 1942 Jack's younger brother, Robert, had begun his pilot training in Canada. He also later served in England and flew with Jack's former squadron, 453. Robert was also killed whilst flying with the Squadron on the 14th April 1944 whilst dive-bombing a V1 rocket site in France. He was buried in Abbeville. Both brothers were only 21 years old when killed.

Whilst he was still on Malta, Jack had written a letter to his mother to be opened only on his death:

My Dear Mother
By the time you receive this letter you will have officially been informed of my death.
This is just to let you know that I am quite satisfied with my life and

the way it has ended.

I entered this war with the knowledge that I had a rather small chance of coming out of it alive. I was under no false impressions. I knew I had to kill- and perhaps be killed. Since I commenced flying I have spent probably the happiest time of my life. I loved flying more than most things, and, if I had come through the war alive, I should probably have killed myself in civil flying. I am not just being fatalistic- I honestly think I would rather have ten years of action and thrills than 50 years of security in some stuffy office.

Since I have been in the service I have met more real friends than I could ever hope to meet in a lifetime of peace. Not just self styled friends who talk platitudes to one's face, and, when it is conducive to their own well-being are quite prepared to disown your friendship; but men who daily risk their lives to save yours. There is nothing like the element of danger to seal a friendship.

I have seen a lot of men killed and have often wondered how I managed to escape alive from some shows, but I know that when the time comes I am quite prepared to face it.

Do not grieve too much, Mother. My life was not wasted. To date I have destroyed 11 enemy aircraft, which squares the account to the nation for my training. I am not sorry it happened this way. If I could live my life over again I would certainly have made a lot of changes, but I should still have flown in the war, and tried to accomplish what I have. What better way to die than fighting against odds in the service of one's country.

Above all, Mother dear, I have proved to my satisfaction that I was, at least, a man.

God Bless You
John

At Jack's former school, Grafton High School, a memorial plaque was placed in his memory. It stated: **In memory of F/Lt J. W. Yarra DFM Enlisted April 1940 Killed in Action 10-12-1942 off Flushing- Coast of Holland.**

Flight Lieutenant John William Yarra DFM aged 21 is remembered on the Air Forces Memorial at Runnymede, Surrey. On Panel 108. In his home country of Australia his name is located on Panel 105 in the Commemorative Area of the Australian War Memorial, Campbell, Canberra.

The Spitfires

There were sixteen dismantled Spitfires transported in large wooden crates by the freighter M.V. Cape Hawke from England to Gibraltar, where they were assembled on the quay at night and loaded on to the aircraft carrier HMS Eagle, to continue their epic journey to the island of Malta. All were of the

Malta Spitfire fitted with a Vokes tropical filter beneath the identification letter N
(F Galea)

Mark VbT variant, having, to prevent the intake of dust into the engine, the prominent Vokes tropical air filter fitted beneath the cowling, although the additional drag incurred reduced the speed of the aircraft. Of the 24 different marks of Spitfire produced, the MkV was built in the greatest numbers with 6,787 produced in total.

Mark V

Production problems with the MkIII Spitfire arose due to its ongoing improvements, that required extensive re-tooling of the production line be undertaken. In addition, the Merlin XX engine to be fitted to this mark was in short supply. This then led to the creation of the MkV. The MkV was a MkI or MkII with a Merlin 45 engine. This engine only had one supercharger, not two as had the Merlin XX, and so was easier to produce. It not only gave a better performance at higher altitudes, but Carburettor improvements also meant that there was no loss of power in zero gravity manoeuvres. The majority of these aircraft were built at the Castle Bromwich, Birmingham, factory and came into RAF service from January 1941.

There were three main types of wing produced for the Mark V with the 'B' variant the most used format, with over 3,500 built including the Malta Spitfires, these were armed with two 20mm Hispano cannon, with 60 rounds each per gun, and four .303 machine guns, having 350 rounds each per gun. The oil cooling system on the early versions was found to be insufficient leading to high oil temperatures; consequently the air intakes under the port wing were enlarged to allow more airflow.

The original intention had been to supply Malta with the standard Spitfire MkVb, but, because of the distance that was to be flown, it was decided to use the tropicalised Spitfires as these were fitted with an oil tank with a greater capacity, allowing sufficient oil to be carried to cover the extra range that would be gained by the use of the long-range auxiliary fuel tanks.

(Figures for a MkV aircraft without a Tropical Filter)
Wingspan: 36'10   Wing Area: 242 Sq Ft   Length: 29' 11
Height: 9' 10"
Weight: 5,065 lb (empty)   6,525 lb (loaded)   Ceiling: 37,500 ft   Range: 475 Miles   Speed: 370 mph

The Malta Spitfires On HMS Eagle: March 7th 1942
To reduce the weight, and therefore fuel consumption, all of the Spitfires had their four Browning machine guns removed from the wings whilst at Gibraltar, and flew with only the two Hispano cannons for protection, one in each wing both loaded with 60 rounds. Many of these cannons, when they had been tested on the flight deck on March 6th were found to require adjustment before they would operate correctly.

The Spitfires carried a total fuel load of 174 gallons, 84 in the main tanks and 90 in the auxiliary tank, along with 6 gallons of engine oil; the total aircraft weight was in the region of 7,330lbs. The Air Ministry believed that after take off and climbing there would be sufficient fuel for approximately 940 miles in still wind conditions. Although the Captain of the Eagle would decide the departure point, it was not to be any further than 670 miles from Malta to allow a good margin of safety. It was recommended to the pilots that they use their main tanks during take off but then switch to the auxiliary tank when at height. It was suggested that the tanks be retained and not discarded unless the pilot felt he had insufficient fuel to reach Malta. If the tanks were jettisoned the reduced airflow drag should allow approximately 100 additional miles of range.

Only one pilot, Plt Off Peter Nash, in AB336, in fact, dropped his tank, although Flg Off Norman Lee who flew AB337 advised that he had had only one hour fifteen minutes endurance from his auxiliary tank. No pilot reported any problems regarding take off or handling of the aircraft during the three hours forty-five minutes flight time it took to reach the island.

Information given to the Air Ministry in London from Malta Air HQ, stated the average fuel consumption was 130 gallons per hour, and noted that the guiding Blenheims flying at an air speed of 140 knots was considered too slow and a speed of 150 to 160 knots would better suit the Spitfires.

Some aircraft also had arrived with flat Accumulators, presumably from the extra electrical consumption required by the fuel pumps for the auxiliary tanks, the suggestion was made that they, in future, had their own units.

The sixteen Spitfires had been taken from a pool of aircraft awaiting deployment to North Africa, and wore the paint scheme for that theatre of Dark Earth and Middle Stone, with Sky Blue undersides. The topside colouring was considered unsuitable for Malta where a good deal of the time the aircraft would be flying above the sea, so they were over painted in a Grey Blue, and then had the code letters GN painted in white signifying 249 Squadron, along with a different identifying letter for each aircraft. Before they went into action replacement, .303 Browning Machine guns were fitted and harmonised so that the bullets would all converge at a set distance, normally around 250 yards. By July 1942, with the greater number of squadrons and Spitfires on Malta, 249 Squadron adopted the code letter T on their aircraft, 603 Squadron used X, 126 Squadron MK and 185 Squadron used GL.

The Operation Spotter aircraft were already fitted with VHF radios for communication with each other and the ground. They also carried IFF, Identification Friend or Foe, an electronic device emitting a signal to the radar stations on Malta showing it to be an allied aircraft. Flt Lt Philip Heppell noted that the Spitfires were fitted with De Havilland airscrews, which were prone to leaking hydraulic liquid over the windscreen obliterating the view.

On March 9th Squadron Leader Stan Turner and Pilot Officer Robert 'Buck' McNair tested a Spitfire, each with a wingman, McNair flying AB262. The aircraft were flown around the island to aid identification to the gun sites. The Spitfires were deemed ready and would go into action for the first time the following day.

AB262 MkVbT
First flown: 24/1/42
Passed to 8 Maintenance Unit: 30/1/42
249 Squadron aircraft code on Malta: GN-B
Flt Lt P.W.E. Heppell of 249 Sqn claimed an Me109 10/03/42
Sqn Ldr S.B. Grant of 249 Sqn claimed an Me109 probable 11/03/42
Damaged beyond repair during an air raid in Kalafrana workshop 7/4/42
Struck Off Charge: 11/4/42

AB264 MkVbT
First flown: 24/1/42
Passed to 8 Maintenance Unit: 30/1/42
249 Squadron aircraft code on Malta: GN-H
Plt Off P.A. Nash of 249 Sqn claimed a Ju87 25/03/42

Flt Lt R.W. McNair claimed a shared Ju88 26/03/42
Sgt T.R.D. Kebbell of 1435 Sqn claimed a Ju88 on 11/10/42
Passed to US Air Force: 1/10/43. Middle East: 31/8/44

Operation Spotter Spitfire Mk Vb AB264 on Malta in March 1942 (F Galea)

AB329 MkVbT
First flown: 28/12/41
Passed to 6 Maintenance Unit: 10/1/42
Struck Off Charge: 6/5/42

AB330 MkVbT
First flown: 29/12/41
Passed to 8 Maintenance Unit: 4/1/42
249 Squadron aircraft code on Malta: GN-C
17/3/42 Crashed into sea off Filfla island Flt Sgt Ian Cormack killed, he is
believed to have blacked out during a dive, or more probably to have been
shot down.
Struck Off Charge: 17/3/1942

AB331 MkVbT
First flown: 30/12/41
Passed to 8 Maintenance Unit: 4/1/42
Flown off HMS Eagle by Flt Sgt David Ferraby

Damaged beyond repair after an air raid on Takali 21/3/42
Struck Off Charge: 31/3/42   Flying Hours Listed: 15:35

AB332 MkVbT
First flown: 31/12/41
Passed to 8 Maintenance Unit: 6/1/42
Flown off HMS Eagle by Sgt Robert Sim
249 Squadron aircraft code on Malta: GN-N
Crashed at Gharghur on return to Takali flying with 126 Squadron, the pilot
Canadian Jim Stevenson was killed 18/10/42

AB333 MkVbT
First flown: 2/1/42
Passed to 8 Maintenance Unit: 4/1/42
Unserviceable as parts had been taken from it for the other Spitfires so did
not fly off on the March 7th, but was Flown to Malta off HMS Eagle by Plt Off
John Yarra on 21st March 1942.
Struck Off Charge: May 1942   Flying Hours Listed: 10:50

AB334 MkVbT
First flown: 3/1/42
Passed to 8 Maintenance Unit: 4/1/42
Flown off HMS Eagle by Sgt John Tayleur
249 Squadron aircraft code on Malta: GN-J
Shot down by Me109s March 18th 1942, Plt Off Harry Fox baled out over the
sea but was not found.
Flying Hours Listed: 19:15

AB335 MkVbT
This aircraft may have had the name Stockbridge painted on it after the
donation of £5,000 towards its purchase from the Stockbridge Spitfire Fund
in Hampshire.
First flown: 5/1/42
Passed to 8 Maintenance Unit: 11/1/42
249 Squadron aircraft code on Malta: GN-F
Plt Off P.A. Nash of 249 Sqn claimed an Me109 probable 10/03/42
Sgt V.P. Brennan of 249 Sqn claimed a shared Ju88 26/03/42
Plt Off P.A. Nash of 249 Sqn claimed a shared Ju889 probable 28/03/42
Plt Off J.A. Plagis of 249 Sqn claimed an Me109 and a Ju88 plus a share of

another Ju88 1/04/42

Plt Off J.A. Plagis claimed a Me109 and a Ju87 also on 1/04/42

On April 2nd 1942 Plt Off D. W. McLeod an American flying with 126 squadron baled out wounded after the aircraft caught fire under an attack by Me109s, he was rescued slightly wounded from his dinghy in the sea east of Kalafrana.

AB336 MkVbT
First flown: 7/1/42
Passed to 8 Maintenance Unit: 11/1/42
Flown off HMS Eagle by Plt Off Peter Nash
The American Hiram 'Tex' Putnam was killed on April 20th 1942, flying with 126 Squadron he was attacked by Me109s, his aircraft then struck a radio mast at Siggiewi and crashed in the Ta'Kandja valley. This aircraft is also noted as earlier having been destroyed on the ground.
Struck Off Charge: 18/4/1942   Flying Hours Listed: 15:20

Spitfire believed to be AB344 in January 1942, the small protrusion beneath the fuselage between the undercarriage is a support for an additional fuel tank
(S Morgan)

AB337 MkVbT
First flown: 7/1/42
Passed to 8 Maintenance Unit: 11/1/42

Flown off HMS Eagle by Fg Off Norman Lee.
249 Squadron aircraft code on Malta: GN-A
Fg Off W.R. Daddo-Langlois of 249 Sqn claimed a shared Ju88 probable 30/03/42
Rhodesian Plt Off Douglas Leggo was shot down and killed by a Me109 on March 30th 1942, he baled out but his parachute failed to open sufficiently before he hit the ground.
Struck Off Charge: 30/3/1942   Flying Hours Listed: 15:55

AB338 MkVbT
First flown:8/1/42
Passed to 8 Maintenance Unit: 26/1/42
Flown off HMS Eagle by Sgt Ray Hesselyn
On April 6th 1942 Luqa airfield was heavily bombed AB338 was one of two Spitfires destroyed beyond repair.
Struck Off Charge: 7/4/1942   Flying Hours Listed: 4:40

AB341 MkVbT
First flown: 10/1/42
Passed to 6 Maintenance Unit: 29/1/42
249 Squadron aircraft code on Malta: GN-E
Flt Lt R.W. McNair of 249 Sqn claimed Me109 shot down 20/03/42
Destroyed beyond repair after a Ju88 bombing raid on April 28th 1942
Struck Off Charge: 28/4/1942   Flying Hours Listed: 19:15

AB343 MkVbT
First flown: 14/1/42
Passed to 6 Maintenance Unit: 30/1/42
Flown off HMS Eagle by Plt Off John Plagis
249 Squadron aircraft code on Malta: GN-D
Australian Kenrick Murray became the first of the Malta Pilots to be killed on March 10th when this aircraft was shot down by a Me109, he baled out but his parachute failed to open correctly before he struck the ground, he died later that evening of his injuries.
Struck Off Charge: 19/3/1942   Flying Hours Listed: 7:45

AB344 MkVbT
First flown: 17/1/42

Passed to 6 Maintenance Unit: 30/1/42
Flown off HMS Eagle by Flt Sgt Paul Brennan
249 Squadron aircraft code on Malta: GN-M
Plt Off R.A. Sergeant of 249 Sqn claimed a shared Ju88 23/03/42
Flight Lieutenant H.A Johnston was returning to Takali with an oil leak on
20th April, when he followed a Ju88 bomber low across the airfield his aircraft
was caught in the blast of a bomb which threw him into the air out of control,
he was able to bale out safely. This aircraft is also listed as destroyed in the
workshops of Kalafrana on 18th April 1942.
Flying Hours Listed: 14:20

AB346 MkVbT
First flown: 24/1/42
Passed to 8 Maintenance Unit: 2/2/42
Flown off HMS Eagle by Flight Lieutenant Philip Heppell.
249 Squadron aircraft code on Malta: GN-K
Plt Off J.A. Plagis of 249 Sqn claimed an Me109 probable 10/03/42
Flt Lt W.C. Connell of 249 Sqn claimed a Ju88 shot down 15/03/42
Sgt V.P. Brennan of 249 Sqn claimed an Me109 shot down 17/03/42
Plt Off R.A. Sergeant of 249 Sqn claimed an Me109 probable 18/03/42
Plt Off J.A. Plagis of 249 Sqn claimed a shared Ju88 probable 28/03/42
On April 8th 1942 Flight Lieutenant Philip Heppell was attacking bombers
over the Grand Harbour, when his aircraft was hit by an anti aircraft shell, he
was subsequently blown out of the aircraft, but parachuted safely to land in
a bomb crater.
Struck Off Charge: 9/4/1942   Flying Hours Listed: 23:25

Out of the first sixteen Spitfires to operate from Malta, (including John
Yarra's AB333, which was unable to take off on March 7th but arrived with
the next delivery on March 21st), four aircraft were shot down and lost into
the sea, four others crashed onto the island and were destroyed. Five Spitfires
were destroyed during bombing raids whilst on the ground. Two others are
listed as struck off charge in early April without reason, but these were also
probably the result of bomb damage, there being no protective blast pens at
that stage. Only one Spitfire survived to leave Malta, this was AB264, which
is noted as being transferred to the Middle East in August 1944.

The Battle Of Malta Is Won

Although the first 15 Spitfires had reached Malta safely, the island would continue to suffer from a lack of food and other vital supplies, until the Allies had gained a much greater air and naval strength in the Mediterranean area, this would require many more Spitfires than it was possible to send in the spring of 1942. However, the RAF and Fleet Air Arm were still on the offensive, flying the small number of Blenheims, Wellingtons and Swordfish bombers that were available on Malta. They carried out bombing raids against airfields in Sicily and against Italian shipping that was supplying Axis troops in North Africa

Malta was in desperate need of food and fuel, no convoy of supplies had been able to reach Malta during February 1942, but another attempt was made the following month. On March 20th a convoy (MW10), set out from Alexandria comprising of four merchant vessels, the Breconshire, Talabot, Pampas and the Clan Campbell. These ships between them were carrying around 26,000 tons of supplies, with an escort of ten destroyers, and three cruisers to protect

Residents of Valletta collecting water from a stand pipe
(B Lazell)

them. On the third day out, and on the outskirts of the Grand Harbour, the Breconshire was hit and severely damaged by three bombs. Less than an hour later, the Clan Campbell was also attacked and sunk within sight of Malta. An unsuccessful attempt was made to tow the Breconshire to harbour. She eventually drifted without power or steering gear, coming inshore at the far eastern end of the island at Zonker Point and was then taken in tow to the bay at Marsaxlokk. Despite the anti aircraft guns and the efforts of Hurricanes and Spitfires to defend the vessels, all three ships were subsequently bombed. Whilst in the Grand Harbour, the Talabot was partially sunk, the Pampas set on fire with the Breconshire sunk at Marsaxlokk. However, work continued day and night to recover what food and oil supplies were possible from the ships. The arrival of the convoy provoked a further response from the Luftwaffe with over 2,159 bomber sorties flown, dropping 1,870 tons of explosives between March 24th and April 12th. Although the targets were the harbour or the airfields, the close proximity of Malta's towns and cities meant that they also suffered from bombs poorly aimed or released too early or too late. Over 10,000 buildings were destroyed or damaged in April 1942 alone, and 300 civilians perished, the highest number in a month since the war began. The population also suffered from the loss of gas, electricity and water supplies to their homes or the underground shelters where many now lived. With the houses being built of stone there was though no risk of the large firestorms, which were later seen in other cities throughout Europe during heavy bombing raids. Most days there were at least three raids on Malta with over 170 bombers striking each day. The constant interceptions of the large bomber fleets by the RAF increased losses of their fighters, sometimes only half a dozen Hurricanes or Spitfires were available at any one time.

**Anti aircraft gunners man a Bofors postion protecting the
Grand Harbour (B Lazell)**

The anti aircraft guns played their part in breaking up the bombing runs and bringing down the Ju88 and Ju87s, but levels of ammunition became so low that restrictions on the numbers of shells fired to fifteen per gun were brought in, except on the days when another delivery of Spitfires was due to reach the island.

On April 15th 1942 Sir William Dobbie, the Governor and Commander in Chief, was pleased to inform the population of Malta of the award of the George Cross from King George VI, in recognition of the bravery of the people of Malta during the ongoing siege. This was the highest possible award that could be bestowed on a civilian group. The medal was later taken around the towns and villages of Malta and Gozo, so that everyone had a chance to view it. A cable sent from the King stated:

'To honour her brave people I award the George Cross to the island fortress of Malta to bear witness to a heroism and devotion that will long be famous in history.'

Lord Gort presented the George Cross to Sir George Borg,
The Chief Justice of Malta on September 13th 1942 (B Lazell)

The many Army units on Malta waited for the anticipated invasion, guarding and keeping watch over the 90 miles of coastline around the island. Approximately 2,500 soldiers were also based at the three airfields, supporting their RAF colleagues by providing the manpower to fill in the large craters constantly made by the bombing, they kept the runways open and created dispersal areas to spread the fighters and bombers over a large area. They also assisted with the building of protective pens that sheltered the aircraft from the blast and shrapnel of the bombs. Sandbags were found not to be suitable, so thousands of empty petrol tins were filled with sand or stones, these, along with blocks of stone from damaged buildings, created the protective walls. Over a three-month period, over 200 of these pens were built for the various aircraft on the island.

In April the pounding of the bombers continued with over 6,728 tons dropped on the airfields, dockyards and harbours, forcing the small flotilla of submarines based at Malta to withdraw to safety in Alexandria for several months. On April 7th the 2,000th air raid warning since the start of the war sounded, this day also saw the destruction, during the bombing of Valletta, of the city's famous Royal Opera House.

**The Royal Opera House in Valletta before and after
the 2,00th bombing raid on April 7th 1942 (B Lazell)**

With the numbers of serviceable fighters depleted to around a handful, British fighter aircraft could not meet every incursion of Malta's airspace. On some days Malta's defence rested on the anti aircraft gunners alone, who responded gallantly with their highest monthly total so far of 102 enemy aircraft destroyed. On one occasion an improvised tactic to confuse the enemy raiders when no fighters were available resulted in the loss of two German aircraft. Group Captain 'Woody' Woodhall described the events:

'The Hun bombers came over in force with quite a large fighter escort. It happened that there were several fighter pilots with me in the Operation room, one of whom was a Canadian with an unmistakeable voice. I put him at the microphone at a stand-by radio set and proceeded to give him dummy orders. He replied just as if he were flying a fighter. This, we suspect, caused a cry of 'Actung ! Spitfire ! To go over the German radio. In any case two 109s enthusiastically shot each other down without any British aircraft being airborne.

'This knowledge that the Germans intercepted our orders stood us in good stead. We claimed that Pilot Officer 'Humgufery shot down the two Huns.'

On April 14th another attempt was made to send provisions to Malta, two convoys set off at the same time from opposite sides of the Mediterranean. The 'Vigorous' convoy left Alexandria in the Middle East, comprising of eleven merchant ships, with an escort of seven cruisers and twenty-eight destroyers. Convoy 'Harpoon' left from Gibraltar with six merchant ships escorted by a battleship, two aircraft carriers, 14 cruisers, 4 minesweepers and 17 destroyers. The cruiser HMS Welshman also made her way to Malta, part of the time under the protective cover of the convoy. The 'Vigorous' convoy soon came under attack from aircraft and E-boats and, with most of the ships damaged and short of ammunition, plus the added threat of possibly being intercepted by the Italian Naval battle fleet, the attempt was abandoned, and the ships returned to port.

The 'Harpoon' convoy battled its way to Malta against Italian naval ships and the Luftwaffe, but only two merchant ships, the Troilus and Orari, managed to get through, with 25,000 tons of supplies were able to be off loaded. HMS Welshman also successfully reached the Grand Harbour with further supplies of ammunition. However, the oil tanker Kentucky, carrying valuable supplies of oil and petrol, had been sunk. The failure of the convoys meant even further restrictions to the already small food rations available from the Victory Kitchens, these had been set up as communal feeding areas providing one meal a day to the Maltese people. With no further attempts to send a convoy possible until August, life on Malta became even harder.

At the end of April some of the German air units were transferred from

Sicily to other frontline areas resulting in less bombing raids against Malta. April 29th had seen 220 sorties against Malta, the following day there were only 68, and these were mainly from high flying Italian bombers. RAF Photo Reconnaissance aircraft had spotted another danger though, three new airfields were being created on Sicily, and it was believed that these were for the use of gliders that would be used later for an invasion of Malta, although this never occurred.

One of the 1,250 German and Italian aircraft that were shot down over Malta by allied pilots and the anti aircraft gunners (B Lazell)

The decrease in bombing allowed Malta some breathing space after the heavy bombing of March and April. Another delivery of Spitfires was flown in on May 9th and this time plans had been made for the quick turn around of the aircraft. Once landed they were refuelled, rearmed and put straight back into the air, flown by an experienced Malta pilot, in some cases within six minutes of having touched down. This time the Spitfires would not be destroyed on the ground when the bombers came over, as had many of the April delivery.

Early the following morning the fast cruiser HMS Welshman again entered the Grand Harbour with another cargo comprising mainly of ammunition for the guns, along with smoke canisters; these were later deployed when information was received from the Operation Room of an incoming raid, the billowing smoke concealing areas of the Grand Harbour and dockyards. The surrounding anti aircraft guns created even more smoke, with the restriction on the number of shells they could fire having now been lifted. The British fighters knew the barrage over the harbour would not stop for them and many took the chance to dive into the barrage after the Stuka bombers, which were particularly vulnerable when they pulled out of the bottom of their dive. Flt Lt 'Nip' Heppell was one British pilot who survived being shot down by the guns around the Grand Harbour.

A second delivery of Spitfires reached Malta during May turning the tide of air supremacy towards the defenders. The Italian and German bombing raids were now much smaller in number but were still backed by a large fighter escort. With night raids becoming more prominent, the Bristol Beaufighter night fighters, which had replaced the Hurricanes, now started to have their successes against the bombers.

The harsh conditions of Malta had taken there toll on General Sir William Dobbie, the Governor of Malta, and during May he was recalled back to England and replaced by Field Marshall Lord Gort VC. June continued as before with another two deliveries of Spitfires. Malta now became more offensive with nearly 200 Allied bombing sorties made between May 26th and July 27th against shipping, ports and airfields. Two more deliveries of Spitfires provided another 59 fighters during July. The fighters now also became more offensive, before they had stayed close to the island to defend it against the raids, now, more and more they would go out to intercept the bombers and their escort at sea, often turning them away before they reached the island. This new tactic had come from Air Vice Marshall Keith Park who had taken over as the Air Officer Commanding from Air Vice Marshall Hugh Lloyd on July 14th. Park, a New Zealander, had been heavily involved in the air fighting and the tactics of fighters during the Battle of Britain.

Part of his Special Order of the Day stated:

"Our fighter strength has during June and July been greatly increased, and the enemy's superiority in numbers has long since dwindled. The time has now arrived for our Spitfire squadrons to put an end to the bombing of our airfields by daylight. We have the best fighter aircraft in the world, and our Spitfire pilots will again show their comrades on the ground that they are the best fighter pilots in the world."

The RAF now held command of the air around the island of Malta, but any convoy still had to travel over a thousand miles of hostile waters to provide the desperately required food supplies to the starving population. Scabies, malnutrition and gastro enteritis were rife on the island, even drinking water was rationed in some areas. No supplies had entered the Grand Harbour for two months. If the next convoy failed to arrive then Malta would certainly be forced to surrender very soon afterwards.

On August 3rd convoy WS21S, now more commonly known as Operation Pedestal, sailed from the Clyde, Scotland. It contained the largest number of warships ever gathered together as escort for a single convoy. Among the vessels was an oil tanker, the Ohio, borrowed from the Americans but sailing under a British flag with a British crew under the command of Captain Dudley Mason. There were also 13 fast merchant ships, carrying a total of around 85,000 tons of supplies. The cargo was divided amongst the ships so that each ship carried a quantity of aviation spirit, kerosene, ammunition, bombs, coal, flour and other food items, so if only a few of the vessels got through there would be some of all the required items. Prior to their sailing each ship, including the Ohio, had been fitted with additional Bofors, Browning and Oerlikon anti aircraft guns to defend against the anticipated air attacks.

The naval escort was in two parts, Force X would sail all the way to Malta and contained four cruisers and eleven destroyers. Force Z contained four aircraft carriers, including HMS Eagle, two battleships, three cruisers and fourteen destroyers. This group would return to Gibraltar once the Sicilian Narrows had been reached. The submarines of the Tenth Flotilla, which had since returned to Manoel Island on Malta, would also guard against any Italian naval ships threatening the convoy.

A week after setting sail the convoy passed through the Straits of Gibraltar and into the Mediterranean. The following day (August 11th) the convoy was spotted by an Italian submarine. Later, in the early afternoon, another submarine, the German U73, penetrated the convoy and fired four torpedoes at a distance of 500 metres at the aircraft carrier Eagle. All four torpedoes struck their target on the port side of the carrier, she quickly began listing, men and aircraft sliding from her deck into the sea. Within eight minutes she had disappeared below the surface. The ship, which had previously carried nearly 150 Spitfires to the take off position for their flight to Malta, including the Operation Spotter pilots, sank with the loss of 160 members of her crew.

One of the other aircraft carriers in the convoy, HMS Furious, continued the work started by the Eagle with 37 Spitfires being launched on their flights to Malta, she then turned and returned to Gibraltar. The events of the day were not yet over. At 8:00pm around 36 torpedo bomber aircraft approached the convoy. The carriers Victorious and Indomitable flew off fighters in defence. Three of the bombers were brought down by the fighters and anti aircraft guns, with no further damage to any of the ships.

The morning of August 12th saw several attacks on the convoy from German and Italian aircraft. Three bombs from a Ju88 hit the merchant ship Deucalion, which, being severely damaged, was abandoned and later scuttled so as not to fall into enemy hands. Axis submarines continued to stalk the convoy. An Italian Submarine, the Cobalto, was depth charged forcing her to the surface where she was rammed and sunk by the destroyer HMS Ithuriel, who then stopped to pick up her 41 surviving crew members.

In the early evening over 100 German bombers attacked the ships, HMS Foresight was so badly damaged that later she had to be sunk. The aircraft carrier HMS Indomitable became the target for 40 Stuka dive-bombers, with three bombs damaging the flight deck and starting fierce fires, but she was able to continue at a reduced speed. Nine of the bombers were believed destroyed. At 7:00pm the ships of Force Z, as planned, turned to return to Gibraltar. The ships of Force X continued with their charges to Malta. Within thirty minutes torpedos fired by the Italian submarine Axum struck two of the destroyers. The Cairo was too badly damaged to continue and, with her crew taken off, she was sunk by gunfire. The Nigeria, hit from the same salvo of six torpedoes, partly flooded but did not appear to be sinking, but, not being able to keep up with the convoy, she returned to Gibraltar. The Captain of the Axum had aimed well; he had also struck another ship in the convoy, the Ohio. Fires had broken out on the deck, but it did not appear too serious and twenty of the crew fought the flames. The engine room had though been damaged and the huge tanker for a time wallowed stationery without power, the convoy continuing to pull away leaving her behind. Admiral Burroughs, who had now transferred to the Ashanti after damage to his ship the Nigeria, had checked on Ohio's predicament. Half an hour later the fires had been put out, and Ohio was underway again despite several large holes in her bulkheads and fuel seeping out of the tanks, damage to her steering gear hampered her progress.

The German bombing continued. The Brisbane Star was hit by a torpedo in the bow and withdrew from the convoy but continued to Malta closer to the shoreline of North Africa. The Empire Hope survived several near misses but was eventually hit and set on fire, her crew later forced to abandon the ship. At 9:00pm, in the last aerial attack of the day, the Clan Ferguson was also hit by a bomb from a Ju88, with one huge explosion tearing her apart, she quickly sank. An Italian submarine later rescued 53 of her survivors.

In the early hours of the morning of the 13th the convoy was attacked by fast manoeuvrable torpedo carrying E-boats both, Italian and German. The cruiser, Manchester, was hit from close range damaging her steering gear and flooding the engine rooms, she later had to be abandoned and scuttled. The merchant ship Santa Elisa was also hit by a torpedo setting her cargo of fuel ablaze and forcing the crew to take to the lifeboats. The Almeria Lykes was another struck by a torpedo on her port side and with her forward bulkheads torn open, she began to sink. The attacks continued until first light with two more of the merchant ships, the Wairangi and Glenorchy, both set on fire and lost. One other ship, the Rochester Castle, was also hit but, despite the damage, she was able to keep up a good speed of 13 knots and stayed in touch with the other ships.

During the night an Italian naval fleet of two cruisers and eleven destroyers approached to intercept the convoy. These vessels had been monitored for the last two days by RAF aircraft, who were well aware of the damage that they could do to the weakened ships of the convoy. There were insufficient bombers on Malta to attack this fleet so it was decided to try and trick the Italians into withdrawing. In the early hours of the morning of the 13th a small force of Wellington bombers found the Italians, which they then bombed, and, by dropping flares, they lit up the area exposing the ships. One of the Wellingtons then sent a non-coded signal calling in other, imaginary aircraft into the attack. The Italians, aware that they were too far away from their own protective aircraft, and having picked up the signal, began to feel very vulnerable and started to alter their course. To further encourage their withdrawal another message was sent calling the Wellingtons once again to illuminate the ships for a bombing attack to be made by a large force of non-existent Liberators. The Italian fleet turned back to its home port driven away by nothing more than intimidation and bluff. Their ignominy was further compounded during their withdrawal when torpedoes from the Malta based submarine Unbroken damaged two of the Italian cruisers.

Another danger had passed, but at 8:00am the air attacks began once more when 12 Ju88s attacked the convoy. Two of the aircraft dived down to bomb the Waimarama. The bombs from the first aircraft struck her in two places, resulting in a huge explosion and fire, which caught the second attacking Ju88 sending it crashing into the sea. Only 27 of the Waimarama's crew of 107 survived to be rescued by following ships. The sea surrounding the ship was covered in burning fuel, which the Ohio pulled hard to one side to avoid as she was still leaking her own cargo of highly inflammable fuel.

The convoy, which was still over 150 miles away from Malta, was now reduced to just four merchant ships and the Ohio, which became the focus of the next attack made by over 60 Stuka dive bombers. Several of the bombs fell very close throwing up huge spouts of water that crashed down onto the decks. The guns on the Ohio fired back relentlessly, one of the Stukas was hit and careered headlong into the side of the ship, breaking up, its fuselage remaining on the deck. No sooner had the Stukas left than a group of 20 Ju88s began their attack, again several bombs fell very close buckling Ohio's plates. One explosion was so great it lifted the ship out of the water. The fires to the boilers were blown out and again the ship was without power for half an hour before she could get underway, this was for only a short while before her engines stopped for the final time. An attempt was made by the destroyer Penn to tow the tanker but the damaged steering gear on the Ohio just sent her around in a circle. When another air attack came in the Penn quickly cut the tow. Although the main attack had been against the oil tanker, another one of the valuable merchant ships was lost when the Dorset was hit by bombs from a Ju88, flooding her engine room and setting her on fire, she sank within twenty minutes.

At 2:00pm it was decided to take the crew off the Ohio rather than endanger them during the rest of the day. They were taken aboard the Penn where most of them quickly fell asleep from sheer exhaustion. Later, under the cover of darkness, they again boarded her to try to save the ship.

The other merchant ships had continued their epic voyage to Malta and, after midday on August 14th they had come under the protection of the Spitfires from the island, which circled protectively overhead. At 6:15pm, led by minesweepers searching the waters ahead for danger, three battle damaged ships, Port Chalmers, Rochester Castle and the Melbourne Star, entered the Grand Harbour to the rapturous cheers of the Maltese and fellow servicemen. The Brisbane Star, which had been damaged by torpedo on the 12th, had continued to Malta close to the North African coast, away from the convoy. In French territorial waters she was stopped and boarded by French officers wanting to intern the ship and crew, but, after drinks with the Brisbane Star's Captain, they were persuaded to let her continue. Having outwitted a following U-boat, the merchant ship entered Grand Harbour adding her cargo to that of the other three ships. Malta, at last had food to keep the people fed, but without fuel for the Spitfires there was still the danger that the siege would force a surrender

The Ohio, although very low in the water, was still afloat, the minesweeper Rye had come out from Malta to assist with attempts to tow her in. The Penn found, as before, with the damaged and holed bow and unusable rudder, the ship could not be towed without her pulling to one side trying to circle. The Rye then attached a line to the centre of the ship and both began to tow, this overcame the problem but only around four knots could be reached. Just when things appeared to be improving, four Ju88s approached low, and from behind the Ohio, making it difficult for the Rye and Penn to train their guns against them. A bomb crashed through the Ohio exploding two decks down in the engine room and the order was given out to abandon the ship, as it was believed she would surely sink. Although severely damaged, she stayed afloat. Later a further attempt was made to tow the tanker with Rye at the bow and Penn at the stern countering her tendency to turn, but after only a short time both towlines broke. The destroyer, HMS Bramham that had been standing by suggested towing from the side to counter the swing, which the Penn attempted, but with the large heavy tanker so low in the water, she was unable to move her and it was decided to wait until the next morning to reassess the situation.

The oil tanker Ohio approaching Malta under the protection of the Island's Spitfires in August 1942
"The Gallant Ohio" by Robert Taylor. (Aces High Aviation Gallery)

Further attempts to tow were made early on the morning of August 15th by the Penn, Rye and another destroyer the Ledbury with some success, until, with less than fifty miles to Malta, the ships were attacked by Ju88 bombers, quickly followed by nine Ju87 Stukas. These were successfully driven away by Spitfires from Malta, but one bomb fell close to the rear of the Ohio blasting away the rudder and creating another hole in the ship. The minesweeper Speedy from Malta had now also come to assist the others, her Commander decided the best method to save the tanker would be to tow her with a destroyer attached to each side. The Penn was still attached to the

369

starboard side, and the Bramham secured herself to the Ohio on her port side. The three ships headed once again for Malta, the speed held down to five knots so as not to risk the Ohio breaking up.

At around 7:00am, with the outline of the buildings of Valletta visible, the tanker limped closer with her two supporting ships still lashed either side. Several times the tow lies were broken but the tired and exhausted crews quickly re-secured the vessels. With the fear of an attack even at this late stage by submarine, the minefield at the entrance to the Grand Harbour was carefully negotiated. As they had waited the previous day for the arrival of the merchant ships, the people of Malta packed every vantage point to watch and cheer the ships as they entered the harbour. The crews were visibly moved by the ovations they received. At 9.30am, with the aid of the harbour's tug boats, the Ohio was finally tied up at Parlatorio Wharf. It had taken five days from the Straits of Gibraltar to reach Malta, but it had seemed like a lifetime for the crew of the Ohio. The lives of hundreds of others involved in Operation Pedestal had been lost in the attempt.

Without the 55,000 tons of supplies that the convoy brought, the island would have been forced to surrender during September 1942. This was, though, still only a postponement. Malta still suffered many air attacks, particularly during early October as the RAF and Malta based submarines continued to inflict great losses on the Italian ships providing fuel, food and ammunition to Rommel's troops in North Africa. The weakened German forces were attacked on October 23rd at El Alamein by General Montgomery's Eighth Army and were soon forced to retreat. On November 8th 1942 British and American forces landed in French North Africa during Operation Torch resulting in additional German forces being transferred away from Sicily to Africa.

The siege of Malta finally came to an end on November 20th with the safe arrival of all four of the cargo ships of Operation Stoneage, which had set out from Alexandria, bringing a further 35,000 tons of supplies. Malta continued to play its part in the war particularly during the allied landings on Sicily in May 1943. In September that year the people of Malta stood on the high vantage points once again looking out to sea, cheering and celebrating, but this was not another supply convoy, they were gazing at over 75 Italian naval vessels, from battleships and submarines, to smaller motor torpedo boats, all having anchored off the island after the earlier surrender of Italy. Admiral Sir Andrew Cunningham sent what would become a famous message to the Admiralty:

"Pleased to inform their Lordships that the Italian battle fleet now lies

at anchor under the guns of fortress Malta."

Malta had paid a high price for her victory during the Second World War with over 1,500 civilians killed, and 3,720 injured. 40,000 buildings were demolished in the bombing including eleven churches, with approximately 100 other churches or religious buildings damaged. Malta had been the most bombed place on earth.

718 aircraft had been delivered via aircraft carrier to Malta during 25 Operations, which included 333 Hurricanes and 367 Spitfires, 34 aircraft were lost during the deliveries. In the air battles over Malta the RAF lost 547 aircraft destroyed. RAF fighters and the island's anti aircraft guns destroyed over 1,251 German and Italian aircraft. The RAF pilots, including the sixteen from Operation Spotter, had more than played their part.

Bibliography

185 The Malta Squadron: Anthony Rogers (Spellmount Ltd 2005)
249 At War: Brian Cull: (Grub Street 1997)
Aces High: Christopher Shores and Clive Williams (Grub Street 1994)
Against All Odds: RAAF pilots in the Battle For Malta 1942: Lex McAulay (Century Hutchinson Australia 1989)
Bader: The Man And His Men: Michael Burns (Arms And Armour 1990)
Bader's Last Flight: Andy Saunders (Grub Street 2007)
Barney Barnfather: Life On A Spitfire Squadron: Angus Mansfield (The History Press 2008)
Buck McNair: Canadian Spitfire Ace: Norman Franks (Grub Street 2001)
Churchill And Malta: Douglas Austin (Spellmount Limited 2006)
Diary Of An 'Erk' With S.O.M.P.: S J Revell (Held at RAF Museum, London)
Five Up: 'Laddie' Lucas: (Sedgewick and Jackson Ltd 1978)
Flying Start: Hugh Dundas (Stanley Paul and Co Ltd 1988)
For Your Tomorrow: Errol W Martyn (Volplane 1998)
Gifts Of War: Henry Boot and Ray Sturtivant (Air Britain Publication 2005)
Hess: A Kiwi Malta Ace: James Sutherland. (Regal Books 2000)
Kenrick Newton Lathrop Murray: David and Simon Thornton (Privately Published)
Kiwi Spitfire Ace: Jack Rae (Grub Street 2001)
Lonely Warrior: The Journal of Battle of Britain fighter Pilot Jean Offenberg, DFC: Edited by Victor Houart. (Souvenir Press 1956)
Malta: Blitzed But Not Beaten: Philip Vella, (Progress Press Co Ltd 1985)
Malta Convoy: Peter Shankland and Anthony Hunter (Fontana Books 1963)
Malta: The Hurricane Years 1940-41: Christopher Shores, Brian Cull, Nicola Malizia (Grub Street 1987)
Malta: The Spitfire Year 1942: Christopher Shores, Brian Cull, Nicola Malizia (Grub Street 1991)
Malta: The Thorn In Rommel's Side: Laddie Lucas (Stanley Paul 1992)
Rhodesians Worldwide Magazine: Volume 11 Issue 2 (1995)
Skies Of Fire: Alfred Price (Cassell & Co. 2002)
Soldier, Sailor & Airman Too: The Fighting life of Group Captain A.B. 'Woody' Woodhall: Martin Woodhall (Grub Street 2008)
Spitfire Mark V Aces: Dr Alfred Price (Osprey 1997)

Spitfires Over Malta: Brian Cull with Frederick Galea (Grub Street 2005)
Spitfires Over Sicily: Brian Cull, Nicola Malizia, Frederick Galea (Grub Street 2000)
Tattered Battlements: Tim Johnston (William Kimber and Co Ltd 1985)
The Air Battle Of Malta: (HMSO 1944)
The Battle Over Malta: Anthony Rogers (Sutton Publishing Ltd 2000)
The Guns Of Hagar Qim: The Diaries Of Stan Fraser 1939-1946: Stanley Fraser (Bieb Bieb Enterprises Ltd 2005)
The Hurricats: Ralph Barker (Pelham Books 1978)
Those Other Eagles: Christopher Shores (Grub Street 2004)
Wing Leader: Johnnie Johnson (Chatto & Windus1956)